**Security Policies
of Developing
Countries**

Security Policies of Developing Countries

Edited by
Edward A. Kolodziej
University of Illinois
Robert E. Harkavy
The Pennsylvania State University

LexingtonBooks
D.C. Heath and Company
Lexington, Massachusetts
Toronto

Library of Congress Cataloging in Publication Data

Main entry under title:
Security policies of developing countries.

Includes edited papers from a symposium held May 1980 which was organized by the Office of Arms Control, Disarmament, and International Security, the Dept. of Political Science, and the School of Social Sciences of the University of Illinois.

Includes index.

1. National security—Congresses. 2. Underdeveloped areas—Military policy—Congresses. I. Kolodziej, Edward A. II. Harkavy, Robert E. III. University of Illinois at Urbana-Champaign. Office of Arms Control, Disarmament, and International Security. IV. University of Illinois at Urbana-Champaign. School of Social Sciences.

| UA10.5.S4 | 355'.03301724 | 79-1547 |
| ISBN 0-669-02897-5 | | AACR2 |

Copyright © 1982 by D.C. Heath and Company

Published simultaneously in Canada

Printed in the United States of America

International Standard Book Number: 0-669-02897-5

Library of Congress Catalog Card Number: 79-1547

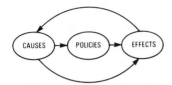

Policy Studies Organization Series

General Approaches to Policy Studies

Policy Studies in America and Elsewhere
  edited by Stuart S. Nagel
Policy Studies and the Social Studies
  edited by Stuart S. Nagel
Methodology for Analyzing Public Policies
  edited by Frank P. Scioli, Jr., and Thomas J. Cook
Urban Problems and Public Policy
  edited by Robert L. Lineberry and Louis H. Masoti
Problems of Theory in Policy Analysis
  edited by Philip M. Gregg
Using Social Research for Public Policy-Making
  edited by Carol H. Weiss
Public Administration and Public Policy
  edited by H. George Frederickson and Charles Wise
Policy Analysis and Deductive Reasoning
  edited by Gordon Tullock and Richard Wagner
Legislative Reform
  edited by Leroy N. Rieselbach
Teaching Policy Studies
  edited by William D. Coplin
Paths to Political Reform
  edited by William J. Crotty
Determinants of Public Policy
  edited by Thomas Dye and Virginia Gray
Effective Policy Implementation
  edited by Daniel Mazmanian and Paul Sabatier
Taxing and Spending Policy
  edited by Warren J. Samuels and Larry L. Wade
The Politics of Urban Public Services
  edited by Richard C. Rich
Analayzing Urban Service Distributions
  edited by Richard C. Rich
The Analysis of Policy Impact
  edited by John Grumm and Stephen Washby
Public Policies for Distressed Communities
  edited by F. Stevens Redburn and Terry F. Buss
Implementing Public Policy
  edited by Dennis J. Palumbo and Marvin A. Harder
Evaluating and Optimizing Public Policy
  edited by Dennis J. Palumbo, Stephen B. Fawcett, and Paula Wright
Representation and Redistricting Issues
  edited by Bernard Grofman, Arend Lijphart, Robert McKay, and
  Howard Scarrow
Administrative Reform Strategies
  edited by Gerald E. Caiden and Heinrich Siedentopf

Specific Policy Problems

Analyzing Poverty Policy
  edited by Dorothy Buckton James
Crime and Criminal Justice
  edited by John A. Gardiner and Michael Mulkey
Civil Liberties
  edited by Stephen L. Wasby
Foreign Policy Analysis
  edited by Richard L. Merritt
Economic Regulatory Policies
  edited by James E. Anderson
Political Science and School Politics
  edited by Samuel K. Gove and Frederick M. Wirt
Science and Technology Policy
  edited by Joseph Haberer
Population Policy Analysis
  edited by Michael E. Kraft and Mark Schneider
The New Politics of Food
  edited by Don F. Hadwiger and William P. Browne
New Dimensions to Energy Policy
  edited by Robert Lawrence
Race, Sex, and Policy Problems
  edited by Marian Lief Palley and Michael Preston
American Security Policy and Policy-Making
  edited by Robert Harkavy and Edward Kolodziej
Current Issues in Transportation Policy
  edited by Alan Altshuler
Security Policies of Developing Countries
  edited by Edward Kolodziej and Robert Harkavy
Determinants of Law-Enforcement Policies
  edited by Fred A. Meyer, Jr., and Ralph Baker
Evaluating Alternative Law-Enforcement Policies
  edited by Ralph Baker and Fred A. Meyer, Jr.
International Energy Policy
  edited by Robert M. Lawrence and Martin O. Heisler
Employment and Labor-Relations Policy
  edited by Charles Bulmer and John L. Carmichael, Jr.
Housing Policy for the 1980s
  edited by Roger Montgomery and Dale Rogers Marshall
Environmental Policy Formation
  edited by Dean E. Mann
Environmental Policy Implementation
  edited by Dean E. Mann
The Analysis of Judicial Reform
  edited by Philip L. Dubois
The Politics of Judicial Reform
  edited by Philip L. Dubois
Critical Issues in Health Policy
  edited by Ralph Straetz, Marvin Lieberman, and Alice Sardell

Contents

Preface and Acknowledgments

This book is a study of the security policies of selected, but key, developing countries. Chapter 1 sketches the rationale for this collective enterprise. It outlines several dimensions along which the security role played by developing states can be measured or evaluated. It also presents a framework of analysis guiding the country-specific contributions made by the authors. Stipulated are a set of analytic categories corresponding to the decisions facing each state in fashioning its security policies. Authors were asked to filter their discussions through these common categories in order to facilitate comparisons and generalizations across cases. The last section of chapter 1 details some of the major problems encountered in defining the scope of the book and bringing it to timely publication.

Chapters 2 through 15 examine the security policies of fourteen developing states. These states have a significant impact on the security systems of their regions and, in some instances, on the global environment. The examples are illustrative, not exhaustive. Constraints of space and of the availability of authors confined us to a limited list of states. They provide, nevertheless, a broad yet representative sample of the varying patterns of security behavior of developing states to support the major conclusions of the analysis.

A final chapter, drawing largely on the preceding chapters, but going beyond them when evidence and logic advise, develops a set of provisional generalizations about the security role of developing states and the principal factors influencing their behavior. This *tour d'horizon* may be useful for students and practitioners seeking a brief, if necessarily simplified, overview of a very complex subject. The chapter also serves to identify where more work has to be done to improve our knowledge about the relevant actors and the significance of the security policies of developing states.

Although this book was intended not to join the current debate over the evolution of security threats in the developing world but to assist long-range efforts to prepare the groundwork for the systematic study of regional and global security, it contributes—as an added if unintended boon—to the present discussion of American security policy. The experts assembled for this book have much to say that both qualifies and contests the assumptions and expectations underlying the current debate between two schools of thought that have emerged in the late 1970s and early 1980s. The first, or what might be termed the *geopolitical* school, places the Soviet Union and the role of force at the center of U.S. security concerns. The second or *regionalist* persuasion emphasizes local sources of conflict and the greater role of economic and political factors over military force as determinative of global and regional power relations.[1] Geopolitical analysts stress the East-West confrontation and view the developing world as a major arena for big-power competition; regional conflict is thus the occasion for superpower intervention. Regionalists accent North-South differences; they insist on the autonomy and saliency of what formerly was termed *low politics*, including such issues as competition for resources, trade-investment flows, and the role of multinationals in economic development.

These chapters suggest that both a geopolitical and a regional perspective are needed, but neither alone provides a fully reliable model with which to explain or predict the evolutionary development of regional and international security. Much of what appears to be purely local competition, like the Arab-Israeli conflict, can be fully understood only by appeal to a geopolitical model. On the other hand, many of the specific determinants of local conflict, including deeply rooted national, ethnic, ideological, and religious rivalries, can be fully explained only by reference to a regionalist view. The picture emerging from this discussion also suggests that the sources of regional and global conflict are greater in number than a strict application of geopolitical thinking might admit, while the centers of independent military power and initiative are more numerous and the capacity of these centers to resolve "deadly quarrels" is more pronounced than regionalists would have us believe. The Soviet Union cannot be defined away by focusing on economic and political development, nor can the use of force by local powers be seen as a function of big-power manipulation or as an issue of lesser significance to developing states than economic expansion and internal political stability.

Acknowledgments

Acknowledgment must also be made of several people and institutions whose assistance was invaluable in organizing this book and bringing it to publication. John Stremlau of The Rockefeller Foundation was helpful at a crucial stage in securing a grant to hold a conference in May 1980. The Office of Arms Control, Disarmament, and International Security, the Department of Political Science, and the School of Social Sciences of the University of Illinois also provided valuable financial, administrative, and secretarial assistance. Hertha Vandiver and Janie Carroll were invariably cheerful and ingenious in unravelling the financial tangles associated with this book and the May conference. Mary Anderson did most of the organizational work for the spring meeting and was unfailingly reliable in doing the typing chores for final publication. Sumit Ganguly and Jeffrey Starr, graduate students in the Department of Political Science, pitched in at key points to sustain momentum. Richard Merritt, head of the Department of Political Science, and Robert Crawford, director of the School of Social Sciences, provided support throughout. Stuart Nagel guided arrangements with Lexington Books and provided back-up assistance and financial aid. Antje Kolodziej lent expert help with editorial work.

We also owe special thanks to the contributors and to their (and our) spouses without whose help and encouragement this book would never have appeared.

Note

1. These geopolitical and regionalist themes are discussed in various measure by the authors of two recently published Adelphi papers. See International Institute for Strategic Studies, *Third World Conflict and International Security*, Adelphi papers nos. 166 and 167, vols. 1 and 2, respectively; see especially the penetrating article by Shahram Chubin, "The United States and the Third World: Motives, Objectives, and Policies," in vol. 2, pp. 19-33.

**Security Policies
of Developing
Countries**

1

Introduction

Edward A. Kolodziej
and *Robert E. Harkavy*

This book examines the security policies of several important developing countries. Until recently, developing states have tended to be treated as clients or proxies of the superpowers or of one or the other of the developed states, like France (for example, francophone Africa). This perspective has increasingly less relevance to the significant and enlarging security functions these states now discharge. They are often as capable of manipulating other states as they are susceptible to being influenced from abroad. Other developing and developed states are targets of their security policies. The behavior of militarily more powerful states, such as the United States and the Soviet Union, is subject to more influence and control by these ostensibly weaker powers than is currently appreciated. It is misleading and even potentially mischievous to view them exclusively as objects of big-power security and arms-control policies. Some states—Israel and Cuba for example—have impressive military establishments relative to their size and resources. Others, like South Africa and India, are building large and sophisticated forces. None perceive themselves either as totally dependent on other powers or as so constrained that they are without a margin of maneuverability in projecting force abroad. In some measure, all attempt to pursue independent foreign and security policies that respond to their perceived needs.

Knowledge of how international security systems and regional subsystems are organized and operate hinges increasingly on our understanding of the important roles that developing countries play in these realms. These roles are of sufficient magnitude to denote these states as emerging regional powers and, in certain defined areas, as global actors. Through the use or threat of force the regimes in control of these states can determine outcomes in their conflicts with other states; the monopolies they exercise over domestic means of violence are sufficient to control their indigenous populations in those instances where loyalty must be more commanded than elicited. Designating these countries as emerging powers contrasts their military growth with their often more retarded economic, social, and political development.

Some Indexes of Developing State Military Power

Several prominent indicators point toward increasing expansion of the quantity and quality of arms in the possession of developing states and in

1

their ability to use and service sophisticated equipment. Table 1-1 compares the military expenditures of developed and developing states between 1969 and 1978. Several surprising trends are highlighted. Much of the 16.7 percent growth in world military expenditures since 1969 is attributable to the developing countries. During this period the military spending of developed states rose from $320 billion to $345 billion in constant 1977 dollars, an increase of 7.8 percent, while expenditures among developing states jumped from $63 billion to $102 billion or 61.9 percent. If Oceania is considered primarily as a developed area, the developing states outstrip the percentage increase in developed-state spending in every region. Most prominent is the Middle East, which recorded increases of 200 percent; Latin America and South Asia registered slightly more and slightly less than a 70 percent increase in military expenditures, respectively. In these three instances the rate of military spending exceeded the growth in gross national product (GNP). Meanwhile, North American military expenditures declined almost 23 percent, partly due of course to the withdrawal of the United States from Vietnam.

The ratio of military expenditures to GNP also shows the developing states spending proportionately more of their economic resources for defense than developed states. Although the ratio of military spending to GNP fell for developed states by one and a half percentage points (6.8 to 5.3 percent), the similar spending ratio for developing states held more steady, falling only one-half of a percentage point, from 6.0 to 5.5 percent. During this period GNP increased by almost 80 percent. These GNP-military spending ratios are confirmed in per capita expenditure data. The developed states registered no change on this scale, while the developing state percentage advanced by almost 30 percent.

The trends suggested by these expenditure figures are mirrored in the growth of the armed forces of the developing countries. All of the world's increase was attributable to the substantial expansion of developing states' military forces. While the armed services of the developed countries were shrinking by almost 10 percent, those of the emerging world were being enlarged by just less than three million, expanding by 22 percent between 1969 and 1978. In this connection, Africa has changed most in the ten-year period. Armed forces are estimated to have increased from 684,000 to 1,335,000 or 95.2 percent. The Middle East follows with a 62 percent increase and then, surprisingly, Latin America, which has no outstanding military conflicts similar to those in Africa and the Middle East, registered a gain of almost 35 percent in personnel under arms.[1]

When the level of analysis focuses, as in table 1-2, on individual country behavior, the picture of expanding military spending in emerging states becomes sharper and more arresting. In all but one instance (Nigeria whose military spending declined after the Biafran war), the countries listed have

Table 1-1
Military Expenditures, GNP, per Capita Military Expenditures, Armed Forces, and Armed Forces per 1,000 of Population, Global and Regional Data, 1969 and 1978
(billions of dollars)

	Military Expenditures (1977 constant dollars)			GNP (1977 constant dollars)			Military Expenditures/ GNP		
	1969[a]	1978	Percentage Change	1969[a]	1978[a]	Percentage Change	1969	1978	Percentage Change
Global									
World	383	447	16.7	5,746	8,348	45.3	6.7	5.4	-19.4
Developed	320	345	7.8	4,698	6,490	38.1	6.8	5.3	-22.1
Developing	63	102	61.9	1,048	1,858	77.3	6.0	5.5	-8.3
Regions									
North America	136	105	-22.8	1,663	2,174	30.7	8.2	4.8	-41.5
NATO Europe	51	64	25.5	1,322	1,771	34.0	3.9	3.6	-7.7
Warsaw Europe	125	165	32.0	1,040	1,528	46.9	12.1	10.8	-10.7
Africa	5	7	40.0	140	212	51.4	3.3	3.1	-6.1
East Asia	38	52	36.8	743	1,340	80.3	5.1	3.9	-23.5
Latin America	4	7	75.0	258	439	70.2	1.7	1.6	-5.9
Middle East	10	30	200.0	101	225	122.8	9.8	13.4	36.7
Oceania	3	3	—	85	118	38.8	3.6	2.5	-30.1
South Asia	3	5	66.7	91	136	49.5	3.3	3.3	—

	Military Expenditures per Capita			Armed Forces (in thousands)			Armed Forces per 1,000		
	1969	1978	Percentage Change	1969	1978	Percentage Change	1969	1978	Percentage Change
Global									
World	107	103	-3.7	24,830	26,639	7.3	7.0	6.2	-11.4
Developed	324	324	—	11,830	10,755	-9.1	12.0	10.1	-15.8
Developing	24	31	29.2	13,000	15,884	22.2	5.1	4.9	-3.9
Regions									
North America	605	432	-28.6	3,560	2,180	-38.8	15.9	9.0	-43.4
NATO Europe	167	198	18.6	3,146	2,746	-12.7	10.3	8.5	-17.5
Warsaw Europe	365	447	22.5	5,434	6,162	13.4	15.8	16.7	5.7
Africa	15	16	6.7	684	1,335	95.2	2.3	3.3	43.5
East Asia	29	33	13.8	6,983	8,234	17.9	5.5	5.4	-1.8
Latin America	16	20	25.0	1,111	1,500	35.0	4.1	4.4	7.3

Table 1-1 *(continued)*

	Military Expenditures per Capita			Armed Forces (in thousands)			Armed Forces per 1,000		
	1969	*1978*	*Percentage Change*	*1969*	*1978*	*Percentage Change*	*1969*	*1978*	*Percentage Change*
Middle East	103	245	137.9	909	1,469	61.6	9.4	11.9	26.6
Oceania	206	142	−31.1	96	87	−9.4	6.3	4.2	−33.3
South Asia	4	5	25.0	2,028	2,102	3.6	3.2	2.4	−25.0

Source: Arms Control and Disarmament Agency, *World Military Expenditures and Arms Transfers 1969-1978* (Washington, D.C.: U.S. Government Printing Office, 1981), pp. 33-36.

^aRounded to nearest billion.

Table 1-2
Military Expenditures, GNP, per Capita Military Expenditures, Armed Forces, and Armed Forces per 1,000 of Population, Selected Regional States, 1969 and 1978

	Military Expenditures[a] (1977 constant dollars)			GNP[e] (1977 constant dollars)			Military Expenditures/ GNP		
	1969	1978	Percentage Change	1969	1978	Percentage Change	1969	1978	Percentage Change
Africa									
Nigeria	1,887	1,742	−7.7	19.4	41.4	113.4	9.7	4.2	−56.7
South Africa	770	1,618	110.1	28.8	38.4	33.3	2.7	4.2	55.5
Ethiopia	64	94	46.9	2.5	3.4	36.0	2.6	2.8	7.7
Somalia	18	60	233.3	0.4	0.4	—	5.1	13.8	170.6
Morocco	170	421	147.6	6.5	11.4	75.4	2.6	3.7	42.3
East Asia[b]									
North Korea	1,002	2,112[c]	110.8	5.4	9.0[c]	66.6	18.7	23.4[c]	25.1
South Korea	645	2,112	227.4	16.7	38.7	131.7	3.9	5.5	41.0
Thailand	309	670	116.8	10.9	20.3	86.2	2.8	3.3	17.9
Malaysia	207	615	197.1	7.1	13.6	91.5	2.9	4.5	55.2
Indonesia	184	1,480	88.8	24.4	47.3	93.9	3.2	3.1	−3.1
Middle East									
Iran	2,970	9,866	232.2	35.9	69.3	93.0	8.3	14.2	71.1
Iraq	1,343	1,988	48.0	9.7	22.0	126.8	13.8	9.1	−34.1
Egypt	707	1,261	78.4	7.4	14.9	101.4	9.6	8.5	−11.4
Syria	370	1,095	195.9	3.7	7.0	89.2	10.1	15.7	55.4
Saudi Arabia	1,921	9,574	398.4	17.6	59.6	238.6	10.9	16.1	47.7
Israel	1,943	3,643	87.5	9.6	15.0	56.2	20.3	24.3	19.7
Latin America									
Argentina	738	1,459	97.7	38.0	48.4	27.4	1.9	3.0	57.9
Brazil	1,587	1,623	2.3	79.4	173.9	119.0	2.0	0.9	−55.0
Cuba	302	437[d]	44.7	6.9	7.0[d]	1.4	4.4	6.2[d]	40.9
Peru	286	699	144.4	8.7	12.2	40.2	3.3	5.7	72.7
South Asia									
India	2,267	3,394	49.7	75.6	106.2	40.5	3.0	3.2	6.6
Pakistan	631	844	33.8	10.6	16.5	55.7	5.9	5.1	−13.6

Table 1-2 *(continued)*

	Armed Forces (in thousands)			Armed Forces per 1000			Military Expenditures (1977 constant dollars)		
	1969	1978	Percentage Change	1969	1978	Percentage Change	1969	1978	Percentage Change
Africa									
Nigeria	110	204	85.4	2.0	2.8	40.0	34	24	−29.4
South Africa	55	78	41.8	2.5	2.9	16.0	35	59	68.6
Ethiopia	45	233	417.8	1.8	7.5	3.2	2	3	50.0
Somalia	18	54	200.0	6.7	15.9	1.4	6	17	183.3
Morocco	70	115	64.3	4.5	5.8	28.9	11	21	90.9
East Asia									
North Korea	410	632	54.1	29.7	34.9	17.5	72	120^c	66.7
South Korea	620	600	−3.2	19.3	15.6	−19.2	20	54	170.7
Thailand	175	250	42.9	4.8	5.5	14.6	8	14	75.0
Malaysia	46	82	78.3	4.3	6.2	44.2	19	46	142.1
Indonesia	358	250	−30.2	3.0	1.7	−43.3	6	10	66.7
Middle East									
Iran	225	350	55.5	8.0	9.6	20.0	105	270	157.1
Iraq	90	140	55.5	9.9	11.2	13.1	147	159	8.2
Egypt	230	350	52.2	7.1	8.8	23.9	21	31	47.7
Syria	75	225	200.0	12.3	27.4	122.8	60	133	121.7
Saudi Arabia	60	50	−16.7	10.0	5.7	−43.0	320	1,088	240.0
Israel	100	165	65.0	34.5	44.6	29.3	670	984	46.9
Latin America									
Argentina	160	155	−3.1	6.8	5.8	−14.7	31	54	74.2
Brazil	360	450	25.0	3.9	3.9	—	17	13	−23.5
Cuba	140	210	50.0	16.7	21.6	29.3	36	80	122.2
Peru	75	125	66.7	5.7	7.5	31.6	21	41	95.2
South Asia									
India	1,510	1,300	−13.9	2.8	2.0	−28.6	4	5	25.0
Pakistan	390	518	32.8	6.1	6.3	3.3	9	10	11.1

Source: Arms Control and Disarmament Agency, *World Military Expenditures and Arms Transfers 1969-1978* (Washington, D.C.: U.S. Government Printing Office, 1981), pp. 38ff.

[a] In millions of dollars.

[b] Data on Vietnam not available.

[c] Data for 1977.

[d] Data for 1975.

[e] In billions, rounded to nearest one-hundred million.

allocated more real resources to military forces in 1978 than in 1969 measured in constant 1977 dollars. In eleven out of twenty-two instances increases in spending have more than doubled. For Somalia, South Korea, and Iran, these expenditures rose more than 200 percent over this period, with Malaysia and Syria almost at that level. Saudi Arabia exceeded all other states, with an increase of almost 400 percent. In only two cases did per capita expenditures decrease: ten dollars per person in Nigeria and four dollars per person in Brazil.

A glance at armed forces levels provides additional evidence of the increase in military capabilities of developing-state armies. Only five of the twenty-two states listed in table 1-2 as a representative sample of regional powers decreased personnel under arms (South Korea, Indonesia, Saudi Arabia, Argentina, India). On the other hand, overall military spending for these five countries grew, whether measured in total expenditures or in per capita outlays. This suggests that more funds were being spent on military equipment and on improving the quality and efficiency of these national armed forces, measured by their acquisition of newer and more sophisticated equipment.

Table 1-3 summarizes trends in the acquisition of increasingly sophisticated military hardware among developing states. Developing states have achieved considerable increases in firepower, range, and reliability over the entire spectrum of ground, sea, and air systems. Table 1-3 reinforces the image of an increasingly diffuse international security system, characterized by a rising number of centers of military force. In 1950, SIPRI indicates that no third-world state had supersonic aircraft or missiles and only one possessed armored fighting vehicles, such as tanks or armored personnel carriers. By 1960, 38 countries had heavy armor in their inventories; 26 had modern warships; and yet only one state (Taiwan) had supersonic aircraft. Ten years later the numbers have increased dramatically in all these categories. Moreover, by 1977, almost 50 emerging states deployed supersonic aircraft, some as advanced as those found in the air forces of developed states. These included MiG 23's (North Korea, Syria, Iraq), Jaguars (Oman and Ecuador), Mirage 3's and 5's (17 states), and F-5's (16 states).[2] Over 80 developing states by then possessed heavy armor; 42 had various missile capabilities; and 67 disposed modern warships in their navies, which have usually emphasized fast, light ships with impressive destructive capabilities.

The upward trends in the military-expenditures and weapons-acquisition data found in the preceding tables are reinforced by an examination of the arms imports of these states in table 1-4. Using five-year averages for 1969-1973 and 1974-1978, the developing countries clearly outdistanced the developed states in the amount and rate of growth of arms imports. Part of this trend, however, can be attributed to decreased arms trade within the

Table 1-3

Number of Third-World Countries with Advanced Military Systems, 1950, 1960, 1970, 1977

	1950	1960	1970	1977
Supersonic aircraft	—	1	28	47
Missiles	—	6	25	42
Armored fighting vehicles	1	38	72	83
Modern warships	4	26	56	67

Source: Stockholm International Peace Research Institute (SIPRI), *World Armaments and Disarmament: 1978* (New York: Crane, Russak, 1978), pp. 238-253. *Armored fighting vehicles* refer only to post-World War II design equipment.

North Atlantic Treaty Organization (NATO) alliance and Western Europe's lessened dependence on the import of U.S. equipment. In 1969-1973, the developing states accounted for 71.2 percent of all transfers; in the next five-year period of 1974-1978, the percentage rose to 76.0 percent. Correspondingly, the rate of growth is also impressive since the base for the imports of developing countries is greater to start with than for developed countries. The former jumped their imports by nearly 49.2 percent; the latter increased by just over 16 percent.

Table 1-4

Arms Imports by Five-Year Averages

(millions of constant 1977 dollars)

	Imports		Percentage Change
	1969-1973	1974-1978	
Global			
World	12,044.2	16,838.4	39.8
Developed	3,463.2	4,039.6	16.6
Developing	8,580.6	12,798.6	49.2
Regions			
North America	366.2	307.0	− 16.2
NATO Europe	1,760.8	1,734.4	− 1.5
Warsaw Europe	1,501.0	2,219.0	47.8
Africa	463.2	2,645.4	471.1
East Asia	4,052.4	1,728.8	− 57.3
Latin America	434.4	857.6	97.4
Middle East	2,552.0	6,038.6	136.6
Oceania	163.6	170.4	4.2
South Asia	461.4	644.6	39.7

Source: Arms Control and Disarmament Agency, *World Military Expenditures and Arms Transfers 1969-1978* (Washington, D.C.: U.S. Government Printing Office, 1981), pp. 117-120.

The breakdown in table 1-4 reveals that the greatest rate of increase in arms imports was in Africa, including North Africa. Many of the states, especially those south of the Sahara, are among those with the lowest per capita income. Over the last five years, imports into Africa increased more than 470 percent over the previous five-year period. The Middle East is also a leader with an increase of slightly more than 136 percent. Paralleling the rate of increase in military power, Latin America is in third place in arms imports, followed by South Asia. Only East Asia declines as a result of the end of the Vietnam War. Table 1-5 identifies arms imports by five-year averages for several regional countries. It presents a more detailed picture of the dynamics of arms imports at the local level.

Table 1-5
Arms Imports by Five-Year Averages for Selected States
(millions of constant 1977 dollars)

	Imports		
	1969-1973	*1974-1978*	*Percentage Change*
Africa			
Nigeria	23.2	44.6	92.2
South Africa	85.2	126.2	48.1
Ethiopia	14.4	310.2	2,054.2
Somalia	22.4	105.8	372.3
Morocco	10.2	191.6	1,778.4
East Asia			
North Korea	175.4	105.0	−40.1
South Korea	391.4	293.8	−24.9
Thailand	83.2	65.4	−21.4
Malaysia	35.6	60.2	69.1
Indonesia	21.6	59.2	174.1
Middle East			
Iran	503.0	1,826.2	263.1
Iraq	255.8	1,093.4	327.4
Egypt	721.2	252.2	−65.0
Syria	492.8	705.4	43.1
Saudi Arabia	93.0	608.8	554.6
Israel	336.8	1,013.2	200.8
Latin America			
Argentina	55.0	73.6	33.8
Brazil	85.6	132.4	54.7
Cuba	59.4	135.0	127.3
Peru	71.0	206.4	190.1
South Asia			
India	256.4	384.6	50.0
Pakistan	124.4	162.2	30.4

Source: Arms Control and Disarmament Agency, *World Military Expenditures and Arms Transfers 1969-1978* (Washington, D.C.: U.S. Government Printing Office, 1981), pp. 123-158.

Significantly, these patterns appear to be a function of the levels of regional conflict and, of course, a function of petrodollar recycling. Moreover, the superpower competition fuels regional arms races since the superpowers are in most cases the principal suppliers of regional rivals. The Soviet Union is a major or principal supplier of Ethiopia, North Korea, Algeria, and Syria; the United States also supports its clients in Asia (South Korea) and the Middle East (Saudi Arabia and Israel).[3] Morocco, among others, is a partial exception to this pattern, receiving twice as many arms from France as from the United States to sustain its war in the western Sahara.[4]

More revealing than arms imports perhaps is the increasing tendency of developing countries to produce their own weapons either indigenously or under license. These arms include heavy armor, supersonic and subsonic aircraft, helicopters, missiles, and warships. Table 1-6 contrasts the number of states manufacturing various categories of weapons in 1965 and 1976. The list has now grown to approximately thirty states.[5] The factors conditioning and prompting this growth are varied and complex, but most prominent among these is a desire to be increasingly independent of foreign suppliers and the pressures that they can exert over a nation's security interests. The views of Brazilian Air Force Minister Joelmir Campos de Araripe Macedo are typical of those found among third-world elites concerned with national security: "The time has come to free ourselves from the United States and the countries of Europe. It is a condition of security that each nation manufacture its own armaments."[6]

A Comparative Approach to the Study of Security Policy

Although these general indexes underscore the importance of developing countries for regional and global security, they tell us little about what factors, or what combination of factors over time, explain these trends. They tell us even less how security systems are organized and operate. Part of the answer to these questions lies in knowledge of the specific security policies pursued by states and their ruling regimes. What is needed, furthermore, is an accumulation of such studies guided by a common analytic framework (1) to facilitate systematic study in terms of the same set of security imperatives and constraints confronting all states in defining and executing security policy; (2) to permit comparisons between states along the same range of categories of action and decision that are examined; and (3) to trace the impact of these separate state policies on global and regional security systems. With the knowledge derived from such studies of the security behavior of individual states, we should be able to deepen our

Table 1-6
Domestic Defense Production in Developing Countries, 1965, 1975, and 1979

	Aircraft			Missiles			Armored Fighting Vehicles			Warships			Small Arms			Electronics			Aircraft Engines		
	1965	1975	1979	1965	1975	1979	1965	1975	1979	1965	1975	1979	1965	1975	1979	1965	1975	1979	1965	1975	1979
China	x	x	x	x	x	x	x	x	x	x	x	x	x	x	x	x	x	x	x	x	x
India	x	x	x	x	x	x	x	x	x	x	x	x	x	x	x	x	x	x	x	x	x
Israel	x	x	x	x	x	x		x	x		x	x	x	x	x	x	x	x		x	x
South Africa	x	x	x	x	x	x		x	x		x	x	x	x	x	x	x	x	x	x	x
Brazil	x	x	x	x	x	x		x	x		x	x	x	x	x		x	x	x	x	x
Argentina	x	x	x		x	x		x	x	x	x	x	x	x	x			(x)			
Pakistan	x	x	x		x	x			x	x	x	x	x	x	x		x	x			
Chile	x[a]	x[b]		x[c]	x[d]	x				x			x	x	x		x				
Egypt		x	(x)			x						x	x	x	x						
Iran		x	?										(x)	x	x		x	?			
Indonesia	x	x	x										x	x	x						
North Korea		x	x								x	x	x	x	x						
South Korea		x	x								x	x	(x)	x	x						
Philippines		x	x						x		x	x	x	x	x						
Singapore		x	x								x	x		x	x						
Taiwan		x	x		x						x	x		x	x	x	x	x			
South Vietnam		x				x				x			(x)	x	x	x	x	x			
North Vietnam		x	x								x	x		x	x						
Colombia		x	x							x	x	x									
Dominican Republic											x	x		x	x			[f]			
Mexico			x							x	x	x	(x)	x	x						
Zimbabwe		x								x	x	x[e]	(x)	x	x		x				
Thailand		x	x					x	x			x[e]		x	x						
Guyana										x											
Peru											x	x					x	x			
Saudi Arabia														x							
Gabon											x	x									
Bangladesh											x	x									
Burma										x	x	x									
Nepal														x	x						
Malaysia														x	x			x			

Table 1-6 (continued)

	Aircraft			Missiles			Armored Fighting Vehicles			Warships			Small Arms			Electronics			Aircraft Engines		
	1965	1975	1979	1965	1975	1979	1965	1975	1979	1965	1975	1979	1965	1975	1979	1965	1975	1979	1965	1975	1979
Venezuela												x[e]									
Sri Lanka												x[e]									
Trinidad												(x)[e]									

Source: International Institute for Strategic Studies, *Strategic Survey, 1976* (London: 1977), p. 22 and updated with Stockholm International Peace Research Institute, *World Armaments and Disarmament* (New York: Crane, Russak, 1979), pp. 152-167 and 1980, pp. 44-56. It has generally been assumed that a country with a production capability in 1975 will have that capability in 1979; Iran is taken as an exception.

Note: (x) = no definite information available on whether production underway.

[a] Production of aircraft terminated in mid-1960s.

[b] Advanced plans to start aircraft production under license within the framework of AMIO (Arab Military Industrialization Organization) arrested after Camp David due to Saudi-Egyptian differences.

[c] Production of missiles terminated in 1965.

[d]

[e] Advanced plans to start missile production under license within the framework of AMIO.

[f] Domestic defense production underway either as indigenous development or under license.

understanding of the sources of international conflicts and the process by which conflicts are initiated, articulated, managed, and resolved insofar as they imply the use or threat of violence. We should also have a greater grasp of the role that force and threats play in internal and external regime policies and policymaking.

For the purposes of this book, policy refers to the decisions and actions of state regimes to produce desired outcomes. For a state to have a policy it must not only seek certain definable outcomes but must also have some capacity or chance of affecting the behavior of its own people or regimes and peoples abroad in these intended ways. If one has aims, but no ability to shape outcomes, one has more a hope or aspiration than a policy; if one can produce outcomes but not define aims, one manifests power but no policy. The two need to be combined to qualify as a policy. By *security* policy, we mean that set of decisions and actions taken by a government to preserve or create an internal and external order congenial to its interests and values primarily (although not exclusively) through the threat or use of force.

To guide—though not to dictate—the studies that follow, nine dimensions of security policymaking are stipulated. These include:

1. elite assumptions about the international system within which national military force must operate; whether, for example, the structure is constraining or permissive, hostile or benign, legitimate or illegitimate;
2. the definition of military (and nonmilitary) threats to the domestic political regime or nation-state or both; the national objectives to be supported by the use or threat of military force; and the regional and international security structure implied by its security policies and behavior;
3. the military doctrinal response to these threats and opportunities, requiring the use or threat of force;
4. the force levels and weapon systems organized to respond to the previous three levels of decision and action;
5. the announced strategies to communicate to, or to conceal policies from, allies, adversaries, and neutrals as well as subordinates (military elites, functionaries, et al.) and the coordination of coercive and noncoercive instruments of power;
6. the human and material resources, including advanced technology, needed to respond to security imperatives while addressing internal socioeconomic demands;
7. the marshalling of public opinion, political parties, and interest groups to support regime and national objectives and policies;
8. the creation of political incentives and controls to direct the military establishment to support defined objectives; and
9. alignment strategies with allies and adversaries to maximize security objectives, including arms-control measures.

The chapters that follow encourage optimism that these nine stipulated categories of strategic policy are appropriate for a comparative analysis of strategic policy because in greater or lesser measure each of the states and elites under review has had to confront, and continues to confront, hard choices at each posited level of decision and action. Approaching security policy from the perspective of the hard choices that ruling elites must make in discharging their security functions provides a clearer and operationally more relevant picture of the security policies of these states and their principal determinants than would be the case from a simple recounting of the announced policies of these countries or from a tedious description of their armed forces or deployment. Also by stressing the political choices and compromises that structure every state's security policies, the relation of military policy to other state policies and goals can be illuminated. Highlighted, too, will be the roles played by different interstate and intrastate groups in defining a state's security policies. Approaching security policies from the actual problem-solving framework within which political decision makers must work injects a note of realism into the discussion. Working within a common analytic framework that is susceptible to adaptation, given the particular mix of problems faced by a specific state, permits relevant comparisons while not ignoring the specific differences among countries.

The categories to be applied to elite decision and action in the domain of security policy derive from the inherent requirements of organizing violence and using or threatening it for varied purposes, whether these are designed to influence the behavior of other countries and ruling elites, to repress or control domestic opposition, to preserve order, to do all three, or to accomplish any other goal that might be appropriately specified as attainable through force. If it can be reasonably claimed that these categories of comparison must be observed in some fashion if a state's governing regime is to maximize its chances of achieving posited aims through threats or the application of violence, it does not follow that elite groups within a state or between states will define the substantive content of these several categories in the same way even under similar circumstances. What may be a problem for one country may not be for another. A closed society, like Vietnam, may have little trouble controlling its communication strategies to influence the behavior of allies and adversaries. The government in Israel, subject to open criticism and democratic rule, cannot fully control the statements or behavior of other domestic actors, nor can the prime minister always count on the public support of his own cabinet ministers. On the other hand, countries like Pakistan, Syria, and Iraq have special problems with military intervention in civil affairs. If each of these states faces problems in acquiring, producing, and transferring arms or in influencing a reluctant protector or in marshalling public support for its security policies, each must develop its own solutions to fit its unique circumstances.

The security policy of a state may be seen to be decided and executed within a framework composed of two conceptually different, but operationally fused, political processes. The first is interstate in character and encompasses the bargaining and negotiating among nations for advantage in which force or its threat is a basic medium of exchange. The second process is intrastate and involves all aspects of a state's domestic politics and decision-making institutions that play a part in defining its security policies to respond to external imperatives. It is very difficult to separate any one function of the nine dimensions of security policymaking already outlined and classify it solely as a derivative of the interstate or the intrastate process. If one assumes a static conception of security policymaking, it is perhaps conceivable, for example, to argue that conceptions of external threat are totally defined by external conditions. Yet how elites and public opinion within a state define the external environment, whether as menacing or supportive or as acceptable or intolerable, also determines in part what kind of international environment will develop. A state's security policies would appear to be a compromise between the imperatives confronted within each of these intertwined processes. Strategic policy may thus be viewed as both an independent set of factors affecting the environment to which it is directed and as an outcome or derivative of the environment within which it is formed.

Like Clausewitz's notion of pure war by which real war can be examined and evaluated, the categories stipulated above provide ideal forms against which the actual behavior of states and their elites can be uniformly observed and experience accumulated. These responses and reactions may be patterned, ordered, informed, and calibrated relative to means and ends or, contrariwise, they may be discontinuous, fragmented, and contradictory. Whatever the case, the accumulating decisional and action chains that crystallize form a unique structure and dynamic appropriate to each nation's needs and condition. On the other hand, the composite of these case studies provides the basis for generalization across cases to identify common features in all of them or clusters of commonality that can advance our understanding of how global and regional security systems work.

Figure 1-1 suggests how this process of decision and action may be conceived and portrayed. The process model is divided into three phases identified by roman numerals. Although these three phases are depicted as sequential in time, they are in reality simultaneous. The first (roman numeral I) includes a set of varying internal and external input factors that prompt, elicit, or compel elite responses to security problems. The number of input factors that might be specified for all states and those that apply to a particular state are too numerous to be cited. The factors noted are illustrative, not exhaustive or determinative.

Elite responses to input stimuli result in two distinguishable output phases. The first of these, or intervening phase (roman numeral II), constitutes the substantive decisions and actions taken over time by a nation's elite to form the major components of a state's security policies. This phase includes the nine dimensions of security-policy decision making previously sketched. These responses lead to yet a third phase (roman numeral III), characterized by the impact that a state's strategic policies have had on the global and regional security environment and the feedback effect on those policies. They may have had the intended effect on other elites or on the physical parameters limiting action; they may have been frustrated by countervailing elite reactions; or some mix of success and failure will result. The feedback on the field of input factors prompting elite decision making leads to the creation of a new equilibrium of forces that either reinforces, weakens, or affirms, although sometimes under new conditions, the security policies and position of the ruling coalition within a state.

In the third phase, two sets of related outputs can be observed. The first refers to security processes, the second to the outcomes of these conflict processes. These dimensions are only briefly sketched here, but are elaborated in the individual country analyses that follow and in the concluding chapter.

Many developing states now play key roles in security processes at regional and global levels that were hitherto reserved to the great powers. They can deny or facilitate the access needed by other states to strategic resources (oil, territory, and the like); act as conduits for the transfer of arms from other states or from their own indigenously produced stocks; send troops, "volunteers," or advisors abroad on behalf of allies; or finance the arms acquisitions and defense efforts of other states. Increasing participation in these processes affords developing states an opportunity to determine the outcomes of conflicts at local, regional, and global levels.

At a local level, developing states now define a wide array of specific security outcomes. They may wish to be recognized as a nuclear power, as with India's explosion of an atomic device in 1974. Or, they may seek to hold key but vulnerable strategic areas (Israel's retention of the Golan Heights after the 1967 war). They may also strive to deter an enemy attack on their homeland (Cuba's reliance on the Soviet Union to forestall U.S. incursions), or successfully coerce an adversary to withdraw from a strategic salient (Vietnamese pressure to effect U.S. departure from Southeast Asia). They may also contribute significantly to the maintenance or overthrow of another regime. (Saudi money keeps the North Yemeni government afloat; Cuba and Vietnam have also been instrumental in implanting preferred regimes, respectively, in Africa and Asia.) Finally, developing states have a greater capacity than ever before to set regional and global security agendas. They have increased say over what problems will be addressed, in what manner and sequence, and to what degree of salience. For example, questions such as whether a conflict will lead to hostilities (Iran and Iraq) or

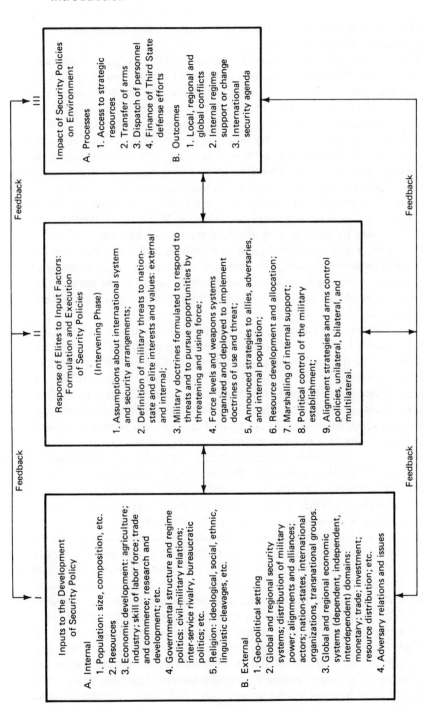

Figure 1-1. Security Policymaking at the Nation-State Level

whether a state will go nuclear (India and Pakistan), fall increasingly within the purview of developing states.

Developing states also shape the security environment in unintended ways. The Truman administration did not seek Chinese intervention in the Korean War, but its decision to cross the 38th parallel inevitably led to that result. The repercussions of Chinese entry into the conflict had a significant impact on American security policy. China and the Soviet Union were identified as coconspirators at the very time that the two Communist giants were splitting apart. In treating the two as unified allies, bent on undermining the U.S. global position, rather than as incipient antagonists open to manipulation for U.S. advantage, Washington's intransigence thrust both into uneasy alignment. An increasingly diffuse and decentralized international system was artificially polarized around the Moscow-Washington conflict; the Cold War was intensified with the attendant risks and costs of armed hostilities on a global scale; American resources and attention were unnecessarily dissipated in isometric exercises of managing tensions partly of Washington's own creation; China was isolated in the world community; and the independence and the freedom of maneuver of other nation-states were constrained.

The impact of the security policies of developing states on regional and global security is, as the Chinese example suggests, likely to grow, not diminish, in the future. The struggles between India and Pakistan or Israel and the Arab states or the Vietnam-Laos-Cambodian triangle have obvious security implications beyond their regional sources. Created from these local conflicts are worldwide alignment patterns that define the larger context within which these primary adversarial relations are worked out. More broadly, webs are created—some discrete, others interlaced—that facilitate or hinder states' achievement of their security objectives. The United States-Cuban conflict further illustrates the point. Moscow's sponsorship of the Castro regime raises a seemingly regional struggle to global proportions. Similarly, Cuban intervention in Ethiopia and Angola affects United States security interests in Africa—and those of the African states.

There is evidence that decision makers are sensitive not only to specific outcomes that they favor or oppose at a nation-state level but also seek to break or bend the constraints set by regional and global security systems on which their narrower objectives depend. French security policies under President Charles de Gaulle, for example, must be understood in these inclusive terms.[7] The French *force de frappe*, whatever its operational capabilities in deterring foreign aggression, was the centerpiece of the Gaullist attack on the rigid bipolar international security system that grew out of the superpower conflict after World War II. De Gaulle argued that the system was unstable and illegitimate: unstable because it increased the risks of war since an armed clash between the superpowers or their clients could provoke a global conflagration; illegitimate, because Moscow and Washington usurped the security roles of other states whose performance was the primary source of the moral and legal authority of the nation-state and because the smaller states might be dragged into war against their own interests. France's withdrawal from NATO, its pursuit of an independent security policy, and its promotion of detente were policies aimed at changing the rules of behavior and enlarging its own possibilities of maneuver and independent action and those of other states within an altered international security regime. France's initiatives, when combined with others, such as those of the nations of the nonaligned movement, did eventually contribute to a more diffuse, decentralized international system and a far more complex (and confusing) set of regional and global security systems.

Scope and Organization of the Book

If analysts possessed systematic and readily available knowledge of each phase of nation-state security policymaking (a wildly optimistic assumption), the support factors shaping regime and nation-state strategic policies and the perceived and real impact of these policies on other actors and on the geopolitical environment could be more clearly explained and, potentially, controlled. Comparative analysis obviously cannot meet all our needs in these areas, but it can be helpful. First, from a methodological viewpoint, the actual decisions and actions of real regimes and countries are examined in the chapters that follow within a common framework of analysis. Instead of ascribing the same behavior to all states to satisfy the analyst's need for logical consistency and forced uniformity, the multiplicity of specific factors surrounding, conditioning, and determining elite choice in the security domain can be taken into account. At the same time the search for generalizations across cases—the thrust of theory—can inch along since the same set of categories of behavior is applied to all political actors.

A comparative approach essentially makes no assumptions about how a ruling elite will specifically behave in acquiring or using military power; only that along the dimension of security policy sketched above it must fashion some response or take initiatives—wittingly, consciously, intentionally or not—if it is to shape the environment in desired ways. Generalization is then rooted in experience. Observations are potentially subject to empirical verification. Knowledge developed in this manner can also be accumulated and modified as new evidence about elite and national behavior in the security-policy domain is recorded.

A comparative approach to security policy, built on the discrete observations of different observers, admittedly poses major problems for consistent and systematic observation. The biases of the observer will almost inevitably intrude and flaw objective analysis. This study runs these risks in the interests of generating tentative hypotheses and substantive knowledge of how the global and security systems are structured and how nations, working through the elites in control of their governments and armed forces, relate to each other in circumstances implying the use or threat of force.

A country-specific rather than a regional analysis has certain advantages. First, it focuses on how the parts of a larger regional and transregional security system work. We have to know how the parts operate in order to understand how the larger systems to which these parts are attached function. We do not have nearly as much information as we need to generalize confidently about these groupings. Through this book we hope to encourage the accumulation of country-specific studies, guided by a common comparative framework, in order to produce more solid knowledge than we now have about them. Through such an approach we can avoid positing the existence of regional and global constraints that may be more in the mind of the observer than a conditioning factor in the behavior of the actor who is being studied. Notions like regional and global security can then be built up from their components. Indeed, most of the states in this volume do not confine their behavior to the geographic area of their immediate regional setting but act on a larger stage with implications that go well beyond their locales. Security systems develop, like tapestries, from these strands of activity. We hope to follow these strands and to identify patterns made by the actors themselves rather than impose preconceived notions on state security behavior.

Second, a country-specific approach to comparative analysis highlights patterns across regions that might otherwise be obscured if a regional bias were introduced too early into the analysis. For example, the country chapters reveal the profound and pervasive effect that modernization has had on national armed forces across regions. While the impact is variable and the rate of change differential, all of the states under study are subject to the compelling force of technological innovation. Civilian and military technology, which motors modernization, is being diffused throughout the globe and is tending to encourage a structural convergence on national armed forces. This convergence both widens and narrows the options available to ruling elites. Developing states can now project greater amounts of lethality at greater distances more rapidly and accurately than ever before, but they are also limited to the menu of responses endemic to these weapons.

This book could conceivably be organized on any one of several principles. All states, developing and developed countries separately, or some selected mix of each, might have been examined. Space and data limitations precluded the first two options. Focusing on developed states would have required us to go over some well-trodden ground, although the approach would have been different. Mixing selected developed and developing states was an intriguing possibility, and might well have been pursued if the gaps in the current literature about the security policies of developing states had not been so obvious. As editors we concluded that a book devoted primarily to developing states would have the greatest value at this time for students and practitioners in international relations and, specifically, for those interested in regional and global security and arms-control problems. These states also provided a challenging terrain on which to apply a comparative framework of analysis. If it works for them, it is likely to be applicable to more developed countries with more advanced and complex security systems.

As editors, we faced several problems in deciding on what states to study. Constraints included space, the availability of analysts willing and able to work within a comparative-security framework, and the amount of support we could get for the project. Several criteria were relevant in choosing the fourteen states studied in this book. All have impressive military establishments measured by spending relative to per capita expenditures or GNP, number of personnel under arms, complexity of their organization, or sophistication of military equipment at their disposal. To these were added considerations of the arms-production, procurement, and transfer policies and the security and foreign-policy alignment strategies that they have pursued in the recent past. The strategies, organizational structures, and national and international processes used by these states to make, buy, or sell arms are elaborate, intricate, and generally multinational. All are central actors in the regional security systems of which they are a part and many have been key players in regional and even global conflict situations.

Not all states meeting these criteria have been included. Algeria, Libya, Taiwan, and North Korea, for example, do not appear. It might also be argued that China should have been included or that Israel and even South Africa should not be grouped with developing countries. The lack of available researchers and the problem of space forced some unwelcome choices. The literature on China is abundant and we felt that we could make a more useful contribution by focusing on states that have received less attention. Israel and South Africa are too important to exclude simply in terms of their economic development; if wealth were a standard for exclusion, Argentina or Iraq would also have to be dropped. Our aim is to present a sufficiently representative grouping of states to provide some clearer idea than we have now of the significant and increasingly important role that these emerging powers (most of which are still economically underdeveloped) play in defining and articulating the organization and rules, however incomplete, fractured, or refracted they may be, of global and regional security systems.

Finding analysts for the various countries studied in this book also proved more formidable than we had anticipated. The number of researchers that have the requisite country-specific, regional, and analytic skills in security policymaking is small. Several who were contacted were otherwise committed; others were reticent about working within a comparative framework. We also discovered that analysts rarely knew each other or their work across regional lines. This circumstance became an additional justification for the enterprise but an obstacle as well. The participants in the symposium from which this book emerged are a diverse group, and molding them into a working team has posed numerous problems because of their different personal styles, backgrounds, and settled methodological and substantive views. Guidelines were written to encourage uniformity and coherence, and these have been observed, although in different measure, by the contributors. A two-day symposium, held at the University of Illinois in May 1980, allowed the contributors and editors to meet each other—many for the first time—and to criticize and perfect their respective efforts. Gaps quickly surfaced and lapses were more easily identified than would have otherwise been possible through written communication with busy and harassed analysts. Each analyst subsequently revised his or her paper into the form in which it appears here, and the editors completed work on their introduction and on the concluding chapter. These efforts were moved to completion as rapidly as possible even at the sacrifice of some papers to facilitate timely use by students and practitioners of security policy and policymaking. Much work still needs to be done. We hope this book will provide impulse and guidance for other studies.

Notes

1. Accurate data about the strength of current national armed forces compared to their composition ten years ago are not readily available. That the trend is in the direction indicated by table 1-1 is suggested by a comparison of the military capabilities of developing states listed in the annual publication of the International Institute of Strategic Studies. See their publication, *The Military Balance* for 1965-66 and 1980-81, passim, and compare with ACDA source cited in table 1-1.

2. Stockholm International Peace Research Institute (SIPRI), *World Armaments and Disarmament: 1978* (New York: Crane, Russak, 1978), pp. 240-241.

3. China and the Soviet Union share almost equally as arms suppliers to North Korea, with the Soviets slightly ahead over the period 1974-1978, having sent $220 million in arms to Chinese transfers of $190 million. Arms Control and Disarmament Agency, *World Military Expenditures, 1968-1977*, p. 160.

4. See Stephen J. Solarz, "Arms for Morocco?" *Foreign Affairs* 53 (Winter 1979/1980):278-299.

5. There are several useful sources that sketch increasing Third World production gains. The bedrock source is SIPRI's annual *World Armaments and Disarmament*, which has a chart of indigenous and licensed third-world production. The 1971 SIPRI publication, *The Arms Trade with the Third World* (New York: Humanities Press), is also useful although now outdated. For a recent brief overview with citations to other works see Michael Moodie, "Defense Industries in the Third World: Problems and Promises," in *Arms Transfers in the Modern World*, eds., Stephanie G. Neuman and Robert E. Harkavy (New York: Praeger, 1979), pp. 294-312.

6. Quoted in Moodie, "Defense Industries," p. 298. See other similar views of third-world elites reviewed in Moodie's article. For an Indian perspective that mirrors these sentiments, see K. Subrahmanyam, *Defence and Development* (Calcutta: Minerva Associates, 1973), and Rajesh K. Agarwell, *Defence Production and Development* (New Delhi: Arnold Heinemann, 1978).

7. See Edward A. Kolodziej, *French International Policy under De Gaulle and Pompidou: The Politics of Grandeur* (Ithaca: Cornell University Press, 1974).

Part I
Latin America

2 Argentina

Edward S. Milenky

The formation and implementation of national-security policy in Argentina provides an important case study for understanding pressures that many developing nations, particularly those not located in regions with high levels of international tensions, experience. These pressures include "small state" status, internal security, and economic security and development. Small states are those that cannot guarantee their security exclusively through their own capabilities and must therefore rely on cooperation with other states, processes, institutions, or on attempts to balance or manipulate forces in the international system.[1] Internal security includes the intrusion of outside forces and the competition of domestic elites to secure and to maintain power. Economic development becomes economic security when elites perceive a connection between industrialization, the maintenance of military power, and the achievement of a higher international status, particularly when many of the required inputs are controlled by other nations.

Argentina is an advanced developing country, a key Latin American nation, and a rising middle power with a growing global role. Although it does not face any overwhelming external military threats, successive governments have been intensely concerned with internal security, a higher degree of economic growth and independence, and with providing a basic capability to respond to threats along the country's frontiers. In practice, security policy has been broadly defined, including matters other than the use of military force and blurring many of the classical distinctions between foreign and domestic policy. Furthermore, while there are core doctrines and generally recognized threats there is also substantial disagreement among elite groups concerning the way in which the nation will go about obtaining its security objectives.

Assumptions about the International System

Historical experience and economic imperatives are two of the most important influences on Argentine elite perceptions of the international system and Argentina's place within it.

A profound sense of lost status and continuing national crisis color all strategic thinking. The Great Depression ended a long period of continuous economic growth fueled by the export of primary products to world markets, a per capita income equal to much of Europe and the British dominions, and political stability. Since 1930 Argentina has experienced a series of *coups d'états* and growing political violence. Although the country has undergone rapid economic growth and industrialization since World War II, it has never regained its comparatively high standing. Consequently, the pre-1930s period is regarded as a golden age, and the country's relative decline in international standing is regarded as a serious obstacle to achievement of economic security. There is a widely shared determination to recover the country's rightful place as a high-status influential power.[2]

Economic conditions, which are partly attributed to the country's loss of status and international influence, compound this sense of crisis. A boombust economic cycle is linked to beef and wheat exports that face unstable world markets. Domestic mismanagement and disputes over the distribution of income and the nature of social policy have frequently compounded foreign-exchange crises and contributed to the country's having the world's highest inflation rate. The large and continuing role of foreign firms and capital in the Argentine economy—British until World War II and those of the United States since then—compounds a strong sense of national vulnerability and external dependence. Higher international status and influence are seen as necessary to redressing the allegedly unequal balance in Argentina's international economic relationships.

Weak nationalism compounds this sense of lost status and external vulnerability. Communal solidarity and commonly shared symbols are poorly developed because of a tradition of family-centered loyalties and the dislocations of large, recent, European immigration, rapid urbanization, and industrialization. In the absence of a fundamental social revolution these tensions, which the economic cycle exacerbates, remain unresolved. As a result, nationalism tends to be directed against perceived external threats, which often provide the most ready source of unity.[3]

Geopolitics has made a contradictory contribution to the Argentine world view. Remoteness from the main centers of international conflict and location within the traditional sphere of U.S. strategic concerns has contributed to a sense of security. However, Argentines have more frequently expressed resentment of U.S. domination of the hemisphere and their country's apparently diminished ability to pursue its aims on the global level. The net result is a traditional sense of marginality or nonparticipation in world politics.[4] Insofar as Argentine elites believe that they are dependent on world markets and economic relationships for national well-being, this condition threatens national security by reducing the country's ability to secure its economic viability.

On the regional level Argentina's relative position also seems to be eroding. Traditionally, Argentina considered itself a European nation by virtue of culture and population, with a higher standard of living than its *mestizo* neighbors; these elements made it the natural leader of Latin America and assured the country's regional security. Leadership of a Latin American bloc of countries in the security sense was a means for achieving more important economic goals, such as better terms of trade and access to advanced industrial technology. However, Brazil has surpassed Argentina in industrial development and is receiving increasing international recognition as an emerging world-class power. Oil-rich Venezuela and Mexico have also emerged as rivals for the leadership of Latin America. By virtue of its still potent revolutionary mystique and connection to the Soviet Union, Cuba has emerged as a potential ideological threat, and even a military threat, should Cuba choose to give support to domestic insurgents. As a result, the regional environment now contributes to Argentina's sense of insecurity and marginality.

Two distinct ideological influences have developed in response to these feelings of insecurity and marginality. Each suggests an explanation and possible alliances. Since the nineteenth century some sectors of the economic and social elite, particularly in Buenos Aires, have aspired to a "European connection" in culture, political ideas, and national self-identification. This European connection would reinforce Argentina's sense of distinctiveness in Latin America and provide a rationale for the pursuit of leadership. In the psychological sense it would provide an extraregional link that would overcome the country's sense of marginality in world affairs. In practice, pursuit of the European connection has given a strong extraregional thrust to the Argentine world view, reinforcing the attention the leadership pays to the country's global position.[5]

The participation of Argentine technocrats in international organizations, particularly development banks and aid organizations, the rise of the third world, and the country's continuing economic and social crisis have given credibility to Marxist and dependency models. Although these approaches vary in specific content, most accept the conclusion of Raul Prebisch, the Argentine executive secretary of the Economic Commission for Latin America, that developing countries are located in the exploited raw-materials-producing periphery of a global economic and political system dominated by a central group of industrialized countries. Acceptance of this approach in Argentina leads to a profound sense of grievance, exploitation, and domination, which appears to explain the country's loss of status and power since 1930.[6]

All of the foregoing factors have combined to produce a widely shared view within the Argentine foreign-affairs community of the international system as hierarchical, dominated by political and economic inequalities, and therefore, as threatening to national security. Because Argentina has lost relative status since 1930 it is less able to promote economic growth at home and to secure its politica. and social system against powerful external forces, such as foreign economic pressures and political influences, that have caused internal disruption. Insofar as these forces reduce the ability of any government to achieve its objectives they promote domestic political and social instability and threaten its grip on power. If Argentina is dependent on external forces, it is also less than secure in a violent, unfriendly international order.

Definition of Threats to Regime and Nation

The Argentine world view leads to the identification of specific internal and external threats to national security. Some require a military response, but most will be ameliorated by the internal mobilization of economic and political resources. Nearly all threats requiring the possible use of military force derive from the location and character of the country's frontiers and neighbors.

Historic and growing inequality in population and industrial production is the source of the threat from Brazil. From the perspective of some Argentine geopolitical analysts, Brazil has been expanding since the nineteenth century, first by absorbing weakly controlled border territories from its neighbors and now by extending its economic and political influence within the southern cone of South America. Traditionally, Uruguay, Paraguay, and Bolivia have formed a buffer, but Brazil is seen as successfully bringing these countries within its orbit by expanding trade, communications, and transportation links.[7]

An internal frontier, the Plata Basin system of international rivers, brings easy access to the Argentine heartland. Development of the choicest hydroelectric dam sites requires cooperation with other riparian states and in many instances negotiation with Brazil, the upstream state. Moreover, Argentine strategists have assumed that the economic links and associated trade and transportation linkages that evolve as a result of hydroelectric development will determine in large measure the balance of influence beween Argentina and Brazil in the buffer states. In this context the Brazilian-Paraguayan agreement to construct the world's largest power dam at Itaipu on the Parana River just north of the Argentine frontier was a strategic defeat.[8]

In the case of Chile the prospect of military conflict is greater because of a long history of boundary conflicts along the Andes and in the waters south of Tierra del Fuego. In 1978 both countries called full military alerts after the failure of negotiations to settle the boundary in the Beagle Channel south of Tierra del Fuego. Since the nineteenth century Argentina has attempted to protect its southern coast by securing an agreement with Chile to divide the southern waters along the line of Cape Horn, roughly the boundary between the Atlantic and Pacific Oceans. Chilean claims in the channel would have crossed that line and forced Argentine ships to navigate Chilean waters to reach Argentine ports along southern Tierra del Fuego. Both countries also eye the potential petroleum reserves in thousands of square miles of continental shelf lying within the 200-mile economic zones of three disputed islands south of the Beagle Channel.[9] As of late 1981 the dispute was still in the hands of a mediator appointed by the Vatican.

Aside from the territorial-waters dispute Argentina and Chile have frequently been at odds over extensive Chilean migration, often illegal, into Argentina's underpopulated southern provinces. This immigrant population is regarded in Argentina as another form of territorial pressure made all the more acute by the growing unwillingness of Argentines to settle those remote and arid areas.

All neighboring countries are potential sanctuaries for political dissidents or guerilla forces. Frontier areas are remote, underpopulated, and have in some instances long histories of involvement in smuggling. The Defense Ministry's October 1973 security plan for frontier regions refers to the threat of "migratory intellectual minorities." Argentine governments have claimed repeatedly that terrorist groups from neighboring countries and Argentina cooperate regularly in exchanging arms, training, information, and sanctuary. The unexplained murders of Chilean dissidents in Buenos Aires and of Argentine exiles in Brazil suggest also that such cooperation may extend to the security forces of area governments. For logistical reasons and because of the Latin American tradition of sanctuary it would be difficult for Argentina to use overt military force across its frontiers. However, Argentina has maintained a longstanding interest in preventing the establishment of radical, left-wing regimes in the buffer states and Chile. Some Latin American sources claim that the Argentine military provided small-arms aid to Uruguay in its struggle against the Tupamaro guerillas and that it may even have shipped some weapons to Chilean General Augusto Pinochet shortly after the overthrow of Salvador Allende.[10]

The South Atlantic is another area in which the use of force may be contemplated. Naval patrols are needed to enforce Argentina's claim to a 200-mile territorial sea and to secure the country's long, exposed coastline. Soviet support for Cuban intervention in Angola and Soviet naval and ocean surveillance activity operating out of West African ports seem to threaten the sea lanes from the Persian Gulf and to indicate a decline in the effectiveness of the U.S. security umbrella. To date Argentina has been unwilling to contemplate hemispheric or global peacekeeping activities in this area aside from a few joint naval exercises conducted periodically with the United States. Independence in foreign and security policy still takes precedence.

Unresolved territorial issues are also a problem in the South Atlantic. Great Britain has been unwilling to contemplate ceding the Falklands-Malvinas Islands, which Argentina claims. Although Argentina is a party to the Antarctic treaty, it maintains active territorial claims, which overlap those of Chile, and has attempted to establish a sovereign presence there by maintaining an air base and scientific stations, and by conducting periodic civil-aviation activities. However, for the present, the foreign-affairs community appears to have opted for long-term diplomatic pressure to maintain its position.

These specific external issues notwithstanding, the military and civilian leadership regard internal security, political disorder, and economic instability as the greatest threats to national well-being. A long history of political instability combined with the boom-bust economic cycle has seriously weakened the country's ability to meet internal social and political demands and to secure its international objectives. Beginning in the early 1960s internal violence intensified into a virtual civil war among the military; Perónist, Trotskyist, and Marxist guerillas; and disaffected labor and middle-class groups prone to direct action, even spontaneous rebellion. In response, the military developed a strong counterinsurgency capability. Since the March 1976 coup that overthrew the government of Isabel Perón, the armed forces appear to have the upper hand, but thousands of Argentines and resident foreigners have disappeared and are presumed dead. The lasting bitterness of this conflict will keep the military on a state of alert and involved in politics as the ultimate guarantors of the regime for the foreseeable future. The military also believes that the potential for foreign involvement through assistance to domestic dissidents or through ideological influence remains high, as evidenced by its censorship of allegedly Marxist publications and repeated military purges of universities, publishing firms, and unions of "Marxists" and radical Perónists.

Continued economic disorder is considered as serious a threat to national security as political disorder. As noted above, nearly all sectors of the elite agree that Argentina is highly dependent on the international environment for the achievement of its basic economic goals of stability and development. The country's relatively weak, unequal position in the world economy and consequently reduced international status impede its ability to negotiate for such vital inputs as technology, critical industrial goods and raw materials, and markets for its products and, over the longer term, to achieve greater independence from the vagaries of foreign economic pressures that have contributed to the continuing political crisis. Hence, improved economic performance is regarded as necessary to achieve stable government and to support such standing armed forces as the nation may require.

Doctrinal Responses: The Strategies of National Security

In response to assumptions about the nature of the international system and specifically perceived threats, the Argentine foreign-affairs community has developed two general approaches to the formulation of specific national-security doctrine: the classic liberal and the statist nationalist schools. There is substantial agreement between the two groups on the specific threats and long-term problems that national-security doctrine must confront, but substantial disagreement on responses, ideological interpretations, and force-development strategy.

Classic liberals identify Argentina as a nearly developed, Western nation that has failed to achieve its economic potential and a more substantial role in world affairs because of political instability, internal economic mismanagement, and failure to come to terms with the requirements for viable international economic relationships. They would renegotiate international economic relationships so as to improve prospects for agricultural products exports, the country's best foreign-exchange earners. Export-oriented industrialization and continued foreign investment would be used to promote national development and ultimately to reduce external dependence. As long as no dependence for critical technologies or raw materials is involved, this group would accept trade with the Soviet Union. If international accounts are balanced, then Argentina will be able to negotiate for the critical inputs needed to assure a greater degree of security from foreign economic pressures and the vagaries of world markets. Fundamental reliance is placed on the private sector and the establishment of internationally competitive domestic industries. On major East-West security issues, classic liberals would align with the United States and Western Europe as long as Argentina retains the freedom to protect its vital foreign markets. With respect to force development, this group would seek to import foreign weapons systems and technology where cost advantages outweighed domestic production. On internal security questions, classic liberals have resisted U.S. human-rights pressures and emphasized Argentina's need to restrain the role and influence of allegedly Marxist or third-world-oriented political groups. Supporters of this position include large landowners, businessmen from the larger locally owned and multinational corporations, and the predominant elements of the officer corps of the armed forces. The present government of General Jorge Rafael Videla is drawn mainly but not exclusively from this group.[11]

Statist nationalists see Argentina as a predominantly Latin American or as an advanced developing country kept subordinate in the international system by its position as a supplier of raw materials. Extensive central planning and state-controlled corporations operating in key sectors would be used to create a heavy industrial base with maximum autonomy and independence from outside sources of supply and influence in order to liberate the nation from a hierarchical and unequal international order. Statist nationalists have been hostile to foreign investment, particularly in security-related basic industries and energy production, except when forced to consider it for reasons of economic expediency. In contrast to classic liberals this group when in power has been more attracted to the Non-Aligned Movement and the Group of 77 as vehicles for lobbying against the established international economic and political order and for negotiating arrangements for favored treatment.

Statist nationalists, particularly in the armed forces, have supported indigenous arms production and basic industry as directly relevant elements in the creation and maintenance of national power and independence. General Juan E. Guglialmelli (retired), at one time a leading spokesman for the military developmentalists, a group that emerged within the Superior War School, has summed up the doctrine bluntly: "A nation which does not have basic industries is a castrated country because basic industries are the virile elements."[12] Since the 1940s, when Argentina as a neutral was unable to purchase arms just as Brazil was expanding its production capabilities and armed forces as a participant in the U.S. Lend-Lease Program, the military has managed an expanding local weapons industry that has served to promote civilian industrial development and to guarantee the armed forces some security of supply for basic items as well as moderately sophisticated ships, tanks, and light aircraft. In general, the statist-nationalist approach to national-security policy is supported by the majority of intellectuals, urban professionals, businessmen from the poorer interior provinces, union leaders, and members of the Perónist and Radical political parties, which together probably still command a majority of the electorate.[13]

Philosophical differences aside, the two approaches to national-security policy have many operational elements in common. Neither regards the use of force as very likely. Each assigns priority to economic growth and stability as the main elements in securing the nation against an essentially unequal, probably hostile international system that has denied Argentina the opportunity to realize its full potential, and that has contributed through adverse economic pressures to the continuing political crisis. Both schools agree that such foreign economic pressures must be ameliorated, although classic liberals would opt for freer and more balanced trade whereas statist nationalists are inclined more toward the immediate pursuit of industrial and technological autarchy, particularly in arms production.

Both groups favor an independent foreign policy as the best means of preserving the nation from the full impact of its internationally subordinate position. However, classic liberals would in the most serious confrontations choose the United States and Western Europe, whereas statist nationalists would opt for neutrality or a third-world orientation. The Videla government did not hesitate to break the U.S. grain boycott with massive sales to the Soviet Union, an example of the priority assigned to economic interests, but it did agree not to attend the Moscow Olympics, and it condemned the

Soviet invasion of Afghanistan. The governments of the second Perónist era, 1973-1976, negotiated massive trade deals with Cuba in defiance of the U.S. boycott but did not hesitate in repressing domestic leftists and former supporters of Salvador Allende who had sought asylum in Buenos Aires. In all of these instances, economic security and internal security, defined as the freedom to suppress potential enemies of the regime, took precedence over other objectives as key national-security concerns.

With respect to regional and local security issues the two sides have few fundamental differences. Statist nationalists would pursue leadership of a Latin American bloc of nations more vigorously and would tend to be more suspicious of Brazil as the country's major rival. Responses to frontier problems are largely in the military's hands and hence outside the scope of the broader debate over general national strategy.

The major disagreements between the classic liberal and the statist nationalist schools, then, revolve around the pursuit of economic policy as it relates to freeing Argentina from a generally recognized external dependence and threatening subordinate international position, the degree of alliance or support each would extend to the United States or the third world, and the attitude toward the link between industrialization and national security. Statist nationalists posit a more direct, immediate link requiring highly autarchic policies, particularly in arms production, whereas classic liberals favor negotiating for technology transfer and arms in the context of a long-term drive for independence in which the private sector has the primary role.

The Domestic Scene: Political Forces, the Military Establishment, and the Regime's Objectives

The high priority assigned to internal security and economic well-being makes the domestic political process highly relevant to the formation and implementation of security policy in Argentina. A set of long-term political and power relationships has prevailed under both civilian and military governments. A dominant president presides over a political team that includes representatives of the principal factions within the armed forces, either classic liberal or statist nationalist business groups, depending on the dominant character of the regime, and either direct representatives of labor or individuals who can negotiate with labor. Key team members for national security questions serve as economy minister, foreign minister, and as commanders of the three armed services. Economic interests are represented in the state secretariats within the Economy Ministry. Groups excluded from direct participation in the political team are still consulted, if only because they retain the power to affect policy through direct action. Corporatist inclinations in Argentine political culture favor a paternalistic, authoritarian state that consults with vertically organized interests, classes, and groups, each of which claims to speak for an entire socioeconomic category of persons.[14]

Internal economic and social demands that compete with national-security priorities enter the political process through such consultations. The landed elite benefits the most from classic liberal policies favoring reliance on agricultural-products exports and balanced international accounts, which may require internal economic austerity. Urban and professional groups gain the most from statist nationalist support for autonomous industrialization, which creates new managerial opportunities and makes union cooperation with government policy more critical. In the absence of fundamental political consensus and stable institutions, supporters of each policy approach have tended to see their interests as mutually exclusive. Dissidents have resorted frequently to violence or other forms of direct action such as strikes, riots, and demonstrations. In this fashion internal security and economic security have become linked to each other and to broader questions of power and social justice within Argentine society.

The armed forces occupy a special position as a semiautonomous political force that has been capable of seizing power almost at will but incapable of governing effectively without some broader base of civilian support, especially among key economic interests. Historically, they have regarded themselves as the ultimate guardians of the national interest, interpreted variously according to statist nationalist or classic liberal perspectives. The three commanders of the armed forces represent these interests directly as near coequals to the president under civilian regimes and as a formal junta with a monopoly of the governing power under military regimes.

Guardianship, in the form of an independent veto over the actions of the sitting president, relates most directly to internal-security questions, broadly defined to include control over internal violence and threats to the regime such as strikes and relations between the government and suspect political groups. After the 1955 Liberating Revolution (a military coup) ousted Perón, the three service commanders closely monitored contacts between successive governments and the former dictator. Arturo Frondizi was overthrown for seeking too close an electoral alliance with the Perónists, but the 1972 settlement, which allowed Perón to return from exile and permitted Perónist candidates in the 1973 elections, was approved. Perón and the military chiefs cooperated in 1973 in ousting Perónist President Hector Campora, who had appointed left-wing Perónists as foreign and interior ministers, tolerated a rash of industrial strikes, and eased control over various left-wing Perónist groups. Aside from these political actions, the military has assumed direct and sole control over all counterinsurgency and counterterrorist actions. The importance of this issue is indicated by patterns of troop deployment away from the frontiers and into the major cities. Cordoba, the country's second industrial center after Buenos Aires and traditionally the center of Perónist unionism, student protest, and the scene of the most violent clashes in recent years between police and army units and the guerillas, has become the second most important post for army and air force officers, with some of the most senior generals within each service as garrison commanders.

All three services have insisted on maintaining access to foreign weapons, weapons technology, and training opportunities. Since the controversy over human rights, Western Europe has displaced the United States as the favored source. Furthermore, France and Germany have been willing to consider coproduction and licensing arrangements for complete or partial local manufacture while the United States has not. Under the Ongania government, 1966-1970, the army instituted Plan Europa, a program to obtain license or coproduction agreements for European armaments.[15] Even though reliance on imported technology, technicians, and armaments predates it, the plan was the first long-range attempt to link such acquisitions to a comprehensive security policy in the statist nationalist mode. Army missions to Europe have negotiated arrangements for producing the French AMX light tank by assembling imported components, and in 1979 an agreement was signed with a West German firm to produce, in both West Germany and Argentina, a family of armored vehicles that includes the Argentine medium tank (or TAM), a light tank, and an armored personnel carrier. The navy has built destroyers jointly with Britain and assembled two submarines in its own yards from West German components. In the 1950s the air force experimented unsuccessfully with prototype jet fighters, using British Rolls-Royce engines made under license, but since then has concentrated on building light transports and the Pucara counterinsurgency aircraft using indigenously designed and manufactured components.[16] The three services would probably resist any attempts by the government to curb their apparently considerable autonomy in negotiating such arrangements.

There are also some service-specific interests. Ranking navy officers have supported rapid development of the Plata river system to forestall Brazilian domination of what they regard as an internal frontier and have pressed for the resources to patrol the nation's claim to a 200-mile territorial sea.[17] The army has staked out relations with Brazil as its special concern. Army generals have frequently served as special envoys and ambassadors to Brazil. In 1961 the army forced President Arturo Frondizi to annul the Uruguiana agreements, which proposed a settlement of outstanding issues and closer consultations.[18] The army has also assumed the leading role in local arms production through its control of the Bureau of Military Factories, the DGFM, which appears to supervise the air force's National

Bureau of Aeronautical Manufacturing and Research (DINIFIA) and the navy's State Naval Shipyards and Factories (AFNE). In the past, each service has had links to state-owned steel, aluminum, and vehicle production firms through officers serving in key managerial positions and support for defense-related projects. However, given the present government's determination to close or sell state firms to the private sector, the future of such links is in doubt.

Inter-service rivalries over arms production and government policy exist but are less important than ideological factions that tend to find support in each branch. The army is clearly predominant in politics by tradition and superior land-based manpower. However, in the present government, power is shared equally at least in the formal sense through the junta of commanders; a Legislative Advisory Commission composed of equal numbers of army, navy, and air force officers; and a careful allocation of cabinet positions among all three arms of the military. This arrangement reflects the cross-service alliance of moderate and extreme conservatives that supports the present regime.

The Argentine policymaking process has some definite impacts on the content of security strategy. The armed forces function as a veto group that is sufficiently united on nonideological issues to force acceptance of its bureaucratic interests and, frequently, its views on other questions. On broader political and economic questions the divisions in the Argentine polity are responsible for the prominence of internal security and economic growth as national-security issues. Both issues affect the ability of the government of the day to retain power.

Human, Material, and Technological Resources and Constraints

Available resources determine in part what strategies are available to Argentine decision makers. Potential for economic diplomacy is critically important because of the importance of economic growth and ultimate achievement of greater independence from global economic pressures. Although the use of military force is considered improbable, the country still maintains standing forces for internal security and frontier defense. Hence, the ability to raise and sustain those forces, including satisfaction of their arms requirements, should also be considered. All of these factors are functions of the country's human capabilities, technological and industrial accomplishments, and natural resources.

In terms of basic resources Argentina is well-endowed. Although productivity lags behind North American and Australian levels, the humid pampa is still one of the world's greatest agricultural regions. By the early

1980s offshore drilling may eliminate even the present 10-percent oil-import requirement, and the large resources of coal and hydroelectric potential on the river systems promise to provide the basis for long-term self-sufficiency in energy. By the year 2000 nearly 23 percent of electricity may be supplied by the nuclear-energy program, which is supported by large reserves of uranium.

Industrial and technological potential are uneven. With nearly 28 percent of GNP of industrial origin and a per capita income of $2,100, Argentina approaches the economic level of the lower-ranking members of the Organization for Economic Cooperation and Development (OECD). Steel, vehicles, and capital equipment are strong sectors but depend heavily on foreign technology, capital, and multinational corporations. The locally owned private sector tends to be fragmented into small, undercapitalized firms with obsolete equipment, although the government has been successful in encouraging the formation of consortia to bid on hydroelectric and nuclear-energy projects. State-owned industries in petroleum, vehicles, aluminum, and railroads, historically deficit-ridden and featherbedded, are being sold to the private sector with as yet unforeseeable effects.

In general, potential for local research and development activities is low, although Argentine scientists have won international recognition in medicine, nuclear energy, and geophysics. Most industrial patents are of foreign origin. The emigration rate for scientists and engineers is high; scientific and technical research institutions—including the universities—are weak, fragmented, and poorly funded. Furthermore, dependence on foreign technology and licensing agreements shows no sign of decreasing.

These disadvantages notwithstanding, Argentina has achieved some impressive results when scientific and technological resources are concentrated on long-term projects that have some immunity from political interference. As noted above, the military has chosen with some success to produce basic and moderately sophisticated weapon systems tailor-made for internal security and frontier defense, including light transport aircraft, counterinsurgency aircraft, locally designed and built ships as large as frigates, machine guns, and most ammunition for artillery and infantry needs.[19]

Aircraft production, probably the most technologically demanding activity undertaken by the Military Factories, illustrates Argentina's potential and limitations in local arms production. Since the 1960s DINIFIA (the Air Force's National Bureau of Aeronautical Manufacturing and Research) has concentrated on light transport and counterinsurgency aircraft. The IA-50 Guarani II twin-engine transport, and the IA-35 Huanquero, a single-engine transport, have been on active status with the air force for nearly twenty years, including a version of the Huanqero armed with a Browning machine gun. The IA-58 Pucara, described as a multipurpose attack aircraft for offensive reconnaissance and fire support in land and sea operations, particularly for counterinsurgency, was designed in 1968 and put into production in 1974 with twin, turboprop engines made locally under French license. As of 1977 fifteen Pucaras were in service, and an equal number were on order. As of mid-1980 DINIFIA had also produced the IA-46 Ranquel, a light monoplane for agricultural applications and was developing the IA-60 Pucara jet attack fighter, a trainer based on the Pucara airframe, and the Cicara CH-11 helicopter trainer, which would apparently use an engine imported from the United States.[20]

Based on this experience it is possible to conclude that Argentine design and production capabilities are impressive by developing-country standards and appear sufficient to produce rugged, long-life systems that do not require highly sophisticated technology. However, the combination of fairly short production runs and some continued dependence on foreign inputs probably means that cost per unit is high, although partially offset by foreign-exchange savings, experience gained, and security of supply. Moreover, Argentina has been able to extend its capabilities significantly by securing coproduction and licensing agreements for more ambitious projects such as submarines, although not for ultrasophisticated items such as jet fighter aircraft.

Additional evidence of Argentine technological potential under appropriate managerial and financial incentives comes from the country's nuclear program. Established in 1950, the National Atomic Energy Commission (CNEA) has exhibited a capacity for long-range planning and development and continuity under various governments. It has designed and built several of its own research reactors and it recently exported a research reactor to Peru. Nuclear-power development is based on the heavy water, natural-uranium design that does not require foreign enrichment services. Atucha I, the country's first power reactor, went into service in 1974. Atomic Energy of Canada, Ltd. is building the second station in Cordoba Province, and contracts with West German and Swiss firms were signed recently for a third reactor and a heavy-water plant, respectively. CNEA's 1975 to 1980 plan proposed investment of a total of $3.7 billion in the nuclear program, with the ultimate objective of creating an indigenous technology and industry. International safeguards administered by the International Atomic Energy Agency are applied to all facilities, although Argentina has not signed the nonproliferation treaty.[21]

Manpower resources for military forces are limited. The country's twenty-six million people are largely concentrated in a few large cities, with one-third in greater Buenos Aires alone, within a territory half as large as the continental United States. However, there are few if any ethnic tensions that might impede the recruitment or use of manpower among a population overwhelmingly descended from Spanish, Italian, German, English, and Irish immigrants with smaller numbers of Indians and *mestizos* (Indian-Spanish mix). A high literacy rate, one of the best educational systems in Latin America, and generally excellent standards of health and nutrition make up for some of the lack of numbers. Universal conscription applies to males at age eighteen.

In conclusion, Argentina has important resources that can be applied toward the achievement of its national-security objectives. Agricultural potential is large, but Argentina has yet to regain the strategically significant share of world grain markets it enjoyed in the 1920s. The quantity and sophistication of industrial production and exports is increasing but continued dependence on foreign capital and technology combined with the historic boom-bust economic cycle and its associated domestic political and social tensions are severe weaknesses. A high degree of energy security will help to promote an end to external economic dependence and will provide flexibility to foreign policy. However, if the experience of smaller industrial economies elsewhere in the world is any guide, Argentina is unlikely to acquire the more complete technological autarchy it is seeking. Given the low probability of major military conflict, a small population is less of a liability than its concentration in a few urban centers, which prevents a more even pattern of economic development.

Strategies, Policies of Alignment, and Military Posture

Resources are only as useful as a state's ability to translate them into operational requirements. In this respect Argentina's record is mixed. Scarce human and material resources can be mustered for long-term projects, as in the arms and nuclear industries, but Argentina has frequently been frustrated by its status as a middle power and by its history of political instability and low social cohesion.

Military forces appear well-matched to their projected missions of internal security, land frontier defense, coastal patrol, and maintenance of a strategic-political counterweight to the forces and ambitions of neighboring countries. As table 2-1 illustrates, the Argentine defense budget is modest on a world scale.

Equipment inventories are poor but improving as the pace of local manufacture and foreign purchase has been stepped up. Historically, the three services have suffered from obsolete equipment, some of which is still of World War II vintage, and highly diverse stocks. In addition to the domestic production activities of the Military Factories system, which have already been described, the armed forces have apparently experienced no difficulties in purchasing advanced foreign equipment from European

Table 2-1

Comparative Military Spending Levels: Argentina, Brazil, Latin America, and Developing Countries

Item	Argentina	Brazil	All Latin America	Developing Countries
GNP (1976 in millions of constant dollars)	36,081	116,748		
Military spending as percentage of GNP (1976)	2.4	1.3	1.8	6.3
Military spending as percentage of central government budget (1967-1976)	13.4	19.2	13.4	40.6
Standing forces per 1,000 of population	6	4	4	5
Actual standing forces (1976)	155,000	450,000		

Source: *World Military Expenditures and Arms Transfers 1967-1976* (Washington, D.C.: Arms Control and Disarmament Agency, 1978).

suppliers, including tanks, Mirage II jet fighters, and capital ships.[22] A rough balance in such sophisticated systems has been successfully maintained with Brazil and Chile.

Involvement in politics poses the greatest obstacle to the military's mission, particularly in maintaining internal security. There is a long tradition of factionalism, secret lodges, defiance of formal command structures by ambitious officers, even rebellion and armed confrontations between the services and elements of the services. In the early 1960s army factions fought tank battles in the streets of Buenos Aires, and air force planes bombed the naval base at Belgrano, south of Buenos Aires. Divisional and service commanders have been forced to retire under threat of insurrection by their own units. Alliances of civilian and military figures have cut across the unity of the armed forces. As a result, high-level political control of the military for internal purposes is weak and frequently subject to interfactional negotiations.

In the past, extended periods of military rule have made the armed forces unpopular with the civilian population. Politicians in uniform have proved no more adept at various times in resolving Argentina's fundamental social and economic conflicts than have civilian politicians. Moreover, the unions, middle-class groups, and students have been able to cause the armed forces to lose face in violent confrontations. One notable example was the "cordobazo," a mass street battle and general strike that shook the industrial city of Cordoba in May 1969. This apparent loss of control contributed to the military's decision to overthrow the government of General Juan Carlos Ongania in June 1970. The military's inability to either repress or come to terms with the Perónist movement during the military's first experiment with extended rule, the "Argentine Revolution" of June 1966 to May 1973, eventually led to direct talks between the commanders and the exiled Juan Perón and their decision to permit the elections in May 1973 that placed Hector Campora, Perón's personal representative, in the presidency. In brief, the target of force used in support of internal security has been ambiguous because violence and other forms of direct action, such as strikes and massive disobedience of government policy, have been used by nearly every major political group acting alone or in alliance with elements of the military itself.

Internal problems aside, there is no evidence to suggest that the military would not be effective in applying force against a clearly identified foreign enemy. Under most circumstances action would be limited to repelling any challenge to Argentine frontiers or territorial waters. In nearly all of the incidents that have occurred, the army and navy have not engaged in hot pursuit into neighboring countries but have also not hesitated in asserting established claims and jurisdictions.

Some fragmentary evidence suggests that Argentina would be prepared to use overt and covert force to prevent the establishment of a radical, Marxist-oriented regime in one of the buffer states. Argentine political and military elites, with the exception of the Perónist left and some small pro-Castro groups, have feared the potential internal influence of neighboring radical regimes. During the Argentine Revolution period of military government an extensive debate took place over the opposing concepts of "ideological frontiers," which required all efforts to isolate pro-Castro forces within the hemisphere and full support for the U.S. boycott of Cuba (the position of army hardliners and President Ongania), versus accommodation with "ideological pluralism," which would allow pragmatic relationships with all regimes. President Lanusse adopted the latter position and eventually came to terms with the existence of the Allende government in Chile. Following Allende's overthrow, however, there were unconfirmed charges by Argentine leftist groups that Perón shipped tear gas and small arms to the new military government. There have also been repeated claims about cooperation among the military security forces of Argentina, Uruguay, Chile, and Brazil in controlling, even executing, each other's political dissidents and exiles, particularly those suspected of Marxist sympathies, a broad definition that has included former Chilean Christian Democrats and members of Uruguay's Colorado party as well as those with pro-Castro inclinations.[23]

More direct action within neighboring countries has been used or at least contemplated. Latin American sources alleged that Perón aided the successful 1952 coup of the Bolivian MNR party, and that President Ongania was prepared to cooperate with Brazil in occupying Uruguay in the event of a victory by the Tupamaros. Small quantities of arms were supplied to Uruguayan President Bordaberry, and cooperation was given in denying sanctuary in Argentine territory to Tupamaro guerillas.[24] Were similar situations to arise in the future the military would probably provide aid, including arms and advisers, to the nonradical contenders—even over the objections of the president. Overt invasion is far less likely because of the armed forces' limited long-range logistical capabilities, possible opposition from Brazil, and the intense diplomatic pressures that the United States and other Latin American countries would mobilize.

Aside from limited operations, largely on a covert basis, in neighboring countries threatened with a radical takeover, Argentine civilian and military elites have not contemplated the use of armed force on a regional or global basis. Argentina has not volunteered for United Nations peacekeeping duties. General Ongania's proposal to assist the United States in its 1965 landings in the Dominican Republic did not receive wide support. Military and scholarly journals devoted to strategy and security have generally not dealt with large-scale troop or naval deployments away from Argentine territory, nor is there other evidence, such as press statements and tactical formations, to suggest that such action has been regarded seriously.[25]

The military has evolved other, more usable operational strategies for pursuing national-security objectives. Military-to-military diplomacy is used frequently, particularly within Latin America. Members of the present junta and lower-ranking officers have traveled frequently to Santiago or received their Chilean counterparts for talks on the Beagle Channel dispute. Independent military missions have attempted to sell arms to neighboring countries and to buy arms in Europe. Officers and cadets from other Latin American countries have been trained in Argentine military educational establishments.

Military aid and sales have been used with very modest success. Between 1967 and 1976 a total of $22 million in weapons was exported, most of which was probably ammunition and small arms. The Pucara aircraft has been offered unsuccessfully to Bolivia, Peru, Libya, and South Africa. An improved version, the Pucara B, was exhibited at the Le Bourget Air Show in Paris in 1979, reportedly attracting some interest from the Dominican Republic and Venezuela.[26] It is possible that Argentina may develop a modest export market for fairly simple, rugged, easily maintained weapons systems in developing countries.

Alliances are another tool for improving the nation's security situation but the traditional Argentine doctrine of an independent foreign policy has very much limited their use. As noted earlier, most elites assume that the United States will deter any major Soviet thrust and will restrain Cuba. Classic liberals have favored the maintenance of military sales, training relationships, and the Inter-American Treaty on Reciprocal Assistance. In

1973 army officers in this group resisted Campora's attempts to side with Peru in weakening the treaty and in terminating the U.S. military-assistance group in Argentina.[27]. All factions, however, resisted U.S. attempts to link military assistance to Argentine human-rights compliance, and they accepted termination of the agreement in 1977. Should there be a global U.S.-Soviet confrontation, statist nationalists would opt for neutrality, while classic liberals would give at least tacit support to the United States.

Within Latin America, Argentina has preferred to maintain a balance of power while avoiding formal, lasting alliances. Brazil is a rival but also an important partner in restraining radical forces within the southern cone. In mid-1980 Argentina and Brazil had settled their dispute over the use of Parana River hydroelectric sites, signed an agreement for cooperation in nuclear energy, and were negotiating a significant expansion in bilateral trade. Both countries were motivated by their perceptions of declining U.S. influence and willingness to restrain Cuba and the Soviet Union and by the prospect of greatly expanded trade and technical cooperation.[28] On the other hand, formal alliance is unlikely because of the deeply ingrained Argentine tradition of independence in foreign policy, the suspicion engendered by the power and economic disparity between the two countries, and the muted, but ongoing, contest for influence in the buffer states. Rather, the new cordiality should be seen as another expression of Argentine pragmatism and flexibility, displayed on other occasions with all of its neighbors, in securing a regional balance. This time Argentina was responding to Chile's hostile posture over the Beagle Channel, the rise of radical regimes in Central America and the Caribbean, and the opportunity to promote trade expansion, particularly in critical industrial products.

This same attitude carries over into Argentina's response to growing Soviet naval activity in the South Atlantic and the Cuban presence in Angola and other West African states, a change signifying a shift in the area's balance of power and another example, in the Argentine view, of declining U.S. influence. Southern-cone foreign ministers have discussed strategic cooperation in the South Atlantic, possibly including South Africa, on several occasions since 1975, most recently in October 1979. Argentina and Brazil have held bilateral talks on at least one occasion in 1976 on the same subject.[29] Formal arrangements are unlikely because Brazil has important economic and cultural links to Angola, Mozambique, and other African states that an avowedly conservative ideological bloc, especially one including South Africa, would threaten. Argentine-Chilean relations are too unsettled, and, militarily, Argentina would gain little through formal association with other weak naval powers. These disadvantages notwithstanding, such consultations do provide evidence of Argentina's continuing efforts to restrain the growth of radical influences in its vital southern-cone region.

With respect to its economic-security goals Argentina has used its trade and investment policies to bargain for foreign technology and production rights for key industrial and military equipment. Large state-controlled contracts and preferential access to the national market are used as inducements for foreign suppliers. Recent examples include agreements with France and Germany, respectively, for coproduction of tanks and submarines. The Soviet Union won a contract to supply turbines to the Salto Grande dam because it promised to transfer all technology and manufacturing know-how. Conversely, the Soviet Union rewarded Argentina for several years of growing trade expansion by allowing it to replace the United States as a grain supplier. Argentina succeeds as the discriminating consumer of high-technology products because it is able to play the classic small-state role of balancer and beneficiary of competition among larger states.

Argentina has used its own growing technological and industrial capabilities and its ability to supply goods with fewer political strings than either the United States, the Soviet Union, or Western Europe to bid for support in Latin America. In 1974 then President Juan Perón concluded a major agreement to supply automobiles and trucks built in Argentina by U.S. firms to Cuba in an effort to outflank his domestic critics on the left and to secure a new market. Peru, viewed as a strategic counterweight to Chile, has been the target of an Argentine industrial-products sales campaign for several years. In 1979 Peru accepted Argentina's offer to construct a nuclear-research center using two research reactors designed and built by CNEA. Such sales broaden the country's export base, provide opportunities to reduce costs by producing on a larger scale, and undergird attempts to build longer-term security relationships.

In addition to economic diplomacy, Argentina has attempted to use bloc bargaining within international organizations, the nonaligned group, and the Group of 77 to promote selected security objectives. The United Nations Law of the Sea talks and regional Latin American conferences on maritime questions have been used to promote a claim to a 200 mile-territorial sea. Within the nonaligned nations and the UN General Assembly, Argentina has packaged the Malvinas question with other less-developed country (LDC) anticolonial issues in a series of resolutions aimed at Great Britain. Prior to the recent settlement with Brazil, Argentina used these same tactics to garner international support for its position on the use of Parana River hydroelectric resources. Multilateral settings and formal international organizations are useful because voting procedures and organizational rules can be used to mute power differences for political purposes and to secure a wider forum for the Argentine position.

In conclusion, Argentina finds nonmilitary strategies more useful than the use or threat of force to promote its security objectives. Its immediate, regional environment is relatively secure from any serious military challenge. Political challenges from potentially unfriendly groups and governments are met by working for a balance of power and by avoiding rigid alliances, while tacitly relying on the United States to secure the area from Soviet or Cuban penetration. Military forces and arms-production capabilities support these objectives by providing a shield against overt territorial intrusion, but their main purpose is to maintain the regime of the day in power. Argentina attempts to bargain for strategically significant goods and technology by playing off the major suppliers and using its national market as a lure.

Conclusions

The Argentine experience illustrates that some aspects of international conflict derive from the interaction of intra-state objectives that have become linked to and politicized by present trends in the international system. Above all, Argentine decision makers are attempting to create what they understand as the classic nation-state, an entity with high levels of self-sufficiency, sovereignty in the sense of autonomy in decision making and enforcement, and a high degree of impermeability to outside influences. The most serious security problem for all groups is the country's perceived external dependence, which affects internal security and the ability to achieve economic objectives.

Economic policy has become central to these efforts to create the national state because of the rise in Argentina, as in other societies, of the "organizational state." In Gunnar Myrdal's definition, the organizational state assumes a widening responsibility for the social and economic welfare of its citizens through planning and an inward-looking control over all influences that affect this process. Internal politics becomes the "revolution of rising entitlements" in which organized interest groups struggle over the allocation of public resources and guarantees and the nature of the state's comprehensive plan for society.[30]

This process affects the international system in two ways. First, more effective planning requires the consolidation of the nation-state and escape from or control over external influences. Second, for most countries the goals of the organizational state can only be realized if there is access to external sources of technology and material resources. In smaller and developing nations both pressures are particularly acute because national identity and communal solidarity are weak, undermining the planning and implementation machinery and the consensus that keeps the range of demands manageable. Also, many key industrial and technological resources must be imported. In Argentina, the range of demands is not manageable within the current political process and a large number of external inputs is required. This becomes a security issue because national viability and the stability of the regime are threatened. Statist nationalists would respond by substituting to the greatest possible degree internally mobilized resources for external inputs, whereas classic liberals would attempt to mitigate dependence by diversifying it.

Argentina's choice of means to advance its national security is a consequence of broader international trends that affect the state-building process. The growth in exclusivity, the breakdown of dominant world patterns of authority and jurisdiction in favor of dispersed authority, allows small states greater freedom of action but also exposes them to neighboring and regional powers that have also acquired greater freedom. Hence, Argentina responds with a freewheeling economic and diplomatic bargaining style.

The second great influence is interdependence, the growing importance of shared resources and global networks of exchange to the well-being of individual states. Interdependence is the product of industrial-technological changes combined with the spread of organizational-state politics. It has made high politics of trade, resource technology, and monetary matters, all of which are critical to the success of internal planning and maximization of welfare. The linkage of international status with level of industrialization by many sectors of the Argentine elite reflects these concerns and perceptions of new forms of vulnerability.

As a result, security policy in Argentina and other developing countries is more than concern over military preparation and the military balance. It touches all areas of national life. For the international system as a whole this development introduces new forms of conflict as states attempt to manage a wider range of shared resources, networks of interaction, and mutual vulnerabilities.

Notes

1. Robert Rothstein, *Alliances and Small Powers* (New York: Columbia University Press, 1968) p. 5.

2. See for example, Felix Luna, *De Perón a Lanusse* (Buenos Aires: Editorial Planeta Argentina, 1974) and Mario Amadeo, *Hoy, ayer, y mañana* (Buenos Aires: Ediciones Gure, 1956).

3. James Scobie, *Argentina, A City and a Nation* (New York: Oxford University Press, 1971), p. 218; for an Argentine interpretation see Mariano Grondona, *La Argentina en el Tiempo y en el Mundo* (Buenos Aires: Editorial Primera Plana, 1967).

4. H.S. Ferns, *Argentina* (London: Ernest Benn, Ltd., 1969), pp. 246-257 for a discussion of marginality; for an analysis of ethnic influences

on the national outlook see Ezequiel Martinez Estrada, *X-Ray of the Pampa,* trans. Alain Swietlicki (Austin: University of Texas Press, 1971). This work, originally published in 1933, has been highly influential in Argentine intellectual history.

5. For an important Argentine analysis of the European connection, especially during the nineteenth century, see Jose Luis Romero, *A History of Argentine Political Thought,* trans. Thomas F. McGann (Stanford, Calif.: Stanford University Press, 1963), esp. part III.

6. United Nations Economic Commission for Latin America, *The Economic Development of Latin America and its Principal Problems,* UN DOC E/CN.12/80/ Rev 1, April 27, 1950, authored by Raul Prebish is the most important work in this group. See also Edward S. Milenky, "Problems, Perspectives, and Modes of Analysis: Understanding Latin American Approaches to World Affairs," in *Latin America: The Search for a New International Role,* eds. Ronald G. Hellman and H. Jon Rosenbaum (New York: Sage-Halsted, 1975), pp. 93-95 on development of these approaches, and Milenky, *Argentina's Foreign Policies* (Boulder, Colo.: Westview Press, 1978), chapter 1, for a more complete analysis.

7. For a geopolitical analysis see the writings of Juan Enrique Guglialmelli, especially his "Cuénca del Plata o Cono Sur," *Estrategia,* no. 28 (May-June 1974). *Estrategia* is the foremost Argentine journal of geopolitics.

8. Julio E. Sanguinetti, "Geopolitica de la Cuénca del Plata," *Estrategia,* Nos. 19-20 (November 1972-January 1973); Juan E. Guglialmelli, "Cuénca del Plata o Cono Sur (a Proposito de la VI Reunion de Cancilleres del la Cuénca del Plata)," *Estrategia,* No. 28 (May-June 1974); for current statements see *La Prensa,* Buenos Aires, 8 June 1979, p. 5, for comments by retired Admiral Issac F. Rojas, a leading strategist and former junta member (1956), and a speech by the current navy commander, Admiral Armando Lambruschini, *Clarin,* Buenos Aires, 5 October 1979, pp. 5, 57.

9. "Argentina, Year of the Spark," *Economist,* 30 December 1978, pp. 34-35; and text of an interview with the army commander-in-chief, General Roberto Viola, in *Defensa* (Madrid), November 1979, pp. 16-19.

10. *La Opinión* (Buenos Aires), 12 August 1973, p. 2; Vivian Trias, *Uruguay y sus Claves Geopolitícas* (Montevideo: Ediciones de la Banda Oriental, 1972), pp. 77-79; *La Opiniòn,* 12 May 1974, p. 2 on arms to Chile.

11. See speech by present Economy Minister José Alfredo Martinez de Hoz, Buenos Aires domestic radio, 3 April 1976, for a contemporary version.

12. "Palabras del Señor General de Brigada Juan E. Guglialmelli, Director del Centro de Altos Estudios y Escuela Superior de Guerra, al Clausurar el 17 Curso de Coroneles (11-xii-1964)," *Revista de la Escuela Superior de Guerra* (November-December 1964):116.

13. For a Peronist version see *Juan Perón en la Argentina 1973, sus*

Discursos sus Dialogos, sus Conferencias: Plan Trienal 1974-1977 (Buenos Aires: Vespa Ediciones, 1974) and compare to similar military views by a retired general in Osiris Villegas "Estrategia para el Futuro," *Revista de la Escuela Superior de Guerra,* 70 (November-December 1973).

14. Howard J. Wiarda, "Law and Political Development in Latin America: Toward a Framework for Analysis," in *Politics and Social Change in Latin America,* ed. Howard J. Wiarda (Amherst: University of Massachusetts Press, 1974), pp. 209-210; and Kalman H. Silvert, "The Costs of Anti-Nationalism: Argentina," in *Expectant Peoples, Nationalism and Development,* ed. Kalman H. Silvert (New York: Random House, 1963), p. 355.

15. The history of the plan appears in Eduardo Juan Uriburu, *El Plan Europa, un Intento de Liberación Nacional* (Buenos Aires: Cruz y Fierro Editores, 1970); and Stockholm International Peace Research Institute (SIPRI), *Arms Trade with the Third World* (Stockholm: Almquist and Wiksell, 1971), pp. 694-697.

16. Arms production data from SIPRI, *Arms Trade,* pp. 760, 864; SIPRI, *World Armaments and Disarmament, Yearbook* (Stockholm: Almquist and Wiksell, 1974 and later years); and International Institute for Strategic Studies, *The Military Balance* (London, 1970-1979), and *Défense Interarmées* (Paris), 19 March 1979, pp. 26-30.

17. For example see the following work by a retired admiral and former Junta member Isaac Francisco Rojas, *Intereses Argentinos en la Cuenca del Plata* (Buenos Aires: Ediciones Libera, 1975).

18. Alberto Conil Paz and Gustavo Ferrari, *Argentina's Foreign Policy 1930-1962,* trans. John J. Kennedy (South Bend, Ind.: Notre Dame University Press, 1966) a work written for the Foreign Ministry's in-service institute.

19. For complete documentation on the Argentine arms industry see Edward S. Milenky, "Arms Production and National Security in Argentina," *Journal of Inter-American Studies and World Affairs,* August 1980.

20. *The Military Balance (1977-1978),* p. 67 for a listing of aircraft. See also *La Opinión,* (Buenos Aires) 13 November 1979, p. 10 for history of the Puccara.

21. For a summary of the nuclear program see verbatim text of an interview with the president of CNEA, Rear Admiral Carlos Castro Madero, in *Confirmado* (Buenos Aires), 3 August 1978, pp. 18-21, and *Nuclear Engineering International,* October 1978, p. 10. On the nuclear plan see *Clarin* (Buenos Aires), 17 September 1978, economic supplement pp., 8-9.

22. *The Military Balance* (1977-1978), p. 67.

23. *La Nación* (Buenos Aires), 2 January 1974, pp. 1, 5, 7; on security forces see *La Opinión* (Buenos Aires), 9 August 1975, p. 8.

24. Trias, *Uruguay,* pp. 77-79.

25. Based on the author's survey of such periodicals for 1960-1978.

26. *La Opinión*, (Buenos Aires) 13 November 1979, p. 10.

27. Ibid., 2 September 1973, p. 2 and 4 September 1973, p. 3.

28. See text of interview with Argentine Foreign Minister Brigadier General (ret.) Carlos Washington Pastor, *Clarin*, (Buenos Aires) 17 May 1980, pp. 9, 25; *O Globo* (Rio de Janeiro), 12 May 1980, p. 4.

29. *O Estado de São Paulo*, 12 January 1980, p. 5 and *La Nación* (Buenos Aires, 12 April 1976, p. 1 (air edition).

30. Gunnar Myrdal, *Beyond the Welfare State* (New York: Bantam Books, 1967), pp. 20, 54-55, 119-120, 131. See also Daniel Bell. "The Future World Disorder", *Foreign Policy*, no. 27 (Summer 1977):131-132.

3 Brazil

David J. Myers

Underlying Assumptions

The military has governed in Brazil since 1 April 1964, when General Humberto Castelo Branco ousted President João Goulart. During 1979 Brazil inaugurated its fifth consecutive military officer as president. The generals and their allies currently portray the civilians who governed between 1930 and 1964 as either corrupt or incompetent, especially in the pursuit of national security. Only men in uniform are seen as trustworthy guardians of national-security interests. Since the early 1950s, military intellectuals have devoted considerable attention and energy to explicitly setting forth their view of Brazilian national-security interests.

The best summary of the Brazilian military's national-security thinking appears in the *Basic Manual (Manual Basico)* of the Brazilian National War College *(Escola Supérior de Guerra [ESG])*. The 1976 edition of the *Basic Manual* proclaims that national security has four dimensions: the political, the economic, the psychosocial, and the military.[1] These dimensions are found in both the internal and external arenas.

Internally, the military sees national-security threats as deriving from the tendency of great powers to interfere in the domestic affairs of lesser ones. Interference is said to be aimed at exploiting preexisting insecurities. Three kinds of insecurities are common to "lesser states," especially those in the developing areas. Most important are *national insecurities*. War College theorists see these as related to the lack of resources, deficiencies in industrialization, and financial insecurities. *Cultural insecurities,* a second category, are tied to the "ignorance" of some sectors when they "participate in the political process." Although ignorance is never satisfactorily defined in the *Basic Manual,* it seems to imply that the masses demand a level of wealth redistribution that would make significant capital formation impossible. *Moral insecurities* constitute a final category. They are related to the confrontation between generations, the clash of ideologies, the struggle between classes, and the pace of technological change. ESG doctrine portrays the Soviet Union as the principal, but by no means the only, exploiter of these insecurities.[2]

Students at the ESG are taught that as domestic tensions generated by insecurities reach critical levels, maintaining order becomes increasingly difficult. A breakdown of internal order, by undercutting the state, reduces the capabilities of the institution most responsible for maintaining an overall sense of national well-being. When domestic insecurities threaten to get out of hand, dealing with them detracts significantly from the ability of the government to pursue its international-security interests. For the Brazilian military, therefore, maintaining domestic tranquility is the first order of business in the national-security arena. What this means operationally is best understood by focusing on: (1) the procedures favored for handling domestic threats to the regime; (2) the strategies pursued in the international arena; and (3) the continuing capability of the ESG doctrine to dominate Brazilian national-security thinking.

Handling Domestic Threats to National Security

From the day he assumed the presidency on 7 September 1961 until his ouster on 1 April 1964, João Goulart maneuvered in hopes of changing the balance of political and economic power inside Brazil. Had he succeeded, businessmen, landowners, and the middle class would have been the great losers. Peasants, slum dwellers, and workers would have come out ahead. Important elements in the officer corps opposed Goulart, and in retaliation he encouraged noncommissioned officers and enlisted men to organize for collective bargaining. The officer corps saw this as an assault by the president against their control of the military and removed him from office. Once in power the generals and admirals began to implement policies based on the national-security doctrine of the Superior War College.[3]

The first important group of policies implemented by the military sought to strengthen the power and authority of state institutions in relation to those of the interest groups and political parties. Goulart's actions were seen as having weakened the state relative to the industrial unions, the peasant leagues, and the growing numbers of violence-prone slum dwellers. In its weakened condition the state was vulnerable to a Castro-style takeover. The Cuban dictator's success in destroying the traditional Cuban military had alarmed the Brazilian officer corps to an unprecedented degree, and this largely explains why even leftist generals abandoned Goulart after he indicated support for unionization of the armed forces.[4]

Superior War College doctrine, as suggested earlier, saw atheistic communism as the mortal enemy of Christian civilization. Given the leftist orientation of the Brazilian masses, if the state was to prevent a slide into communism it would have to be given sufficient capabilities to overwhelm those seeking to plunge Brazil into a chaos from which it would emerge bound to the Soviet Union. Therefore, not only was a strengthened state apparatus necessary to maintain a culturally Christian social milieu, it was also a requisite for pursuit of what the generals initially saw as the bottom line of Brazil's true international interest: membership in the Western bloc.

The first military president, General Humberto Castello Branco, attempted to establish a controlled democracy in which elements considered dangerous to national security as defined by Superior War College doctrine would be permitted to continue most of their activities as long as they accepted the fact that they would not be allowed to control important policymaking positions in the state apparatus. Neither military hard-liners nor those being controlled were satisfied with this approach. During October 1965 it was abandoned for a more repressive policy that abolished the historic political parties and deprived those who had dominated Brazilian politics between 1945 and 1964 of their political rights.[5]

Controlled democracy's second incarnation, the Humanized Revolution of President Arturo Costa e Silva (1967-1968), proved equally unsuccessful. During December 1968 the military demanded that its controlled congress lift the immunity of a member whose criticism of the armed forces' handling of internal-security problems they considered disrespectful. The refusal of congress to comply, even given the growing intensity of urban guerrilla warfare, convinced most generals that Brazil's national security could only be preserved by dealing more harshly with political dissent.

The subsequent promulgation of Institutional Act Number 5 notified opponents of the military's willingness to use draconian measures against all who challenged the regime. Most significantly, it gave the president authority to recess the national congress and call it back into session. It also set aside the military constitution's own limitations on the president's right to intervene in state and local governments and to appoint mayors and governors. Finally, the act empowered the president—after consultation with the National Security Council and without regard to constitutional guarantees—to suspend the political rights of any citizen for ten years and to cancel federal, state, or municipal electoral mandates.

Institutional Act Number 5 remained in force for more than a decade, until 6 January 1979.[6] It provided the legal framework for ending the political careers of many party and interest-group leaders who had managed to retain their political rights during the early years of the military revolution. Accompanying Institutional Act Number 5 was a dramatic expansion of the National Security Law that hit particularly hard at the press and the media. Article 34, for example, stipulated two to four years imprisonment for "moral offense to anyone in authority" and Article 45 provided penalties of up to four years for the crime of subversive propaganda, which included the use of any means of communication as a vehicle for adverse psychological warfare against a public entity or public official. Taken together, the new National Security Law and Institutional Act Number 5 gave the military and police counterinsurgency units a green light to intensify their campaign against the urban guerrillas. They were so successful that within two years the level of organized violence declined in the cities to the point that the guerrillas no longer constituted a significant threat.

Brazil's national-security-minded regime assembled an impressive array of institutions to enforce compliance with its policies. First and foremost an expanded and strengthened National Security Council provided the mechanism through which generals and admirals could oversee the civilian cabinet and advise the president before major decisions became final.[7] Implementation of controlled democracy in 1964, and of the harder line after December 1968, involved creation and expansion of the National Intelligence Service (SNI). The SNI's authority combines jurisdictions and power given in the United States to the Central Intelligence Agency and the Federal Bureau of Investigation. One measure of SNI influence is that Brazil's last three presidents—Emilio Medici, Ernesto Geisel, João Figueiredo—have served as directors of the SNI. The military also established a group of institutions to investigate, harass, and on occasion liquidate opponents of the regime. Every state, for example, possessed its own Department of Political and Social Order (DOPS) and Operations Center for Internal Defense (CODI). Operacion Bandeirantes (OBAN), however, struck more fear into the hearts of dissidents than any other of these institutions. Many saw it as a front for the infamous death squads.[8]

President Medici used the strengthened state apparatus ruthlessly against opponents of the regime. His successor General Geisel, however, softened Medici's most repressive policies. This was partially because the hard line had been successful in eliminating all but a few urban guerrillas, partially because a growing number of officers believed that continuing Medici's approach would alienate middle-class supporters of the regime, and partially because of Geisel's personal preferences. Geisel labeled his more moderate stance "decompression".

Between 1976 and 1980, despite continuing resistance on the part of hardliners, Geisel convinced the armed forces to gamble that social peace could be maintained using a variation of the less repressive but twice abandoned "controlled democracy." During January 1979 Geisel canceled Institutional Act Number 5 and introduced modifications in the National Security Law that eliminated many provisions empowering the government to curtail political rights. During March 1979 President João Baptista Figueiredo took office, and in June he signed a bill granting amnesty to all who had not taken up arms against the regime.[9] This opened the door for a return from exile of politicians who controlled Brazil during the 1945-1964 democratic regime.

Despite these rapid and sweeping changes the military has not abandoned its mission of preserving domestic tranquility. President Figueiredo personally has worked with consultants from the West German Social Democratic party to forge a new government party that will replace the discredited Renovating Alliance (ARENA). He and his military advisors also have fragmented the opposition into several competing political parties as well as guiding the debate over which procedures will be used to select the next chief executive during 1984.[10] In summary, the resurrection of controlled democracy in no way suggests that the generals will be reluctant to intervene in domestic affairs when issues of national security are being decided.

The other group of policies related to the internal dimension of national security focused on economic development and growth. As early as 1953 Superior War College strategists listed economic growth and development as a "permanent national objective."[11] Amaral Gurgel, a prominent Brazilian social scientist, analyzed the content of President Medici's speeches and found economic development and growth to be the theme most often mentioned. This suggests that Medici pursued hard-line policies not only because he believed that they would bring social peace, but also because he assumed that without social peace, economic growth and development were impossible.

Medici's basic strategy for stimulating growth and development, like that of the military regime's other presidents, was to entice multinational corporations into investing in Brazil. Inducements included tax holidays, generous terms for depreciating equipment, and liberal regulations on profit repatriation. These policies were successful, at least in the short run. Between 1968 and 1974, the years of the "Brazilian Miracle," gross national product spurted ahead at an annual average rate of 10 percent.[12] Inducements even proved sufficient to attract foreign capital into high-risk ventures in the Amazon basin. Development of the Amazon was seen as a national-security-related matter for two reasons: it provided an alternative pole of attraction for northeastern peasants who otherwise would migrate to the already overcrowded slums of Rio de Janeiro, São Paulo, and Belo Horizonte; and it moved Brazilians into a sparsely settled but resource-rich zone that the military feared might become attractive to developed countries as their own economic situations deteriorated.

A policy of attracting investment by the multinationals did not imply to the generals that they were surrendering control over Brazil's economy. Indeed, they used many of the industrial processes transferred by the multinationals to develop one of the Southern Hemisphere's most sophisticated defense industries. Automobile companies thus produced armored vehicles, commercial aviation factories manufactured military aircraft, and the petrochemical industry made fuel for the growing family of Sonda rockets. In both defense and civilian industries the generals increasingly forced foreign companies into joint ventures with private Brazilian capital or with state corporations. New tax incentives were also offered for the purpose of encouraging businessmen to reinvest their profits inside Brazil. Nevertheless, in 1976 the Brazilian economy was more dependent on money markets and investment from the industrialized countries than it had been in 1964, the first year of military rule.

Much of the economic miracle's industrial development was predicated on the continuing availability of abundant and inexpensive energy, even though Brazil remained sadly deficient in fossil fuels. Consequently, sharp increases in the price of imported petroleum after 1973 dramatically slowed economic growth. During 1975 the rate of economic growth fell to 4 percent, and in 1976 and 1977 it hovered around 5 percent.[13] Seen in this light, the controversial purchase from West Germany in 1975 of a complete cycle of nuclear-energy technology was the rational policy of a nationalistic government determined to reduce its dependence on forces in both the industrialized and developing countries over which it has little control.

In summary, the internal dimensions of Brazil's national-security policy involves a commitment by the military to preserve social peace and stimulate economic modernization and Brazilian competitiveness in the global struggle for markets and resources. The internal dimension of national security is thus seen as blending into the international.

Handling International Threats to National Security

External threats focus attention directly on foreigners, rather than on those inside Brazil who do the bidding of foreigners in seeking to weaken the existing regime.[14] During the 1980s, Brazilian national-security policymakers foresee four first-order "external" threats or problems: (1) continuing Argentine military and economic power along the southern and southwestern frontier; (2) a contingency that the Bolivarian countries to the north and northwest (Péru, Ecuador, Colombia, and Venezuela) might transform the Andean Pact into an anti-Brazilian alliance; (3) concern that the East-West military-political balance not shift to restrict Brazil's capability to maneuver between the two superpowers; and (4) uneasiness that Brazil's extreme dependence on imported energy will absorb most of the capital needed to develop an economy capable of supporting great-power status. The responses of Presidents Geisel and Figueiredo to these threats, while building on the initiatives of their predecessors, represent a departure in that for the first time Brazilian strategy is global and almost totally disassociated from the United States or any other Western power.

Threats from the South

Brazilian foreign policy traditionally encouraged nationalism in Paraguay, Uruguay, and Bolivia as a tactic for guarding against the reabsorption of these countries into Argentina. Throughout the nineteenth century, and as recently as the first Perón era (1945-1955), Buenos Aires had indicated a desire to recover these "lost" territories. Most Brazilian army field maneuvers, consequently, have assumed that the primary army mission with regard to South America would be to repel an Argentine invasion from the south.[15] Subsequent to halting such an invasion, Brazilian army units would be expected to pursue the aggressor forces as they retreated into their homeland.

During the past century Brazil has always maintained that it would not contemplate using military force against its neighbors, aside from military operations connected with repelling an invasion. Article 7 of the 1967 constitution goes so far as to forbid wars of external conquest and aggression. Nevertheless, on several occasions during the 1960s and 1970s Brazilian saber-rattling echoed along the southern frontier. The most notable incident occured in October 1973, when forces sympathetic to Uruguay's Tupamaro urban guerrillas began to exhibit surprising strength as that country's presidential campaign unfolded.[16] Several days prior to the balloting Brazil indicated extreme displeasure over the possibility that the Tupamaros might have sympathizers in the Uruguayan national executive by conducting large-scale military maneuvers along the Brazilian-Uruguayan frontier. Tupamaro sympathizers, for whatever reason, went down to defeat.

Two years earlier Brazil made no effort to conceal its relief that General Hugo Banzar had ousted Juan Torres from power in Bolivia. There was some evidence that Banzar had received assistance from Brazilian pilots whom leftists claimed had flown reconaissance missions against the Torres forces. The Bolivian and Uruguayan incidents suggest that under given calculations of risk and benefit Brazil will not hesitate to flex its military muscles if this strengthens ideologically compatible elements in neighboring countries.

The Brazilian military of 1980 was larger and better equipped than at any other time in its history. The army, with a strength of 182,000, consisted of eight divisions, two independent infantry brigades, one parachute brigade and five jungle infantry brigades. Each of the eight divisions boasted up to four armored or mechanized infantry brigades. These armored forces were largely aging medium and light tanks, although 35 modern XIA2 tanks had been integrated into the maneuver units and another 35 were on order. Finally, the Brazilian armored brigades relied on 120 of the domestically manufactured Cascavel armored carriers and an undisclosed number of the new Brazilian-built Sucuri armored combat cars.[17]

Brazilian air-force strength includes 50,000 personnel, 142 combat aircraft and a wide variety of support aircraft and facilities. The three basic air-force missions are to support army maneuver units in combat, to protect Brazilian cities from air attack, and to provide the air links necessary for Amazon development. Until late in the 1960s, most Brazilian military aircraft were purchased from the United States. However, Washington's restrictions on the sale of supersonic fighters to Latin America caused the Brazilians to loosen their historic links with North American suppliers. At present, most Brazilian supersonic aircraft are of French origin and most subsonic aircraft are being manufactured locally. The navy also is attempting to equip itself with domestically produced weapons systems. Brazilian-made patrol boats are now used in the Amazon and along the country's 4,600 miles of coastline. However, the navy has tended to lag behind the other services in gaining an independent footing.

The Brazilian army is deployed into four armies and two commands. Its best maneuver units and most sophisticated hardware are assigned to the Second Army, with headquarters in São Paulo, and the Third Army, with headquarters in Puerto Alegre. It is these forces that have responsibility for guarding southern Brazil against possible military moves by Argentina. The First and Fourth Armies, in contrast, are largely concerned with maintaining internal order. The Amazon Command focuses on occupying and developing the northern third of the country, and the Planalto Command concentrates on insuring tranquility in and around the capital city of Brasilia. Historically, Argentina attempted to maintain superiority in relation to Brazil's Second and Third Armies. The Argentine strategy was to offset Brazil's greater numbers with advantages in training and weaponry.

Brazil's growing conventional military capabilities convinced the Argentines during the late 1960s that they would have to explore the nuclear option more seriously. Argentine activity relating to nuclear weaponry goes back to 1950, when General Juan Perón created the National Atomic Energy Commission. The overenthusiastic general subsequently announced that Argentina had discovered the secret of the hydrogen bomb, only to have it then "discovered" that the discovery was a bluff. Attention subsequently shifted to developing a capability to generate electricity from nuclear fuel.[18] Progress along these lines was minimal until 1968 when General Ongania, then president of Argentina, signed a contract with Siemens of Germany for construction of Latin America's first nuclear-power generating facility, Atucha 1. Atucha 1 commenced operation during 1974.

General Ongania gave the nuclear-power contract to Siemens, despite a lower bid by Westinghouse of the United States, because the Siemens technology was based on a natural-uranium reactor. This freed Argentina from dependence on the U.S. monopoly over enriched uranium and accompanying controls over waste that could be reprocessed into weapons-grade materials. During the late 1970s Argentina's supply of plutonium from Atucha 1 passed beyond the critical threshold for weapons production.

The Siemens contract with Argentina led Brazil to pressure Westinghouse, which had been selected to build Brazil's first nuclear-power plant, to install a full-cycle system and not reclaim spent fuel that could be transformed into plutonium. With U.S. law prohibiting such an agreement, Brazil turned to Western Europe. On 27 June 1975 Bonn and Brasilia signed a comprehensive agreement involving the massive transfer of West German nuclear technology to Brazil.[19] The deal covered six basic items: uranium exploration and mining, uranium enrichment, fuel fabrication, reprocessing of spent fuel, and power plants. Its centerpiece envisioned the sale to Brazil of up to eight giant reactors, together worth between $7 billion and $8 billion. These reactors were to accelerate Brazilian nuclear-energy capabilities toward the goals of 10,000 megawatts of electricity-generating capacity by 1990 and of producing 41 percent of the total energy supply by 2010.

By including provisions to sell a uranium-enrichment plant and a facility for reprocessing spent fuel—from which plutonium could be extracted—the Brazilian-West German agreement could eventually alter the South American military balance. As of mid-1980 the Tlatelolco nuclear nonproliferation treaty bound neither Brazil nor Argentina.[20] In both countries projected or existing plants for preparing and recycling nuclear fuels might easily be used for the production of nuclear weapons. As a hedge against this contingency, Bonn had insisted that Brasilia accept an elaborate system of international inspection. However, nobody seems to know how technological safeguards are to be implemented after the enrichment and reprocessing plants with weapons-making potential are delivered.

The widely publicized Brazilian-West German agreement caused Argentina to place even greater emphasis on its nuclear-energy program. In late 1979 President Jorge Videla of Argentina announced his government's irreversible decision to build a third nuclear-power plant using natural uranium, and he accepted the Swiss bid for construction of a heavy-water plant. The Swiss were persuaded to abandon even the questionable safeguards of the 1975 Brazilian-West German agreement.[21] This convinced the Brazilian military that in the event of a confrontation between the two countries Argentina intended to produce a nuclear bomb. Given Argentina's edge in trained nuclear scientists and greater capacity to reprocess spent fuel from nuclear-power plants, President João Baptista Figueiredo decided to dampen Brazil's escalating nuclear competition with her southern neighbor.

During late 1979 President Figueiredo sent the head of NUCLEBRAS, the Brazilian nuclear authority, to Buenos Aires to explore possible avenues of nuclear cooperation with Argentina. Just prior to the NUCLEBRAS president's departure, Argentina and Brazil signed an agreement that settled the perennial problem associated with hydroelectric development in the River Plate Basin. Without settlement of these issues, which many thought some day might lead to armed conflict between the two nations, nuclear cooperation between them would have been impossible.

In early 1980 Brazil and Argentina exchanged high-ranking nuclear delegations to prepare a broad nuclear-cooperation agreement. A formal treaty between the two countries was signed during President Figueiredo's visit to Argentina the following. May. It called for two-way technical cooperation to minimize dependence on third countries and for joint ventures in producing nuclear-reactor components and uranium and fuel elements. As of this writing it is too early to assess how substantial such cooperation will be in practice.

Events in 1979 and 1980 signaled that for the present Brazil recognized the impossibility of attaining hegemony along her southern frontier. During much of the 1970s there had been a great deal of speculation about Brazil being on the verge of achieving domination over Paraguay, Uruguay, and Bolivia, the buffer states in which Buenos Aires and Brasilia historically competed for influence. The economies of important frontier provinces in these buffer states had fallen under Brazilian domination and Brazilian peasants were drifting across the international boundaries into mushrooming Portuguese-speaking settlements. Historically, similar migrations had preceded substantial territorial gains for Brazil when Portuguese-speaking pioneers petitioned for incorporation into their homeland. From this perspective, Argentina's ability to force Brazilian cooperation in nuclear and hydroelectric matters suggests that despite the latter's growing economic and conventional military power Argentina remains sufficiently strong to prevent any undesired change in the territorial status quo.

Threats from the North and the Northwest

Along the north and northwestern frontiers, the vastness, low population density, and relative isolation of the Amazon Basin have shaped the thinking of Brazilian national-security planners. The Brazilian Amazon, with just under 5 million square kilometers, encompasses 64 percent of the overall Amazon Basin and 42 percent of Brazil's total land area. Nevertheless, only 5 percent of all Brazilians live in the Amazon. Throughout the 36 percent of the basin that eight other countries share (ranging from Peru with 15.9 percent to Guyana with 0.1 percent), as well as within the Brazilian Amazon, the population is confined to a few important cities and scattered Indian settlements. Historically, this vast emptyness provided an almost impenetrable buffer between the effective populations of Brazil and her northern and northwestern neighbors.

Brazilian national-security doctrine, as indicated earlier, stressed national integration and industrialization as prerequisites for attaining great-power status. From this perspective, Amazon development was important for at least three reasons. First, the region contained great agricultural and mineral resources that could provide valuable exports and reduce imports. Also, growing migrations from the impoverished northeast had created potentially explosive situations in the slums of southern industrial cities such as Rio de Janeiro and São Paulo. The government gambled that by opening the Amazon it could provide attractive growth poles away from the industrial south. Finally, the armed forces believed that in a period of increasing global scarcity it was essential that Brazil more effectively occupy and control its resource-rich but underpopulated north.[22]

President Humberto Castelo Branco underlined the military's commitment to development of the Amazon when in 1966, during the closing months of his administration, he created SUDAM as a special regional-development agency with authority in both the north and the northwest. Castelo Branco felt that SUDAM would help in overcoming what he saw as a major impediment to the region's development, the lack of capital. The drive to attract capital into the Amazon also led to establishing the city of Manaus as a duty-free zone and to reorganizing the government's Bank of the Amazon. Rechristened the Amazon Development Bank, this organization became a major conduit for public-sector investment into the north.

SUDAM and the Bank relied heavily on fiscal incentives, granting exemptions from taxation for ten years in some cases. Brasilia thus assigned the private sector an important role in Amazon development. Exemption from taxation and other fiscal incentives had three purposes.[23] The first was to stimulate investment in facilities that would complement military efforts to strengthen and expand the region's basic economic infrastructure, especially in transportation, communication, and electric energy. A second basic purpose involved credits for entrepreneurs in the areas of mining, lumbering, and cattle raising. Finally, increasing investments in agriculture and a new fishing industry were to make the region self-sufficient in food production by 1985.

Economic development in the Amazon was accompanied by a reorganization and strengthening of the armed forces in the area. The Amazon Command, a major military force ranking just below the four armies in importance, had been headquartered historically near the mouth of the Amazon River, in the city of Bélem. The command's presence was strongly felt in the lower Amazon, with the upper Amazon, except for Manaus, being largely neglected. In 1967 the General Staff acted at the direction of President Arturo Costa e Silva and shifted the command's headquarters to Manaus. The relocated and reorganized Amazon Military Command included special subordinate commands in Acre-Rondonia, Roraima, and at the mouth of the Amazon.[24] As part of this westward shift of military power the air force also upgraded its installations in Manaus, although Bélem remained the overall air force command center for the Northern region. Similarly, the navy, with a mission of defending the coast as well as controlling the inland waterways, retained Val de Cans on Guajara Bay, some five miles from Bélem, as the center of its Fourth Naval District. Additional patrol craft capable of operating in the upper Amazon, however, were added to naval inventories.

The heaviest burden of strengthening the military's presence, not surprisingly, fell to the army. Army engineers built major installations in the Amazon at Tabatinga, Macapá, Boa Vista, Porto Velho, and a host of minor bases along the frontier from Bolivia to French Guiana. These activities mandated an increase in the number of engineer battalions attached to the Amazon Command. In addition, the Amazon Command received authorization for five new jungle battalions of 600 men each.

Construction of a basic transportation infrastructure has been one of the most important tasks in the army's Amazon development mission. Responsibility for road construction involved army engineer battalions in the much publicized Trans-Amazon Highway, a 3,500-mile link between Recife on the Atlantic coast and the Peruvian border. Other major Amazonian highways being built and maintained by the army include the 1,000-mile link between Cuiabá and Santarem, a connector between Manaus and the Venezuelan border, and the Northern Perimeter highway. The latter road, more than 2,000 miles in length, seeks to open the Amazon Basin north of the river, just as the Trans-Amazon Highway did in areas to the south. Although the Trans-Amazon Highway was finished during 1975, the Northern Perimeter roadway lags far behind its mid-1977 completion target. Soaring petroleum prices and balance-of-payment deficits since 1974 have significantly reduced the government's ability to develop the Amazon and raised questions about the advisability of shifting transportation investment from highways to railroads. Completion of the Northern Perimeter road has been pushed back at least into the mid-1980s.[25]

Brazilian efforts between 1967 and 1980 to exploit the Amazon, even given recent slowdowns, have altered the geopolitical balance in northern South America. For the first time, Peru, Colombia, Venezuela, Guyana, Surinam, and French Guiana must contend with an effective Brazilian presence on their Amazonian frontiers. Concerning the latter three, one remains a colony of France and the other two achieved independence only recently.[26] With a combined population that barely exceeds two million, they are by far the smallest and least influential countries in continental South America. Thus, the growth of effective Brazilian power suggests eventual Finlandization of these three, with some possibility that they could suffer the fate of Estonia, Latvia, or Lithuania. Although the latter contingency seems unlikely at present, it might materialize as the byproduct of rising tensions between Brazil and its northern Spanish-speaking neighbors.

Successes in projecting Brazilian power throughout the once lightly held Amazon Basin alarmed the national-security policymaking establishments of the Andean Pact countries as early as 1972. Despite Brazilian Foreign Office (Itamaraty) assurances that Brazil had no territorial ambitions, the Andeans' relatively haphazard efforts to exploit their own Amazonian peripheries made Brazilian achievements appear threatening. Rumors circulated in Caracas, Bogotá, and Lima that "their" Amazonian indians were speaking Portuguese as a second language, rather than Spanish, and that the Brazilian Indian Service controlled native populations throughout the entire Amazon Basin.[27]

In February 1973 Venezuela's president, Rafael Caldera, toured the Andean countries seeking to develop a common pact position with regard to growing Brazilian power in the Amazon. Subsequently, Caldera met with Brazil's president, Emilio Medici, at the border town of Santa Elena de Uairen. Although the two presidents signed a joint declaration reaffirming the principles of nonintervention, Medici refused to treat Caldera as a spokesman for other Andean Pact countries. The two delegations did not get on well and the Venezuelans returned to Caracas with heightened misgivings about Brazilian intentions along South America's inner rim.

Caldera's tour and the Santa Elena meeting prodded the Itamaraty to develop a strategy that insured that the Andean Pact did not evolve into an anti-Brazilian alliance. The strategy contained three elements. First, Brazil proposed new or additional bilateral treaties of friendship and cooperation with each of the Andean Pact countries. These treaties were negotiated and ratified by the end of 1979. Second, Brazil approached countries having Amazonian territories, and this included most Andean Pact members, with a proposal to join an organization that would coordinate the development of their respective Amazonian regions. It was implied that within such an organization Brazil would share the knowledge and technology it had gained in developing its Amazon. On 2 July 1978, after a series of conferences in which the Andeans weakened the powers that Brazil initially proposed for the organization's secretariat, representatives of Venezuela, Colombia, Ecuador, Peru, Bolivia, Guyana, Surinam, French Guiana, and Brazil signed the Amazon Pact Treaty.[28]

Finally, during 1979 the Itamaraty initiated a campaign to convince the Andeans that they should join with Brazil in a continent-wide economic union. The Andeans responded by inviting Brazil's foreign minister to a meeting of Andean Pact foreign ministers in Lima during January 1980. Although Brazil's presence was well received, concern persisted among the Spanish-speaking delegations that their Portuguese-speaking neighbor would come to dominate any organization that merged the Andean and Amazonian Pacts.[29] Argentine participation also remained a point of disagreement. Nevertheless, the likelihood of the Andean Pact evolving in an anti-Brazilian direction was far more remote in 1980 than it had been in 1973. From this perspective, Brazilian diplomacy under Presidents Medici,

Geisel, and Figueiredo was successful in reducing the probability of the one geopolitical event along the northwest and northern frontier that could seriously threaten Brazilian national security.

Threats Deriving from the
East-West Conflict

Soon after the newly installed military regime proclaimed its opposition to communism and support for the "Christian West," the United States responded with large-scale economic assistance, police training, and counterinsurgency technology. Brasilia drew closer to Washington than at any time since the two had collaborated against the Nazis in World War II. However, the official U.S. presence in Brazil made nationalist Brazilians increasingly uncomfortable, and by the end of the 1960s a significant reduction in U.S. government personnel was underway. In 1975 Brazilian-American relations underwent a severe strain when President Ernesto Geisel entered into the previously mentioned agreement with West Germany that provided for the transfer of a complete cycle of nuclear-fuel technology. The Ford administration's opposition to the accord, however, was short-lived. Secretary of State Henry Kissinger did not consider it worth jeopardizing relations with a major ally. In a dramatic about-face he signed a special memorandum of understanding with his Brazilian counterpart, Foreign Minister Antonio Azevedo da Silveira. The memorandum established a twice yearly system of ministerial-level consultations. It was an arrangement reserved for major U.S. allies like Great Britain, and President Geisel considered it a centerpiece of his national-security policy.[30]

The Carter administration dramatically reversed its predecessor's pro-Brazilian policy. Soon after Jimmy Carter took office he shocked, angered, and dismayed the Brazilian foreign ministry by announcing his extreme displeasure over Brazil's purchase of nuclear-power technology from West Germany. Carter not only labeled this a first step toward acquiring nuclear weapons, which President Geisel denied, he also pressured West Germany, unsuccessfully as it turned out, to cancel the agreement. Carter's behavior strengthened the hand of conservative nationalists who argued that major-ally status was a hoax when it entailed knuckling under to U.S. efforts at retaining monopoly over the technology used in Brazil's nuclear-power industry. The same conservatives were also outraged over Carter's public condemnation of alleged human-rights violations in Brazil.[31]

At the beginning of the 1980s, Brazilians of all political persuasions had come to believe that the United States needed Brazil at least as much as Brazil needed the United States. The military regime stated repeatedly that it could handle internally generated threats to public order, and Cuba's ability to export its revolution to Brazil without Soviet assistance was not taken seriously. The generals, however, remained distrustful of Soviet imperialism, and herein lay the principal reason why they muted their expression of outrage over Carter's attempt to scuttle their nuclear agreement with West Germany. Thus, while abolishing the joint Brazil-United States military commission, President Geisel stopped short of withdrawing ratification of the Interamerican Treaty of Reciprocal Assistance (TIAR). TIAR bound Brazil and most other Latin American states to the United States in case of an extrahemispheric attack on any member nation.[32] Also, Geisel allowed the Brazilian navy to continue its annual UNITAS maneuvers with the United States. UNITAS focused on keeping the South Atlantic and the strategic Atlantic narrows open in case of a war between the North Atlantic Treaty Organization and the Warsaw Pact.

Even given its growing Niteroi-class destroyer fleet, Brazil lacks the capability to defend the South Atlantic and Atlantic narrows by itself.[33] Brazilian naval forces are configured primarily for the coastal defense of population centers between Rio de Janeiro and Puerto Alegre in the extreme south. Brazil cannot engage simultaneously in coastal patrol and escort or other activities. Antisubmarine capabilities also remain limited, and as of early 1980 neither the United States nor Western Europe was willing to supply the electronic-detection equipment needed to upgrade them. Without assistance from the U.S. fleet, therefore, Brazil is unable either to keep open its lifeline to Europe or to defend its coast against hostile Soviet naval power.[34]

Since the early 1970s, Brazilian national-security planners have assumed that all-out war between the two superpowers is improbable. Therefore, while continuing to participate in UNITAS exercises, Brazil has not joined in a regional South Atlantic Treaty Organization that Washington hoped would have provided an institutionalized regional multinational military capability. Also, alliance with the United States in the event of conflict between NATO and the Warsaw Pact does not guarantee that Brasilia will back Washington every time the United States opposes Soviet expansion, even in areas bordering on the South Atlantic.[35]

Angola represents an excellent case in point. Despite extreme unhappiness over Soviet-Cuban intervention in the Angolan civil war, Brazil was among the first countries to recognize Agostinho Neto's Marxist government.[36] It was initially considered likely that Neto would repay the Soviets by providing them with their first major naval installation in the South Atlantic. Brazil's decision to recognize Neto indicates that the potential for commerce with the former Portuguese colony and friendship with oil-rich Nigeria, one of Neto's major backers, had become more important than support for the West against the East. The linkage of economic development and national security that characterizes Brazilian national-security doctrine thus produced a political-strategic decision that would have been difficult to predict using the more narrow definition of national security common in Western Europe and the United States. It also suggests that if United States and Brazilian economic interests continue to diverge, Brazil will assume an increasingly neutral position in most manifestations of the East-West struggle short of all-out war.

Threats Deriving from Extreme Dependence on
Imported Energy

Although Brazil must import some nonferrous metals to operate modern industries, its lack of success in locating domestic petroleum creates the shortage that most clearly threatens economic growth and development. Industrialization between 1964 and 1973 was predicated, erroneously, on the availability of abundant supplies of inexpensive imported petroleum. With each Organization of Petroleum Exporting Countries (OPEC) price rise, despite a rapidly expanding export capability, Brazil's balance of payments has deteriorated. During 1979 Brazil imported roughly 1,050,000 barrels of petroleum per day, at an annual cost of almost $10 billion.[37] Its trade deficit in 1979 was $2.7 billion, and its total foreign indebtedness approached $47 billion.[38]

In addition to leading the world in substituting alcohol for petroleum as a liquid fuel, Brazil has pursued an export-diversification strategy to cover the costs of petroleum and other imports. A category of exports in which Brazil is having increasing success, and one with great implications for the South American military balance, is the production of conventional arms. *Business Week* estimates that by the 1980s Brazil will be marketing $500 million worth of military hardware annually—equal to the armaments exports of France or Great Britain during the early 1970s.[39] These arms have proved especially attractive to Brazil's Middle Eastern oil suppliers. For example, Libya, Qatar, and Iraq are among the most important customers for the previously noted Cascavel, a light armored vehicle that mounts a 90mm cannon and carries laser range-finders.

Brazil's state-owned Empresa Brasileira de Aeronautica (Embraer) is already the world's sixth-largest general aviation company. Its twin-engine Bandeirante, developed originally for exploring the Amazon, has been sold worldwide for military and civilian use. Embraer also builds the two-seat Xavante jet for advanced training and ground support under license from Italy's Aeronautica Macchi.[40] On the aerospace side, there are the Sonda rockets. The Sonda III, used for meteorological studies, continues to interest Taiwan as a ballistic missile, and the Sonda IV is the step up to launching communications satellites. President Geisel underlined the government's continuing commitment to Brazil's aerospace industry in 1978 when he expanded and modernized the scientifically oriented missile base at Barreira do Inferno.[41]

Brazilian arms are especially attractive to third-world countries since they are comparatively simple, high quality, and free of ideological ties. Because of the growing demand for Brazilian arms, and given that Brazil must increase exports to compensate for rising petroleum prices, the state continues to assign a high priority to investment in what already is the largest and most sophisticated conventional-weapons industry in South America. As a major arms supplier, Brazil will be able to exert greater pressure on its neighbors and to increase its influence in the emerging commercial markets of black Africa, the Middle East, and Asia.

Conclusions: The Continuing Capability of ESG National-Security Doctrine to Dominate

Those who govern Brazil hold that if their country is to fulfill its destiny—achieving a position of dominance in South America and of global power and influence—support must be maintained for the Escola Superior de Guerra (ESG) national-security doctrine. The ESG itself continues to be a major source of political socialization for military and civilian elites. Graduate war courses provide an opportunity for mixed teams of civilians and officers to study and analyze contemporary Brazilian problems. The Armed Forces General Staff Course, for officers only, alerts future military leaders to their national-security-related responsibilities. The ESG alumni association has grown in numbers and prestige, and the association's magazine, *Segurança e Desenvolvamento*, disseminates the latest national-security thinking to an influential audience of professionals and businessmen.

The ESG and its doctrine are not without detractors. Immediately following the 1964 revolution most leftists saw both as evidence of U.S. penetration and domination of Brazil. Although many believe that this remains the case, others have been pleasantly surprised by the increasingly nationalist policies being advocated by ESG strategists and by the ruling military. In foreign affairs especially, Brazil's more independent posture has met with approval from leftists as well as conservative nationalists. Should the leftists come to power during the next decade, Brazil might tilt more toward the Soviet Union, but the policies pursued in relation to other South American countries and the third world would not differ substantially from those of the Figueiredo government. It is also unlikely that tilting toward the Soviet Union would entail "Cubanization." Satellite status is incompatible with great-power aspirations and Brazil's economy is closely tied to the capitalist West. Finally, Moscow simply does not possess sufficient resources to pursue its higher priority security interests and sub- sidize the transformation to socialism of the economy of a nation with more than one hundred twenty-five million inhabitants.

The future of the ESG's internal national-security formulas remains cloudy. General Golbery Couto e Silva, perhaps the leading national- security strategist, has been given a mandate by President Figueiredo to preside over a return to the most open political system Brazilians have enjoyed in more than a decade.[42] Golbery's strategy is to retain the state's ability to depress redistributive demands and accumulate capital for development while restoring many political freedoms. Structurally, this is to be accomplished by creating a broad-based "official" political party, the Brazilian Social Democratic Party (PSD), behind which ESG-mandated economic development can occur. Opponents are to be dispersed among several political parties, each presumably too weak to effectively challenge the military regime. Whether or not Golbery is successful in institutionaliz- ing this system must await the results of elections still very tentatively planned for 1982 and 1984.

Notes

1. Escola Superior de Guerra, *Manual Básico* (Rio de Janeiro, 1976), p. 418.

2. Ibid., pp. 415-417, 436-437.

3. Alfred Stepan, *The Military in Politics: Changing Patterns in Brazil* (Princeton, N.J.: Princeton University Press, 1971), part VI.

4. Ronald M. Schneider, *Brazil: Emergence of a Modernizing Authoritarian Regime 1964-1970* (New York: Columbia University Press, 1971), pp. 91-107.

5. Peter Flynn, *Brazil: A Political Analysis* (Boulder, Colo.: Westview Press, 1978), chapters 2, 10.

6. *Latin American Weekly Report,* 5 January 1980, p. 5.

7. United States Army, *Area Handbook for Brazil* (Washington: Department of the Army pamphlet 550-20, 1975), pp. 220-221.

8. Flynn, *Brazil*, pp. 434-435; *The New York Times*, 14 June 1970, pp. 1 and 26.

9. *Latin American Weekly Report,* 25 January 1980, p. 9.

10. *Latin American Regional Reports: Brazil,* 14 March 1980, pp. 1, 5.

11. Wayne A. Selcher, "The National Security Doctrine and Policies of the Brazilian Government," *Parameters,* 7, no. 1 (1977), p. 16.

12. Edmar L. Bacha, "Issues and Evidence of Recent Brazilian Economic Growth," *World Development,* 5, nos. 1-2 (1977), pp. 47-67.

13. Jonathan Kendell, "The Economic Miracle in Brazil Is Over," *The New York Times,* 8 February 1976, p. 5.

14. *Manual Básico,* p. 447.

15. Frank D. McCann, "Development of Brazilian Military-Strategic Thinking" (Paper read to Brazil Seminar, Columbia University, 18 May 1978), pp. 9-10.

16. *O Estado de São Paulo,* 26 October 1973 and *O Jornal do Brasil,* 26 October 1973.

17. International Institute for Strategic Studies, *The Military Balance 1979-1980* (London, 1980), pp. 76-77.

18. C. H. Waisman, "Incentives for Nuclear Proliferation: The Case of Argentina," in *Nuclear Proliferation and the Near Nuclear Countries,* eds. Onkar Marwah and Ann Schulz (Cambridge, Mass.: Ballinger, 1975), pp. 279-293.

19. Edward Wonder, "Nuclear Commerce and Nuclear Proliferation: Germany and Brazil, 1975," *Orbis* 21, no. 2 (Summer 1977):277; and Norman Gall, "Atoms for Brazil, Dangers for All," *Foreign Policy,* no. 23 (Summer 1976):155-201.

20. John Redick, "Regional Restraint: U.S. Nuclear Policy and Latin America," *Orbis* 22, no. 1 (Spring 1978):161-200.

21. John Reichertz, "Brazil Forges Nuclear Link with Argentina," *Weekend Australia,* 29 March 1980, p. 9.

22. H. Jon Rosenbaum and William G. Tyler, "Policy Making For the Brazilian Amazon," *Journal of Inter-American Studies and World Affairs* 13, no. 4 (July-October 1971):410-417, and Frances M. Foland, "A Profile of Amazonia," *Journal of Inter-American Studies and World Affairs,* 13, no. 1 (January 1971):62-63. Also see *Correio Brasiliense* (Brasilia), 2 February 1973.

23. The most recent analysis of Brazilian efforts in the Amazon is Norman Gall's five-part "Letter from Rondonia," *American Universities Field Services Reports—South America,* nos. 9-13 (1978).

24. Brazilian Army Public Information Service, *Sentinels of the Amazon,* n.d., pp. 1-8, 54-55.

25. *Correio Brasiliense* (Brasilia), 10 June 1973 has a useful summary of the government's plans to develop highways in the Amazon. Also see Gall., "Letter from Rondonia," part 1.

26. Guyana gained independence in 1966, and Surinam became independent in 1975.

27. Interview, 27 February 1974, with a high Venezuelan government official active in CONDESUR, the Amazon development agency.

28. *El Nacional* (Caracas), 18 May 1978 contains a detailed discussion of the Amazon treaty from the Venezuelan perspective.

29. *Latin American Weekly Report,* 25 January 1980, p. 5.

30. U.S. Department of State, Bureau of Public Affairs, Office of

Media Services, *Major Statements on Latin America by Secretary Henry A. Kissinger, Made During His Visits to Venezuela, Peru, Brazil, Colombia, and Costa Rica; February 1976* (Washington, D.C.: U.S. Department of State, 1976), pp. 15-19.

31. Margarete K. Luddeman, *Nuclear Technology From West Germany: A Case of Disharmony in U.S. Brazilian Relations* (Washington, D.C.: Georgetown University Latin American Studies Program, Occasional Paper No. 1, 1978), p. 10.

32. The language of the Inter American Treaty of Reciprocal Assistance is almost identical to that used in the 1948 North Atlantic Treaty. The text of the Inter American Treaty of Reciprocal Assistance is reprinted in *The Dynamics of International Politics*, eds. Norman J. Padelford, George A. Lincoln and Lee D. Olvey (New York: MacMillan, 1976), Appendix A.

33. Margaret Daly Hays, "U.S. National Security Interests in Latin America" (Unpublished paper presented at Middle Atlantic Latin American Studies Convention, April 1980), pp. 13-20.

34. Interview with a United States naval officer who commanded nuclear submarines that patrolled the South Atlantic during the late 1970s.

35. Alexandre S.C. Barros, "The Diplomacy of National Security: South American International Relations in a Defrosting World" in *Latin America: The Search for a New International Role,* eds. Ronald G. Hellman and H. Jon Rosenbaum (Beverley Hills, Calif.: Sage Publications, 1975), pp. 131-149.

36. Wayne Selcher, *Brazil's Multilateral Relations Between First and Third World* (Boulder, Colo.: Westview Press, 1978), pp. 231-233.

37. *Latin American Weekly Report,* 1 February 1980, p. 1.

38. *Latin America Regional Report: Brazil,* 14 March 1980, p. 8.

39. *Business Week,* 31 July 1978, pp. 45-46.

40. *Latin American Weekly Report,* 7 December 1979, p. 68.

41. Michael Arkus, "Brazil's Spectacular Space Age Launch Site," *The Christian Science Monitor,* 3 July 1975, p. 10.

42. *Latin America Regional Report: Brazil,* 14 March 1980, p. 1.

4 Cuba

Carla Anne Robbins

There are forty thousand Cuban combat troops stationed in Africa. These troops played a central role in Communist victories in Angola and Ethiopia. In the past two years Cuba has increased its involvement in Central America and the Caribbean as well. Cuban weapons and advisors provided important support to the Sandinistas during the Nicaraguan revolution. Rumors of Cuban aid for insurgents in El Salvador and Guatemala are still unconfirmed.

Cuba's commitment of troops to Africa raised the specter of a new form of internal conflict: big-power military competition by proxy. Cuban foreign policy has thus become important to any study of recent changes in the international system. The Cuban case is particularly appropriate for a study that questions theoretical assumptions about the limited power of developing states in the international arena.

The Cuban case is contrary to all expectations. In terms of size, resources, and level of development, Cuba is one of the developing states least capable of conducting an aggressive foreign policy. Nevertheless, Cuba does just that. Moreover, Cuba's foreign policy is in many significant ways determined autonomously. Although Cuba's current policies in Africa have strengthened Soviet interests in strategic areas of the continent, there have been times when similar Cuban policies directly challenged Soviet interests in the third world. In the mid-1960s Cuba tried to export revolution to Latin America over the protests of its Soviet allies, even after Moscow threatened to cut off deliveries of oil.

The basis of Cuba's foreign policy is an ideological commitment to proletarian internationalism: a commitment to promote nationalism, socialism, and antiimperialism throughout the third world. Although ideology has traditionally played an important role in the Cuban policy process, it has at times had to face the pragmatic limitations of internal security and external defense. Cuba's security policy, like that of all states, is the result of a complex interplay of many factors on both international and domestic levels.

In comparative terms, Cuba's foreign policy has been far less constrained than that of most developing states. Cuba's basic security is guaranteed by the Soviet nuclear umbrella. Cuba also receives all of its arms free of charge from the Soviet Union. As a result, Cuba's decisions to send arms or military aid abroad are exempted from the traditional competition for scarce resources that plague most developing countries.

Cuba has been relatively unconstrained by its international alliances as well. Cuba has a special relationship with the Soviet Union. Cuba is economically and militarily dependent on the Soviet Union, yet maintains a remarkable degree of political autonomy. Not only have the Cubans pursued their own policies both at home and abroad, they have also apparently been able to influence Soviet policy choices. The Cubans appear to have played a central role in the Soviet decision to aid Agostinho Neto's Popular Movement for the Liberation of Angola (MPLA) in the Angolan civil war.

Cuba's special relationship with the Soviet Union can be traced to an unusual set of historical circumstances. As the first socialist revolution in the western hemisphere, Cuba became a very valuable ally for the Soviet Union in its competition with the United States and China for influence in the third world. During the 1960s—the period of the developing Sino-Soviet split—Moscow repeatedly pointed to its support for Cuba as evidence of its strong commitment to third-world revolution. More recently the Cubans have served as a go-between for the Soviets in the Nonaligned Movement and on the battlefields of Africa. Castro has often drawn on his unique bargaining position to guarantee Soviet support for Cuba, to deflect Soviet demands on Cuba, and to broaden Soviet commitments to the third world.

Cuba's power is not unlimited. Cuba suffers from many of the problems that constrain the independent action of most developing states. The Cuban economy, while subsidized, is still very weak. The commitment of forty thousand Cuban troops to Africa, over half of whom are reservists, must inevitably place new strains on an already overburdened economy. Cuba is also a client state. Ultimately, its survival as well as its ability to pursue an aggressive foreign policy depends on Soviet aid. Most immediately, the Cubans lack the transport capability to move men and weapons overseas without Soviet help.

The nature of Castro's revolution—socialist and antiimperialist—has also created a set of implacable enemies for Cuba both at home and abroad. The most threatening has been the United States. For twenty years Cuba has had to defend itself against U.S.-supported exile attacks, a U.S.-imposed economic embargo, and U.S.-imposed political isolation.

Finally, Cuba's own ideology has placed particular constraints on its choice of foreign policies. Cuba claims to be a member of both the socialist bloc and the third world. Cuba's ability to move freely between the two has won the nation a degree of international prestige that far outweighs its size and resources. Thus Cuba has gained a surprising amount of leverage with the Soviet Union. But Cuba's efforts to combine the interests of these two constituencies has placed it in a tenuous international position. The defeat of Cuba's bid for a seat on the U.N. Security Council soon after the Soviet invasion of Afghanistan is only the most recent reminder of Cuba's dilemma.

How Cuba Views the World

The revolution that brought Fidel Castro to power was committed to a broad program of social change at home and antiimperialism abroad. The increasingly radical nature of those goals created three security challenges for the Castro regime: internal defense, external defense, and the effective propagation of proletarian internationalism.

The most immediate security challenge was internal defense. When Castro's band of guerrillas came to power in January 1959 they were unknown to most Cubans. The few rebel policy statements that had leaked through Batista's censorship spoke only in vague terms of agrarian reform and social and political freedoms. The new regime also lacked organizational support outside the Sierra. Without minimizing Castro's heroism, it must be recognized that Castro came to power almost by default. Batista's authority had become increasingly illegitimate; eventually it disappeared completely. His army deserted; the United States cut off aid. Castro stepped into the power vacuum.

Once in power the full contours of the revolution's radicalism became clear. From agrarian reform the new regime quickly moved to nationalize almost all sectors of the economy. In April 1961 Castro declared that he was a Marxist-Leninist. As the radical nature of Castro's programs solidified, so did his opposition. Plantation owners were soon joined by factory owners, professionals, and bureaucrats—most of Cuba's privileged classes. After Castro's turn to socialism, some of his own rebel army deserted him.

Most of the opposition left Cuba. A few, however, did choose to stay and fight, and, like Castro, they formed guerrilla bands and took to the hills. There were probably never more than one thousand anti-Castro guerrillas. But Castro's own rebel army never numbered more than two thousand.

At the same time that Castro's army was fighting counterrevolutionaries in the Escambray mountains, the regime was facing a more subtle form of opposition in the cities, that of political consciousness. Castro tried to recreate the consciousness of the Cuban people not only to guarantee support for the new regime but also to fulfill the ideological mission of creating communism in Cuba.

In sum, the requirements of internal defense entailed three separate tasks for the new regime: to defend against internal insurrection, to build the institutions to administer the revolution, and to transform the Cuban people into "new Communist men and women."

External defense against U.S. invasion and exile attacks was the second security challenge confronting the Castro regime. The U.S.-Cuba split was not inevitable. In the first months after the revolution both parties made a number of cautious overtures, but there was strong distrust on both sides.

U.S. hostility toward the new Castro regime can be explained by the volatile combination of the Monroe Doctrine and the Cold War. Cuba's fear of U.S. intervention can be traced to 1898 when the United States intervened in the Cuban War of Independence, commonly known as the Spanish-American War. The 1954 U.S.-backed overthrow of the Arbenz regime in Guatemala reinforced in Fidel Castro's mind this long-standing Cuban fear of U.S. intervention and domination.

In this atmosphere of mutual distrust, events quickly overtook actors. In January 1961 the United States and Cuba officially broke relations. The immediate cause was the refusal of U.S. refineries in Cuba to process Soviet crude oil and the subsequent Cuban decision to nationalize the plants. Three months later Castro's worst fears were realized when the United States launched the Bay of Pigs invasion.

In October 1962 the world was brought to the brink of war over the Soviet right to install nuclear weapons in Cuba. Washington and Moscow went eyeball to eyeball, and Moscow flinched first. The resulting compromise, which included a no-invasion pledge from the United States, was intended to placate the Cuban leadership. It did not. Castro was incensed with Khrushchev for going over his head and conducting the negotiations with Kennedy directly.

Despite the no-invasion pledge, the Cubans continued to fear a U.S. attack. The findings of the Church subcommittee's 1976 investigation of the Central Intelligence Agency (CIA) suggest that these fears were not unfounded. During the 1960s the CIA funded insurgency within Cuba, exile attacks, and a whole range of dirty tricks intended to destabilize the Castro regime. In addition, the U.S.-imposed embargo on trade and the political isolation of Cuba were, in Havana's view, tantamount to acts of war. The landing of U.S. marines in the Dominican Republic in 1965 and the escalation of the Vietnam War added to Cuba's sense of insecurity.

It must be emphasized that for much of the 1960s the Cubans also suffered from grave doubts about their alliance with the Soviets. The missile crisis made them painfully aware of their military dependence on the Soviets and unsure of the fidelity of the Soviet commitment to Cuba's defense. Moscow's refusal to get directly involved in the Vietnam War exacerbated these fears. If the Soviets could abandon the Vietnamese in their fight with the United States, might they not some day abandon the Cubans in a similar situation?[1]

The real strain in Cuban-Soviet relations developed over the issue of the correct strategy for promoting revolution in Latin America. Cuban advocated armed struggle. Moscow sought change in Latin America through the more incremental and political united-front strategies followed by most of the region's Communist parties. This debate did not long remain in the realm of ideology. In 1966 The Cubans and Soviets found themselves on opposite sides of the barricades. Castro's government openly supported the Venezuelan FALN guerrillas' attempts to overthrow the Leoni regime. At the same time Moscow tried to extend its influence in the region by establishing diplomatic relations with the Leoni regime. The Cubans reacted strongly. They accused the Soviets of betraying the international revolution to further their own state interests. It is said that it was in the context of this debate that the Soviets cut back on their deliveries of oil to Havana.[2]

The third security challenge confronting the Cubans was their own commitment to proletarian internationalism. In July 1960 Castro summed up that commitment when he said, "We promise to make an example of our country that will turn the Andes into the Sierra Maestra of the American Continent."[3] This was not an empty promise. In the first months of the Cuban revolution the Cubans launched attacks agains the Dominican Republic, Haiti, and Panama.

Proletarian internationalism has strong roots in Cuba's history and revolutionary philosophy. As early as the 1898 U.S. intervention the Cubans learned that their own revolution was unavoidably an international affair. The Cubans have also known the benefits of foreign support. Two of their most famous revolutionary heroes were not Cuban nationals: Maximo Gomez, a hero of the 1898 revolution, was a Dominican; Che Guevara was an Argentine. Even today, the revolution still could not survive without Soviet aid. The Cubans feel that it is thus their duty to aid other struggling movements and regimes.

Proletarian internationalism has its pragmatic sources as well. Cuba's attempts to export revolution to Latin America were aimed at overcoming its hemispheric isolation and developing new allies. The export of revolution was also an effort to defend Cuba against outside aggression. In 1967 Guevara outlined a plan to tie down U.S. resources and divert U.S. attention from Cuba and Vietnam by creating, "Two, three, many Vietnams."[4]

Internationalism has also played a central role in Cuban-Soviet relations. Cuba's campaign for internationalism was a bid to strengthen Soviet commitments to the third world in general, and Cuba in specific. It was also an attempt to assure that Cuban-Soviet ties were strong but not overly binding. Cuba's commitment to internationalism validated Castro's claims to leadership of the third-world revolution and reinforced his bargaining position with the Soviets.

In recent years the Castro regime has become more secure. U.S. defeats in Vietnam and Angola have convinced Cuba that the balance of international forces has shifted in favor of the socialist bloc. U.S. efforts to improve relations with the Cuban government also contribute to this new sense of security. Even though the efforts at rapprochement have foundered on the issue of Cuba's involvement in Africa, there is little doubt in either

Washington or Havana that the United States has finally accepted the permanence of Castro's regime.

Cuba's Latin American neighbors now also appear less hostile. Cuba has diplomatic and trading relations with almost every regime in the hemisphere. The new independence (and anti-Americanism) of the Latin American regimes has led them to defy the U.S.-imposed economic and political sanctions on Cuba. The Cubans have also changed their attitude and have gone to great lengths to reassure their neighbors that they have no intention of exporting revolution or intervening in the internal affairs of any state—unless they are invited in.

The Cubans have resolved many of their difficulties with the Soviets. Cuba has abandoned those policies that the Soviets termed adventurist, while the Soviets have in turn taken a more aggressive interest in the third world. Soviet aid to Cuba has also increased markedly since the early 1970s.

Until the recent exodus of Cuban refugees it appeared that the Cubans had resolved their internal-security problems, as well. Two symbols of the regime's growing sense of security were the decisions to free a large number of political prisoners in 1979 and to open its doors to Cuban exiles. It is difficult to predict now how the mass exodus will affect the Castro regime.

The Angolan involvement did a lot to improve Cuba's international position. Not only did it demonstrate to the Soviet Union the continuing utility of its alliance with Cuba, it also did much to reaffirm Cuba's position as a leader of the progressive third world. Cuba was elected head of the Nonaligned Movement six months after the Angolan victory. At the same time Cuba's expanding role in Africa has increased its vulnerability in the hemisphere. In 1976, amidst rumors of an impending Cuban involvement in Namibia, then-Secretary of State Kissinger threatened Cuba with direct U.S. retaliation should Cuba increase its military presence in Africa. This would certainly have violated the 1962 U.S.-Soviet agreement on Cuba—and it is not clear whether Kissinger was bluffing. His threat did not, however, surprise the Cuban leadership, which has consistently refused to lower its guard. Castro summed up Cuba's continuing distrust of the United States when he said. "Our defense can never depend on the good faith of the imperialists."[5]

Cuban Security Policies

To meet the challenges of internal security and external defense the new Cuban leadership first implemented a program of local militarization and then set about building a sophisticated armed force. At the same time they established close political and military ties with the Soviet Union. To meet their commitment to proletarian internationalism the Cubans pursued a wide variety of programs ranging from guerrilla insurgency in Latin America, to peaceful foreign aid in Africa, to the present large-scale military commitments in Angola and Ethiopia.

From 1960 to 1965 the regime fought a second guerrilla war. This time, however, Castro's army was the government force and the guerrillas were the enemy. The Castro regime sent ten times the number of troops against the Escambray banditos as the number committed by Batista.[6] In the cities, at the same time, the new regime sought to simultaneously defeat its internal enemies and integrate the local population into the revolution with a far-reaching program of local militarization. The first mass organization created was the National Militia. This was an all-volunteer, civilian army. By 1961 it claimed over 300,000 members. The militia was sent to fight the Escambray guerrillas and the Bay of Pigs invaders.

In September 1960 the militia idea was broadened to include the entire Cuban population with the creation of the Committees for the Defense of the Revolution (CDR). CDRs were set up on every block, in every work place. Their membership claimed young and old alike. Neighbors kept tabs on neighbors and reported any irregularities of consciousness or behavior. The CDRs also performed local police duties, guarding against the more mundane crimes as well as counterrevolutionary acts.

The army also played a central role at the top of Cuban society, institutionalizing the revolution and implementing its programs. When Castro seized power he disbanded the old bureaucracy. He did not have a trained bureaucracy or political party to take its place, so the rebel-army leadership became the new administrators. Although the army was really the only institution available for the job, it was also not a bad choice. During the years in the Sierra the army had been called upon to administer a whole range of social programs in the liberated territories: hospitals, schools, small industries. They had also levied taxes and promulgated new laws, including a new penal code and a land-reform law.[7]

By the late 1960s the military was to extend its participation into the production sector. During the 1970 "Ten Million Ton" campaign, the military cut 20 percent of the harvest, built roads, laid railroad tracks, and built housing for the cutters. Seventy-thousand troops participated.[8]

To meet the challenges of external defense the Castro regime first established a close alliance with the Soviet Union. It then set about creating a highly sophisticated military force to develop as much self-sufficiency as possible. The Cuban-Soviet alliance is the product of Castro's most successful political maneuvering. The Soviets were at first hesitant about committing their support to Cuba. They did not wish to jeopardize their newborn détente with the United States and at the same time they feared that any strong commitment on their part might provoke a U.S. attack on the Castro regime. Finally Castro appeared to be something of a dark horse to the Soviet leadership: he was not a Communist, he didn't even have a party's backing.

The Cuban-Soviet alliance grew incrementally. The first economic agreement was signed in April 1959. In February 1960 the Soviets sent Cuba its first aid: a $100 million credit to buy industrial equipment. Three months later Cuba and the Soviet Union established diplomatic relations. The pace increased over the summer of 1960. First the U.S. refineries refused to process Soviet oil, then the Cubans nationalized the refineries. The United States retaliated by cutting its order for Cuban sugar by 700,000 tons. Three days later the Soviet Union picked up the slack, increasing its own contract for the same amount. At the same time Khrushchev made his first commitment to the Cubans:

> I would like to call attention to the fact that the United States is clearly plotting criminal action against the Cuban people . . . It would be wise not to forget that the United States is no longer at an inaccessible distance from the Soviet Union. Figuratively speaking, should the need arise, Soviet artillery can support the Cuban people by missile fire if the aggressive forces from the Pentagon dare intervene in Cuba.[9]

Limited arms shipments from Eastern Europe began soon after. That July Raul Castro travelled to Moscow where he received assurances that the bloc would defend Cuba against economic ruin in the face of the U.S. embargo. Although these commitments were intended to reassure the Cuban leadership, they were still only qualified commitments. The "figuratively speaking" of Khrushchev's statement left the Cuban leadership feeling insecure and unprotected.

In April 1961 Castro took a major step toward binding the Soviet Union permanently to Cuba's defense when he declared himself a Marxist-Leninist. A second important step was taken a few weeks later when, by turning back the Bay of Pigs invasion, the Cubans proved that they were not destined to become a second Guatemala. Still, it was another year before Moscow finally recognized that Cuba had "embarked on the path of building socialism" and fully committed itself to Cuba's survival.

Since 1962 the Soviets have not shirked their responsibility. As of 1978 Soviet military aid totaled close to $1.5 billion. Soviet subsidy of the Cuban economy is estimated to be around $8 million per day.[10] That aid has known limits. As a result of the missile crisis the Soviets have only been able to give the Cubans arms "for defensive purposes." This means that Cuba's survival still depends on the U.S. no-invasion pledge and on the deterrence of the Soviet nuclear umbrella. Cuba's security below the nuclear level depends on its own military forces. A detailed description of Cuba's current military capabilities will be addressed in a separate section later.

Cuba's internationalist policies began in the first year of the revolution with Cuban-supported guerrilla attacks on several Caribbean dictatorships. In the mid-1960s Cuban insurgents joined guerrillas fighting in Venezuela, Bolivia, Colombia, Guatemala, and Peru. It must be emphasized that all of these attempts to export revolution were not official acts of the Cuban government. The internationalist fighters were all volunteers who resigned their official positions before going overseas. These missions were small—there were never more than a few hundred Cubans fighting in all of Latin America—and poorly provisioned. The Cubans had few arms of their own to spare, and the Soviets generally refused to support armed struggle in Latin America.

Cuba sent its first military aid to Africa in 1960: arms and medical personnel to the Algerian Liberation Front. A year later in Ghana the Cubans established their first permanent overseas military mission. Cuban troops first saw active combat in the 1963 Algerian-Moroccan border dispute, during which Cuba committed some 300-400 troops. In 1964 Guevara conducted a three-month tour of Africa. It was during this trip that the Cubans first contacted the leadership of the Angolan MPLA. During the mid-1960s Cuba also established close contacts with progressive regimes in Congo-Brazzaville, Guinea, and Equatorial Guinea, sending military and political advisors to train presidential guards and militias.[11]

In the early 1970s Cuba abandoned the export of revolution to Latin America. There are a number of explanations for this decision; the simplest is that the policy was not working: Cuban-supported guerrillas suffered defeat after defeat. Also, by the early 1970s Cuba could no longer afford an independent foreign policy. Failures in its development programs demanded the country's full resources, Castro's full attention, and an increase in Soviet aid. This was not the time to place strains on the economy or the Cuban-Soviet alliance. By the early 1970s other policy options also became available. Allende's election in Chile and a leftist military coup in Peru held out new opportunities for Cuba to end its hemispheric isolation. These developments also placed a new premium on national sovereignty.With a growing number of states seeking to normalize relations with Cuba, the Cubans had to recognize the norms of conventional international behavior.

Although Cuba abandoned the export of revolution it did not abandon its commitment to internationalism. Instead of supporting insurgents Cuba now concentrated on building good state-to-state relations in the third world. The government sent earthquake relief to Peru, Honduras, Guatemala, and Nicaragua. In Guyana it built a fishing port; in Jamaica, schools, dams, and waterworks. Outside of Latin America it increased its humanitarian aid as well. By the mid-1970s there were an estimated five thousand Cuban advisors serving overseas in twenty countries on three continents.[12]

In 1975 in Angola Cuba began a new phase of internationalism. For the first time Cuban military forces were committed to front-line overseas combat. The record suggests that the Cubans did not originally see the Angolan involvement as a new departure for Cuban foreign policy. Their first commitment was a limited number of military-technical advisors to help the MPLA learn how to use their new Soviet weapons. It was only after the intervention of South African regulars on the side of the National Front for the Liberation of Angola (FNLA) that the Cuban leadership decided to send combat troops.[13] In November 1977 Cuba embarked in Ethiopia on its second full-scale overseas military involvement. The sequence of events leading to the commitment of some seventeen thousand troops is similar to the Angolan case. First the Cubans sent technical advisors, then the massive intervention by Somali forces across the Ethiopian border into the Ogaden led the Cubans to make a full-scale military commitment.

During the past two years Cuba has increased its involvement in the Caribbean and Central America. There are several thousand Cuban advisors now serving in Nicaragua, Grenada, St. Lucia, and until recently Jamaica. The Cubans have, however, refused to commit themselves militarily in the region. During the Nicaraguan revolution the Cubans sent no troops and only limited arms—two planeloads of light weapons, according to CIA reports.[14] It is important to note that in Nicaragua Cuba's efforts were matched, even exceeded, by the efforts of Costa Rica, Panama, Mexico, and Venezuela. The Cubans are no longer revolutionary outlaws. Their aid in the region has been limited primarily to technical and political advice.

Cuba's Armed Forces

Cuba today has one of the largest and most professional militaries in the developing world. In Latin America only Brazil, with twelve times the population of Cuba, has a larger standing force. The competence and versatility of the Cuban military has been proved by Cuba's recent victories in Angola and Ethiopia.

In late 1970 the Cuban army began a drastic reduction in size and professionalization. The goal was to establish a smaller, more modern force whose functions could be augmented by an easily mobilized reserve. From a force level of 250,000 in 1970 the number of the standing forces was cut to 100,000 by 1974. At the same time a clearer delineation of functions was effected. In 1973 the Army of Working Youth (EJT) was created to take over the production responsibilities previously performed by the regular army. Today there are an estimated 120,000 men in the regular standing forces, another 60,000 ready reserves, 175,000 to 200,000 second-line reserves, and about 100,000 members of the Army of Working Youth.

The size reduction was accompanied by an upgrading in equipment and organization. The Cuban military now models its organization, strategy, and tactics closely on those of the Soviet military. Supply and maintenance methods have also been greatly improved since the early 1970s. The reduction in size has thus not impaired the military's combat preparedness. The new system has been designed to rely heavily on the ready reserves that can be mobilized within four hours of call-up. The reserves train at least forty-five days a year, and since over half of the troops sent to Africa were drawn from the reserves, thousands have also had combat experience.[16]

Even with the professionalization and upgrading of equipment, the Cuban military is still an organization primarily committed to defense. According to the U.S. Defense Intelligence Agency (DIA), the Cuban military is "capable of providing a tenacious defense of the island." They also have the capability for quick strikes off the island into the Caribbean and the southern United States. But they do not have the capability to conduct a large-scale offensive war. The Cubans have neither the air nor the naval equipment to transport medium to heavy weaponry off the island nor are they equipped for the large-scale movement of troops. For the African involvements the Cubans had to depend on the Soviet Union for both troop transport and heavy equipment.[17]

Looking at the Cuban performance in Africa one begins to understand how successful the military reforms have been. For Angola the Cubans developed a dual command structure, rotating high-ranking members of the armed forces between Angola and Cuba. The Cubans now have two full sets of military commanders with experience both in Cuba and overseas. In Angola and Ethiopia the Cubans also demonstrated their ability to work closely with the Soviet military for transport, supply, and strategic planning.

The effect of the African involvements on the Cuban military is not clear-cut. It has given the *military as an institution* an important new mission and a new claim on the Cuban budget. The Cuban leadership announced that for 1978 its expenditures for military and security forces would be 8.6 percent of the budget. The only time a higher percentage was reported was during the early 1960s fight against internal insurrection.[18] The effect on the Cuban *military organization,* on the other hand, has been negligible. According to members of the U.S. DIA, the Cubans have not significantly changed their military organization or training procedures since getting involved in Africa. As one expert put it, "The Cubans already had the capability to fight the Angolan war long before Angola. Angola just proved to them and to us what we already knew. There really was no need to reorganize."[19]

The only noticeable strain on the military imposed by the Angolan involvement was on the availability of highly trained fighter pilots. At one point in the spring of 1978 U.S. intelligence reported that an estimated fifty Soviet fighter pilots had been sent to Cuba to replace Cuban pilots serving in Africa.[20]

Since the Cuban victories in Africa, Soviet aid has improved significantly. The new hardware Cuba has received includes T-62 tanks, some 15-20 MiG-23 Floggers, a FOXTROT-class submarine, and a number of BM-21 multiple rocket launchers.[21] Although the payoff has been real it should not be overemphasized. The Cubans are still receiving primarily second-line Soviet armaments that are well within the parameters of the 1962 agreement.

The Cuban-Soviet Alliance

Over the past few years many of the traditional fears about the Cuban security threat have been resurrected. The increasing closeness of the Cuban-Soviet alliance when coupled with such recent developments as the new Cold War and the growing instability in Central America have once again raised the specter of Cuba as a strategic threat to the United States or as a base for hemispheric subversion.

These fears are generally unfounded. The Soviets have been careful to keep to their half of the 1962 agreement. In 1970 they tested the parameters of that agreement when they tried unsuccessfully to build a base for nuclear submarines in Cienfuegos Bay on the southern coast of Cuba. Since the Cienfuegos affair there have been no other known attempts to use Cuba as a strategic-operations base.

There have, however, been several peaceful Cuban-Soviet projects in recent years that *could* be interpreted as having some military-security implications. In 1965 the Cubans and Soviets began a joint program for oceanographic research intended to improve Cuba's fishing capabilities. As part of that project they have mapped out the Caribbean, the Gulf of Mexico and the entire southern coastline of the United States. This intelligence has certainly been of use to both the Cuban and Soviet navies. It also appears that some Cuban fishing boats are commanded by Soviet officers and may be used for surveillance missions.

Another program with possible security implications is in the field of nuclear energy. Since the late 1960s the Soviets have given Cuba an atomic reactor, a nuclear-physics lab, and radiochemical isotope lab. The Cubans, who have no coal or petroleum and only a limited hydroelectric potential, consider the reactor to be essential to their economic development. Although the Soviets have given the Cubans a reactor, it is unlikely they would ever give them any opportunity to develop an independent nuclear capability. The issue of nuclear weapons has long been a source of strain between

Havana and Moscow. The Cubans want control of their own defense, whereas the Soviets refuse to provoke the United States into a repetition of the 1962 crisis. The Cubans have repeatedly refused to sign the nuclear-nonproliferation treaty, insisting on the right of small states to develop their own defense systems. The Soviets, as cosponsors of the treaty with the United States, are committed to limiting the spread of nuclear arms to the third world.

A more overt demonstration of the Cuban-Soviet military alliance has been the increase in the number of, and upgrading of the type of, Soviet submarines calling at Cuban ports. The implications of these visits are more political than strategic. These are diesel-powered, not nuclear-powered submarines. Moreover, the use of Cuban ports for refueling and servicing only provides a marginal increase in their on-station time in the Caribbean. On the other hand, their regular calls at Cuban ports are a clear assertion by the Soviets of their right to operate openly and freely in the region.

The presence of Soviet combat troops in Cuba requires some attention—if only because of its celebrity. The troops, according to Castro, have been in Cuba since the 1962 missile crisis, the remnants of some twenty-thousand Soviet troops originally sent to protect the missile installations. Their present function has not yet been determined, but several possible explanations have been suggested: that they are training the Cuban military to allow an even closer integration in future campaigns; that they are training the Cubans in subversive techniques for Latin America; that the troops are there to protect Soviet electronic-monitoring installations alleged to be in Cuba; that the troops are a Praetorian Guard to protect Castro from his own army. The best explanation is that they are a tripwire. Ever since 1962 the Cubans have had their doubts about the fidelity of the Soviet commitment to Cuba's defense, and these troops may well be hostages to that doubt.

The degree of Cuban-Soviet collaboration in Angola has not been fully established. The Soviets obviously did not oppose Cuba's involvement—they had been provisioning the MPLA since the early 1960s. And yet there is evidence to support Cuba's claim that the decision to commit combat troops was a Cuban and not a Soviet decision. It was not until January 1976—six months after the first Cuban advisors arrived in Angola and two months after the Cuban troop airlift began—that the Soviets decided to lend Cuba much-needed transport planes. In Ethiopia, however, there was no doubt about the coordination of Soviet and Cuban forces. Cuban troops were flown over on Soviet planes; once in Ethiopia they were provided with Soviet arms and heavy equipment.

Communist victories in Angola and Ethiopia have led some analysts to suggest that Moscow and Havana have developed a new division of labor in the third world: the Soviets provide the arms, the Cubans provide the advisors and, when necessary, the troops. The prediction is for an increase in such activities. Although there is no doubt that both sides have found their collaboration in Africa to be mutually beneficial, I would hesitate to predict unlimited repeats of their joint performance. When and where their interests coincide they will undoubtedly be willing to work together again. A recent instance where their interests did *not* coincide was in Eritrea. The Soviets were apparently committed to aiding their Ethiopian allies in the suppression of the Eritrean nationalists. The Cubans, however, had too many ties with the Eritreans—they trained Eritrean guerrillas in the 1960s—to join the fight. The Cubans did not choose to commit their troops to Eritrea, publicly refusing the appeals of the Ethiopian regime.[22]

International Constraints

Cuba is a creation of the international environment. Had it not been for the Cold War, it is unlikely that the Soviet Union would have been willing to commit itself to Cuba's survival. Had it not been for the Sino-Soviet split, and Cuba's position in the third world, it is unlikely that the Soviet Union would have tolerated Cuba's claims to autonomy and outright opposition. Nevertheless, Cuba's international position has, at times, also exercised certain constraints on Cuba's ability to guarantee its national security.

Since the missile crisis the U.S.-Soviet relationship has exercised real constraints on the Cuban-Soviet alliance. The 1962 agreement has limited Soviet military aid to Cuba. The Soviet desire to build détente with the United States has also led to major disagreements between Havana and Moscow about the conduct of Cuban foreign policy in the region. In recent years the Soviets have become less susceptible to U.S. efforts to link U.S.-Soviet relations to Cuban policies. The Soviet leaders refused to restrain their Cuban allies even after two U.S. administrations had directly linked Cuban policies in Africa to the fate of Strategic Arms Limitation Talks (SALT) negotiations.

Cuba's dual commitment to the socialist bloc and the third world has also been a source of major dilemmas in its choice of foreign policies. Cuba's early commitment to violent revolution assured it a leadership position among the more radical third-world states, but at the same time strained Cuban-Soviet relations almost to the breaking point. Cuba's abandonment of armed struggle and recent efforts to move the nonaligned nations closer to the socialist bloc pleased its Soviet allies but led a number of third-world leaders to question Cuba's claims to nonalignment. The defeat of Cuba's bid for a seat on the U.N. Security Council in the wake of the Soviet invasion of Afghanistan was a major blow to Cuba's and Castro's prestige as the leader of the nonaligned nations.

Despite recent strains it is doubtful that the third world will abandon the Cubans. Cuba remains an attractive role model and a convenient ally—particularly because of its alliance with the Soviet Union. Despite professions of nonalignment, when it comes to military conflict, it is still a bipolar world. When threatened by their neighbors, nationalist leaders know they will be forced to swallow their pride and fear of big-power interference and turn to one of the blocs for military aid. For those states who can turn to Cuba the humiliation is much less onerous and the aid just as adequate.

What Cuba can and cannot achieve in the third world will be defined by the interests of the individual states. Cuban aid will certainly foster tolerance for Cuban ideas on socialism and anti-Americanism. It is unlikely that this aid will lead to a fundamental shift in the policies of any states, at the very least because Cuba sends aid to movements and regimes that already share its outlook.

Revolutions can be aided and abetted, but they can't be exported. The cause of revolution in the third world today is not Cuban support but the instability, poverty, and repression that leads people to rebel. Even if there is a revolution the Cubans cannot use their influence to turn other states into Soviet puppets. Even if those states were willing (which is unlikely), the Soviet Union is not. In Peru, Chile, and Nicaragua, Moscow has made it clear that it will not take on the financial burdens of another Cuba.

Cuba's experience in Angola should make this clear. Despite predictions of doom, the victory of Cuban-backed MPLA forces has not turned Angola into a Soviet puppet. Angola today is aligned with the socialist bloc. But the Gulf Oil rigs in Cabinda province continue to pump as Cuban troops stand guard. And the Angolans have refused Soviet requests for military bases.

Domestic Constraints

Cuba's choice of security policies has been generally free of domestic political challenges or constraints. No doubt this is due to the fact that Cuba has a closed political system. But it goes beyond that. Cuban society has demonstrated a remarkable degree of consensus from top to bottom about security issues. The siege mentality of the early years has easily justified any demands made by the military on the national budget or on the lives of the Cuban people.

The Cubans have managed to avoid the civil-military split that in many lesser developed countries has led to praetorian politics. The high degree of elite consensus can be traced to Cuba's particular revolutionary experience: the fusion of military and civilian roles in the liberated territories, the small size of the elite, and the continued dominance of Castro's leadership.

The high degree of local support can also be traced to the revolutionary experience. The siege mentality created by U.S. hostility and attack and by Cuba's isolation in the hemisphere reinforced rather than undermined popular support for Castro's regime. Popular support for internationalism follows logically from the revolutionary experience as well. Moreover, during the 1960s the practice of internationalism placed very few strains on either the Cuban budget or the population. The small number of internationalist fighters were all volunteers.

Today there appears to be some new questioning about foreign policies at both the elite and mass levels. Enterprise managers have raised questions about the effect on production of the large commitment of reserve forces overseas. Not only have the enterprises lost workers, they have also had to pay the salaries of the reservists out of the enterprise budgets.[23]

On the local level there are an increasing number of Cubans who are tired of the rationing of food and the unavailability of consumer goods. Although this situation existed long before Angola, the Angolan involvement has focused and heightened the discontent. A common question being asked is, "Why send goods and food and workers overseas when we barely have enough to feed ourselves at home?"

There also appears to be a growing resentment of military service. In a speech to the First Party Congress in 1976, Castro called for a change in popular attitudes toward the military. For the first time since the revolution the Cuban military has had to confront the problem of troop insubordination. In *Verde Olivo*, Cuba's military magazine, there was a detailed description of disciplinary procedures, soon after the commitment to Angola.[24]

The source of this new resentment of the military is not clear. Explanations range from disaffection toward serving in Africa particularly, to disaffection toward serving overseas for a prolonged period of time (an experience Cuba's armed forces have never had before), to a more general disaffection toward military service that seems common to all militaries when they are not defending their own homelands. The state of the Cuban economy has not allowed the government to offer the sort of incentives for military service that we find in the United States today. During the same First Party Congress address, Castro spoke of the need to improve the salaries and living conditions of the armed forces.

There is no doubt that there is local disaffection in Cuba. The tragic sight of tens of thousands of Cubans crowding onto small boats to escape to the United States attests to this fact. Most of this disaffection can be blamed on the failures of the economy, failures that the regime has begun to admit are the result of its own mismanagement, rather than just the fault of imperialism. The Cubans also have had terrible luck in 1980. Disease destroyed almost 25 percent of the sugar crop and 80 percent of the tobacco crop. The complaint heard over and over again from refugees as they arrived in Miami was that there was not enough food, jobs, or opportunities. Some of the disaffection must also be traced to political discontent in general and specific discontent with Cuba's foreign policies. But what must be recognized before jumping to any conclusions about popular resistance to "Cuba's Vietnam" is the continued, strong local support for internationalism. The pride felt by many Cubans in their nation's international role acts as a buffer to discontent and to social unrest.

Notes

1. Castro's speech of 1 May 1966 is quoted in Jacques Levesque, *The USSR and the Cuban Revolution* (New York: Praeger, 1978), p. 123.

2. For a detailed discussion of the Cuban-Soviet conflict see D. Bruce Jackson, *Castro, the Kremlin, and Communism in Latin America* (Baltimore: Johns Hopkins University Press, 1969); F. Parkinson, *Latin America, The Cold War and the World Powers, 1945-1973* (Beverly Hills: Sage Publications, 1974); Brian Crozier, "The Satellization of Cuba" in *Conflict Studies*, no. 35 (May 1973).

3. Fidel Castro quoted in Levesque, *The USSR and the Cuban Revolution*, p. 91.

4. For a full text of Guevara's speech see K.T. Fann and Donald C. Hodges, eds. *Readings in U.S. Imperialism* (Boston: Porter and Sargent, 1971) pp. 357-370.

5. Fidel Castro quoted in Jorge Dominguez's monumental work, *Cuba: Order and Revolution* (Cambridge, Mass.: Harvard University Press, 1978), p. 363.

6. Ibid, p. 346.

7. For an insightful analysis of civil-military relations in Cuba see William M. LeoGrande, "The Politics of Revolutionary Development: Civil-Military Relations in Cuba, 1959-1970," *The Journal of Strategic Studies* 1 (December 1978).

8. Dominguez, *Cuba*, p. 358.

9. Khrushchev quoted in Levesque, *The USSR and the Cuban Revolution*, p. 17.

10. "Impact of Cuban-Soviet Ties in the Western Hemisphere," *Hearings before the Subcommittee on Inter-American Affairs of the Committee on International Relations*, House of Representatives, 14-15 March 1978, p. 2.

11. William M. LeoGrande, "Cuba's Policy in Africa: 1959-1980" (Berkeley, Calif: IIS Monograph, July 1980).

12. An overview of the variety of Cuban foreign-aid programs is available in Jorge I. Dominguez, "The Armed Forces and Foreign Relations" in *Cuba in the World,* Cole Blasier and Carmelo Mesa-Lago eds. (Pittsburgh: University of Pittsburgh Press, 1979) pp. 53-86.

13. Gabriel Garcia Marquez, "Operation Carlota: Cuba's Role in Angolan Victory," *Cuba Update,* no. 1 (April 1977).

14. Graham Hovey, "U.S. Study Says Cuba Plays Cautious Role in Nicaragua," *The New York Times,* 4 July 1979, p. A3.

15. Defense Intelligence Agency, *Handbook on the Cuban Armed Forces,* DDB-2680-62-79, April 1979, p. 1-10.

16. Ibid., p. 2-2, 2-6.

17. Ibid., p. 1-5, 1-6.

18. "Budget Law for the State for 1978," *Granma,* 23 December 1978, p. 4.

19. Personal interview with members of DIA.

20. "Soviet Pilots in Cuba," *The San Francisco Chronicle,* 25 May 1978, p. 1.

21. *Handbook,* pp. 2-9, 2-11.

22. "Fidel Presents Playa Giron National Order to Lt. Col. Mengistu Haile Mariam," *Granma Weekly Review,* 30 April 1978; Castro speech of 26 April 1978, quoted in *Granma Weekly Review,* 23 July 1978.

23. Fidel Castro's address to the First Party Congress notes this fact; reproduced in *First Congress of the Communist Party of Cuba, December 17-22, 1975* (Progress Publishers: Moscow).

24. Jorge Dominguez notes this point in his *Cuba,* p. 363.

Part II
Asia

5 Pakistan

Stephen Philip Cohen

The toad beneath the harrow knows
Exactly where each tooth-point goes;
The butterfly upon the road
Preaches contentment to that toad.
　　　　　　　　—Rudyard Kipling[1]

In early 1980 Pakistan's President Mohammed Zia Ul-Haq rejected an ambiguous American offer of military and economic assistance. A wave of resentment and relief went through Washington—resentment because it was thought that Pakistan was so threatened that Zia's rejection was an insult, and relief because the United States would not become more closely associated with a state that only a few months earlier had stood by while the U.S. embassy in Islamabad was besieged and burned out. Further, Pakistan had been discovered in an apparently successful attempt to circumvent U.S. nuclear nonproliferation efforts.

In many ways Pakistan was and is thought to be the epitome of a crazy, irresponsible military dictatorship. Although U.S. reactions were not altogether unjustified, they did indicate how little Washington actually understood what was once its most "allied of allies" and how far apart the two states were in their perceptions of Pakistan's security requirements and on the proper American role in the region. A full year later, a new American administration has apparently increased the 1980 offer tenfold, and negotiations are underway for a multi-billion, five year package of economic assistance and military sales credits, featuring a number of F-16 aircraft. Yet, even with a sympathetic administration, there have been serious misjudgments, and not a few members of the Reagan administration have anticipated access to Pakistani air and naval facilities, or even the stationing of American troops on Pakistani soil. It is improbable that such facilities will be offered, but that they are discussed (although promptly rejected by the Pakistanis) inspires no more confidence than the miserly Carter offer.

Research for this chapter was supported in part by a Ford Foundation fellowship in arms control and international security in 1977-1978, and travel support was received from the University of Illinois and the Inter-University Seminar on Armed Forces and Society in 1980. I am grateful to the Ministry of Defense, Government of Pakistan, and the Pakistan Army for the opportunity to visit a number of training facilities and active units and conduct interviews with retired and serving officers. None of the foregoing institutions is in any way responsible for any error of fact or interpretation.

In the course of this chapter—and this is the goal of all comparative analysis—I shall attempt to temporarily transport the reader from the vantage point of the road to that of the toad. This is difficult because Americans are maladapted to understand the security of such states as Pakistan. For example, the United States has not had a serious border conflict in this century and its two neighbors are economic dependencies; Pakistan's neighbors are hostile giants and its borders have seen armed conflict since the creation of the state. For Americans war is a matter of choice, not survival; for Pakistan a future war is not likely to be a matter of choice, and it certainly may lead to the destruction of the state. Americans manage the threat of nuclear annihilation by esoteric doctrines of deterrence and compellence; Pakistanis are just entering the nuclear era, but without full comprehension of the risks and dangers of nuclearization and certainly without the technical and scientific resources even to begin competition with its regional rival, India, and the new regional superpower, the Soviet Union. There are other critical points of departure, but these are sufficient to make the point: Pakistan belongs to that class of state whose very survival is uncertain, whose legitimacy is doubted, and whose security-related resources are inadequate. Yet these states will not disappear nor can they be ignored. Pakistan (like Taiwan, South Korea, Israel, and South Africa) has the capacity to fight, to go nuclear, and to influence the global strategic balance (if only by collapsing). It is also in a strategic geographic location, surrounded by the three most populous states in the world and adjacent to the mouth of the Persian Gulf.

There are three other aspects of Pakistan's society that make it an especially interesting case among middle-range states. First, like Israel, Pakistan was formed to protect and further a particular religion. Second, Pakistani society is enormously complex and diverse, with a number of ethnolinguistic divisions, and it includes part of the world's largest tribal society. Almost all of its population belongs to a linguistic or cultural group that has ties in neighboring countries. The Baluchis, for example, can be found not only in Iran and Afghanistan but in the Soviet Union as well, where Baluchi is taught in school. Finally, the military in Pakistan has been deeply involved in politics almost since the creation of the state. Indeed, some soldiers argue that the army preceded the state of Pakistan and hence has the right to engage in ortho-political surgery. None of these three characteristics endears Pakistan to the liberal West (nor, in most cases, are Pakistanis themselves pleased with their situation). Pakistan is hardly the current preferred model of political and economic development, but that is not the issue.[2] It is an important country to understand precisely because it displays in acute form so many of the problems of intermediate-range developing states. An understanding of Pakistan's recent past—civil war, ethnic conflict, economic de-development, political chaos, military inter-

vention, nuclear acquisition, and religious resurgence—may be one
substitute for an over-the-horizon political radar.

Pakistan's External World: Perceptions, Strategies, Responses

Perceptions of the International System

There is a special Pakistani world view, highly pluralist in nature. At one
and the same time Pakistanis see themselves as anticolonial yet descendants
of a militant, conquering religion; Pakistan is clearly located in South Asia
but it is also Middle Eastern in character and tradition; until recently
Pakistan was the most allied of American allies, yet it is now nonaligned; it
is small, vulnerable, and surrounded, yet possesses one of the world's
toughest armies and will perhaps soon have nuclear weapons. It is no
wonder then that Pakistanis see their environment as threatening *and*
reassuring, often simultaneously. This pluralist—if not confused—world
view can be traced back to Pakistan's origins.

Pakistan was created because of the temporary conjunction of two
struggles: that of Indians against British colonial rule, and of some (but not
all) Indian Muslims against the domination of Indian Hindus. Many Indian
Muslims saw the British as allies against the Hindus, yet they also sought an
independent homeland, free from British domination. The result was
Pakistan. Thus, unlike virtually all other Islamic states today, Pakistanis
were fighting *two* enemies: Western imperial domination and a different but
powerful cultural-religious system. The struggle against the British and the
West is over, but almost all Pakistanis (and Bangladeshis, for that matter)
still fear continuing conflict with "Hindu India." Since the creation of
Pakistan was strongly opposed by most Hindu politicians (and a number of
Muslim leaders as well, some of whom remained in India), the feeling persists that India has not reconciled itself to the permanent, autonomous, and
Islamic status of Pakistan. Or, put another way, most Pakistani elites are
concerned that the very existence of Pakistan is a goad to India; as long as
Indian leaders attempt to maintain a secular state, they claim, a truly
religious state such as Pakistan is a provocation and a threat to the stability
of India.

Pakistanis retain an interest in the fate of the millions of Muslims in
India or under Indian control, as in Kashmir. Early Pakistani hopes that
these Muslims would somehow develop ties to Pakistan have been tempered
by the fear that Pakistan would be swamped by refugees; this, plus the fact
that many millions of Muslims seem perfectly content to live in India, raises
the basic question of the identity of Pakistan itself as a homeland for per-

secuted Indian Muslims. Should the Indian Muslims be written off? Are they no longer true Muslims—in that they are living in a state dominated by another religion and culture? Or, perhaps, in secret moments of self-doubt, was Pakistan some kind of cosmic error, and would Pakistanis be better off within a powerful, independent, and relatively secure India where they would form an enormously powerful voting bloc? Here, as in very few other areas of the world, perceptions of the international system are directly related to national identity and may lead one to question the very existence of the state.

A second Islamic path leads Pakistan to look to its Muslim neighbors to the west, especially Iran, Afghanistan, and the oil-rich Persian Gulf states. Pakistan has been among the leaders in attempts to forge Islamic solidarity. But it has often found that the Islamic world is no less fickle than the West; in times of crisis some Islamic states have come to Pakistan's assistance—usually in token fashion—while others have been neutral. Pakistan has developed substantial economic and cultural ties with some of the Gulf states, but Islam has not bridged the differences between it and Iran and Afghanistan. Indeed, Islam now creates major difficulties in both cases: Pakistani security elites are concerned about the capture of the Iranian revolution by Shi'ite fundamentalists, and the Soviet operations against Afghan Mujahiddin place Pakistan between its fellow Muslims, who are being brutally crushed, and the vastly superior Soviet occupation forces. Blunt and explicit public Soviet threats remind Pakistanis of their vulnerability.[3]

Layered over this belief in their special religious role are Pakistani perceptions of a historically predestined geostrategic destiny. Pakistan comprises the western and northern reaches of the old British Indian Empire. It was the last area to be conquered by the British; indeed, large parts of Pakistan were never directly ruled by them. Beyond Pakistan lie territories and kingdoms that became the modern state of Afghanistan. It was in Afghanistan that the expanding British and Russian empires met and clashed in the "Great Game" of Kim, Kipling, and Lord Curzon. Since the old British Indian Army was preoccupied with defense of the frontier against Russian influence, the young Pakistani officers who received their training from the British came to share the view that Pakistan inherited the responsibility of protecting the entire Indian subcontinent from Russian-Soviet advances.[4] Pakistanis took this role seriously, not least because it led them into alliance with the British and Americans in the 1950s and served as the justification for massive arms transfers from the United States, membership in Southeast Asia Treaty Organization (SEATO) and the Central Treaty Organization (CENTO), and a staunch anticommunism at home. It is little consolation to the present Pakistani leadership that their concern about Soviet penetration in Afghanistan was not taken seriously in 1978; Pakistan may be the country that cried wolf once too often.

A concern with Soviet influence also led the Pakistanis to a close relationship with the People's Republic of China (PRC) long before journeys to
Peking became fashionable.[5] Here there was another factor at work: both
states saw India as a security threat as India's ties with the Soviet Union
grew rapidly in the 1960s.[6]

Pakistan's image of itself as the guardian of the Khyber Pass against
Soviet expansionism implies a powerful military capability. Until recently
most Indian strategists vehemently disagreed with this view. They saw a
strong Pakistan as disruptive. Their image of regional stability envisioned
Pakistan as an Afghanistan, a weak, not a strong, buffer. A strong buffer
attracts attention, a weak one can be maintained by agreement among the
concerned major powers and is not likely to go off on adventurous paths.
This difference in perception of what causes instability and of whether
Pakistan should play an active or a passive buffer role is critical and we
shall return to it below. I believe it to be one of the most important agenda
items in any discussion of how to meet Soviet aggression in South Asia and
how to curb nuclear proliferation.

To summarize: Pakistan's perception of the international environment
is complex and multilayered. It defines the world in its own terms, as do
most other states: it is Islamic, having strong but ambivalent ties to Muslims
in India and other predominately Muslim states; it is astride the historic invasion routes to South Asia, but neither its neighbors nor the superpowers
agree that it is necessarily geopolitically important because of that; it seeks
to play a role in regional and international affairs and has an enormous
pool of trained, educated manpower, yet it is surrounded by two giant states
(India and the U.S.S.R.) that make Pakistanis feel insecure and threatened.
Those historic friends of Pakistan that have resources (the United States,
Britain, some Arab states) are distant and unreliable; nearby friends are either
unreliable (Iran) or otherwise occupied (China) with their own security.

Threat Analysis

If strategy is defined as those matters affecting the integrity and existence of
the state, then Pakistan must have one of the most complex and multilayered
strategic threat analyses of any state in the world. To the east Pakistan faces
India, a state with vastly superior industrial resources and a much larger
human base;[7] to the West lies Afghanistan, never a friendly power, but now
occupied for the foreseeable future by the Soviet Union. At home—the
third front—there are important grievances to which the military is especially
sensitive. One stems from the widespread dislike of military rule per se—even
within the officer corps itself there is considerable opposition to its contin-
uation. Another grievance is that the military is drawn largely from the

Punjab, and continued military rule is seen as a cover for Punjabi predominance. In two of Pakistan's provinces there are important populations with strong ethnic and tribal ties across the border in Afghanistan; even on the Indian frontier there is an unresolved dispute over the status of Jammu and Kashmir.[8] Thus, domestic Pakistani politics remains intimately linked to political relations with Pakistan's neighbors; any analysis of threats to Pakistan's security must emphasize this overlap between internal and external problems.

Additionally, many Pakistani elites, especially in the military, raise questions about the loyalty of their "intellectuals, poets, and professors" to both Islam and the state of Pakistan. A fear held by some generals is that such ideologically "impure" groups constitute a massive fifth column.

On the ground, specific conventional military threats can be identified. To the east, Pakistan shares a long frontier with India; much of that frontier is ideal tank country and both states maintain the bulk of their armored forces along the Punjab-Rajasthan-Sind line. Two major wars have been fought over that frontier; at its northern end there is a ceasefire line that is appropriate guerrilla territory. Parts of the ceasefire line are observed rather ineffectively by a token U.N. presence that serves no real peacekeeping function. Pakistan's only port, Karachi, is close to the Indian frontier. It can be attacked by land and air and can be blockaded very quickly by any state (such as India) with a moderate naval capability.

To the west is the Durand line, the historic frontier between British India and Afghanistan.[9] Until recently the Durand Line was publicly challenged by the Afghan government, although its legitimacy now seems to be accepted on both sides. However, as we noted, a number of major tribes straddle this frontier. Almost a million tribal people have sought refuge with their kinsmen in Pakistan as a result of Soviet military activity; more will follow.

When military assistance to Pakistan was being publicly discussed in the United States in early 1980, it was often asserted that such assistance was useless because Pakistan was helpless in the face of the Soviet threat. In fact, this is not the view of the Pakistan military themselves. They analyze the threat from Afghan/Russian forces in the following way. First, if, for some reason, the Soviet Union wanted to undertake a massive invasion of the Northwest Frontier Province (NWFP) there is little that Pakistan could do to stop them. However, there is little incentive for the Soviets to undertake an invasion that leads them away from the strategic prize of the Persian Gulf. Second, a massive Soviet push through Baluchistan, either toward the Arabian Sea or en route to Iran, makes somewhat more strategic sense but might precipitate American intervention whether or not there was a Pakistan-U.S. agreement. Pakistan itself could do little that would prevent the Soviets from achieving such an objective but, as in the first case, it could at considerable risk to itself resist with ground and air forces.

Third, far more likely, but far more containable, would be direct Soviet or (Soviet-supported) Afghan attacks on refugee camps in Pakistan—some of which are within artillery range of Afghanistan and most of which could be struck by air or ground raids. Although Pakistan could not prevent such attacks, it might do some damage to the attackers and retaliate upon support facilities in Afghanistan. It could also increase the flow of weapons to the Afghans, offer training to them, and allow Pakistani "volunteers" to join them, as the Indian government allowed Indian Army personnel to join the Mukti Bahini. There is no evidence that Pakistan has done any of these things, but they could form part of a response to Soviet-Afghan pressure on Pakistan's highly permeable border.

Finally, there remains the possibility of long-haul Soviet support for Baluchi and other tribal groups in their continuing struggle against the government of Pakistan.[10] Such a struggle could probably be contained by the present Pakistani government; if it could not, it might affect the integrity of the state, its economic base, and the loyalty of most of its citizens.

Besides these conventional strategic threats to Pakistan—which may well involve rebels acting in support of or simultaneously with an external power—Pakistanis are virtually unanimous in their perception of a military nuclear threat.

Their concern obviously stems from the 1974 explosion of an Indian nuclear device. However, there is some evidence to indicate that Pakistanis took the nuclear issue seriously before that.[11] Indeed, as we shall argue, the idea of a nuclear weapon dovetails nicely into overall Pakistani strategic doctrine. In any case, the nuclear program was apparently continued by the military after they removed Zulfiqar Ali Bhutto from power in 1977. This is an involved and complicated issue, but Pakistanis define the nuclear threat this way. First, Indian possession of several nuclear weapons must be assumed. Second, such weapons are directly primarily against Pakistan, not China. Pakistani strategists generally ridicule the idea of India catching up with the Chinese or that there are any serious grounds for an India-China conflict. Third, if Pakistan is the target then the Indian bomb must have a military as well as a political rationale. They generally see it as enabling Indian conventional forces to seize the rest of Kashmir from Pakistan or even to dismember all of Pakistan; nuclear weapons held in reserve as a threat against Lahore, Karachi, Islamabad, and other vital targets would effectively paralyze Pakistan and make it unable to resist. Fourth, they conclude, a modest, "limited" Pakistani weapons program is essential to deter India's nuclear forces. These factors explain their pursuit of fissile material through both the reprocessing and enrichment routes and perhaps through other channels of which we are not yet aware.

Strategic Doctrine

The preparation of strategic doctrine in Pakistan closely resembles an attempt to hit multiple moving targets from a moving vehicle. Not only are the forces and threats to Pakistan in constant flux but the capacity of the state itself to respond to such threats has dramatically changed within a short time. For example, in 1965 the decision not to defend East Pakistan was reaffirmed and only token forces were stationed there. This neglect of East Bengal contributed to growing separatism in that province;[12] however, the units necessary to control that separatism could not be released from West Pakistan because the Indian military continued to pose a threat there. Another example: Pakistan is faced with the prospect of incursions along the Durand Line but it cannot risk a massive transfer of forces to its western frontier for fear of leaving its border with India open to attack. Yet it must not run the risk of allowing incursions to occur now because of the relatively weak political position of the military in the country; one major military defeat might mean the end for those responsible for strategic planning. In both of these cases Pakistan did not (or does not) have the resources to enable it to fight a two-front war, yet there were (and are) compelling political reasons to prevent it from redefining the strategic threat so that it would not have to fight such a war. One of these reasons was and is the hope that outside powers will provide substantial military assistance to Pakistan (or, in the case of China, create a two-front problem for India), but even this outside support is unreliable and unpredictable. Despite Pakistan's essential strategic dilemma—it is a big enough state to play the game but not big enough to win—it has evolved a *strategic style*, which might also be called a strategic doctrine. What follows are the main components of that style, which has remained remarkably consistent over the years.

Given Pakistan's size and location, as well as the terrain along its eastern border with India, its strategists have always been attracted to the doctrine of the offensive-defense. That is, in time of heightening crisis, Pakistan has not hesitated to be the first to employ the heavy use of force to gain an initial advantage. This was clearly the pattern in 1965 and possibly in 1971; in both cases it was thought that a short, sharp, war would achieve Pakistan's military as well as political objectives. However, this strategy has always assumed the availability of high-performance armor and aircraft and superior generalship, given India's larger territory and population. Looking at a map, it is easy to see why Pakistanis have always been reluctant to adopt a strategy of trading space for time: a number of vital Pakistani population and transportation centers are located near India and there is little room to defend them.

Second, Pakistan has usually regarded war as an opportunity to bring outstanding conflicts to the attention of the international community and to mobilize its friends among the Islamic world and fellow alliance members and, more recently, the PRC. But over the years the world has grown tired of Indians and Pakistanis shooting at each other. Pakistan cannot count on anyone caring much about a new war with India, and at the same time its capacity to avoid defeat at the hands of the Indians has been sharply reduced. War for political purposes now represents an enormous risk to the survival of the state.

A third component of Pakistani strategic doctrine has been to use military force to deter an Indian attack. In recent years this has become the dominant theme of Pakistani defense planners since they realize that the risk of initiating war becomes greater. Bluntly put, the Pakistanis hope to kill as many Indian soldiers as they can, raising the *cost* of Indian victory to unacceptable levels.[13]

In view of the Soviet occupation of Afghanistan, Pakistani strategists have now begun to develop a strategic doctrine to deal with various kinds and levels of threats from the west. As we indicated above, present force levels are adequate to deal with insurgency and limited probes by conventional Afghan forces across the border. But no forces would be adequate to deal with a major Soviet thrust backed by the threat of nuclear attack on troop concentrations or urban areas. Pakistan is forced to play a very dangerous game: maintaining enough of a military presence to deal with and thus deter limited probes, but not so large a force that the Soviets will fear Pakistani intervention on behalf of the Mujahiddin or that forces facing India are depleted.

Two different kinds of strategic responses have been widely discussed in Pakistan and must be noted here. We have already referred to the likelihood of a Pakistani nuclear capability. This would, according to many Pakistanis, neutralize an assumed Indian nuclear force. Others point out, however, that *it* would provide the umbrella under which Pakistan could reopen the Kashmir issue. A Pakistani nuclear capability paralyzes not only the Indian nuclear decision but also Indian conventional forces, and a brash, bold, Pakistani strike to liberate Kashmir might go unchallenged if the Indian leadership was weak or indecisive. To a lesser extent such a nuclear force might enhance Pakistan's deterrent along the Durand Line. A major incursion into Pakistan could trigger a Pakistani nuclear response, directed against "purely military" targets in Afghanistan or the Soviet Union itself. This may seem extreme, but it is nothing other than NATO doctrine transferred to the South Asian environment.

A second strategic doctrine was widely discussed in Pakistan a number of years ago and may yet be revived by some future government. This may be termed a people's guerrilla war. It grows out of three military traditions, all of them familiar to the Pakistan Army. It argues that instead of relying for deterrence and defense upon very expensive and very high-technology

weapons, nuclear or conventional, that Pakistan train and arm its population so that any invader would be unable to occupy the country. The cost of
victory would be so great that such an invader, presumably India, would
have to retreat or would be deterred from attacking. A variation on this
people's guerrilla war involves a more activist strategy: train and arm
friendly populations in the territory of your enemy, tying him down in a
hundred places.[14] Of course, this strategic doctrine borrows from American
Special Forces training imparted to many Pakistanis, recent Chinese writing
(which they have studied), and the two-thousand-year-old tradition of tribal
guerrilla war that is found in Pakistan's NWFP and Baluchistan.

People's guerrilla war is unlikely to be favored by the current military
leadership of Pakistan. It had been tried earlier in Kashmir and was not successful. Whether this was due to the unwarlike character of the Kashmiris or
to poor planning is not clear. What is certain is that the military of Pakistan
favor regular, conventional formations, except for light patrol and police
work in the tribal areas. Further, it is highly unlikely that a relatively unpopular regime will supervise the widespread dispersal of small arms and explosives to its own population. Finally, Pakistanis have the terrible example
of Afghanistan before their eyes. The Afghans have a proud and ancient
martial tradition, but this has merely slowed down the Soviet military
machine; the price of their resistance is fearful. For many Pakistanis an accommodation—even with the Indians—might be preferable to Cambodiazation.

The strategic choices open to Pakistan never were terribly attractive and
are now increasingly risky and limited in number. It would be suicide for the
Pakistan Army to provoke a confrontation with the Indian forces today;
even managing limited incursions from the Indian or Afghan frontier runs
great risks of escalation. Above all, there remains the new possibility of active Indian-Soviet cooperation, based on the 1971 Treaty of Friendship,
which places Pakistan in a hopeless strategic position. As one distinguished
retired general phrases it: "I have eaten many chicken sandwiches, but this
is the first time I have ever realized what it is like to be the chicken."
However, a full assessment of Pakistan's strategic problem is not complete
without looking at two additional factors: the weapons and manpower that
Pakistan is able to devote to its defense.

Force Levels and Disposition

A brief examination of Pakistan's defense effort further clarifies the
strategic dilemma of that state. The numbers and quality of weapons held
by the Pakistan military is determined by factors largely beyond their control: the attitudes of weapons suppliers and financial supporters and the

slow growth rate of the Pakistani arms industry. The actual *disposition* of forces was severely limited by geography even before the 1980 Soviet invasion of Afghanistan; that event complicates even the simplest defense task. We will look at the geomilitary problem in this section and take note of Pakistan's arms-production capabilities in the context of a discussion of allies and arms suppliers.

When the British ruled South Asia the old Indian Army had four major tasks. One was internal security; large numbers of troops were stationed in cantonments located outside major population centers, and they could move rapidly from these cantonments to trouble spots. Another role was to patrol the long—and sometimes undefined—frontier with India. Third, the military was used intermittently as an expeditionary force; Indian and Pakistani army units even today carry such places as Cassino, Peking, Lhasa, Basra, El Alamein, Burma, Saigon, and Japan on their battleflags. Finally, the Indian Army maintained a series of forts and posts in the Northwest and engaged in a number of campaigns to check an advancing Russian Empire.

With some modification the Pakistan military today still carries out internal security, border patrol, and expeditionary tasks. (The latter now take the shape of thousands of officers and men serving as pilots, gunners, advisors, and training cadres in a number of foreign military establishments, especially in the Middle East.) But it has, in effect, given up the task of checking Russian/Soviet advances in exchange for a new role, that of preparing for conventional ground war against India. Most of the Pakistan army's 400,000 soldiers and approximately 900 tanks are dedicated to the long border with India. There is a clear discontinuity between the self-image of the Pakistan military as the legatees of the British side in the "Great Game" of Central Asian politics, balancing out the Russians, and the reality of Pakistani troop dispositions. There is also a substantive reason for the discontinuity; in 1947-1948 Pakistan could not afford to maintain a far-flung and costly series of forts—let alone challenge the Soviets in Afghanistan or elsewhere—without the complete backing of a major power and, at the same time, be expected to defend against India.[15]

Thus, Pakistan's main-line forces, organized into approximately twenty divisions, grouped into six corps, largely face east, not west. One corps, based in Peshawar, probably has two infantry divisions within it; another, located in Quetta, is in the process of formation, but four major corps containing most of Pakistan's armor face the Indian Army in the east.[16]

The troops that actually patrol the border, especially along the Afghan frontier and in Kashmir, are usually not regular army but belong to one of several special units. Units such as the Mohmand Scouts, the Pishin Scouts, and the Khyber Rifles are raised from local tribes but are officered by regular Pakistan Army officers on deputation. Although quite small in numbers, they effectively combine romance, firepower, and mobility. Because of their local ties, their actual use is a serious political as well as military decision—they may be fighting their own kinsmen. Yet when they are used it is often seen as a local matter; their presence is considerably more acceptable than that of regular Pakistan Army units that may be drawn from distant provinces. These scouts thus stand somewhere between the regular army and the local police units, with some of the firepower of the former and the local contacts and mobility of the latter.

Pakistan did have a major urban-oriented paramilitary force—the Federal Security Force (FSF)—but it was disbanded after Zulfiqar Ali Bhutto was removed from power. The FSF was resented by the military and hated by the population. Today, regular army units stationed near urban centers have auxiliary "aid to the civil" responsibilities when the police are unable to cope.

As a topographical map indicates, there are special problems associated with the defense of Pakistan. Lahore and the main north-south railway, canal, and road transportation systems are very close to India and must be protected at all costs with static formations. Pakistan's only port, Karachi, is eight-hundred miles away from Islamabad and far from the likely scene of major combat in Kashmir and the Punjab. The two most rebellious provinces, Baluchistan and NWFP, do not have well-developed road or rail systems except for the Khyber-Peshawar area. Quetta, the capital of Baluchistan, is screened by a number of small mountain ranges, although it does have rail connections. But the rest of Baluchistan is both inaccessible and inhospitable. Thus, the army concludes that it cannot count on quickly moving units around Pakistan during a major crisis. New threats—such as that from the Afghan border—require new units, and Pakistan would probably like to raise several new divisions dedicated to the Durand Line.

Before 1980 the Pakistan Air Force (PAF) was entirely oriented toward the Indian border.[17] Aircraft had been used along the Afghan frontier for patrolling purposes and occasionally for punitive raids on rebellious tribes. The situation is now transformed. Most of Pakistan's major military airfields placed well back from the Indian border; this now means that they are very close to the Afghan frontier and major Afghan military airports. Published reports indicate that the Soviet Union has introduced a large number of aircraft and missiles into Afghanistan, supplementing aircraft already supplied to the Afghan Air Force. Some of these aircraft are less than a minute's flying time from Pakistan, and the PAF finds itself vulnerable to a surprise attack from the west. It must assume that if there were to be major Soviet or Afghan incursions into Pakistan—in hot pursuit of Afghan tribesmen or for purposes of harassment—that PAF airfields would be under attack. This has led the PAF to state that it has a minimal requirement of improved advanced-warning and surface-to-air missile (SAM) systems and substantial numbers of new high-performance aircraft.[18]

Weapons Acquisition and Arms Transfers

This discussion of the possible expansion of the army and air force brings us to one of the central constraints on the Pakistan military—their dependence upon outside sources for weapons.

Pakistan is a very large country and possesses a substantial pool of educated, trained manpower. However, it cannot manufacture a crankshaft.[19] Pakistan became completely dependent upon the United States in the 1950s for all major and most minor kinds of equipment, and it was not until 1965 when American arms transfers were practically terminated that Pakistanis began to think seriously about building up an indigenous arms industry. Since 1965 there has been considerable progress in that direction, largely with Chinese and French help, but Pakistan is still dependent for new tanks, armored personnel carriers (APCs), aircraft of all kinds, soft-skinned vehicles, artillery, electronics, radar, fire-control systems, and many other items. Pakistan does produce virtually all of its light infantry weapons (the excellent G-3 rifle and a machine gun both built under West German license), most ammunition, shells, explosives, and recoilless rifles and mortars; it has recently acquired the capacity to completely rebuild and reconstruct its seven hundred Chinese supplied T-59 tanks and its French Mirage III aircraft. It will soon be able to rebuild the Chinese F-6 (MiG. 19) aircraft and it can undertake major repairs on most of its heavy armored vehicles.[20]

Since a number of these projects are geared to an international market— the Mirage rebuild facility expects to handle aircraft from all over the Middle East and Asia—it can be said that Pakistan belongs to the category of intermediate arms supplier. It must acquire the most advanced equipment from others, yet it is also capable of supplying simpler arms. Since some of these projects have been bankrolled by Saudi Arabia and other Arab states, there is some truth in the claim that Pakistan hopes to become the arsenal of the Islamic world. But this is a long-term prospect fraught with difficulties and risks, and Pakistan cannot wait until it develops an indigenous capacity to manufacture high-performance weapons. For these it must turn to the commercial international arms market or to its friends.

Except for the Chinese, who have earned a reputation among the Pakistanis for their steadfastness, reliability, and tact—if not for the quality of their technology—the fact is that Pakistan no longer has friends who are reliable suppliers of key weapons, whether for cash or credit, or as a grant.[21] The French will sell Mirage and other weapons, but for cash—which means reliance upon the states that will provide it. The United States has had an extremely restrictive policy of arms transfers to South Asia since 1967, a policy that was virtually identical to that adopted by Jimmy Carter as a global arms-transfer policy in 1977.[22] The Soviet Union has provided a limited number of T-55 tanks to Pakistan but demanded a settlement of the Kashmir issue as the price of further assistance. In almost all other cases there are special obstacles, and indeed few other states make the kinds of weapons that Pakistanis feel they must have. Pakistan *has* acquired a small number of weapons from a large number of states, but on an irregular basis. This presents serious problems of compatibility. For example, the artillery comes from the United States, China, Great Britain, Italy, and North Korea; this raises difficulties of coordination, ammunition supply, and training—although Pakistani gunners claim that because of their weapons diversity their personnel are among the most flexible and innovative in the world.[23]

Two factors stand in the way of Pakistan's attempts to acquire high-performance aircraft and substantial amounts of armor and other weapons. One, alluded to earlier, is cost. By any standards, Pakistan is not a rich country and its economy has been in serious trouble since the 1971 war with India.[24] Further, the acquisition of a modern weapon represents only the beginning of its cost: a rough figure is that 50 percent of the original price will have to be spent on repairs, spare parts, and replacements; in some cases this work must be done in the country of origin.

But another restriction on arms transfers is of equal importance. It is that *politically* many potential arms suppliers do not wish to incite India's wrath. The Indian government has long had an obsession with preventing the transfer of any weapons to Pakistan, and only the recent Soviet invasion of Afghanistan has caused them to think the problem through. India and Pakistan are in many ways quite similar states, yet India is larger and more powerful. Very few Western and even very few Islamic states want to alienate India for the sake of an arms sale to Pakistan. Only China, for obvious reasons, and France—which sees Pakistan as an entry route into the Islamic world and in any case sells little to India—have recently provided major weapons to Pakistan. Until recently, Pakistan could only come out second best in such a competition with India. It remains to be seen whether Pakistan will benefit from the recent events in Iran and Afghanistan.[25]

For Pakistan, the recent failure of outside powers to provide it with substantial numbers of weapons has given impetus to what was an ongoing process of rethinking basic policies. Pakistan has become a nonaligned state; its current leadership has attempted to maintain good relations with India and yet not sever its ties with China. It has acted with restraint in its handling of the Afghan refugee problem. All this may indicate that Pakistan has despaired of receiving the kind and quantity of weapons that some of its generals claim are necessary to defend the state. If so, and this remains speculation, the weapons-acquisition tail may wind up wagging the strategic-policy dog.

Internal Foci of Security

Observers of the old united Pakistan often remarked on the wide cultural, linguistic, and economic differences between West and East Pakistanis. Many of them accurately predicted the destruction of Pakistan, but not until recent years has the same attention been given to the striking differences between Sindhis, Baluchis, Pathans, and Punjabis[26] and to differences within some of these provinces, differences based on urbanization, commercial and land-tenure patterns, and even subregionalism and the presence of the world's largest tribal society.

One of the central characteristics of Pakistan is the permanent tension between centrifugal and centripetal forces. It is important that Pakistan's diverse tribal, plain, agricultural, and urban populations be knit into a reasonably unified society. Yet even before the British came to South Asia, whenever a strong central government has tried to impose its rule the reaction has usually been revolt. Recent grievances vary: there have been major language riots in Sind—Urdu, the national language of Pakistan, is not truly indigenous to any part of the country; when Bhutto tried to impose his party's rule in Baluchistan an extended guerrilla war broke out and lasted several years. During some of that period the NWFP was in a partial state of rebellion. The military had a difficult time coping with these domestic insurrections and simultaneously manning the Indian frontier. Most recently Bhutto himself was deposed as a result of widespread protests over alleged vote rigging.[27]

Yet if the central government fails to impose its authority over rebellious or partially integrated regions of Pakistan, there is some concern that this might itself lead to an actual attempt at independence. This was the logic that led to the brutal, and perhaps because of that, ineffective, attempt to repress Bengali subnationalism. The choices are not pleasant: concede all grievances and run the risk of inciting demands from other provinces or subgroups in the society as well, or draw a line and stand firm, possibly forcing a region into open rebellion. One policy may lead to a de facto independence or a federalism so loose that Pakistan ceases to be a state; the other may to the same end after extensive bloodshed.

Since Pakistan was created as a homeland for Indian Muslims there has always been the hope that Islam itself would be the glue that kept Pakistan together in time of crisis. There are certain limits to this. First, there are important sectarian and theological differences among Pakistani Muslims. There is a minority population of Shi'ites and several sects that do not conform to Islamic orthodoxy.[28] Second, there are a number of political parties and movements that urge greater Islamicization, but these tend to be ultraconservative in their social and economic outlook. They thus antagonize large numbers of urban dwellers and Muslims who have a more relaxed view of the ideal of an Islamic state, and who do not believe that the Koran can be a guide to modern life without interpretation. Pakistani politicians and the military have tried virtually every combination of orthodox and conservative Islam, socialism, capitalism, federalism, and unitary state structure; there have been demagogues and liberals, technocrats and incompetents, and although Ayub Khan was able to provide stability for ten years, he was unable to devise a system that allowed for the orderly and peaceful transfer of power.[29] In terms of security policy this has had two important consequences: there has not been consistent leadership or a continuity of policymaking even in defense matters, and there has been repeated intervention of the military into Pakistani politics.

The Pakistan Military and Politics

There are armies that defend their nation's borders; there are armies that are concerned with protecting their own position in society; and there are armies that defend a cause or an idea. The Pakistan Army does all three. From the day Pakistan was created it has been active in helping to establish internal order and in protecting Pakistan's permeable and often ill-defined borders. During this period it has used its power and special position within Pakistan to ensure that it received adequate weapons, resources, and manpower. Unlike India, where civilians dominate the defense policy process, the military in Pakistan are chiefly responsible for all strategic and structural decisions, and attempts to reduce their role in the decision-making process have never been successful.

Decision Making

The so-called British tradition of civilian control over the military was a mixed legacy for both India and Pakistan.[30] One strand, which has become the dominant feature of the Indian defense policy process, emphasized the ultimate authority and responsibility of civilian officials and has led to a complex series of fiscal and administrative restraints on the Indian military. However, there was another component of the tradition, one that emphasized the authority and status of the military commander. Although independent India managed to cut away at the special role of the military just as it enhanced the power of civilian politicians and bureaucrats, it was not until a few years ago that Pakistan—then led by Bhutto—tried to do the same. For years the head of the Pakistan Army has had a special position within the government and effectively dominated the policy process; defense policy usually led, rather than followed, foreign policy. This was true even when Ayub Khan gave up command of the army since his commander-in-chief, Mohammad Musa, was a close personal friend and not an independent thinker. The pattern continues today; Mohammed Zia Ul-Haq retains his position as Chief of the Army Staff and has made himself President of Pakistan as well. Clearly, as he has said, the former position is more important than the latter.

The military does not claim to be pleased with an arrangement that gives them complete control over the policy process. Although a few generals feel that increased military influence is desirable, most say they would like to make the present civilian-oriented structure work. Bhutto's reforms of the defense policy process are recognized as necessary and desirable, and a number of generals agree that the inordinate role of the army under the old system did not meet the test of war in 1965 or 1971. The new system, which has only been in operation for four years, is the result of the military's own study of defense policymaking systems in a number of countries.[31] The final product closely resembles the Indian defense policy process in several ways. However, the missing ingredient in the Pakistani system is effective, competent, and responsible civilian politicians and bureaucrats.

The Military and Society

There are many reasons why Pakistani politicians, bureaucrats, and civilian elites compare unfavorably with their Indian counterparts and have never been able to establish a stable civilian government. Some of these are historical: the movement for Pakistan was led by politicians who did not have a strong political base in what became Pakistan; two of the leading figures in the creation of the state died early or were assassinated. There are also difficulties in creating an explicitly Islamic state that is compatible with British parliamentary traditions and an impetus to social and economic modernization.

There are other factors and linkages that may be vital but about which we know very little. Pakistan's economy has been dominated by a handful of families, most of whom were migrants from India.[32] There are important labor and urban groups, many of which also came from India, a fact that has often led them into conflict with local "sons of the soil." Further, Pakistan retains a powerful landowning class and tribal leaders who find it in their interest to oppose modernizing influences. Roads, for example, are a threat to those tribal chieftains who control the smuggling trade, which is a not inconsiderable source of income and power for them.

The point is that the military, which have usually been lumped in with the civil service as part of the government bureaucracy, do have their own connections and ties to Pakistan's rich, its peasantry, its tribes, and even its urban classes. We have only the vaguest notion of how such linkages, especially to the officer corps, affect the political behavior of the military or whether the generals are motivated primarily by organizational and institutional self-preservation. Leftist critics have always accused the Pakistan Army of being descended from and defending the rich and the powerful; although they are hardly social revolutionaries, an increasing number of officers are drawn from middle- and even working-class families—or more importantly, have traditional family ties to the military itself.

This family-like characteristic of the army has contributed to its view that it is the most Pakistani of Pakistan's institutions. Not only does the officer corps believe that it defends society from external enemies, but a number of officers will argue that the military has an important role in ensuring that Pakistani society itself modernizes and yet remains pure and truly Islamic. Not only should the military defend Pakistan, they claim, but Pakistani society must remain worthy of the military. The military was the first all-Pakistan institution—indeed, it existed before the state—and there is still a belief that it is the only one that can keep the country together. A critic would point out that there is more than a little bit of a self-fulfilling prophecy in this argument, since the military have intervened on several occasions when they were dissatisfied with the power or performance of the bureaucracy or the political parties—they will not *let* the latter become effective national institutions.

This is clearly the puzzle of Pakistani politics. The military are reluctant to withdraw from power today because they do not believe that any of the current civilian leaders are capable of running the state to the satisfaction of the military themselves. Not surprisingly, in view of Mr. Bhutto's fate, civilians are reluctant to come forward. There is also no assurance that the military will not try to play a critical behind-the-scenes political role even if formal power should pass to a civilian government as in the Turkish model. But the notion of partial military rule is not accepted by most Pakistanis, whose perspective has been strongly shaped by the British tradition of parliamentary democracy and strong civilian control. The discontinuities between civilian and military opinion on these basic questions are enormous.

However, the generals are also aware that they cannot run Pakistan indefinitely. They have before them the example of Ayub Khan who civilianized himself but was then led into a series of foreign-policy and domestic-political disasters. With a few exceptions the present generation of military leaders freely admit that they do not have the vision or ambition of Ayub— put another way, they know their limits and do not believe that they can retain political power without this affecting the quality and performance of the military itself.

One solution would be some form of national compact or agreement. The military will not satisfy the politicians unless they allow free elections; those parties—such as the Pakistan People's Party, now headed by Bhutto's wife and daughter—with grievances against the military will probably have to promise that they will not seek retribution. At the same time the military may have to be given a constitutional voice in the making of policies that most strongly concern them, such as defense and foreign policy. A staged withdrawal, in both senses of the word, would reassure both the military and civilian politicians that both sides were keeping their promises. Realistically, it is extremely unlikely that this will come about. With Bhutto's death it is not clear whether there is any single party or individual that can effectively run Pakistan even if the military remained neutral. There are no political figures who seem willing to serve as a front for the military, nor has the military offered a coherent, attractive alternative to some form of civilian democratic government, although there is much talk in the officers' messes about a system that suits the special genius of the people of Pakistan.

Conclusion

Pakistan is the only ex-colonial state to have been divided by war after achieving independence. Bangladesh was created partly out of the desire of East Bengalis to achieve national status, partly because the Indian government was willing to hasten the process by military intervention, but certainly in large part because of decisions made by the military leadership of West Pakistan.

Their successors are aware that neither the international nor the domestic environment has improved since 1971. Pakistan is now flanked by the Soviet Union and India; almost a million Afghan refugees have crossed the Durand Line, with more on the way; Pakistan's international friends do not match their verbal encouragement with material support; in terms of equipment the military is in relatively poorer shape in 1980 than it was in 1971; politically, it is even more unpopular, and there appears to be no civilian leadership capable of assuming power. Finally, ethnic, regional, religious, economic, professional, and class groups periodically express their unhappiness with continued military rule. The military leadership is widely perceived as incompetent and some in the military feel that it may be damaging to the army itself. Many Pakistanis and foreigners do not believe that Pakistan will survive in its present form beyond this decade. Pakistan faces the unenviable prospect of becoming a latter-day Poland, partitioned out of existence.

Without underestimating the possibility that civil war, revolution, external invasion, or some other calamity may lead to another vivisection of

Pakistan, there are factors that may enable Pakistan to negotiate the present crisis. First, although unpopular the military leadership are not irrational and are aware of the desperate predicament they are in. Zia and other generals have encouraged debate, discussion, and criticism within the military, although they have not allowed civilians to speak their minds.[33] They are painfully aware of the technical shortcomings of the military, of the regional dominance of India, of the ruthlessness of the Russians, and of the unreliability of their American ex-allies. Nor do they think that the Islamic world—let alone the nonaligned movement—will do very much to help them. They hold the stark but realistic view that they must rely upon their own resources and forge their own path at a moment of great peril. But this path is not immediately apparent to anyone, Pakistani or non-Pakistani.

If, as seems most likely, the military continue in power in Pakistan—or retain a veto over security-related decisions—there is not likely to be a major change in the present strategic style. It represents a consensus within the military hierarchy itself; it is not likely that there will be a change in Pakistan's attempts to maintain a conventional retaliatory capacity in the form of armor, air support, and mobile infantry to punish or raise the price of invasion. Yet Pakistan finds it difficult to raise and maintain expensive armor units, it cannot produce its own high-performance aircraft, and it must commit large forces to the static defense of major urban areas and lines of communication. Increasingly, the strategy of deterrence is stretched thinner and thinner and may lose credibility altogether. The solution for Pakistan may be in the acquisition of nuclear weapons. They would force the enemy out of massed concentrations on the ground and may be used in a punishment strategy. Yet nuclear weapons are hardly attractive to the professional Pakistani officer and pressure for their acquisition has always come from civilians. It is likely that Pakistan will acquire nuclear weapons if it can, but it is not very probable that they will be used as a substitute for conventional ground and air force as long as the military remain in power or retain a veto over security policy.

Should, however, the Pakistan Army be persuaded to withdraw from power and its dominant role in defense policymaking, it is conceivable but not very likely that a future civilian government would reshape both structural and strategic components of security policy. It would be following in Bhutto's footsteps and might pursue an expanded role for nuclear weapons or attempt to create a people's army. We have discussed this above, and it is improbable that the Pakistan Army as it is now constituted would yield power to those who would gut it. Pakistan itself would have to be on the verge of civil war and anarchy for such a radical departure even to be contemplated.

More likely would be a civilian attempt to limit the size, role, and mission of the military without altering its characteristic structure. There are a number of thoughtful officers who have argued that Pakistan could survive with a much smaller military establishment, even without nuclear weapons, and that regional stability and even Indian dominance does not mean the destruction of an independent Pakistan. Some have even argued for a deal with the Soviet Union. The dangers here lie not in the present but in the future. Would a Pakistan subservient to either India or the Soviet Union be required to alter its Islamic character? Would strategic dependency lead to political and cultural penetration, undoing the partition of 1947? Finally, there is the small possibility—considering the events of 1971—that one of Pakistan's neighbors will seize upon its disorder and end the "Pakistan problem" once and for all. If the Pakistan Army were defeated and disarmed, Pakistan could be divided into its "natural" components, each a separate, independent state, each virtually disarmed and under the protective influence of India or the Soviet Union. It is inconceivable that India would want to reabsorb much of the present Pakistan, but it might conclude that an unstable, fragile, nuclear-armed, and hostile Pakistan held greater risks than an immediate war.

Pakistan must thus search for a middle road between concessions that would undo the state itself and a hard-line strategic policy that threatens total war as a form of defense, a policy that leads its neighbors to conclude that it is irredeemably irresponsible. This is especially true in the case of India. Pakistan has little choice but to learn to live with its newly powerful neighbor and to accept its own de facto strategic inferiority. But such acceptance is in turn dependent on Indian statesmanship. If India insists that Pakistan has no legitimate defense needs—as many of its generals and strategists claim—then Pakistan is in an impossible position. But if India recognizes that it has an interest in the continuing existence of a Pakistan that is capable of defending itself—even against India—because that capability is one, but not the only, condition for the integrity of the state, then there may be an opportunity for a general regional-security agreement. Recent statements emanating from India seem to indicate a new realism on this point, and the rest of the world has every reason to encourage such a development; for it is only through regional processes of consultation and negotiation that anything of consequence can be done about Soviet penetration or nuclear proliferation.

Notes

1. From "Pagett, M.P.," in *Selected Prose and Poetry of Rudyard Kipling* (New York: Garden City, 1949), p. 980. Kipling's parody of a reform-minded M.P. who stays in India for three months—in constant fear of climate and illness—only to return as an "expert" on the India problem is still appropriate.

2. Of some historical interest, however, is the fact that for many years Pakistan *was* a highly praised model of development, featuring the encouragement of entrepreneurial adventurism and a strong central authority. One consequence of this was an increase in regional economic disparities and political grievances. For a comparative analysis see Angus Maddison, *Class Structure and Economic Growth: India and Pakistan Since the Moghuls* (New York: Norton, 1971).

3. While in India in February 1980, Andrei Gromyko warned Pakistan that its position as an "independent state" would be undermined if it supported American and Chinese policy. See *The Hindu*, 13 Feb. 1980. These crude threats eventually embarrassed his hosts, who were trying to find a peaceful solution to the Afghan crisis.

4. The classic statement of this view is in the writings of Sir Olaf Caroe. See *Wells of Power* and *Soviet Empire* in particular. For an authoritative Pakistani statement see Aslam Siddiqi, *A Path for Pakistan* (Karachi: Pakistan Publishing House, 1964).

5. For a perceptive study see Shivaji Ganguly, *Pakistan-China Relations: A Study in Interaction* (Urbana: Center for Asian Studies, 1971).

6. Pakistan has received some military equipment and economic assistance from the Soviet Union—perhaps a measure of how seriously the Soviets treat South Asia. It has been a useful lever against the two states—Afghanistan and India—with close ties to the Soviets.

7. See Stephen P. Cohen and Richard L. Park, *India: Emergent Power?* (New York: Crane, Russak, 1978) and John W. Mellor, ed., *India: A Rising Middle Power* (Boulder, Colo.: Westview Press, 1979).

8. The best study of the complex Kashmir issue remains that of Sisir Gupta, *Kashmir: A Study in India-Pakistan Relations* (Bombay: Asia Publishing House, 1966).

9. For a comprehensive study of the border and its people see Sir Olaf Caroe, *The Pathans* (London: Macmillan, 1958; reprint ed., Union Book Stall, Karachi, 1973). The Durand Line is discussed in the context of Afghan history in Louis Dupree, *Afghanistan*, rev. ed. (Princeton: Princeton University Press, 1980). A detailed study of legal aspects of the border is in Mujtaba Razvi, *The Frontiers of Pakistan* (Karachi-Dacca: National Publishing House, 1971).

10. See Caroe for a short discussion of the Baluchis and several of the papers in Ainslie T. Embree, *Pakistan's Western Borderlands* (New Delhi: Vikas, 1977). Selig Harrison has written on the Baluchi issue in "Nightmare in Baluchistan," *Foreign Policy* 32 (Fall 1978):136-160.

11. There are a number of perceptive articles on nuclear strategy and theory in various Pakistani strategic journals. For an indignant Indian view see Major General D.K. Palit (retd.) and P.K.S. Namboordiri, *Pakistan's Islamic Bomb* (New Delhi: Vikas, 1979). A more balanced approach is in

Zalmay Khalilzad, "Pakistan and the Bomb," *Survival* (November-December 1979):244-250.

12. For a Bangladeshi account see Rounaq Jahan, *Pakistan: Failure in National Integration* (New York: Columbia University Press, 1972); an informed Pakistani military eyewitness version is Siddiq Saliq, *Witness to Surrender* (Karachi: Oxford University Press, 1978).

13. There has been a burst of writing in Pakistan on strategic matters. Among the best writings are Lieutenant General (retd.) M. Attiqur Rahman's *Our Defense Cause* (London: White Lion, 1976); *Leadership: Senior Commanders* (Lahore: Ferozsons, 1973); and *Reflections on Infantry* (Lahore: Wajidalis, 1978). See also Brigadier S.K. Malik, *The Quranic Concept of War* (Lahore: Wajidalis, 1979), and almost every issue of the monthly, *Defense Journal* (Karachi) and the quarterly *Strategic Studies* (Islamabad).

14. See the provocative *Raiders in Kashmir* (Rawalpindi: Ferozsons, 1975) by "ex-Major General" Akbar Khan, an associate of Zulfiqar Ali Bhutto and once involved in a conspiracy to overthrow the government. Of great interest was the brief rise of revolutionary military movements in Bangladesh, led by several young ex-Pakistani Army officers. Several of them were hanged after the abortive coups and counter-coups in August-November 1975. A sympathetic account containing the text of several relevant documents and speeches is in Lawrence Lifschultz, *Bangladesh: The Unfinished Revolution* (London: Zed Press, 1979).

15. Arnold Toynbee discusses the withdrawal of Pakistani forces from these forts immediately after independence in the broader historical context of the balance of power in Central Asia and Afghanistan. See *Between Oxus and Jumna* (London: Oxford University Press, 1961), pp. 152-155 and 180ff.

16. Until April 1980, the commanders of four of these corps were also the governors of the four provinces of Pakistan. The jobs have been divided, and all of the corps have new commanders. It should be noted that not all Pakistani divisions have a full complement of equipment such as artillery.

17. The most complete description of PAF history and operations is in John Fricker, *Battle for Pakistan: The Air War of 1965* (London: Ian Allen, 1979), which was written with the cooperation of senior PAF officers.

18. The PAF would like air-superiority aircraft that would enable them to meet and defeat such aircraft as the MiG 21, and possibly more advanced MiG's in Afghanistan. It is highly unlikely that the United States will provide such aircraft. Even if given for the purpose of defending the western border of Pakistan, by their very nature they can be quickly applied to the Indian front.

19. Lieutenant General Abdul Hameed Khan (Retd.) "Organization for Defense," in *Nawa-i-Waqt*, Lahore, 1979 April 10-11 (English translation provided by the author), p. 11.

20. The F-6 and tank rebuild facilities are being provided by the PRC; the Mirage rebuild factory is French-supplied but paid for by Pakistan; the repair facilities of the Pakistan Army have been built up over the years, but with a major American contribution in the 1950s.

21. This may even be true of the Chinese, who are themselves seeking assistance in defense production. It is not clear whether Western suppliers, such as the British or the United States, would allow China to transfer either weapons or production technology to third countries such as Pakistan.

22. See Stephen P. Cohen, "U.S. Weapons and South Asia: A Policy Analysis," *Pacific Affairs* 49 (Spring 1976):49-69.

23. This may well be the case, but it certainly is not true for aircraft. Pakistan used to boast that it had the best-trained repair crews because of the diversity of aircraft flown by the PAF (British, American, Chinese, French); however, this meant that aircraft were limited in their operations, as their spares and maintenance crews could not be distributed to all bases.

24. In comparative terms Pakistan spends more on defense than almost any of the other poorer states of the world; its defense effort is on every relative measure greater than that of India, although its actual force levels are subtantially smaller. For a full analysis comparing India, Iran, China, Japan, and Pakistan, see Stephen P. Cohen, "Towards a Great State in Asia," in *Military Power and Policy in Asian States: China, India, Japan*, eds. Onkar Marwah and Jonathan D. Pollack (Boulder, Colo.: Westview Press, 1980), pp. 9-41.

25. The United States has provided two older destroyers—without surface-to-surface missiles—and a wide range of auxiliary equipment to Pakistan for cash. It is highly doubtful whether it will provide either armor or high-performance aircraft.

26. There are several excellent collections of essays on post-1971 Pakistan. See Ainslie T. Embree, in *Pakistan: The Long View*, eds. Ralph Braibanti, Lawrence Ziring, and W. Howard Wriggins (Durham, N.C.: Duke University Press, 1977); and W. Howard Wriggins, ed., *Pakistan in Transition* (Islamabad: University of Islamabad Press, 1975); a collection dealing with foreign policy is in Masuma Hasan, ed., *Pakistan in a Changing World* (Karachi: Pakistan Institute of International Affairs, 1978), an informed Indian analysis is in Satish Kumar, *The New Pakistan* (New Delhi: Vikas, 1978). It should also be noted that provincial conflicts in the new Pakistan are both moderated and exacerbated by massive internal migration. Karachi has a substantial Pathan and Baluchi population, many Punjabis have settled down in some districts in Sind, and there are many Pathans living in Punjab, especially in Rawalpindi and the districts adjacent to the NWFP. The governments of each province also have a land-settlement scheme for ex-servicemen that is especially important in Sind, Baluchistan, and NWFP. This population movement both helps to create

a "Pakistani" consciousness and simultaneously to strengthen feelings of regional loyalty. The two processes are not necessarily incompatible.

27. The successor government's version of Bhutto's manipulations is contained in the massive *White Paper on the Performance of the Bhutto Regime* (Islamabad: Government of Pakistan, 1979), in three volumes; Bhutto's own rejoinder, written in his death cell, is in *"If I am Assassinated . . ."* (New Delhi: Vikas, 1979).

28. At least one of these sects, the Ahmediya community, was banned by Bhutto's government in 1974. See Ralph Braibanti, "The Research Potential of Pakistan's Development," in *Pakistan: The Long View*, eds. Ralph Braibanti, Lawrence Ziring, and W. Howard Wriggins (Durham, N.C.: Duke University Press, 1977), pp. 464ff.

29. For a perceptive analysis of the role of the military in Pakistan's politics see Gerald A. Heeger, "Politics in the Post-Military State: Some Reflections on the Pakistani Experience," *World Politics* 29 (Jan. 1977):242-262; for a survey of the military's political involvement see Hasan Askari Rizvi, *The Military and Politics in Pakistan*, rev. ed. (Lahore: Progressive Publishers, 1976).

30. For a comparison see Stephen P. Cohen, *The Indian Army* (Berkeley, Calif.: University of California Press, 1971).

31. The text of the "White Paper on Higher Defense Organization" and several accompanying articles is in *Defence Journal* (Karachi) 17 (July-August 1976).

32. For an introduction to the imbalances of Pakistani society and a description of the various civilian groups that contend for influence and power see Robert LaPorte, Jr., *Power and Privilege: Influence and Decision-Making in Pakistan* (Berkeley, Calif.: University of California Press, 1975) and Shahid Javed Burki, *Pakistan Under Bhutto, 1971-1977* (New York: St. Martin's, 1980). In neither of these excellent studies is there much discussion of the social origins, attitudes, and professional interests of the military, the one group that has dominated Pakistani politics for over twenty-two years.

33. The recent (April 1980) reshuffling of the higher command of the army has, according to some observers, improved Zia's position in the military, but at the cost of removing some independent-minded officers.

6 India

Raju G.C. Thomas

As elsewhere and especially in Western-type democracies, the security policy of India is broadly determined by the interplay of various political, economic, and technological factors at both the domestic and international levels. In particular, two interrelated linkages are evident: first, the interactions between domestic parliamentary politics on the one hand and foreign policy behavior on the other; and second, between external strategic pressures and domestic economic priorities.

In the first place, periodic changes in the strengths of political parties and leaders in India as well as political conditions in general have produced some shifts in the country's foreign-policy objectives. Adopted strategies of international alignments, appeasement, or opposition toward the great powers in order to counter or modify regional threats perceived from Pakistan and China, have been influenced by such internal political factors as the personality and clout of a prime minister, the persistence or fall of a dominant one-party system, and other internal religious-ideological divisions. Indian defense policy in the 1950s, for instance, was largely determined by the philosophy and political outlook of Prime Minister Jawaharlal Nehru. Between March 1977 and October 1979, substantial changes in policy were introduced by the newly formed Janata party, which defeated the Congress party at the 1977 general elections. Of similar relevance to Indian security policy is the Muslim-minority question in India, which continues to affect the government's policies on Kashmir and relations with Pakistan, as well as on other international issues in the Islamic Middle East.

In the second place, competing claims to India's scarce economic resources require that Indian defense policy and planning be formulated in the context of the country's economic-development program. Although Indian perceptions of external threats to the nation may at times appear to call for a large-scale defense build-up, domestic economic conditions may preclude such a policy. For India, the basic defense-development dichotomy continues to be this: external threats demand appropriate defense measures to meet or deter them, thus placing a strain on scarce economic resources; the urgency of economic development in India and the need for rapid social transformation demand that defense expenditures be maintained at a minimum, thereby increasing the security risk to the nation. This paradox is further aggravated by the fact that defense potential is dependent on economic growth. A reduction in development expenditure in order to bolster the defense program to meet immediate threats may, in fact, imply less defense potential in the future if such a diversion of resources retards economic growth.

Defense planning and production in India must, therefore, have a minimum effect on development while also ensuring the maximum possible security for the nation. Note, however, that this mini-max balance is a subjective and uncertain condition. A greater diversion to defense would not necessarily increase the security of India if this were to set off counter-defense measures in Pakistan and China. As a consequence, there can be no guarantee that increasing defense programs in India will have achieved compensatory increases in security. Similarly, as Emile Benoit, K. Subrahmanyam, and others have shown, less spending on defense may not produce a corresponding increase in the economic growth rate.[1] This observation may be particularly true where savings from a reduction in defense spending are channeled into noninvestment areas of the economy; or where savings might reduce the total effective demand on defense and defense-dependent ancillary industries.

Such domestic-international linkages and the interplay of political, economic, and technological factors are discussed here first, within a framework based on an *inter-state* perspective. This includes the following analytical categories:

1. India's milieu objectives and general assumptions about the international system
2. military and nonmilitary threats perceived at both the regional and global levels
3. appropriate foreign policies and military strategies adopted to counter such perceived threats, or to modify the international system to produce a favorable security environment
4. defense-program responses that establish various force levels and weapon systems

The second framework is based on an *intra-state* perspective and includes the following:

1. the marshalling of economic and technological resources for the defense effort while paying attention to the needs of national economic development
2. the conduct of domestic politics and bureaucratic processes that attempt to foster consensus among political parties, interest groups, and the military establishment in support of national-security policy objectives

Assumptions about the International System

The Indian historical experience under British colonial rule colored the international outlook of the new independent government of India. On the one hand, the general admiration among Indian elites for British political, administrative, and judicial systems resulted in the adoption of a Western-style parliamentary democracy in India. On the other hand, the Indian nationalist movement and struggle for independence against the British produced a determination not to be pushed into any Western alliance network that might erode India's newly found independence. A similar paradox may be found in the personality and outlook of Jawaharlal Nehru, India's first prime minister and architect of post-independence Indian foreign policy. Despite his aristocratic education at Britain's Harrow, Cambridge, and the Inner Temple, Nehru at the same time had considerable admiration for Soviet socialist planning as well as sympathy for China, which he viewed as a brother Asian state that had been exploited in the past by the European colonial powers. Such conflicting pressures and outlooks partially explain the Indian decision to remain within the British Commonwealth, as well as its refusal to join the American-sponsored SEATO and CENTO defense treaties directed against the communist states.

As will be discussed later, Nehru's decision to adopt a nonaligned policy carried certain security arguments. Nevertheless, it is important to note that its initial practice also carried certain idealistic visions of the nature of world politics. In professing nonalignment and peaceful coexistence with communist states, especially with the neighboring state of China, Nehru implicitly rejected the Western concept of maintaining security through a balance of power among nations. Balance-of-power politics, the traditional practice of European statesmen, was considered volatile and precarious to the maintenance of world peace. According to Nehru, "the normal idea is that security is protected by armies. That is only partly true; it is equally true that security is protected by policies. A deliberate policy of friendship with other countries goes further in gaining security than almost anything else."[2] This belief is in contrast to the realist dictum of British Prime Minister Lord Palmerston who, more than a hundred years ago, stated: "Great Britain has no permanent enemies or permanent friends; she has only permanent interests."

Such visions of the world received a setback after the border war with China in October 1962. During the immediate period thereafter, Nehru regretted that India had been living in a "world of her own creation" and he considered joining the Western military camp. Subsequently, as the Chinese threat receded, a qualified reversal to past assumptions followed. However, the interpretation and application of nonalignment was no longer the same. Under the same banner of nonalignment, a loose political and military alignment with the Soviet Union was pursued in order to deter the possibility of future Chinese military interventions on the subcontinent.

Meanwhile, the rejection of balance-of-power politics continued to be manifest in official Indian positions on various regional and world issues. For example, India has always insisted that Indo-Pakistani issues should be resolved on a bilateral basis. Western and Chinese efforts to arm Pakistan to counter the growth of Indian military power were seen as endangering the peace of the subcontinent, as their policies might tempt Pakistan to seize Indian-held Kashmir by force. According to the Indian position, its dominance would ensure the status quo and peace on the subcontinent, as indeed has been the case since the creation of Bangladesh in 1971. Similar beliefs are implicit in Indian calls for eliminating superpower naval rivalry in the Indian Ocean and for maintaining it as a "zone of peace," and in the Indian rejection of Pakistan's call for creating a "nuclear-free zone" in South Asia unless this principle was extended universally. The success of Indian efforts here are again expected to ensure regional dominance and peace. Needless to say, Pakistan and some of the other smaller states in the region see such attitudes and plans as detrimental to their own national security and independence. Moreover, it is the interlocking global balance-of-power politics that has enabled India to offset the Chinese threat—for instance, through the security benefits that accrue to India from Sino-Soviet rivalry.

The Indian rejection of the balance-of-power concept, however, is also based on the belief that its practice would lead to constant great-power intrusions in the internal affairs of middle and smaller powers. Attempts to produce a military balance between India and Pakistan—two states of completely unequal size at nonmilitary levels—would link regional-conflict issues to global-conflict issues, thus substituting Indian regional dominance for that of one or more of the great powers. The total effect would be less regional independence all around and greater chances of more intensive and extensive wars occuring in South Asia.

Perceptions of Regional and Global Threats

Since gaining independence from Britain in August 1947, India has fought wars with Pakistan in 1948, 1965, and 1971, and with China in 1962. Immediate and visible threats, therefore, continue to be perceived from these two neighboring states. Variations of these two basic threats are essentially two-fold: the possibility of military collusion between China and Pakistan that might result in a two-pronged attack, one of which could be diversionary while the other attained its objective; and indirect threats stemming from other military ties to these two states, such as that of Pakistan with some of the Middle East states, and of China with the United States. Certain internal threats also exist in the form of periodic communal rioting and separatist movements among various groups in India.

In the case of Pakistan, the threat was initially enhanced by its membership in the America-led SEATO and CENTO defense pacts in the 1950s. Although the American purpose in setting up these two treaties was to counter the communist threat to the "free world" stemming from China and the

Soviet Union, Pakistan's purpose in joining the treaty organization was perceived by Indian leaders as directed against India. Nehru in a speech to the Lok Sabha on 29 March 1956 declared that the Pakistan government did not enter "into this Pact (the Baghdad-later CENTO-pact) because it expected some imminent or distant invasion or aggression from the Soviet Union. The Pakistani newspapers and the statements of responsible people in Pakistan make it perfectly clear that they have joined this pact because of India."[3]

The American arming of Pakistan under these two treaties in the late 1950s and early 1960s consequently produced a concentration of defense efforts against Pakistan and considerable strain in Indo-American diplomatic relations. The threat from this direction was aggravated subsequently by Pakistan's use of American-supplied arms against India in the 1965 war, the Nixon administration's tilt toward Pakistan during the 1971 Bangladesh crisis and ensuing Indo-Pakistani war, and the American diplomatic rapprochement with China about the same time. These events and changing security conditions eventually led to the signing of the Indo-Soviet Treaty of Peace, Friendship and Cooperation in August 1971.

Meanwhile, concentration on the Pakistani threat in the 1950s also led to the neglect of the evolving Chinese threat along the Himalayan frontier as the new communist government consolidated its position in Tibet. The Sino-Indian border war in 1962 and the subsequent quasi-alliance forged between China and Pakistan established a dual threat north and west of India. These two basic threats continue to appear more long-term because of unresolved religious, ideological, and territorial differences. No doubt, tensions could ease between India and her two neighbors as some issues are resolved or fade away; however, certain fundamental geopolitical conditions existing in the region will call for continuous security precautions against both states.

More recently and distantly, newer threats to India have surfaced by way of these two traditional adversaries. First, there has been growing economic interdependence and accompanying strategic linkages between the states of the Indian subcontinent and the Middle East. While oil is being exchanged for a variety of Indian and Pakistani consumer and investment goods and labor services, the accumulation of petro-dollars in the Middle East has also led to a large-scale and sophisticated arms build-up in the area. Also, the earlier secession of Bangladesh from Pakistan has provoked the latter state to turn westward to the Islamic Middle East to balance the dominance of India in the subcontinent. Pakistani policies here have included strengthening—until the overthrow of the Shah of Iran in 1979—the Regional Cooperation for Development organization among itself, Turkey, and Iran; the sponsoring of Islamic summit conferences to generate solidarity among Muslim nations; and pushing for an Islamic defense pact including the development of an Islamic nuclear bomb. The Middle East arms build-up may therefore prove relevant in future Indo-Pakistani conflicts since it may strengthen Pakistani ties with Muslim states.

Secondly, the double and more credible nuclear deterrent against China that had hitherto been provided by both the United States and the Soviet Union, has now been reduced to the single and less credible deterrent provided by the Soviet Union alone. The new situation was ushered in with the visit of President Richard Nixon to Peking in February 1972. As a result of that meeting, a Chinese conventional or nuclear threat during a subcontinental crisis was likely to appear more effective because of the cordial and quasi-alliance relationship that had come to exist between the United States and China. The nuclear stalemate between the two superpowers also bolstered the Chinese threat. The American hands-off policy and Soviet inaction beyond verbal condemnations during the Chinese invasion of Vietnam in early 1979—despite the existence of the Soviet-Vietnamese Friendship Treaty—is indicative of likely behavior among the various parties in potential future South Asian crises.

Thus, the prospect of Pakistan developing nuclear weapons in collaboration with other Islamic nations, together with the eroding credibility of nuclear guarantees provided by the superpowers against China, compel India to retain its nuclear option. In this respect, note that apart from the decision to explode a nuclear device in 1974, India's strategy before and after this event has been to maintain the nuclear *option* rather than to become a nuclear power. Indeed, to engage in a nuclear-arms race with China might enhance the Chinese nuclear threat rather than reduce it, because India might find itself always several years away from achieving a deterrent retaliatory-strike capability.[4] Meanwhile, the Chinese may be tempted to preempt and destroy the growing Indian nuclear capability without fear of retaliation.

On the other hand, maintaining the option serves two essential purposes. First, it has been used by India as a bargaining chip to pressure the United States and the Soviet Union into providing more credible guarantees and safeguards. Second, it has enabled India to pressure the existing nuclear "haves," including China, into reducing and eliminating their nuclear stockpiles. For India, proliferation is perceived to be not merely the spread of nuclear weapons among the present "have-nots" (horizontal proliferation), but also the growth of more sophisticated and destructive nuclear weapons among the present "haves" (vertical proliferation). The latter form of proliferation is perceived to be as dangerous to world civilization as the former.

In addition to external threats, certain internal-security problems have existed or continue to exist that may be exploited by outside powers. These include various separatist movements among the Naga, Mizo, Gharo, and other tribal communities in the northeast; the Tamil separatist movement for a Dravidastan in the south; the Sikh movement for a Punjabi Suba in the north—with demands by some extremists in the 1940s for a separate Sikhistan; and the large Muslim religious minority scattered throughout India whose loyalties are still perceived by some extreme Hindu leaders and groups as lying with Pakistan. With the creation of the new states of Nagaland, Mizoram, and Meghalaya out of Assam, and with the separation of the new state of Haryana from Punjab to allow for a Sikh majority there, the northeast tribal and northern Sikh separatist tendencies have largely been diffused. Meanwhile, the Tamil separatist movement led by the now divided Dravida Munnetra Kazagham party has also lost much of its steam. Nevertheless, it is important to note that the *potential* balkanization of India has always been much greater than in the case of Pakistan, although it was the latter country that first experienced disintegration with the separation and independence of Bangladesh in 1971.

Foreign Policy and Strategic Objectives

Assumptions about the international system and perceptions of external threats are reflected in India's strategic objectives and conduct of foreign policy. In the first place, foreign policy is directed toward neutralizing Pakistan's anti-Indian propaganda, especially regarding its claim to the disputed state of Kashmir, two-thirds of which is held by India. Although thwarting Pakistani efforts to seize Kashmir by force lies within the realm of Indian defense capabilities, the possibility still exists of losing the state through international diplomatic pressure at the United Nations and other world forums. In particular, successive Indian governments under Prime Ministers Nehru, Shastri, Gandhi, and Desai have all considered it vital to solicit the support of Muslim states or at least to maintain their neutrality on the Kashmir issue. Such a policy was considered imperative both to demonstrate to the Muslim population of Kashmir external Islamic support for the Indian government's Kashmir policy, as well as to retain the confidence of the large Muslim minority in India. Overwhelming external support for Pakistan from other Muslim nations and a general internal Muslim revolt against the government's policies could make the Indian position on Kashmir as difficult as a direct military attack by Pakistan.

As a consequence, India has always strongly supported the Arab position on the Palestinian issue. Even after the signing of the Israeli-Egyptian Peace Treaty in 1979, India has continued to support the Palestinian cause for fear of alienating the other Arab states. In contrast, there has been little reciprocal support for India's policy on Kashmir, except for mild neutrality in the past from Egypt, together with some Arab admonishments to both parties to settle the Kashmir dispute peacefully. Indeed, during the Indo-Pakistani wars of 1965 and 1971, with the exception of Egypt, Afghanistan, Malaysia, and the Muslim nations of black Africa, most of the other Islamic states, Arab and non-Arab, have tacitly or openly supported Pakistan in varying degrees. Nevertheless, such temporary setbacks in the Islamic world were considered as problems to be overcome through diplomacy, and here India has been largely successful in recent years.

The second major thrust of India's foreign policy is directed toward neutralizing the Chinese threat. Unlike the Pakistani threat, which could be met through an Indian defense build-up, meeting the Chinese threat independently was considered beyond the limits of Indian defense capabilities. In July 1962, three months before the outbreak of Sino-Indian hostilities, the former Chief-of-Army Staff, General K.S. Thimayya, stated that "whereas in the case of Pakistan I have considered the possibility of a total war, I am afraid I cannot do so in regard to China. I cannot even as a soldier envisage India taking on China in an open conflict on its own. It must be left to the politicians and diplomats to ensure our security."[5]

The security of India against China has consequently always rested on external political maneuvering. In a sense, these efforts may appear to contradict India's general rejection of balance-of-power politics since it is the prevalence of such politics at the global level that permits the forestalling of a major Chinese offensive. In the absence of such conditions, the mere threat of a Chinese attack could effectively freeze any Indian military action against Pakistan and permit the latter state to follow a more adventurous policy on the subcontinent.

Efforts to produce security against China may be seen in the varying interpretations and applications of the standard Indian foreign-policy doctrine of nonalignment. In the 1950s Nehru's nonalignment policy was underwritten by the 1954 Sino-Indian Treaty on Tibet.[6] The treaty's preamble included the declaration of *panchshil*, the five principles of peaceful coexistence that essentially charged both sides not to use force to settle disputes between them. In one respect, it was Nehru's confidence in *panchshil* that enabled India to reject Western offers to join their military-alliance system. With *panchshil* appearing to resolve the more proximate Chinese threat problem, the wider declaration of nonalignment was expected to eliminate Soviet hostility.

The Sino-Indian border war of 1962 radically altered that situation. After some initial but hesitant moves to join the Western-alliance network, the doctrine of nonalignment was once again reemphasized. However, declarations of "positive" and "realistic" nonalignment suggested a newer interpretation, and practice thereafter indicated closer ties, both political and military, with the Soviet Union. This tilt was justified and made possible by the intensifying Sino-Soviet rift and by the American unwillingness to arm India at the cost of alienating its ally Pakistan. Nevertheless, American hostility toward China continued until 1971, and this fact in combination with Sino-Soviet hostility provided India with a double indemnity against a Chinese conventional or nuclear attack.

The Nixon administration's unexpected diplomatic approach toward China in 1971-1972, coinciding as it did with the year-long Bangladesh crisis, suddenly made India almost entirely dependent on the Soviet Union. The new situation immediately produced the Indo-Soviet Treaty of August 1971, which included clauses of a quasi-military nature.[7] At the time of its signing the treaty was intended to raise the risk for China of any major military diversion on the subcontinent during an Indo-Pakistan war, although admittedly such an explanation for Chinese nonaction in the 1971 war must remain hypothetical.

Later, in retrospect, the extreme dependence on the Soviet Union since 1970 was viewed as unsatisfactory and efforts were made to reduce it by the new Janata government that assumed office in March 1977.[8] Janata attempts to follow a more neutral interpretation of nonalignment were based on simultaneous efforts to normalize relations with China. Some major shifts away from the Soviet Union were therefore attempted by the Janata government as India's relations with both China and the United States showed improvement. These included the rejection of the Soviet offer to produce the MiG-23 Flogger in India and the selection instead of the Anglo-French Jaguar fighter-bomber; and a search for tanks, submarines, and other weapons in the Western European arms market. However, this search was suddenly aborted with the collapse of the Janata government in October 1979. The return to power of Indira Gandhi's Congress party in January 1980 has produced a reversal to a Soviet-dependent arms-acquisition policy. This reversal may be seen in a $1.6 billion low-interest arms-purchase agreement concluded by India with the Soviet Union in June 1980.

Determining Force Levels and Weapon Systems

With respect to Pakistan, the general Indian policy over the last thirty years has been to maintain a "slight edge" in military capabilities on the ground and in the air. With respect to China, the policy has been to maintain sufficient ground forces for a "holding" operation along the Himalayan border. A deeper Chinese ground penetration into the Indian plains or a major air attack on Indian cities and military installations were expected to be forestalled through great-power diplomacy or even their military action. Countering the nuclear threat from China rests similarly on external nuclear guarantees, although doubts about the reliability of this policy continue to keep alive the nuclear-option debate in India. Policies that determine the force levels and the weapon systems needed to meet the threats from Pakistan and China are therefore fundamentally different. One rests heavily on maintaining capabilities; the other mainly on diplomacy.

The policy of maintaining a slight edge against Pakistan was most easily carried out in the case of the Indian Army, where manpower training and weapons production are relatively simple. The slight-edge policy may be seen at the commencements of the 1965 and 1971 Indo-Pakistani wars. In 1965 the Indian Army had ten infantry divisions to Pakistan's eight, and one armored division to Pakistan's two.[9] Similarly, in 1971 there were thirteen Indian infantry divisions to Pakistan's twelve, while both sides had two armored divisions. By 1979 four more infantry divisions had been raised on either side, as well as some additional independent armored brigades. Army equipment consisted mainly of various tanks and artillery pieces. Here the difference has been the steady increase in the quality and quantity of such weapons on the Indian side, thus reversing the advantage possessed by Pakistan in the early 1960s when sophisticated American arms such as the M-47/48 Patton tanks were supplied under the SEATO and CENTO defense pacts. Today, some 250 aging Patton tanks continue to be deployed by Pakistan, although an additional 700 T-59 medium tanks acquired from China now constitute the backbone of the Pakistani armored divisions. These are complemented by another 100 assorted light tanks, including about 50 T-54/55 tanks briefly supplied by the Soviet Union more than a decade ago. As against this, India acquired some 900 T-54/55 tanks from the Soviet Union between the middle and late 1960s, while another 700 Vijayanta light tanks manufactured in India have also since been deployed. For the 1980s, India has concluded an agreement with the Soviet Union for the manufacture of the T-72 battle tank under license in India, while Pakistan is expected to receive an undisclosed number of the M-60 tank from the United States as part of a larger arms-package transfer.

Since air-force defense programs tend to be more capital intensive and consequently, more dependent on external arms sources and technical assistance, the policy of keeping a step ahead of Pakistan becomes more difficult and less certain. Given the variety of aircraft being obtained by India and Pakistan from several sources, and given also the different missions and quality levels these weapons carry, estimates about who is ahead are more difficult to establish. Quantitative comparisons are less meaningful in the case of the air force than in the case of the army. Broadly, it would appear that Pakistan maintained air superiority until the mid-1960s, with this situation being reversed by the time of the 1971 Indo-Pakistan war.

The arms race in combat aircraft on the subcontinent began with the American decision to supply Pakistan with several squadrons of the then comparatively sophisticated F-86 Sabres, F-104 Starfighters, and B-57B Canberras.[10] At about the same time India responded by purchasing several squadrons of Hunter-MK56 fighters, B-1 Canberra bombers, Mystere-IVA interceptors, and MD-450 Ouragons from Britain and France. Meanwhile, the Gnat interceptor manufactured in India under licensed agreement with Folland Aircraft and Bristol Siddley of Britain, as well as the Indian-made HF-24 Marut fighter-bomber, were in various stages of deployment. By the late 1960s these aircraft were joined by the MiG-21 interceptors manufactured in India with Soviet assistance and by the SU-7B fighter-bomber purchased from the Soviet Union. Pakistan's response to these newer Indian acquisitions was to obtain several squadrons of MiG-19/F-6 interceptors from China, and Mirage-IIIEPs and V's from France. Currently a new arms spiral has been generated with the Indian decision to purchase and later manufacture in India the Anglo-French Jaguar fighter-bomber.[11] On the Pakistani side, earlier efforts to obtain the American A-7 Corsair fighter-bomber failed, and the American offer to sell F-5E interceptors instead has not yet been accepted. Subsequently, however, the Soviet invasion of Afghanistan in December 1979, followed a year later by the advent of the Reagan administration in Washington, resulted in a major American-Pakistani arms agreement. The agreement, reached in June 1981, included a decision to transfer an estimated 100 F-16 modern fighter planes to Pakistan. Even as these negotiations were afoot, New Delhi concluded an agreement with France for the manufacture of the Mirage-2000 under license in India by the late 1980s.

Until the late 1960s neither side had a navy of any serious magnitude and there was virtually no naval arms race on the subcontinent.[12] Consequently, neither side perceived a threat by sea despite India's 3,000-mile-unguarded coastline and Pakistan's ultimate dependence on sea routes between its eastern and western wings should land and air links be cut by India. Under these conditions, wars until 1971 had been confined to land and air. However, since the late 1960s a comparatively modest expansion and modernization of the Indian Navy had begun in response to navy demands in India for greater military balance among the services and the need to protect the growing Indian seaborne trade. Although such belated Indian naval acquisitions did not appear threatening, it nevertheless proved sufficient to overwhelm the neglected Pakistan Navy during the 1971 war. Currently, the Indo-Pakistani naval arms race continues to be relatively low key, although some major naval purchases have been reported in the 1980 Indo-Soviet arms agreement, which included Kashin destroyers and Nanuchka corvettes.

As already noted, there is no serious effort to counter the growth of Chinese military power at all levels—land, air, and nuclear. The only significant defense program against China was the raising of ten mountain divisions equipped with light arms and ammunition in the immediate years after the 1962 Sino-Indian war. The value of these mountain divisions as a form of defense against China may now appear questionable. They could well turn out to be India's Maginot Line—a defense designed to fight another 1962-type Himalayan border war for which India was then ill-prepared. However, the present Indian strength along the Himalayas may prove sufficient if the bulk of Chinese ground forces are drawn and pinned down along the Soviet, Vietnamese, and Korean borders. In any case, these mountain divisions proved unexpectedly useful during the 1971 Indo-

Pakistan war, which for the first time was fought on two fronts, when two or three of these divisions were diverted to the East Pakistan border for the liberation of Bangladesh.

Economic and Technological Constraints

Indian political rhetoric has always emphasized the need for self-reliance and self-sufficiency in defense. In practice this goal continues to remain distant. Even in the case of the Pakistani threat, efforts by India to maintain an edge have proved elusive as Pakistan continued to acquire arms from the United States, China, France, and the Middle East. This in turn has produced countermeasures in India, thereby constantly placing stress on India's domestic economic and technological capabilities. With respect to the Chinese threat, as we have seen, the objective of self-sufficiency has never been seriously attempted although declarations of intent, especially at the nuclear level, persist.

Defense programs in India are shaped by official perceptions of their impact on economic development and are restricted by Indian technological know-how. Ironically, these economic and technological constraints also shape the nature of external threats since adversaries are responding to Indian defense programs in their planning. This has been particularly true in the case of Pakistan. A recent example is the Pakistani attempt, with the financial assistance of Libya, to develop an "Islamic" bomb as a response to the Indian atomic test of 1974. Now, should India attempt to counter present Pakistani nuclear efforts, this is likely to aggravate the Chinese nuclear threat, thereby further increasing substantially the stresses on India's economic and technological resources.

Although Indian defense programs could intensify the arms race in the region, a converse effect is also evident. The modest level of Indian defense spending, which has averaged about 3.6 percent of the GNP—among the lowest of the major countries in the world—has also produced a certain braking effect on the regional arms race.[13] As long as Pakistan was responding to defense programs in India, India could control the nature and pace of the arms race on the subcontinent. Thus Pakistan could reduce its constantly rising economic burden by conceding Indian military superiority within the limits of some acceptable ratio of, say, 2 to 1 or 5 to 3. Neither side need then engage in a crippling and futile arms race. However, this would not resolve Pakistan's sense of insecurity and its goal of annexing Indian-held Kashmir. Nor would the maintenance of such a ratio help India cope with the wider threats perceived from China and to a lesser extent from the Middle East. A freeze in defense programs on the subcontinent would therefore appear difficult to achieve for the present.

The interlocking nature of external threats, defense programs, and economic development is reflected in the composition of the Indian Armed

Services and their weapon systems. In terms of annual budgetary allocations, the Indian Army constitutes the largest of the three Indian services, receiving about 68 to 70 percent of the defense budget.[14] Air force and naval shares have been around 20 to 22 percent and 8 to 10 percent, respectively. This is partly because proposed army programs are usually economically and technologically feasible except for some of the equipment needs of its armored divisions. The Pakistani defense program has responded in kind, thereby justifying the emphasis on army defense programs in India. The case of the more capital-intensive and technologically difficult air-force defense program has been somewhat different. Although Pakistan has often generated the arms race in combat aircraft through various overseas acquisitions, the general unwillingness of Western nations to supply sophisticated arms indiscriminately as well as Pakistan's own economic inability to buy extensively in the overseas arms market has provided restraints until now to what could have been an economically destructive air-force arms race for both countries. However, recent announced Indian and Pakistani acquisitions, respectively, from the Soviet Union and the United States suggest that these constraints have become relaxed. Strangely, in the case of the navy, modest growth of this service in India has not been seriously countered by Pakistan. The policies of both India and Pakistan have been somewhat unusual since naval-defense programs may carry comparatively greater economic and technological spin-offs for the civilian sector of the economy than air-force defense programs. The commercial shipping industry can more readily utilize less-sophisticated ships generated by naval technology than can the commercial air-transport industry. The needed technological know-how in shipbuilding is also simpler than aircraft technology. However, from the Indian standpoint, without many visible Pakistani or Chinese sea-borne threats, prospects for naval-defense growth in India remains limited.

Arguments resting on the complementary nature of defense and development are most forcefully voiced on the issue of India's nuclear option. The spending on India's nuclear-energy program, which has constantly been declared for peaceful purposes, is only 10 percent of the entire defense program, the latter in itself being quite modest when measured as a percentage of the Indian GNP. Although Indian claims that there can be such a thing as peaceful nuclear explosions for mining and irrigation will continue to generate skepticism abroad, more convincing arguments rest on the positive linkages and feedback between military and civilian nuclear research and development. Other arguments by the pro-bomb lobby in India point to the economic benefits that may be obtained through a corresponding reduction in the conventional military program. The costs of maintaining a million men in uniform in the nonproductive activity of security could prove economically more disastrous than a military nuclear program that may carry spill-over economic and technological benefits for the civilian sector.

Domestic Political Considerations

Domestic politics underlying the formulation of Indian security policy may be examined at three levels: the power of prime ministers; the impact of party politics and parliamentary debates; and the influence of the military with civilian defense decision makers.

During the Nehru years from 1947 to 1964, foreign and defense policy making were largely the domain of the Indian prime minister. India's Kashmir policy, nonalignment doctrine, leadership of the third world, its policies toward China and the Soviet Union, friendship with Egypt and attitudes toward the Arab-Israeli dispute, and its Goa policy, were all largely formulated by Prime Minister Nehru. During this time, he was also influenced to some extent by his representative to the United Nations and later defense minister, V.K. Krishna Menon. But ultimate policy was usually formulated by the first Indian prime minister. Although some voices called for stronger action toward Pakistan and expressed doubts about India's Tibetan policy, such dissent was subdued and carried little impact on defense policymaking. Even after the 1962 Indian military defeat in the Sino-Indian war, Nehru was trusted to lead the nation out of the national military and emotional crisis. Nehru's offer to resign along with others who were compelled to do so—Defense Minister Krishna Menon, Defense Secretary O. Pulla Reddy, and Chief-of-Army Staff General P.N. Thapar—was opposed by members of Parliament.

The new national concern and parliamentary debates after 1962 on the state of India's defenses did not produce any significant influence on the formulation and conduct of defense policy until after the death of Nehru in 1964. Thereafter, the impact on policy of Prime Ministers Lal Bahadur Shastri, Indira Gandhi, and Morarji Desai has varied. Unlike the undisputed leadership of Nehru in the prime-ministerial post, all three subsequent prime ministers have had to contend with challengers for the position, and their external policies have been subject to greater scrutiny. An exception to this general condition in the post-Nehru era was a brief period after the exhilarating Indian military victory over Pakistan in 1971 when Mrs. Gandhi carried undisputed popular support and political power. In contrast, the least powerful of the prime ministers has been Morarji Desai, who on two previous occasions had challenged and failed to obtain the prime ministership. Even his eventual selection as prime minister in the Janata government set up in March 1977 was a compromise decision within a coalition and faction-ridden party. Consequently, his ability to direct defense policy without question was comparatively low. Thus, while Nehru's Kashmir policy was virtually unquestioned at home, and while Indira Gandhi was acclaimed for liberating Bangladesh by armed force, Desai's interpretation of nonalignment, his pronouncements on the Sino-Indian border issue, and his nuclear policy, were all subject to condemnations within and outside parliament.

At the second analytical level suggested earlier, that of party politics and parliamentary debates, note that before 1977 the continued dominance of the Congress party in the central legislature had enabled it to wield the responsibility of Parliament as a whole in defense matters. Disapproval by the small and fragmented political opposition could always be disregarded as of little importance since this was expected to have little bearing on the outcome of national elections. At the same time, opposition within the Congress party was usually disciplined by the party whip and dissenting members were made to align themselves with government policy during parliamentary voting. Consequently, shattering military failures such as the NEFA debacle in November 1962 and the Rann of Kutch fiasco with Pakistan in April 1965 could not produce parliamentary pressures sufficient to threaten the continued rule of the Congress party. What occurred then was essentially individual ministerial accountability to the ruling party, much less cabinet responsibility to Parliament as a whole, and little parliamentary control over defense.

These conditions had changed following the defeat of the Congress party at the 1977 general elections. During the brief period of Janata rule from March 1977 to October 1979, there was some resemblance to the two-party parliamentary situation found in Britain. The Congress party had remained a sizeable opposition in the Lok Sabha, capable of displacing the party in power. The ruling party under these circumstances would feel more accountable to parliament as a whole. However, in 1979 with the defections of M.P.s from the Janata party, the loss of its majority in the Lok Sabha, and with the resignation of Desai as prime minister, the performance of the new political system was never seriously tested.

The general lack of parliamentary control over defense policymaking in India is not due merely to the distribution of party seats in parliament; much of the problem is also found in the inability of M.P.s to comprehend the complex nature of strategic questions and military detail. This situation is in part created by the government's overwhelming insistence on secrecy on the ground that disclosure of details of some weapons negotiations or internal weapons-production difficulties would not be in the national interest. Consequently, M.P.s having little information to initiate a serious debate are then obliged to toe the goverment line for fear of undermining national security.

This problem is perhaps partly alleviated by periodic investigations into defense production by some of the standing parliamentary committees: the Estimates Committee, the Public Accounts Committee, and the Committee on Public Undertakings. Although neither their recommendations nor subsequent actions taken by government are drastic, nevertheless these committees perform two useful functions. First, they tend to educate at least the participating M.P.s in the economic costs and efficiency of the defense-production sector in India and indirectly the value of certain defense programs in terms of strategic necessities. Second, the committees have served the limited purpose of maintaining a watch on possible misappropriation or misuse of funds allotted to defense and have generally prevented excessive waste.

Regarding the third level of analysis, the influence of the military on the civilian decision-making process has not been substantial. Military dabblings in national politics are rare and civilian control over the military is virtually complete. Before 1962, the general neglect of the military services was highlighted by the controversy between Defense Minister Krishna Menon and Chief-of-Army Staff, General K.S. Thimayya. Menon, while taking an active interest in the defense system and also pushing for increased defense programs, made no effort at the same time to hide his disdain for the army. He considered it to be a "parade ground army" that continued to be subservient to British traditions and practice. A similar ambivalence toward the army prevailed in general among members of Parliament during this time. The Menon-Thimayya episode had produced an angry reaction in Parliament mainly because of a general dislike for the arrogant defense minister who had managed to gain the confidence of Prime Minister Nehru, rather than because of a concern for army morale and prestige. The air force and the navy did not fare much better than the army. Although there were several sizeable purchases of aircraft for the air force in the fifties and attempts were made to develop an indigenous fighter-bomber, these programs did not attract serious political attention in Parliament. As noted earlier, the navy remained neglected until after 1965.

The 1962 Sino-Indian war and 1965 Indo-Pakistan war served to draw political attention to the needs of the services. However, service input into the defense policymaking process did not increase in proportion to its ability to raise force levels and acquire more weapons. For example, although the navy obtained several new cruisers, submarines, and torpedo boats after 1965, its efforts to continue military collaboration with Britain have largely failed. The Congress party's political shift toward the Soviet Union overrode the naval preference for British vessels. Except for the construction of the Leander-class destroyers at Mazagon Docks in Bombay with British technical cooperation, almost all major naval purchases have been from the Soviet Union. A similar political shift may be seen in the production and purchase deals involving the MiG-21 interceptor and the SU-7B fighter bomber for the air force, and the purchase of several hundred T-54/55 and PT-76 tanks for the army.

The structure of the defense decision-making apparatus in itself limits the role that the services can play on broader defense policy decisions. Until 1962, the policymaking apparatus consisted of a three-tier committee system consisting of the Defense Committee of the Cabinet (DCC), the Defense Minister's Committee (DMC), and the Chiefs-of-Staff Committee (CSC). This three-tier framework was supplemented or appended by a constellation of other advisory and information-gathering committees. The CSC was aided by a Joint Planning Committee that contained representatives of the three services. The CSC had been created on the British pattern under the chairmanship of a service chief who held the position by seniority. This committee was expected to coordinate the activities of the three services and to offer expert advice to the defense minister and through him to the cabinet. The DMC therefore played an intermediary role between the service chiefs and members of the DCC.

After the 1962 war, the DCC was renamed the Emergency Committee of the Cabinet (ECC) to reflect the urgency of the situation and to denote the importance of its deliberations. Although a provision had existed in the past for the attendance of the service chiefs during the DCC meetings, invitations to do so became more regular after 1962. The new attendance policy was an improvement over past arrangements because until 1963 the service chiefs had no formal access to the highest levels of defense policymaking. No doubt they could always approach the prime minister directly if their proposals were repeatedly turned down at meetings of the DMC, but this right was seldom exercised without the knowledge and consent of the defense minister.

In more recent years, the three-tier committee system of decision making has been subject to two further changes to the greater disadvantage of the armed services headquarters. At the top level, the DCC/ECC has been replaced by a Cabinet Committee on Political Affairs (CCPA) whose agenda includes problems of external security, domestic political unrest and violence, and economic crises such as cut-off of oil imports that could affect the underlying stability of the country. The expanded committee, however, has reduced the frequency and importance of the participation by the service chiefs since the CCPA is concerned with an array of other problems not directly connected with defense. Additionally, at the middle level, the DMC has been quietly displaced by a new Defense Planning Committee (DPC) consisting of seven senior civil servants and the three service chiefs. The DPC is presided over by the cabinet secretary and includes the secretary to the prime minister, the secretaries of defense and defense production, and the secretaries of external affairs, home affairs, and the planning commission. The overwhelming representation of civil servants against the military services has again caused some unhappiness at the three armed services headquarters as military inputs into defense policymaking was being further curtailed.

The structural relationship limiting the political decision-making role of the military has not led to any major friction between the services and the civilian decision makers. The Menon-Thimayya episode was more of an aberration and resulted only because of excessive civilian interference in what the army considered their professional domain. Unlike several states of the third world—and more pertinently Pakistan and Bangladesh, which grew out of the same historical and traditional background—the Indian services have been content to maintain their generally apolitical status in conformity with the Western political ethic regarding civilian control over the military.

Prospects

The substance and direction of Indian defense policy have been subject to considerable stresses during the last decade at the strategic and domestic levels. India's strategic environment has undergone substantial transformation during the 1970s. This included the breakup of Pakistan in 1971; the British decision to withdraw its forces east of Suez in 1971, which ushered in superpower naval rivalry in the Indian Ocean; the rapprochement between the United States and China since 1972; the high Indian economic dependency on the Middle East states since the oil crisis of 1973 and the accompanying arms accumulation in this region; India's entry into the nuclear club with the atomic explosion of 1974; increasing Sino-Vietnamese hostility since 1978; the overthrow of the Shah of Iran in 1979; and the Soviet invasion of Afghanistan in late December 1979. At the domestic level there have been various economic crises and political instabilities. The Emergency rule of Prime Minister Indira Gandhi in June 1975 was partly precipitated by the sudden increase in the Indian oil-import burden and poor monsoon rains that left the economy crippled. Subsequent improvement in India's economic health, however, could not stop the collapse of the Congress party at the March 1977 general elections; and continued disunity within the Janata party eventually led to the loss of its parliamentary majority in the Lok Sabha and a return to Congress government in 1980.

Despite these significant changes and events in the 1970s, there are, nevertheless, some improvements in India's strategic environment and domestic political situation. Events in Iran, Afghanistan, and Southeast Asia have tended to preoccupy India's traditional adversaries, whereas the return of Indira Gandhi to power suggests signs of domestic political stability and a stronger defense policy abroad.

Notes

1. For two discussions of the defense-development debate, see K. Subrahmanyam, *Defence and Development* (Calcutta: Minerva Associates, 1973); and Emile Benoit, *Defense and Economic Growth in Developing Countries* (Lexington, Mass.: Lexington Books, D.C. Heath and Company 1973).

2. Jawaharlal Nehru, *India's Foreign Policy: Selected Speeches, September 1946-April 1961* (New Delhi: Publications Division, Government of India, 1961), pp. 79-80. For a discussion see Raju G.C. Thomas, "Nonalignment and Indian Security: Nehru's Rationale and Legacy," *Journal of Strategic Studies* (September 1979):153-171.

3. Ibid., p. 94.

4. For a somewhat different assessment of India's nuclear capability, see Onkar C. Marwah, "India's Nuclear and Space Programs: Intent and Policy," *International Security* (Fall 1977):96-121.

5. Cited by S.S. Khera in his *India's Defense Problem* (New Delhi: Orient Longman, 1968), p. 158.

6. See Nehru, *India's Foreign Policy*, p. 99.

7. For a full text of the treaty, see *Current Digest of the Soviet Press*, 7 September 1971, p. 5.

8. For a more detailed discussion, see Raju G.C. Thomas, "Indian Defense Policy: Continuity and Change Under the Janata Government," *Pacific Affairs* 53 (Summer 1980):500-518.

9. From The International Institute for Strategic Studies, *The Military Balance* (London, 1965-1966 and 1971-1972). For the historical growth of the army, see Stephen P. Cohen, *The Indian Army: Its Contribution to the Development of a Nation* (Berkeley, Calif.: University of California Press, 1971).

10. See chapters on the air force in Lorne Kavic's *India's Quest for Security: Defense Policies, 1945-65* (Berkeley, Calif.: University of California Press, 1967), and Raju G.C. Thomas, *The Defence of India: A Budgetary Perspective of Strategy and Politics* (New Delhi: Macmillan Company of India, 1978; Columbia, Mo.: South Asia Books, 1978).

11. See Raju G.C. Thomas, "Aircraft for the Indian Air Force: The Context and Implications of the Jaguar Decision," *Orbis* 24 (Spring 1980): 85-102.

12. See Raju G.C. Thomas, "The Indian Navy in the Seventies," *Pacific Affairs* 48 (Winter 1975-1976):500-518.

13. Defense/GNP figures are drawn from the *Institute for Defence Studies and Analyses Journal*, 4 (April 1972), and various issues of *The Military Balance*. For an explanation of the budgetary distribution, see Raju G.C. Thomas, "The Armed Services and the Indian Defense Budget," *Asian Survey* 20 (March 1980):280-297.

14. See table 4 in Thomas, *The Defence of India*, p. 147, and tables 2 and 3 in Thomas, "The Armed Services," *Asian Survey* 20 (March 1980): 284.

7 Vietnam

Sheldon Simon

Southeast Asia appears to be a region unsuitable for stable peace. Culturally heterogeneous, its various modern nationalisms have clashed over the past fifty years, echoing the centuries of conflict among predecessor empires. Today, the region is rent by ideological animosities, urban-rural rivalries, competitive economies, population pressures, minority ethnic problems, and troublesome insurgencies.

Moreover, Southeast Asia must cope not only with indigenous rivalries but also with the designs of outside powers. These range from the region's great neighbor, China—which has historically regarded it as an area to be kept in a divided and subordinate condition—to more remote powers over the last century: Western Europe, Japan, the United States, and the Soviet Union.

Vietnam is located in the virtual geographic center of this region of turmoil. Since the ruling Communist party managed to capture popular nationalist sentiments as early as the 1930s, its leadership now sees itself as the rightful successor to the French rulers of all Indochina.[1] The Lao Dong party has also displayed remarkable leadership continuity and solidarity. Despite the protracted stress of forty years of uninterrupted warfare, only one politburo member has defected. In 1979, Hoang Van Hoan, who had lost his post the year before because of avowedly pro-Chinese sentiments, eluded his associates in Pakistan and boarded a flight to Peking. He was warmly received and has since been regularly broadcasting propaganda broadsides against Hanoi's Asian policies. Although several thousand lower- and middle-ranked party members were purged in 1979 to make way for younger technocrats, the central-committee level and above have remained relatively stable.

Vietnam's role conception as regional leader forms the basis for its current conflicts with China and the Association of Southeast Asian Nations (ASEAN, composed of Malaysia, Thailand, Philippines, Singapore, and Indonesia) within Asia and with the United States and Western Europe outside the region. As in the past, this lineup of adversaries also leads to Vietnam's choice of allies—in this case the Soviet Union and its Eastern European associates in COMECON (the Moscow-oriented Council of Mutual Economic Assistance). Little has changed for Vietnam strategically; although the identity of allies and adversaries may vary, the desire on the part of some regional states to constrain Vietnam's ambitions persists. For

Vietnam, the international environment remains constraining, despite the Vietnam Peoples Army (VPA) military victory in 1975 that led to the country's political reunification and subsequently its hegemonic position within Indochina at the end of the decade.

This chapter explores the contemporary evolution of Communist Vietnam's security policy, initially by discussing its view of the international environment both before and after the SRV's (Socialist Republic of Vietnam) 1975 victory and comparing perceived threats to its security during those periods. The chapter then turns to the manner in which the SRV has responded to these threats by means of diplomacy as well as military-force composition and deployment. Tradeoff problems between military and civilian needs for Vietnam's limited resources are assessed along with differing views within the political leadership over economic developmental versus security responsibilities for the military since the end of the second Indochina war. The chapter concludes with a review of Vietnam's politico-diplomatic alignment options and calculations.

Vietnam's View of the International System—
Threats and Supports

As a middle-sized divided state with a legacy of French colonial rule, North Vietnam (the SRV's predecessor) strove for almost three decades to acquire the weapons, organization, and skill to expel the United States from Vietnam and effect a series of coordinated Communist victories in Vietnam, Laos, and Cambodia. Although the Vietminh—who were led by Ho Chi Minh—were doggedly opposed to French colonialism, they were not necessarily anti-Western. Desirous of Western technology for modernization and hoping for Western political support for independence, the Vietminh worked with both the American and British forces in China against the Japanese occupation in World War II. Indeed, elements of North Vietnam's first constitution were drawn from both the U.S. Constitution and Declaration of Independence. This essentially pragmatic view of international politics also led the Vietminh to turn away from the West, however, when Washington and London assisted the French in reoccupying its Indochinese colonies in 1945.

The Vietminh orientation toward China and the Soviet Union beginning in the 1950s may also be explained in essentially instrumental terms. If the French would not transfer power peacefully, then the revolutionaries had to elicit military assistance to force them out. Both Moscow and Peking were eager to oblige, for they, too, wished to expel Western influence from Asia. An alliance was forged that, while waxing and waning, basically remained steadfast until the Vietminh victory of 1975. The history of this alliance, however, demonstrated to Vietnam's Communist leaders that outside powers—even "socialist brothers"—had their own separate goals and were quite prepared to subordinate their smaller allies. Thus, at the 1954 Geneva Conference, which terminated the First Indochina War, both Moscow and Peking pressured the Vietminh to settle for considerably less than their objective: control of all Vietnam. Neither China nor the Soviet Union wished a direct confrontation with the United States at that time, so Vietminh goals were given short shrift. From the late 1950s to the mid-1960s, China seemed more supportive than the Soviet Union, viewing the guerrilla-style revolution of the Vietnam Communist Party (VCP) as a validation of Mao's revolutionary model for Asia. Beginning in the late 1960s, however, as the Vietminh changed their tactics from guerrilla to conventional warfare, China's political influence waned both because Peking advised against this tactical shift, and because the exigencies of the Sino-Soviet conflict proscribed Chinese cooperation with the Soviets in aiding Vietnam. Even in the final months before the January 1973 Paris Agreement that led to America's military withdrawal, both China and the Soviet Union disappointed Hanoi, the latter because it did not respond to the American bombing of Hanoi and Haiphong in order to protect the SALT I negotiations, and the former because it placed détente with the United States ahead of the Vietminh victory.[2]

The VPA's military strategy evolved from underground rural guerrilla origins in the 1930s, heavily influenced by Ho Chi Minh's observations of the Chinese Communist experience in southern China, to the Soviet-supplied conventional field force of the 1970s, which won the battle of Vietnam through the effective employment of modern military machinery against a demoralized, disordered, and crumbling Saigon foe.

The military organizational concept of General Giap, the Vietminh strategist, divided the revolutionary forces into three groups: main force, guerrilla, and village militia. In accord with the Maoist three-stage view of warfare, Communist forces would first take a predominantly defensive approach designed to protect its fledgling army; next, they would harass and disrupt the adversary's position in rural areas through a period of control in the countryside, during which village militia would protect the gains achieved; finally, a general offensive was launched against the enemy's urban enclaves.

This military strategy was premised on a united political front that subordinated the Communists' socialist orientation to the broader appeal of nationhood. The latter became the banner around which diverse political groups would form under Vietminh leadership. In general, this approach proved successful in both the anti-French struggle culminating in the mid-1950s as well as in the anti-American war in the South beginning in the mid-1960s. Despite the Lao Dong's emphasis on political alliance with noncommunist forces, however, the Communists had difficulties with various ethnic and religious minorities—Catholics, overseas Chinese, Hoa Hao, Cao Dai, Meo—who mistrusted either Vietminh politics or the fact that the Vietminh were lowland Vietnamese, a group that had historically persecuted them.

During the second Indochina war, a southern-led guerrilla strategy dominated until the 1968 Tet offensive in which the southern guerrillas were decimated. From that time until the 1975 victory, the fight in South Vietnam was led by northern regulars. Prior to 1968, the VPA chose not to directly provoke the Americans for fear of retaliatory assaults on northern bases before the northern army would be prepared to undertake the brunt of the action. Although it was understood that the VPA could not physically eject the U.S. Army from Vietnam, North Vietnam's purpose was to demonstrate that it could produce a stalemate, rendering the maintenance of U.S. forces on Vietnamese soil an increasingly costly political situation. This strategy, while ultimately successful between 1968 and 1973, also meant that the VPA had to absorb many more casualties than it could inflict upon the United States, thus violating the Maoist guerrilla-war dictum of not moving to the conventional warfare stage until one had overwhelming superiority. China also objected to Giap's compressed version of protracted war after 1968, in large part because it enhanced the Soviet supply role.

Although Communist Vietnam emerged victorious in 1975, seemingly achieving Ho Chi Minh's original dream of uniting Indochina through allied Communist movements, the dynamics of yet another regional conflict had already been set in motion, once again tying outside powers to local dissidents. This time the catalytic element was the Sino-American rapprochement. Growing out of U.S. efforts to enlist China's aid in obtaining a compromise from Hanoi that would facilitate an American withdrawal, the relationship solidified as the post-Mao leadership of Hua Guo-feng and Deng Xiao-bing moved to the right and began to enlist Western aid for both economic modernization and a security buildup against the Soviet Union. As China began to husband its resources for domestic development, it reduced the amount of assistance destined for Vietnam, forcing Hanoi to rely more heavily on the Soviet Union. Vietnam's shift toward Moscow was reinforced by the U.S. decisions neither to provide reconstruction aid in the aftermath of the war nor to normalize relations.

Vietnam's move toward the Soviet Union, however, only fueled China's suspicions that another encirclement policy had begun, just as China reached a modus vivendi with its former U.S. adversary. A number of potential conflict sources between China and Vietnam could be discerned at this time. These conflict sources were rooted in the traditional Chinese belief that the Chinese culture areas of mainland Southeast Asia should defer to China's security needs. Minimally, this meant that no neighboring state could ally with any outside power. Indeed, China's involvement on the Vietminh side for over two decades was designed to realize this principle against a Saigon-Washington alliance. Peking's more recent opposition to Hanoi can also be explained by the same logic—this time opposing a Moscow-Hanoi entente. China's policy toward Vietnam since 1977 echoes the imperial tradition of cutting a recalcitrant tributary state down to size through the withdrawal of aid, the dissemination of propaganda stressing Vietnam's ingratitude for past assistance, and, finally, the use of military force.

Other sources of distrust between the two included disputed land and island territorial boundaries, the future political orientation of Cambodia, and the treatment of ethnic Chinese within Vietnam. The Cambodian issue in particular reveals a kind of parallel view of the international environment from both Peking and Hanoi. Just as China insists that Hanoi must subordinate its security policy to Peking's interests—that is, no ties to outsiders—so Vietnam requires that Cambodia, and Laos, defer to Vietnamese leadership in an Indochina-wide security system.

Vietnam believes it must be treated as the dominant power in Indochina, just as China holds that its preeminent position be acknowledged by the states of mainland Southeast Asia. Since neither Hanoi nor Peking is willing to accept the other's pretensions, the stage is set for a new protracted conflict. Both leaderships believe the other to be following an encirclement policy: China points to the Vietnam-Soviet alliance formalized by the November 1978 Treaty of Friendship and Cooperation; and Vietnam cites China's military assistance to Pol Pot's Cambodia for its raids into western Vietnam during 1977-1978 and, subsequently, China's continued resupply of the Khmer Rouge guerrillas through Thailand to their bases in the Elephant and Cardomon mountains in western Cambodia.

It is interesting that the arguments made both by the Khmer Rouge against Vietnam and by Hanoi against Peking display remarkable parallels. Each larger power in the two dyads sees the smaller as the pawn of an outside state and as an agent of encirclement. Moreover, each smaller state believes that its successful revolution precludes returning to a vassal status vis-à-vis its larger neighbor. Each feels betrayed by its larger neighbor in that the latter had served as an ally for its revolutionary cause and after victory had turned against it.

Although China's hostility, Khmer Rouge belligerence, and the U.S. policy of isolation drove Vietnam toward an alliance with the Soviet Union at the end of the 1970s, this outcome was not inevitable. Indeed, there is considerable evidence that Hanoi wished to avoid choosing sides in the Sino-Soviet dispute, and it wished to construct a new, more positive relationship with the United States after 1975. For almost two years after its victory, the SRV followed moderate policies that actually served to reduce Soviet influence. Hanoi retained membership in such capitalist financial institutions as the World Bank, the International Monetary Fund (IMF), and the Asian Development Bank. It moved slowly in imposing a socialist regimen on the South and resisted Soviet pressure to join COMECON. By the spring of 1977, Vietnam had promulgated a foreign-investment code, thereby demonstrating that the government desired Western capital and technology. Although sources of friction with China existed over the Paracel and Spratly Islands, Hanoi refused to emulate Moscow's anti-Peking line. In order to effect a better relationship with the United States, Hanoi dropped allusions to America's moral and legal obligations to Vietnam. When the United States did not respond, Premier Pham Van Dong visited Western Europe in May 1977 in hopes of finding alternative *capitalist* aid sources.

Stymied in its efforts to avoid inordinate dependence on the Soviet Union, Hanoi finally sought out the Soviets in the summer of 1977. Vietnam was facing a serious drought; reconstruction work had bogged down; food was short, funds for industry were scarce. Moreover, large-scale clashes had broken out along the border with Cambodia, resulting in a hardening of China's attitude. Economically desperate, diplomatically isolated, and militarily under pressure, Hanoi turned to Moscow. The die was cast.[3]

Although China and Vietnam's Indochina neighbors were the most salient components of its regional environment, Hanoi also had to devise a policy toward ASEAN. In the aftermath of the war, ASEAN had emerged as the most dynamic organization in Southeast Asia. Spurred on to politico-economic cooperation by the belief that the noncommunist states of the region had to rely increasingly on their own devices for security, the member states hesitantly managed to transcend several internecine quarrels to devise common positions on a number of regional issues.

From its birth in 1967, ASEAN was viewed with considerable suspicion by Vietnam. Four of its five members had actively assisted the U.S. war effort against Hanoi. In 1970, the association had backed the anticommunist Jakarta Conference on Cambodia. Vietnam saw ASEAN, then, as a replacement for the moribund Southeast Asia Treaty Organization (SEATO), that is, as a vehicle for the maintenance of Western military influence in Southeast Asia. The ASEAN states tried to alter this image by proffering economic assistance to the SRV soon after its 1975 victory and expressing their readiness to establish friendly relations. Hoping to allay Vietnam's fear that ASEAN was simply a convenient vehicle for the continued assertion of American security interests, the association underlined its commitment to the creation of a Zone of Peace, Freedom, and Neutrality (ZOPFAN) in Southeast Asia. Nevertheless, the continued operation of U.S. bases in the Philippines and the Five Power Defense Agreement covering Malaysia and Singapore reinforced Vietnam's suspicions. Moreover,

U.S. statements in 1979 that its security obligations to Thailand remained operative under the Manila Pact further heightened Vietnam's belief that ASEAN was essentially an adversary.

Although Vietnam has refused either to recognize or deal with ASEAN as an association, it has nevertheless courted each member individually, hoping to split ASEAN's united front. Thus, in the summer of 1978, high-level Vietnamese officials visited the five in hopes of creating a modus vivendi prior to the SRV's invasion of Cambodia. Hanoi's goal was to neutralize ASEAN prior to the Cambodia invasion so that its members would not align in opposition with either the United States or China. Quite to the contrary, the Cambodian invasion in fact proved to be a major diplomatic setback for Vietnam. Even those ASEAN states normally oriented more toward Hanoi than Peking, such as Indonesia and Malaysia, were appalled as Vietnam inaugurated a series of acts seemingly designed to repel its noncommunist neighbors in 1978 and 1979. Tens of thousands of refugees fled the country, arriving primarily in Thailand and Malaysia to the increasingly hostile receptions of the local populations. The Vietnamese alliance with the Soviet Union—although precipitated by economic isolation and security concerns about China—was viewed by ASEAN as a major challenge to its ZOPFAN hopes and as a deliberate effort to repolarize Southeast Asian politics by inviting great-power intervention once again. All of this was capped by the SRV invasion of Cambodia, which violated the most important dictum enunciated by Vietnamese leaders to their non-communist neighbors: noninterference in the internal affairs of others.

In essence, Vietnam had made a series of difficult and diplomatically costly decisions in 1978 to dispose of the Khmer Rouge security threat and political challenge, while simultaneously nationalizing the economy of South Vietnam at the expense of the local Chinese population. Benefits from these policies included the establishment of hegemony over Indochina and the full economic integration of Vietnam. The costs are still being paid: (1) virtual total reliance on the Soviet bloc; (2) the alienation of both China and ASEAN; (3) continued hostility from the United States; (4) the incipient reintroduction of great-power rivalry in the region; (5) the establishment of a festering insurgency in western Cambodia, overtly supported by China and tacitly assisted by Thailand; (6) the diversion of scarce resources away from reconstruction and development to the maintenance of an occupation army of two hundred thousand in Cambodia and forty thousand in Laos; and (7) the disruption of the lives of hundreds of thousands of Vietnamese forced to flee the country with barely the clothes on their backs.

The SRV's occupation of and responsibility for what used to be French Indochina has undoubtedly created considerable social and economic strain within Vietnam itself. The expulsion of ethnic Chinese and the exodus of other refugees has deprived the country of a considerable percentage of its professional and technical talent. Moreover, the boat-people phenomenon also depleted Vietnam's coastal fishing fleet. Reports of food shortages and an unemployment rate of 13 percent appeared in 1979 which continued into the early 1980s.[4] To forestall any resulting unrest, tens of thousands of young southerners were conscripted into the army. But this diversion of personnel has only exacerbated production problems in a labor-intensive economy. The loss of Chinese coal miners, fishermen, and dockworkers in the north translated into large shortfalls in coal production (six million tons—below the 1977 level), fish catches, and turn-around time at the port of Haiphong. Subsequently, the drop in coal production ramified into other sectors as anthracite exports to Japan dropped some 42 percent in 1978. Coal-based power supplied to factories and farming cooperatives were also adversely affected.

While Hanoi was providing food aid to Cambodia, it also required 1.5 million tons of imports for itself from the COMECON countries to make up part of a 2.4 million-ton deficit in rice production in early 1979. China's destruction of the phosphate mine at Lao Cai during the February 1979 border incursion has meant that indigenous chemical fertilizer is no longer available for the paddies. In sum, an IMF study concluded, by 1979 Vietnam's debt service in convertible currencies ($US 150 million) had exceeded its exports receipts.[5]

Vietnam's Security Responses to Regional Challenges

Given its modern history of continuous warfare, it is not surprising that although Vietnam is ranked one of the ten poorest countries in the world in per capita GNP, nevertheless it maintains the world's fourth-largest standing army of 1,023,000 men as of early 1979.[6] Befitting its guerrilla origins and Spartan economic base, the army's ground forces number over one million, they are supported by 1,000 heavy tanks (T-34/85, T-54, T-62) and 400 medium tanks (M-47, M-48), most of which were supplied by the Soviet Union but some of which are American in origin, captured in the south in 1975. The latter comprised a major source of firepower against Khmer Rouge guerrillas in Cambodia. The navy and air force are small, the former with only 3,000 men; its mission is confined to coastal patrol. The air force is somewhat larger and more sophisticated (20,000 men, having acquired late-model Soviet aircraft (30 MiG-23/27, 60 SU-7/20) as well as captured U.S. equipment (30 F-5A and 70 A-37B). Additionally, the air force flies some 290 early-model Soviet jets ranging from Korean War-vintage MiG-17s to MiG-21s of the 1960s. There is also an inventory of about 200 captured U.S. helicopters that have seen service in pacification efforts against the Meo in Laos and have been used in Cambodia as well.

At the end of the second Indochina war, Vietnam did not demobilize its military but continued to recruit and provide technical training to military personnel for tasks related to the country's reconstruction. Some of these had strategic implications, as in the building of a road from Danang to Techepone in southern Laos, designed to free the Laotians from dependence on Thailand for access to the sea. The Vietminh military had been deployed in neighboring Laos and Cambodia, of course, during both Indochina wars. They withdrew in 1954 at the insistence of both China and the Soviet Union, foregoing their hope of establishing Communist-led governments in both countries at that time. During the second war, VPA operations shifted from guerrilla to more conventional tactics. Instead of spreading themselves thinly over most of Laos and Cambodia, the Vietnamese Communists concentrated their forces to protect the "Ho Chi Minh Trail" in eastern Laos and Cambodia. In fact, this deployment became an early source of friction between the Khmer Rouge and their Vietnamese allies. The latter limited the activities of the former within what the Vietminh called their security zone despite the fact that the zone was in Cambodian territory.[7]

In the aftermath of the second Indochina war, Vietnam's rhetoric and military behavior seemed contradictory. At the United Nations in 1978, for example, while they opposed general disarmament and called for the use of arms by "patriots struggling to free themselves from the colonial and racist yoke," there was no evidence that Vietnam itself was supplying regional insurgents with any of the military equipment captured from the Saigon inventory.[8] Despite the rhetoric, then, the SRV did not want to be labeled an "exporter of revolution." There was still hope that *modi vivendi* could be reached with its neighbors.

There is also evidence that Hanoi tried to reach a border settlement with the Khmer Rouge in early 1978 after Vietnam's successful thrust into Cambodia's eastern provinces the previous December. But the Khmer Rouge responded by continuing to shell the Vietnamese side of the border, using Chinese-supplied artillery. An alternative interpretation of this period is that Hanoi hoped to effect a coup against the Khmer Rouge leadership that would have brought a group of pro-Hanoi Khmer to power in Phnom Penh and permitted the SRV to forego the difficult decision of outright invasion. A number of allegations have been made by the Pol Pot regime concerning assassination attempts against their leaders from within the party, which began as early as 1976.

Hanoi decided, probably around the spring of 1978, to bring the conflict to an end. The SRV devised a coordinated diplomatic-military strategy to neutralize any Chinese military action by aligning with the Soviet Union and simultaneously building the nucleus of a pro-Vietnam Cambodian national-liberation front drawn from those Khmer who had fled Pol Pot's brutality. Called the Kampuchean United Front for National Salvation (KNUFNS), its leaders consisted of a number of pro-Hanoi Khmer Rouge who had been purged from the party between 1975 and 1978.

The SRV turned to the Soviet Union for final preparations before invading Cambodia, and the Soviets responded by doubling the VPA's arsenal in a period of six months, while the army itself expanded from 615,000 to one million men by early 1979.[9] Vietnam's blitzkrieg invasion of Cambodia was rationalized as assistance to a national-liberation movement that would overthrow a tyrannical pariah regime the demise of which would be greeted with global relief, if not applause. Several of Vietnam's political calculations went awry, however. By overtly backing a "national liberation force," Hanoi besmirched its solemn promises made only months earlier in visits to ASEAN capitals that it would not aid regional insurgents. Moreover, Thailand was suddenly confronted with Vietnamese troops only a few miles from its border. ASEAN and Vietnam found themselves uncomfortably close to confrontation.

In addition to raising diplomatic flak, Vietnam's invasion and occupation of Cambodia provided a favorable regional political climate for China's limited retaliatory incursion in February and March. Although China was called upon to leave Vietnam, in contrast to the reaction to the Vietnamese invasion of Cambodia, international *condemnation* of Peking was muted. And privately, the ASEAN states were gratified that China had demonstrated to Vietnam that it could not engage in foreign adventures with impunity. Thailand particularly welcomed Chinese pledges of military assistance should Vietnam attempt to continue its expansion westward.

Militarily, Vietnam's resources are severely stretched. It has fortified its northern border to deter any new Chinese incursion. Approximately 250,000 troops are billeted in Laos and Cambodia for the indefinite future. The Soviet Union exerted considerable pressure on Hanoi to obtain full base rights at Cam Ranh Bay and Danang in exchange for continuing to underwrite the SRV's economy and provide military hardware. Still, the Soviets made it clear that they would not go to war over Indochina—a region that is not vital to Moscow. Therefore, Hanoi has reinstituted full-scale mobilization for its population to prepare for "peoples war." All able-bodied between fifteen and sixty-four years of age undergo military training for a defense-in-depth against any future Chinese attack.[10]

In the 1979 war's aftermath, Moscow has particularly increased its naval presence in Vietnam. In addition to giving the SRV five naval combat craft, Soviet flotillas now call regularly at Cam Ranh Bay and Danang. Some fifty Soviet-made Badger bombers were seen on Vietnamese airfields protected by one hundred fifty MiG fighters and a new air-defense system employing the SAM-3 missile.[11]

The ASEAN states, led by Thailand as the front-line member, have all increased defense spending. This has been facilitated by additional U.S.

military credits to the ASEAN five on generous terms. Nevertheless, it should be noted that the combined military forces of the five still do not equal either the personnel or firepower of the VPA. More important than its military growth is the fact that Vietnam's belligerence has moved ASEAN further along a politico-security dimension of cooperation. The five are determined to maintain a united front on all dealings with outside powers, particularly Vietnam. Moreover, ASEAN has continued to sponsor resolutions at international meetings condemning Vietnam's action, thus keeping the issue alive. The association has also reluctantly moved closer to China over this issue. And perhaps derivatively, the Philippines and Indonesia seem to be pressing their claims to islands in the South China Sea Spratly chain, complicating Vietnam's maritime position, to China's delight.

Despite its confrontation with Thailand over such issues as the latter's provision of sanctuary for the Cambodian resistance and tacit permission for China's resupply activities through Thai territory, the SRV has not supported Thai Communist Party (CPT) guerrilla actions in northeast Thailand, even though the guerrillas' normal sanctuaries are in Laos and Cambodia. In fact, a rather ironic situation developed during 1979. The Vietnamese could not trust the CPT because of its pro-China orientation. Therefore, the VPA closed the guerrillas' base camps on the Lao and Cambodian frontiers and forced CPT members to cross back into Thailand. Moreover, because China was emphasizing government-to-government relations with Bangkok, Peking, too, cut off supplies. The result has been a precipitous decline in guerrilla activities, an upswing in defections, and the most tranquil security situation in the Thai north and northeast since the CPT was founded in 1960. The longevity of this unusual calm is problematical, however. Broadcasts from Vientiane, Laos suggest that a new CPT, organized by Vietnam, may be in the offing with cadres receiving training and supplies in Laos. The potential to engage in subversion toward Thailand remains a real option for Hanoi.

Tradeoffs between Vietnam's Civilian and Military Needs

All policymakers face the problem of limited resources with respect to demands emanating from both the domestic and international environments of a country. The needs/resources ratio leads to competitive political interests and priorities that, in turn, require choices and compromise. Vietnam is no exception. At war's end in 1975, Vietnam's planners were confronted with an enormous task: the integration of two societies, one austere and centrally regimented, the other chaotic, freewheeling, entrepreneurial, and used to living well beyond its means through external

(U.S.) subsidies. Hanoi wanted to move populations from the agriculturally exhausted north to the underpopulated rural south. But socialist construction in the South had stalled because of the resistance of Chinese businessmen who controlled commerce and the belligerence of the Khmer Rouge whose raids precluded the opening of "new economic zones" along the Cambodian border. By September 1978, the state controlled only 40 percent of the South's retail trade. Most agricultural production found its way into Ho Chi Minh City (Saigon) via the black market. The government was unable to mobilize agriculture in the South even though the South was supposed to compensate for the agricultural shortfall in the North. Because Vietnamese peasants had to buy fertilizer and insecticide on the black market, they refused to sell their crops at the artificially low prices offered by state purchasing agencies. The subsequent inability of the government to provide food reduced the movement of people to the new economic zones to a trickle.[12]

During this same period, the SRV attempted to promulgate a new foreign-investment policy, in part to compensate for the shortfall in domestic savings. A remarkably liberal foreign-investment code was announced in 1977, encouraging external investment in three areas: petroleum, export-oriented industries, and manufacturing. Foreign investors were permitted up to 49-percent equity in joint ventures. This promising beginning in soliciting external reconstruction assistance was sacrificed, however, with Vietnam's invasion of Cambodia. Foreign investors have been loathe to consider the SRV since 1979. The absence of Western assistance has been a particularly hard economic blow since Hanoi had counted on it for one-third of its budget, another third coming from Communist states and the rest from domestic taxation.[13]

By 1979, then, Vietnam's economy was limping badly. Western observers declared that its performance had actually deteriorated when compared with the war years. Thus, its industrial plant was estimated to be running at 55 percent of capacity compared to 65 percent in 1975. Diversion of skilled manpower and resources to the military led to the virtual abandonment of the 1976-1980 Five Year Plan. Problems of bad weather, mismanagement, and cadre corruption lowered food consumption to an average 1,300 calories per day—300 below the World Health Organization minimal-nutrition level.[14]

Coal production and exports have fallen, as imports have jumped, primarily in grain. Although the socialist bloc covers Hanoi's deficits by long-term loans, its deficit with convertible-currency countries is met through commercial loans and credit extensions (*tranches*) from the IMF. What had been a promising start toward reconstruction in 1977 had become a virtual balance-of-payments disaster in 1979 just to finance food imports. Long-term development appears to have been shelved. Moreover, the cessation of Chinese aid in 1978 led to an extraordinary dependence on the Soviet

Union—30 percent of the SRV's rice and virtually all its petroleum, chemical fertilizer, and spare parts for transportation.[15]

Perhaps the major economic/security tradeoff to have been made since 1975 was Hanoi's decision to expel hundreds of thousands of ethnic Chinese in the course of socializing the southern economy. Of the 1.5 million in Vietnam, only 300,000 live in the north. They were, however, involved in crucial sectors of the economy, including coal mining, longshore activities, and skilled factory labor. In the South, overseas Chinese virtually controlled the production and distribution of essential commodities.

Escalating food prices due to bad harvests beginning in 1977 led to considerable popular resentment against the resident Chinese in the South who controlled the rice trade. This coincided with a deterioration in political relations with Peking attendant upon the latter's support for Pol Pot against the SRV. Calculating that Vietnam had little to lose in its relations with China at this point and believing that it was absolutely essential to socialize the South in order to mobilize domestic resources in the face of the severe economic situation, Hanoi decided to nationalize all private trade in the spring of 1978, a measure that affected almost exclusively the Chinese community. Peking subsequently charged that Vietnam also began to expel ethnic Chinese from the North at the same time for alleged fifth-column activity. The SRV was creating a *cordon sanitaire* along the Sino-Vietnam border.

Hanoi's crackdown on the Chinese in both the North and the South placed China in a very difficult position. The SRV may have hoped that Peking would not respond sharply because it would be inappropriate to protect a remnant bourgeois sector within a socialist society. Moreover, any attempt to stand up for the ethnic Chinese would be met with considerable suspicion in the rest of Southeast Asia, a region with which China was bent on establishing cordial relations. Despite these costs, however, China did react sharply. Not to have done so, Chinese leaders believed, could have jeopardized ethnic Chinese throughout the region and undermined China's credibility, especially at a time when China was encouraging its overseas compatriots to invest in the motherland's modernization.

On balance, Vietnam suffered the heavier diplomatic loss as a result of its anti-Chinese action. The boat-people phenomenon, while generating considerable hard currency for the government, repelled world opinion and set the ASEAN states uniformly against Hanoi. Combined with its invasion of Cambodia, Vietnam's treatment of its Chinese residents did more to isolate the country politically than any other action since Communist Vietnam's birth.

Vietnam's Alignment and Future Prospects

From a global perspective, the Vietnam-Cambodia and Sino-Vietnam hostilities have brought the Sino-Soviet confrontation directly into

Southeast Asia. Moscow fears that a China with growing economic strength through modernization will ultimately attempt to shut the Soviet Union out of the region. Soviet leaders conjure up an Asian nightmare in which an entente is established among China, ASEAN, Japan, and the United States, which would effectively exclude Soviet influence. Whereas the Soviet Union's fear is a long-term "hypothetical horrible," China's apprehensions are more immediate. They interpret the Soviet-Vietnam relationship to be a revival of Moscow's encirclement strategy, a view reinforced by the Soviet occupation of Afghanistan, which itself occurred just after Sino-Soviet talks on the possibility of détente had failed.

As argued above, the SRV has opted for Soviet alignment at no little cost but with the belief that only the Soviet Union could both compensate for the cessation of Chinese aid and provide the security guarantee and economic and military support necessary for Hanoi to occupy and pacify Laos and Cambodia. This alignment decision, however, while achieving one basic security goal—control of Indochina—has obstructed the achievement of others: the neutralization of ASEAN; the elimination of America's military presence in the region; and the reduction of Chinese influence. In fact, the SRV's military conquest of Indochina has brought about precisely the coalition of opposing forces it had hoped to prevent. ASEAN has presented a strong united front in opposition to Vietnam's military actions. The association's members have expressed their desire for an enhanced American offshore capability in the region. And China's political capital has risen with its promise of aid to Thailand in the event of any further Vietnamese military moves westward. It would appear that Hanoi's 1976 pledge of nonaggression and noninterference in the internal affairs of its neighbors as well as its promise not to provide military bases to any foreign power held scant credibility since 1979.

Are there opportunities for Vietnam to break out of this impasse? Clearly, the ASEAN states hope so; and, strangely enough, so does China. None of the actors, with the exception of the Soviet Union, is pleased with the polarization of regional alignments. And even the Soviets have reservations about spending $3-5 million per day to sustain *Vietnam's* security interests, a process that undermines the Soviet Union's plans for better relations with ASEAN. Chinese officials have predicted privately that after a few years the Vietnamese will discover how unreliable and heavyhanded the Soviets can be. Then, they will be happy to compromise over Indochina's future in order to improve relations with China, the United States, and ASEAN. That is, China believes that Vietnam will become disillusioned with exclusive dependence on the Soviet Union in the same way that the Chinese did in the late 1950s and early 1960s.

The ASEAN states, too, prefer a more balanced relationship with Vietnam and China. Concerned about their own ethnic Chinese, the ASEAN states are uncomfortable confronting Vietnam and moving toward China as a counterweight to the Soviet-SRV alliance. ASEAN believes Hanoi has a number of incentives for improving relations, including the association's capability to assist Vietnam's economic development through aid to its rubber industry, cooperation on the Mekong River project, and the purchase of Thai rice.

Improved relations with ASEAN could go a long way toward rebuilding Vietnam's stature in the nonaligned movement. Moreover, better relations would slow any ASEAN consideration of the creation of new multilateral security arrangements among the association's members. So long as the ASEAN states continue to define their security challenges as primarily domestic, there is little interest in going beyond bilateral border-control cooperation against insurgents. But, with Vietnam's military forces poised on the Thai border, there is talk in ASEAN councils of the possibility of having to go beyond the association's low security profile to new, stronger guarantees against the SRV challenge. The longer VPA forces remain in Cambodia the more likely that ASEAN military cooperation will evolve. Should that cooperation lead to even closer ties with the United States and China, then Vietnam's regional dominance would be further in jeopardy.

SRV leaders have some hard decisions to make. Any improvement of relations with its neighbors to the north and south will require (1) a military withdrawal from and restoration of the neutrality of Cambodia—in short an abandonment of the Indochina federation; (2) a cessation of the forced exodus of its citizens, particularly the ethnic Chinese, to neighboring countries that see them as both politically and economically destabilizing; and (3) a reduction in Soviet military use of Vietnamese bases. These conditions would greatly reduce Hanoi's political challenge in Southeast Asia, and they would enhance the availability of both domestic and external resources for economic growth.

The Soviets would certainly resist any effort by Hanoi to pull away. From the Soviet perspective, the alliance with Vietnam and, derivatively, Laos and Cambodia when combined with the invasion of Afghanistan create a military cordon around China and establish the Soviet Union as an *Asian* power to be reckoned with. If one adds to this picture a growing blue-water Soviet Pacific fleet and newly reinforced bases north of Japan on the islands of Kunashiri and Etorofu, one can portend that the Soviet alliance with Vietnam and the use of its air and naval bases is part of a larger strategic effort to raise its Asian military profile, intimidate China and Japan, and point to itself as the new dominant superpower in the region. Moscow still has a long way to go to achieve these ends, but they appear increasingly plausible.

The linchpin for this whole process is Cambodia. Although regional actors are prepared to accept Vietnam's domination of Laos—in part because the Pathet Lao have always been highly dependent on the Vietminh—the strength of Cambodian nationalism and the activities of core resistance movements in western Cambodia ensure that Hanoi's occupation will remain a festering sore, threatening constantly to spill over into Thailand and involve ASEAN, the United States, and China. The restoration of neutrality to Cambodia under someone like the peripatetic Prince Sihanouk would go far toward defusing the dangerous situation confronting both Thailand and China. Bangkok would have a buffer separating the traditional rivals once again, while China would have saved face in restoring the independence of a small ally. Vietnam's security would not be threatened because its military establishment would remain far and away the region's strongest in both size and quality.

Despite this sanguine scenario, however, it is unlikely that events will move in the direction suggested above. Hanoi has established control over Indochina. To withdraw would be not only to lose status but also to imply that Vietnam's revolutionary momentum had been reversed. This could create difficult domestic political problems for a regime that has attempted to govern a forcibly unified state through mass-mobilization techniques justified by appeals claiming imminent threats by external enemies. In short, if Vietnam were to relax its external posture, there would be similar pressure to do so internally with what the leadership fears might be unpredictable results.

Additionally, Hanoi sees no acceptable alternative to its Heng Samrin creation. The restoration of Sihanouk would be much too risky, for he might well invite a combination of Thai, Chinese, and U.S. influence into Cambodia; and he may not be strong enough to do away with the Khmer Rouge. Moreover, should a private-enterprise regime be recreated in Cambodia, Laos might, in turn, become restive through the Khmer example.

Vietnam's one major military encounter with China, the February-March 1979 border incursion, resulted in something of a stalemate for both sides. Although the Chinese army devastated the northern parts of five border provinces, leveling towns and local industries, it was fought to a standstill by second-echelon SRV regional forces. Top-line VPA personnel never entered the fray. In the aftermath, of course, Vietnam has stationed regular VPA forces in depth along its Chinese frontier, transferring some personnel from Cambodia. They have been replaced, in turn, by raw recruits from the South, who were seemingly neither effective militarily against the Khmer Rouge or in their relations with the civilian Khmer population. Reports from Cambodia detail allegations of Vietnamese corruption, for example, in the trading of rice for objects d'art and other local valuables. The Vietnamese military has been unable to eliminate Khmer Rouge guerrilla activities, and the Thai border region remains hotly contested. There are even signs of Khmer Rouge hit-and-run actions in the villages of the central provinces. Although this guerilla activity presents no direct threat to the viability of the Heng Samrin government in Phnom Penh, it is the rural areas, after all, upon which the country depends for rice.

Finally, despite the rhetoric concerning a potential ASEAN military alliance or a Sino-U.S. counterpart, the Vietnamese have probably concluded that their reality is far away. Neither ASEAN nor Chinese military capabilities constitute a serious threat to the SRV's survival. And, despite the general Chinese-American rapprochement, there is no indication that significant military cooperation, including joint planning and exercises, is on the horizon. Whatever the capabilities and threats of their potential regional adversaries, Hanoi's leaders seem confident they can cope as long as the Soviet alliance remains firm. And Vietnam appears to be willing to go some distance to insure the relationship—perhaps including the provision of full-scale base facilities at Danang and Cam Ranh Bay.

Unhappily, peace in Southeast Asia seems as far away in the early 1980s as it was a decade earlier, even though the alignments have dramatically changed.

Notes

1. For a very readable and almost poetic account of the rise of the Vietnam Communist Party (VCP) and its nationalist struggle against the French, see Paul Mus and John T. McAlister, *The Vietnamese and Their Revolution* (New York: Harper Torchbooks, 1970).

2. For a good, brief discussion of the differences among China, the Soviet Union, and North Vietnam in the course of the second Indochina war (1963-1975) see Bruce Grant, *The Security of Southeast Asia,* Adelphi Paper 142 (London: International Institute of Strategic Studies, Spring 1978).

3. A useful review of this period and Vietnam's efforts to avoid the polarization of regional politics may be found in Alexander Woodside, "Nationalism and Poverty in the Breakdown of Sino-Vietnamese Relations," *Pacific Affairs* (Autumn 1979):381-409.

4. Nayan Chanda, "Vietnam's Battle of the Home Front," *Far Eastern Economic Review,* 2 November 1979, pp. 44-46. The discussion in this paragraph is drawn from the Chanda article and subsequent research in the region.

5. *The New York Times,* 14 January 1980.

6. Data for this section are drawn from the International Institute for Strategic Studies, *The Military Balance, 1979-80* (London, 1979), pp. 73-74.

7. For a detailed discussion of the relations between the Khmer Rouge and the Vietnamese Communists during the second Indochina war, see Sheldon W. Simon, *War and Politics in Cambodia: A Communications*

Analysis (Durham, N.C.: Duke University Press, 1974); and Milton Osborne, *Aggression and Annexation: Kampuchea's Condemnation of Vietnam* (Canberra: Australian National University Research School of Pacific Studies, Working Paper no. 15, 1979).

8. Stockholm International Peace Research Institute, *World Armaments and Disarmament: SIPRI Yearbook, 1979* (London: Francis and Taylor, 1979), pp. 492-493. See also, Franklin Weinstein, "U.S.-Vietnam Relations and the Security of Southeast Asia," *Foreign Affairs* 56 (July 1978):847.

9. International Institute for Strategic Studies data cited in *The Weekend Australian,* 17-18 February 1979.

10. Eyewitness account by Philippe Devillers, "Vietnam in Battle," *Current History* 77 (December 1979).

11. This information is reported in Douglas Pike, "The USSR and Vietnam: Into the Swamp," *Asian Survey* 19 (December 1979):1166.

12. Cf. Woodside, "Nationalism and Poverty," pp. 392-400.

13. Carlyle Thayer, "Development Strategies in Vietnam: The Fourth National Congress of the Vietnam Communist Party," *Asian Profile*, June 1979, p. 284.

14. Douglas Pike, "Communist vs. Communist in Southeast Asia," *International Security* 4 (Summer 1979):27-28.

15. Pike, "The USSR and Vietnam," p. 1164.

8

Indonesia

Peter Lyon

Indonesia is the world's most geographically fragmented major state. Because of its population, approximately 135-140 million in 1980, making it the world's fifth-most-populous country, the geographical span of its territory (extending for 3,000 miles broadly athwart the equator, from the Andaman Sea almost to Australia), its natural resources, and its strategic location at a major crossroads in the world's circulatory systems for transit, tourism and trade, this uniquely large archipelago state comprising several thousand islands of markedly contrasting size and character undoubtedly is a country of some considerable global as well as regional importance.

The islands of Indonesia—together with those of the Philippines and Papua New Guinea—provide the main land areas, rather like a series of stepping stones, between the Indian and Pacific Oceans. The main, though relatively narrow and shallow, straits are commercially and strategically important sea lanes, especially Malacca, Lombok, Sunda and Ombai-Wetar. Indeed, among the world's main seaway arteries the Malacca Strait is rivaled only by the Strait of Dover and that of Hormuz for the density of its seaborne traffic. It is a potentially critical chokepoint along the sea lanes of communications (SLOCs) connecting Japan and the remainder of the Far East with the Persian Gulf; much of its traffic consists of large oil tankers.

The Indonesian Republic shares land borders with Malaysia (on the large island of Borneo, now known to the Indonesians as Kalimantan) and with Papua New Guinea, an independent state internationally only since September 1975. This archipelago state of thousands of islands nonetheless is dominated by its five principal ones—Sumatra, Java, Celebes, Kalimantan, and Irian. Java, though occupying less than 10 percent of the total land area, is the principal power base and much the most populous with more than 65 percent of the nation's population.

Contemporary Indonesia has been characterized in a variety of ways by informed non-Indonesian commentators as a "sick man on the mend,"[1] as "the Showcase State,"[2] as "a somewhat feeble giant,"[3] as "a fascist military regime" which has perpetrated more than "Ten Years of Military Terror,"[4] and as an inherently unstable and impermanent form of patrimonial-military rule.[5] It is not surprising that such characterizations do not closely coincide with the preferred descriptions and self-images cherished by leading Indonesians themselves.

A politically aware Indonesian, born in Java in the 1930s, and in early

1980 contemplating his country's security situation and prospects for the next decade, would be acutely conscious that he had lived through a Japanese occupation (1942-1945);[6] a guerrilla and intense political-propagandistic war for "national liberation" against the Dutch (1945-1949);[7] a protracted and ultimately successful irredentist campaign to wrest West New Guinea (now named Irian Jaya) from the Dutch (1949-1963);[8] *Konfrontasi* against Malaysia (1962-1966),[9] which also meant limited warfare against Britain, Australia, and New Zealand; some armed revolts and communal killings, especially in the bloody months that were a sequel to the Gestapu affair or the abortive Untung coup of 30 September 1965;[10] and a messy military and political operation in 1975-1977 that eventuated in the incorporation into Indonesia of the former Portuguese colony of East Timor.[11] This is, moreover, a suggestive list of the most prominent episodes, not an exhaustive catalogue. Indonesia has thus experienced much violence since Sukarno proclaimed its independence on 17 August 1945.

The thirty-five years since 1945, moreover, have seen some considerable expansion, several major redefinitions, and some consolidation of Indonesia's national-security concerns by its various incumbent governments. To a considerable extent the national-security preoccupations of successive Indonesia governments from 1945 to 1975 can be viewed phasally, with each phase dominated by a particular goal or struggle.[12] Put more simply, but in a way that does point to one sharp contrast in style and professed priorities, Indonesian security policies are to a considerable extent reflected and personified in the careers of Sukarno—in part from 1945 onward, but especially from 1957 to 1965—and, since 1965-1966, of Suharto. The juncture of those careers does of course sharply demarcate distinct phases of Indonesian diplomatic-alignment orientation, defining wholly contrasting ideological perspectives.

Because there is by now an extensive literature available on aspects of Indonesia's foreign and security policies, some of it of high scholarly quality and some of it tendentiously polemical, this short paper will focus principally on the current situation, at the beginning of 1980, and will cite other works frequently to mitigate the inevitable brevity of treatment offered here and also to indicate where more extensive evidence or arguments for particular points may be found.

Indonesia and the International System

Because the contemporary global system is so complex, unevenly institutionalized, and only very patchily integrated,[13] it follows almost axiomatically that it is not easy to characterize current Indonesian perspectives on it.[14] This is partly because detailed Indonesian statements regarding the nature and provenance of the international system are rare and explicitly articulated generalizations or even stereotypes not prominently on display; but it is also because Indonesian attitudes are more often immediately reactive to events or ad hoc rather than preformulated and general.

To the extent that the contemporary international system can be perceived as functionally layered—with such matters as law of the sea, diplomatic protocol and practice, the "New International Economic Order," and arms procurement and regulation being dealt with separately and specifically with their own agendas and conferences—then any full assessment of Indonesian attitudes and policies would have to appraise each of these many sometimes interacting, sometimes discrete, facets. Here one can only offer some impressionistic generalizations.

In the last few feverish years of Sukarno's political ascendancy he articulated a very expressive romantic-revolutionary view of Indonesia's mission in the world, according to which it was to act as a spearhead and beacon for the world's Newly Emerging Forces (NEFO) in confrontation and competition with the "Old Established Forces." To that end he proposed a conference system, "CONEFO," of these progressive forces to plan common activities. In these mistily defined revolutionary enterprises Indonesia identified most closely with North Korea, China, North Vietnam, and Sihanouk's Cambodian government. Insofar as there was any practical expression of these ambitions, Indonesia dramatically withdrew from the United Nations and Jakarta was the venue for a "Games for the Peoples of the NEFO" held in a stadium newly built with massive assistance and generous credits from China. It is rather ironic that in those years of increasingly florid and grandiose oratory about NEFOs and the like, Sukarno's government managed simultaneously to forge apparently close diplomatic ties with China while securing considerable armaments on easy credit terms from the Soviet Union. Apparently riding imperturbably the waves and ripples of Sino-Soviet hostilities, inasmuch as they then spread into Southeast Asia, Indonesia's radical and declamatory world view indubitably was stridently anti-Western in those days.

For Indonesians the international system is generally perceived through two sets of images. First, it is seen as a global arena dominated by a few big powers, with Indonesia obviously not one of them. Indeed, for many Indonesian leaders the general international system is seen as being essentially exploitive, in which the strong dominate the weak, whenever and wherever they can. Economic imperialism is regarded as a very real threat by many Indonesians: "Our wealth, our resources, make us very vulnerable." Quite often, too, Indonesians conceive of the international system in fundamentally racial terms, as dominated by white or yellow men with brown men treated as inferiors.

Secondly, Indonesians tend to view the international system as being partly compartmentalized, perhaps in some degree institutionalized, in regional terms, with there being no doubt that for Indonesia this operationally significant regional environment is Southeast Asia. Since the late 1960s, and especially since 1975, this has been primarily defined in terms of ASEAN,[15] the Association of Southeast Asian Nations, a regional association of which Indonesia is by far the largest member state.

Undoubtedly the task of ranking Indonesia within the contemporary international system is a highly subjective matter as is illustrated, for instance, in its treatment by Ray Cline in his study *World Power Assessment 1977*. Cline shows that Indonesia ranked fifth in world-population terms and fourteenth in territorial size. In light of its territorial size he places it in a third tier of considerable states ranging from ninth to seventeenth in the world, but he then elevates it, with Iran, by five points because of what is designated "perceived power weight" for "nations occupying crucial strategic locations on sea lanes." Indonesia finally comes out ninth in the world in terms of "perceived power weight." According to Cline, Indonesia was deemed to be ranked thirty-first in world-trade terms in 1975, roughly equal in importance to Singapore and Yugoslavia, but featured tenth in his "Consolidated Rank list," which combines "Critical Mass and Economic Capability"—thus placing it above all other ASEAN countries; Vietnam is positioned in thirty-third place. Cline continually stresses that "if perceptions of world power derived exclusively from population, territory, and economic capability" then the "distribution of lasting elements of power around the globe" could be accurately measured and mapped, but he admits that "in fact, of course, military capability, strategic purpose, and political skill in mobilizing national will" will affect power perceptions and performance substantially.[16] Almost incidentally, he again illustrates Indonesia's remarkable variability when in a section devoted to "Estimates of Equivalent Combat Capabilities," he rates Indonesia very low in relation to each of his principal indices: manpower quality, weapons effectiveness, infrastructure and logistics, organizational quality, and finally, "equivalent units of combat capability."

The Sea and Indonesia's Strategic Space

The sea is a major conditioning medium of Indonesian life, necessarily so for such an archipelagic state. Its diplomacy has, however, underlined this fact particularly since 1957-1958 when, by unilateral declaration and then by its diplomacy at the first UN Law of the Sea Conference, Dr. Mochtar Kusumaatmadja (then a professor at Padjajaran University in Bandung, and now Indonesia's foreign minister) presented the now well known archipelagic principle, according to which territorial waters are defined by drawing imaginary straight lines between the outermost points of the country's outermost islands, with territorial waters and economic zones then being measured from this baseline. Thus Indonesia swiftly laid claim to over 660,000 square miles of ocean and thereby sought to incorporate within its own national waters such important straits used for international navigation as Lombok and Makassar. The principal factor immediately impelling this declaration seems to have been the occurrence of armed dissidence and revolt against the central government from the "Outer Islands"—a long-established Java-centric designation. Thus, at a time when the authority of the Javanese-based government seemed likely to crumble, a defiant definition of the unity and integrity of the archipelagic states and its adjacent waters was asserted. On two subsequent occasions Indonesia has taken further initiatives along similar lines.

In November 1971 Indonesia and Malaysia, both riparian states, denied the international status of the Straits of Malacca and Singapore and claimed that henceforth they were governed by the legal regime of innocent passage through territorial waters. Malaysia had extended its territorial waters from three to twelve miles in August 1969, as had Indonesia in December 1957, and in March 1970 the two governments concluded a treaty delimiting the territorial sea boundary in the Strait of Malacca, which at its narrowest is only about eight nautical miles across. The eastern exit of the adjoining Singapore Strait is less than ten miles wide and is commanded by Malaysian and Indonesian territory. The prime avowed justification for this joint initiative was the need for supervisory regulation of maritime traffic through this congested and, in places, narrow and shallow strait, with its attendant risks of collisions and spillage.

In March 1980, President Suharto formally declared an exclusive 200-mile economic zone (EEZ) for the exploration and exploitation of the waters, seabed, and subsoil surrounding Indonesia's territorial waters. Of itself, declaring such an economic zone is not a revolutionary act. But with the Law of the Sea currently being actively negotiated and redefined, Indonesia inhabits a region in which seven neighboring countries have declared similar zones: Australia, Vietnam, Kampuchea, Japan, Papua New Guinea, Burma, and the Philippines. But Indonesia's declaration, nonetheless, will require the negotiation of median boundaries with four of these countries and also with Malaysia, which has not yet formalized its claim to an EEZ. There is also the possibility of a future dispute with China, which claims islands in the South China Sea, but in the absence of formal diplomatic relations between the two countries this issue is not presently negotiable. Although the overlapping boundaries declared by Papua New Guinea and the Philippines pose no major problems for Indonesia, those with Vietnam, Australia, and Malaysia could prove contentious; in recent years, however, Indonesia has managed to resolve bilateral issues with Australia and with Malaysia relatively peaceably. A most potentially escalatory conflict thus lies with Vietnam, as its definition of an EEZ is not accepted by Indonesia and involves some oceanic tracts that Jakarta has already contracted out for oil exploration. Here, then, is another facet of the post-1975 situation whereby a Vietnam unified by military force is a source of some apprehension for an ASEAN neighbor.

Indonesia has a naval base at Tanjung Uban in the Natuna islands, well northwest of the west coast of Kalimantan and thus commanding the main shipping lanes between west and east Malaysia. In December 1979 a senior Vietnamese spokesman said that the Natunas belong to Vietnam, and Foreign Minister Mochtar Kusumaatmadja was reported to have told Vietnam to keep its "hands off."

Then too, it remains to be seen what will be the final outcome of the Law of the Sea negotiations being conducted under the aegis of the United Nations. Most particularly, it remains to be seen whether, if the negotiations are aborted by a U.S. withdrawal, Indonesia will attempt to enforce restrictions on naval movements through its straits; such continued maritime passage was envisaged as a trade-off for the major powers' consenting to international control of mineral resources on the seabed. Indonesia's position astride several important narrow sea passages makes it a crucial case in this regard. What may be a growing conflict between Vietnam and Indonesia, as well as the remainder of ASEAN, may be seen to have a territorial as well as an ideological dimension. As noted in chapter seven by Simon, Vietnamese policies in Cambodia and in relation to Thailand have further served to draw ASEAN together in what is a burgeoning security as well as economic relationship.

Indonesia's Armed Forces: Structure, Deployment, Functions, and Arms Acquisitions

Indonesia's present political system is substantially and unmistakably a military order and has been so ever since the 1965 attempted coup that triggered a massive military retaliation against, and purge of, the Communist party of Indonesia (PKI), and opened the way for a military government.[17] Since 1965-1966, Indonesia has been run like one huge garrison by the armed forces (Abri).

The military, comprising roughly 0.4 percent of the overall population, has emerged as a distinct ruling elite, controlling all the essential governmental organs and state-owned enterprises. Military involvement in almost every facet of public life has been explicitly rationalized by the *dwi fungsi* (dual function) concept, which claims that the military's role is not simply to protect the nation in wartime, but also to undertake nation-building.

The dominance of the military in Indonesia's present public life can be easily demonstrated. The president is a retired four-star general, and so too is the speaker of the national parliament. The president-director of Pertamina, the state oil company, the chief of Bulog (the national logistics board), and the head of Golkar (the government-sponsored mass political movement) are all two-star generals.

Even where civilians serve as ministers—and in early 1980 there were fourteen civilians in the twenty-four-man inner cabinet—there are numerous generals, admirals, and air marshals to fill the key positions in the administration. Overall, about a third of the Indonesian army is engaged in civil and administrative duties. In the civil service there are generals in most of the top jobs, in an unvarying pattern since the army came to power. In 1966, twenty-three of sixty-four directors-general in the civil service were ranking military officers. This rose to about 50 percent in following years, but has declined somewhat since 1974. However, a survey conducted in September 1979 found that nineteen of the sixty-three directors-general were military men. About half the secretaries-general in the civil service are military men, as are all but two of the inspectors-general.

If the minister is not an Abri man, then the secretary-general invariably is. Only in the Ministry of Mining and Energy is neither the minister nor the secretary-general from Abri, but the inspector-general is. Indeed, in every ministry except justice and health, the inspector-general—a watchdog, who scrutinizes funding and performance—is a ranking military officer.

In certain critical departments and regions the government maintains an all-military dominance. In the Department of Interior, for example, generals predominate. The minister, secretary-general, inspector-general, and each of the four directors-general are from Abri.

Such a pattern is substantially repeated at provincial levels. At the end of 1977, twenty-one of the country's twenty-seven governors were military officers. After a major reshuffle in January 1978, there were still nineteen military governors. In Java, four of the five provinces or special territories have military governors, the only exception being Jogjakarta. Finally, many of the main overseas diplomatic postings and most of the large state-owned enterprises, such as Pertamina, are parceled out to military officers.

With corruption, inefficiency, and red tape rife, Abri cannot convincingly justify its monopoly on grounds of better management or the mastery of technical skills, rightly or wrongly, a widespread staple of the economic-development literature. The most widely employed justification is that, in a country as geographically far-flung and fragmented, and culturally as disparate, as Indonesia, only the military has the authority, the cohesion, and the coercive resources to keep the country together.

Many officers have been trained at Seskoad, the army staff and command school in Bandung, but the very top echelons of the military managers have been sent abroad in droves to military colleges in the United States, Western Europe, and Australia. From 1950 to 1979 some 5,500 Indonesian military personnel attended courses in the United States under what is known as the International Military Education and Training Program (IMETP). But foreign training and the professionalism it was supposed to inculcate have not been entirely successful. Pertamina's multi-million-dollar debacle in 1975 was merely the most sensational scandal, revealing ineptitude and corruption in military-run enterprises.

Critics complain that without effective checks against corruption, favoritism, and red tape, the military can do virtually as it pleases. But in contemporary Indonesia any criticism of the military leads inevitably to the question of subsequent alternatives, and most people acknowledge that there is at present no other institution powerful or cohesive enough to govern the country. The imprint of the military has thus been stamped into civilian life, and its role has involved a diffuse set of functions, spanning traditional security activities, political leadership, and also a leading role in the economy. But whether this osmosis of military practices will ultimately result in genuinely beneficial and irreversible changes, or whether it will turn out to provide only a veneer over traditional Indonesia, is a debatable question.

The Indonesian Army

The current disposition of Indonesia's armed forces is about 94 or 95 battalions, with half of them located in Java (thus reflecting its population density and potential importance). The rest are scattered throughout the archipelago. All are well below their nominal strength, however; some have as few as 300 men, and many of the troops are poorly trained and equipped.

To remedy this parlous situation the army, prompted principally and energetically by General Mohammed Jusuf since his appointment as commander of the armed forces and defense minister in February 1978, has embarked on a program to upgrade 50 of its battalions to a high standard of equipment and training. This process had, by 1980, only just begun and it is too early to see whether it is likely to be completed. Even so, the fifty-one-year-old General Jusuf, a member of the South Sulawesi Buginese nobility, already has put his personal stamp on Abri, and has begun very purposefully what he claims will be a major overhaul of all of Indonesia's armed forces.

In addition to its front-line battalions, the Indonesian army today has the usual support units, including artillery, engineers, signals, armored corps, ordnance, and supply. It also has very large numbers of men in what the army leadership regards as the all-important territorial apparatus. This group, which accounts for perhaps half of the army's personnel, is engaged in providing local security and supporting the army's civic mission. The territorial command extends down to the lowest levels of the population, with a noncommissioned officer stationed in every village.

Included in the army structure but operating under a separate command directly under the army chief of staff are the elite Red Berets, once known as the RPKAD (para-commandos) but now renamed Kopasanda (secret-operations command). The men in this force are trained in intelligence gathering, sabotage, parachuting, and beach landings, thereby fulfilling a role similar to the British Special Forces. There are at present about 4,000 of these troops, but General Jusuf is said to want to increase their members perhaps sixfold. If Indonesia were ever to send forces to help in the defense of a fellow member of ASEAN, it would probably choose a Red Beret unit, or perhaps a battalion from Kostrad, the strategic reserve. This clearly could be no more than a token gesture of support; that is, Indonesia has little capacity for the projection of force outside its own island territories.

Assuming, however, that such a plan were assayed, the Indonesians would have little difficulty getting their troops or equipment to the ASEAN country in question. The air force has a fleet of fifteen C-130 Hercules transport aircraft and, though poor engine maintenance keeps about half of them on the ground at any one time, there would be enough available to carry a modest force overseas with a shuttle service. Six additional C-130 Hercules aircraft are on order. The air force could also, *in extremis,* call on the resources of Garuda, the government-owned civil airline, as it did at the time of the invasion of East Timor in 1975. Garuda currently has a fleet of more than fifty passenger aircraft.

Generally speaking, Indonesia's forces are deployed at least as much, if not more so, against the contingency of internal insurrection. And as noted in one recent press report, the principal potential source of domestic rebellion has changed in recent years, from Communist to Muslim. As Pamela Hollie notes:

Tension between the Government and Indonesia's fragmented Moslem majority, which makes up 90 per cent of the population has been building for years. Two of the most serious rebellions since Indonesia gained independence in 1949 were Moslem-fomented. Extremists repeatedly tried and failed to assassinate the country's first President, Sukarno, who was eased from power by General Suharto in 1966. Only Moslems are capable of posing a challenge to President Suharto's New Order. As a general, Mr. Suharto led army forces that savagely suppressed a Communist coup attempt in 1965, and Communists have since presented no discernible threat . . . If Moslems were united, Indonesia might be ripe for revolution . . . More potent concerns, such as the Government's close association with the military and its domestic and fiscal policies, are not often debated openly. Certain kinds of political meetings are risky. The military quickly puts down demonstrations.[18]

The same analysis proceeds to discuss growing conflict between the Muslim majority and its terrorist groups and the Chinese minority, which is said to control much of Indonesia's commerce. The situation appears comparable to that recently witnessed in Vietnam with the exiling of numerous Chinese-origin "boat people" and, among other things, may presage ethnic conflicts that could sour Indonesia's relationships with neighboring Singapore.

Some analysts believe that at present only half of Indonesia's actual military expenditure is recorded in official budgets. The rest is believed to come from the little-publicized flow of funds from the military's extensive corporate-business undertakings into special accounts at defense headquarters. Thus, profits from the military's entrepreneurial and other business activities help to bridge the substantial gap between the official defense budget and the forces' actual annual expenditures. In the years since military officers began to run businesses seized from the Dutch in 1957-1958, Indonesia's armed forces have become associates in a variety of enterprises, from shipping companies and airlines to hotels and timber concessions. In 1980, as in previous years, well over two-thirds of the money allotted to the military will go to routine expenditures, with the main allocations being pay and allowances, maintenance and travel.

Officially, Indonesia's armed forces receive only a modest share of the country's resources, 3.4 percent of GNP in 1979. Under the 1980-1981 budget, which started to come into effect on 2 April 1980, Abri is to receive $2.1 billion. This is about 45 percent more than the $1.47 billion set aside for Abri in the 1979-1980 budget, but, as the 1980-1981 budget as a whole is up by 51 percent to $16.9 billion, thanks mostly to the government's windfall gains resulting from the devaluation of the rupiah in 1978, Abri's apparent percentage share has fallen. This is in line with a trend that has become increasingly apparent in recent years. Though the national budget has more than doubled in the past five years, from $8.4 billion to $16.9 billion, official military spending has gone up by a more modest 68.4 percent. As a result, the military's known share of the budget has been steadily diminishing from 14.7 percent in 1977-1978 to 12.5 percent in 1980-1981. Its share of the nation's GNP declined from 3.8 percent in 1975 to 3.4 percent in 1979, at a time when the total Indonesian forces also declined somewhat from 266,000 to 242,000 personnel. These figures undoubtedly are reflective of the more benign regional-threat environment in recent years, particularly regarding decreased tensions with neighboring Malaysia.[19]

On the evidence of last year's budget figures, after routine expenditures are covered, a mere $619 million, or 7.6 percent of the total budget, is left over for development spending in the military sector, a heading that includes funds raised domestically as well as through foreign military credits.

One notable feature of the 1980-1981 budget was that the government proposed to finance an increased share of development from domestic sources. This is in line with the heightened emphasis recently placed on self-reliance in the military sector, though the ability and willingness of the government to do this is probably due more to windfall gains from devaluation and from oil earnings than to any remarkable long-term strategy.

The budget papers tabled by President Suharto early in January 1980 typically gave no details about the way Abri's development funds will be spent. There is little additional information in the government booklet dealing with the planned receipts and expenditures. Of the twenty-four separate plan booklets issued by the government, the one for the military is by far the slimmest—a mere four pages, so generalized as to be practically meaningless. By contrast, the booklet on the agricultural sector is a quarter of an inch thick. It is nevertheless generally expected by informed sources that the bulk of these funds will go toward the construction of new barracks and housing complexes and the provision of new training grounds—projects being promoted by General Jusuf.

The balance of Abri's development budget is made up of foreign military credits.[20] Included under this heading are such items as a squadron of F5E Tiger fighters, which the Indonesian air force is buying from the United States in a deal funded through the U.S. Foreign Military Sales (FMS) program. Also included is a figure covering the cost of a year's installments and escalations on the navy's three new guided-missile corvettes, four new high-speed patrol boats, two new West German submarines, and a new training ship.

Military hardware acquired in this way, whether it be jet fighters, ammunition, or even reconditioned armored personnel carriers (APCs), goes down as an undifferentiated lump sum entry in the Abri development budget and is paid off, over varying periods of time, along with other debt-service obligations. No department-by-department breakdown of debt service is given in the budget, and so there is no indication what equipment, military or otherwise, is being paid off in any given year.

On the face of it, foreign military credits of about $200 million a year should be enough to fund what is still, by comparison with many other countries, a fairly modest level of military equipment purchases, even allowing for the purchase of ammunition, always a costly item and one that sits rather awkwardly in the development section of the budget. However, even if the foreign military credits are insufficient for these purposes, the amounts to be found—presumably from Abri's private-sector activities and profits—are probably small in comparison to the routine earnings of Indonesia's military-sponsored business ventures. One Indonesian newspaper editor, known as a critic of the government, remarked that military spending has been "very modest" since the "New Order" government came to power: "In the past when we were still involved in the campaign to liberate West Irian, the military got 60-70 percent of the budget. Now it may be 30 percent, of which only 12 percent or 15 percent is admitted. But even so it shows that the emphasis lately has been on development."[21]

The Indonesian Navy

The Indonesian navy is currently undergoing a drastic overhaul and restructuring. Gone are the heady dreams of demonstrating that the Indian Ocean should really be called the Indonesian Ocean (Sukarno's unilateral renaming in 1964), which were once cynically encouraged by the Soviet Union. Most of the 104 Soviet-built warships acquired in the late 1950s and early 1960s have long since been scrapped or immobilized because of lack of spare parts. The much more modestly sized force now under construction is intended for the patrol and protection of Indonesia's sprawling archipelago.

On paper, Indonesia's navy of over 200 warships appears to be one of the most formidable concentrations of naval power in Asia. But, as such authorities as the International Institute for Strategic Studies (IISS), the Stockholm International Peace Research Institute (SIPRI), and *Jane's Fighting Ships* point out, only a "fairly small proportion" is still operational. Three of the fourteen Soviet Whisky-class submarines acquired during Sukarno's volatile flirtation with the Soviet bloc remain in commission, but only one is still capable of submerged operations. The largest warships still serviceable are four 1450-ton Claude Jones-class destroyer escorts provided by the United States a little over five years ago. Powered by four 9,200 horsepower diesels, they can reach a top speed of 22 knots and carry two triple-torpedo tube sets and 50-caliber guns. Three aging Soviet-built Riga-class frigates are all that is left of a once much-larger force. Their range at 15 knots is 2,500 miles, though theoretically they are capable of 28 knots. Other vessels include two slightly smaller Italian-built frigates of late 1950s vintage, two Soviet submarine tenders that now serve as command ships, and an elderly collection of supply and survey ships, tugs, and landing craft.

Nine new ships are now on order with a view to giving the Indonesian navy the flexibility, modernity, and punch it presently lacks. The nucleus of this new force will consist of three 1,500-ton Dutch Corvettes, each armed with French Exocet MM-38 guided missiles, and four missile-equipped South Korean fast patrol boats. Two 1,400-ton submarines are also being built in West Germany. Naval manpower is undergoing intensive training. The overall personnel size, however, is to be reduced progressively over the next twenty years, from the present 38,000 to 25,000. But the marine commandos, 5,000-strong, will be retained.

The navy is better endowed for troop-transport duties. It has a fleet of passenger ships and landing vessels in its Sea Transport Command and also owns its own shipping line, PT Admiral Lines. Like the air force, the navy could also commandeer private transport, if necessary. But the navy is not well equipped for transporting specialized vehicles, like tanks. It does, however, have a dozen tank-landing craft in the fleet, with another four on order. It has also ordered a number of smaller landing craft from local shipyards.

Suharto's government has sought, wherever possible, to standardize the various subsystems being installed in its new warships. A Dutch-made electronics system will be used, for instance, in all vessels. Dutch naval experts have also mapped out a logistic support system so comprehensive that it is reputed to foresee every flag and lifejacket likely to be needed over the next fifteen years.

Of the nine new ships currently on order, the four 250-ton fast patrol boats are nearing completion in South Korea's Tacoma Marine Industries (KTMI) yard. These boats, armed with surface-to-surface guided missiles and with a top speed of 40 knots, are capable of outpacing and sinking even a large, well-armed warship. They will spearhead the new patrol force formed in 1973-1974, when the Australian government handed over two 146-ton Attack-class boats formerly in service with the Royal Australian Navy. In 1978 the Australians provided six lightweight 16-meter patrol boats built at the Hawker de Havilland shipyard in Sydney. These brought the patrol fleet to about 42 vessels. Included are a dozen of the 36 Soviet-built Komar-class attack boats supplied in the 1960s, six 190-ton Kralje-vica-class ex-Yugoslav patrol boats, and three 147-ton Kelabang-class boats of Indonesian construction. Together these could presumably seal the Malacca strait if the Indonesian government so desired, though that would of course depend on the source and extent of its opposition.

The Indonesian Air Force

What hitherto has not attracted much explicit attention and definition is Indonesia's air space and the use of air power to complement and implement land and naval power. Although Indonesia has had an air force ever since independence and is now the second-largest exporter of light aircraft in Asia after Japan, the air force was somewhat under a cloud during the early years of Suharto's New Order because of the apparent complicity of some of its commanders in the abortive Untung coup.

Until recently, the air force suffered from the general neglect of maintenance, which affected all sophisticated equipment in an atmosphere where there was no planned weapons-procurement policy. Indeed, Geoffrey Kemp has cited the earlier Indonesian case as an example of the gulf that may develop between paper weapons inventories and actual deployable force in the third-world milieu, where prestige considerations may override more pragmatic ones:

> The Soviet Union, eager to assist the far-reaching ambitions of President Sukarno, provided Indonesia with lavish amounts of military equipment, and by 1965 the nominal inventory of major Soviet weapons in the Indonesian navy and air force consisted of the following: Navy—1 heavy cruiser, 5 destroyers, 12 submarines; and Air Force—18 MiG-21s, 42-plus MiG-17/19s, 25 Tu-16s, 25 IL-28s. By all accounts this was an impressive list for a less industrial country at that time and, on paper, it helped to make Indonesia by far the largest military power in Southeast Asia. Yet when Sukarno was overthrown in 1965, it was discovered that virtually none of the Soviet-supplied jet aircraft and warships were operable. The reasons for this extraordinary discrepancy between *nominal* and *operational* inventories were simple: the Indonesians were not capable of operating and maintaining such sophisticated weapons, and the Soviets were quite willing to provide weapons they knew would never be used.[22]

Kemp further points out, however, that Great Britain, then fearing the use of Indonesia's apparent air capability, actually rotated an RAF V-bomber squadron out of Singapore to act as a deterrent against it.

Nowadays, Indonesia's air force deploys a rather modest complement of modern aircraft, with a distinctively *defensive* cast. It has sixteen U.S. F-5s and another sixteen older Canadian-origin Sabre jets. Additionally, it fields sixteen OV-10 aircraft and a considerable number of transports and helicopters, seeming perhaps to denote an emphasis on internal mobility, that is, for domestic insurgency contingencies. Older Soviet Tu-16 and IL-28 bombers, and MiG-15/17/19/21 fighter aircraft are listed by the IISS as "in storage," that is, inoperative.[23]

Arms Acquisition Patterns: Diversity of Sources

Even a cursory glance at Indonesia's present orders of battle—army, navy, and air force—and its recent sources of weapons acquisitions will reveal the almost startling, bewildering number of supply sources involved. Indeed, since the period of nearly sole reliance on Soviet weapons that ended after Sukarno's overthrow in the mid-1960s, Indonesia has had perhaps the single most diversified pattern of arms acquisitions in the entire Third World. That appears to denote an almost insistent, maybe exaggerated, compulsion to avoid even the appearance of dependency, that is, it is a reflection of almost extreme nonalignment. Just what the impact might be on Indonesia's combat readiness, given the complex requirements inherent in coping with the weaponry of numerous suppliers, is not easily ascertained. One might surmise that a heavy cost is involved.

Indonesia's army, for instance, now uses American, French, and Soviet tanks; British, French, and Soviet armored personnel carriers (APCs) and mechanized infantry combat vehicles (MICVs); French antitank missiles; artillery drawn from numerous sources; and helicopters and light aircraft from the United States, the Soviet Union, France, and Yugoslavia. Its navy deploys Soviet and West German submarines; U.S. and Soviet frigates; Corvettes with French sea missiles; patrol craft from West Germany, the United States, the Soviet Union, Yugoslavia, Great Britain, and Australia. Its air force is now more uniformly of U.S. origin, but includes French and German helicopters.

And, if the previous patterns of diversity in acquisition were not extreme enough, what the Indonesian air force now has on order, according to the IISS,[24] seems if anything to represent an extension of such patterns. Those orders involve maritime reconnaissance aircraft from Australia, French transports, retransferred U.S.-origin Skyhawk fighter-bombers from Israel, and trainer aircraft from Switzerland. In particular, Indonesia could face severe problems regarding maintenance and resupply of spare parts if involved in a protracted regional conflict that required provisioning from the outside to keep its war machine functioning. On the contrary, however, its oil revenues are clearly providing considerable leverage in the arms markets, allowing it to shop around and to spread arms deals around to numerous suitors.

There is at present no nuclear dimension in Indonesia's actual or immediate strategic capability. There is, however, a heightening Indonesian awareness that some powers—notably the United States and the Soviet Union, but also China and potentially several others—that transit through or over Indonesia's regional space have a nuclear dimension to their own capabilities. In Sukarno's last years Indonesia made a number of boastful and fraudulent claims about Indonesia's impending nuclear potency. Conceivably, future Indonesian leaders might be interested in a serious project for a nuclear-free Southeast Asia, perhaps along the lines of the treaty denuclearizing Latin America, but there are no immediate signs that such is presently in prospect.

Prospects

Indonesian experience since 1945 and currently prevailing Indonesian elite perceptions converge in according highest security preoccupation to what is happening within what is defined by the national leadership as their country's national security, their national territorial (certainly including territorial sea) space. This does not mean, of course, that there is indifference about the policies of the great powers. Indeed, considerable attention is paid to their activities, actual and potential, especially in Southeast Asia, but Indonesian leaders are relatively pessimistic about their ability seriously to deflect a major power from its chosen course. This pessimism may seem ironic in view of the fact that the record of the past forty or fifty years recurrently has demonstrated that the ambitions -and projects of great powers active in Southeast Asia—the Dutch, the Japanese, the British, the Americans, the Soviets—have rarely, and at best only transiently, been accomplished and, even at their apogees, usually with higher costs and lower rewards than were apparently preconceived. Despite their generally prevailing pessimism about their ability seriously to help structure elements of the contemporary international order, the confidence and expectations of the Indonesian ruling elite have grown regarding their role in the shaping of a regional or subregional order—especially through ASEAN, but also through such ideas as the archipelagic doctrine.

Indonesia today is fundamentally a state run by its military with some technocratic collaborators. It is institutionally sterile and under the surface crust of authority there seethe, as previously noted, several potential and some actually manifest rebellions, ideological challenges, and popular discontents—though in recent years the public manifestations of these have taken markedly discrete forms, geographically and ideologically, and with little or no serious substantive or operational international linkages. This could change, however, particularly if there were to emerge transnational aspects of a Muslim religious upsurge.

Generational change, conspicuous corruption, governmental sterility, acute economic inequalities, communal antipathies, ideological fanaticisms, irredentist or separatist ambitions—such classic ingredients of localized violence are to be found individually or severally in many parts of the Indonesian archipelago today. And, hence, granted the relatively extensive record of recurrent bouts of violence in or near the Indonesian archipelago in the past fifty years, it would not be surprising to find that there were more outbursts in the years immediately ahead.

The Indonesian realm today displays, in summary, a number of features that are characteristic of what has been said by contemporary analysts to help make up a new strategic map:

the highly declamatory politics of a now globalized states-system with about a hundred new state sovereignties

the heightened strategic and economic importance accorded to even very small islands

the ever-shifting geopolitical, geostrategic significance of world energy—especially oil—resources the extension of a country's sea-space and the consequent considerable reduction of international waters

the impact of new weapons technologies

the ever-ramifying aspects of intense Sino-Soviet rivalry

Each of these has important present and potential implications for Indonesian security and shape and condition its present and future role in regional and in international security affairs. By its size and situation Indonesia is inescapably a significant regional factor in Southeast Asia. Its ruling elites are not, on the evidence of recent years, particularly self-confident and successful as regional managers or as producers of regional order in any positive sense, but they can, and at times do, exert considerable negative influence as in effect the approvers or disapprovers of projects and proposals of other powers operating in "their" region. This is hardly a regional ordering or management role in any positive sense; but it is a not insignificant dimension of the operations current in a region characterized by considerable volatility.

Thus far, Indonesia's geography, that is, its archipelagic character, has reduced the prospects for regional conflicts. For the time being, older territorial issues with Malaysia have been submerged within ASEAN. Those with Australia apparently appear more or less resolved. At present Vietnam seems to be the major threat, but only if its recent expansionist policies are carried further so as to threaten Indonesia itself—over maritime demarcations or the possession of islands—or one or more of its new-found partners in ASEAN, either Thailand or the Philippines. A seemingly burgeoning Indonesian security relationship with the United States, albeit not made formal, could place Indonesia in a state of confrontation with the combined power of the Soviet Union and Vietnam. Beside that still hypothetical contingency, however, Indonesia's primary short-term security concerns appear to be internal unless, in addition, assertive policies regarding maritime-transit rights through the straits should produce confrontation with either or even both major global naval powers. Indonesia remains, by dint of location and resources, a strategic prize, and that largely defines its security dilemma with respect to the outside.

Notes

1. *Indonesia, Sick Man on the Mend*, Report to the Committee on Foreign Relations, U.S. Senate, by Senator Joseph S. Clark on a study mission to Indonesia, 1968.

2. Rex Mortimer, ed., *The Showcase State: The Illusion of Indonesia's 'Accelerated Modernisation'* (Sydney, Australia: Angus and Robertson, 1973).

3. Michael Leifer, "Patterns of Indonesian Foreign Policy," in *The Foreign Policies of the Powers*, 2nd ed., ed. F.S. Northedge (London: Faber, 1974), p. 374.

4. Malcolm Caldwell, ed., *Ten Years' Military Terror in Indonesia* (Nottingham: Spokesman Books, 1975).

5. Harold Crouch, "Patrimonialism and Military Rule in Indonesia," *World Politics* 31 (July 1979).

6. Willard H. Elsbree, Japan's Role in Southeast Asia Nationalist Movements 1940-45 (Cambridge, Mass.: Harvard University Press, 1953); Harry Benda, *The Crescent and the Rising Sun* (New York: Morton Publishers, 1958); and Joyce C. Lebra, *Japanese-Trained Armies in Southeast Asia—Independence and Volunteer Forces in World War II* (Singapore: Heinemann Educational Books, Asia, 1977), especially chapter 4.

7. G. McTurnan Kahin, *Nationalism and Revolution in Indonesia* (Ithaca: Cornell University Press, 1952); and B.R. O'G. Anderson, *Java in a Time of Revolution* (Ithaca: Cornell University Press, 1972).

8. A. Lipjhart, *The Trauma of Decolonization: The Dutch and West New Guinea* (New Haven: Yale University Press, 1966).

9. J.A.C. Mackie, *Konfrontasi: The Indonesia-Malaysia Dispute 1963-1966* (London: Oxford University Press, 1974).

10. Harold Crouch, *The Army and Politics in Indonesia* (Ithaca: Cornell University Press, 1978). It contains excellently judicious sections on the 1965 "coup" and on different perceptions of security and diplomacy held by the Ministry of Foreign Affairs under Adam Malik and by leading army commanders.

11. Michael Leifer, "Indonesia and the Incorporation of East Timor," *The World Today* 32 (September 1976); "Indonesia and Timor," *World Review* (Queensland, Australia) 17 (October 1978); and A. Kohen and J. Taylor, *An Act of Genocide: Indonesia's Invasion of East Timor* (A. Tapol, 1979).

12. Leifer, "Patterns of Indonesian Foreign Policy."

13. I have illustrated and elaborated this point somewhat in "New States and International Order," in *The Bases of International Order*, ed. Alan James (London: Oxford University Press, 1973).

14. The most thorough and clear study of Indonesian impressions of the "International System" and of great-power policies known to me is in the book published by Franklin B. Weinstein, *Indonesian Foreign Policy and the Dilemma of Dependence. From Sukarno to Suharto* (Ithaca: Cornell University Press, 1976). It is based principally on interviews conducted and data collected in Indonesia from 1968 to 1970 and during the first quarter of

1973. It now needs to be supplemented by further inquiries. Weinstein's principal interests were the origins and evolution of the Indonesian foreign-policy elite's view of the world and especially of aid and independence.

15. Peter Lyon, "ASEAN and Regionalism," in *New Directions in the International Relations of Southeast Asia* (Singapore: Singapore University Press, 1973); and "ASEAN After Ten Years," for the Institute for Developing Economies, Tokyo (forthcoming).

16. Ray S. Cline, *World Power Assessment 1977. A Calculus of Strategic Drift*, for the Center for Strategic and International Studies, Washington, D.C. (Boulder, Colo.: Westview, 1977).

17. There are quite a lot of good studies of the Indonesian military. See, especially, Guy J. Pauker, "The Role of the Military in Indonesia" in *The Role of the Military in Underdeveloped Countries*, ed. John J. Johnson (Princeton: Princeton University Press, 1962); Peter Polomka, *Indonesia Since Sukarno* (London: Penguin Books, 1971); Harold Crouch, *The Army and Politics in Indonesia* (Ithaca: Cornell University Press, 1978); Harold W. Maynard, "A Comparison of Military Elite Role Perceptions in Indonesia and the Philippines" (Ph.D. diss., American University, 1976), University Microfilms no. 76-19-448. This argument is presented briefly as "Views of the Indonesian and Philippine Military Elites," in *The Military and Security in the Third World. Domestic and International Impacts*, ed. Sheldon W. Simon (Boulder, Colo.: Westview, 1978), pp. 123-153. For this section I have drawn heavily on a number of well-informed articles, mostly by David Jenkins, in the *Far Eastern Economic Review (FEER)*: see especially "General Jusuf," *FEER*, 2 March 1979; "Taking a defensive position," *FEER*, 13 July 1979; "A New Order in the Army," *FEER*, 21 December 1979; "The Military's Secret Cache," *FEER*, 8 February 1980.

18. *The New York Times*, 5 April 1981, p. 6E.

19. International Institute for Strategic Studies (IISS) *The Military Balance, 1980-1981*, London, p. 97.

20. For a perspective view of this subject, see Stockholm International Peace Research Institute (SIPRI), *The Arms Trade with the Third World* (New York: Humanities Press, 1971), esp. pp. 460-467; and SIPRI *Yearbooks*.

21. Quoted in *FEER*, 8 February 1980, p. 72.

22. Neuman and Harkavy, p. 266.

23. *The Military Balance*, p. 69.

24. Ibid., p. 106.

**Part III
Middle East**

9 Egypt

Gabriel Ben-Dor

The security policy of Egypt since the 1952 Revolution is a most intriguing and instructive case study in the prominent role of the military in developing countries on various interstate as well as intrastate levels. Not only were the Free Officers among the first activists in the Third World to establish a radical military regime, but Egypt went on to engage in a variety of regional conflicts, eventually building up a very large military force—nearly 400,000 men in the armed forces (1978-1979), supported by about 500,000 reserves— spending over $2.8 billion directly on defense (about 22 percent of the GNP).[1] In the last generation, Egypt has fought four major wars with Israel; at the same time, its regime has gradually but nonetheless dramatically evolved into a semi-open, multiparty, partly civilianized, postmilitary political system. The pioneer of the military regime in the Third World became the pioneer of the postmilitary regime.[2]

Beyond this, there are three more factors that make the Egyptian case particularly interesting. One is the number of shifts in perception of the global power structure and the swift political responses to these perceptual changes, bringing Egypt to the end of a full circle in a generation, moving from dependence on the British, to nonalignment to a pro-Soviet orientation, to disengagement from that orientation, and finally to a strongly pro-Western orientation. The second is an equally dramatic and profound series of perceptual changes on the regional level, again culminating in a virtual full circle, in two-and-a-half decades transforming the undisputed leader of the Arab world into a virtual outcast among the Arab countries, and the most important external conflict Egypt has been involved in has been dramatically altered with President Anwar Sadat's 1977 initiative and the subsequent Egyptian-Israeli peace treaty in 1979. As these two levels of analysis indicate, Egyptian security policy has been strikingly dynamic, and any attempt to conceptualize and theorize about it must come to terms with this dynamic attribute.

However, the third factor, which is the overwhelmingly important one in understanding Egypt's formulation of national security, is rather static, as it is a given fact of life. The most profound influence on Egyptian policy is the almost hopeless, evergrowing, and constantly huge gap between Egypt's large and consistently increasing population on the one hand (40 million people at the end of the 1970s, growing at the rate of about 1 million

---

Editors' note: This chapter was written before the assassination of President Anwar Sadat on October 6, 1981.

179

per year) and its limited resources on the other. Egypt is still a primarily rural society that is too heavily dependent on a key cash crop—staple cotton, the annual exports of which have averaged about 315,000 tons for decades. In 1975 it had to support a population of 35 million on a cultivated area of less than 6 million acres, although in 1821 a bit over 3 million acres had had to support only 4.23 million people.[3] The resulting widespread poverty and the need to look for every conceivable reform in the countryside—only about 4 percent of Egypt's territory is cultivable—while coping with the enormous pressures and problems created by the influx of millions of impoverished ex-peasants to the ill-prepared cities constantly seem to keep Egypt on the verge of a revolutionary eruption, bankruptcy, or both. Consequently, resources must be marshaled, at worst to keep the economy from breaking down altogether, at best to effect a massive structural transformation—for which huge investments are necessary—whereby the productive capacity of the industrial sector will be radically expanded, the tourist and service sectors will flourish, and the dangerous rate of urban unemployment and underemployment will be more or less overcome.

The fact is that Egypt's own resources simply do not suffice for the maximum goal, and at times they have been proven inadequate even for the minimal goal.[4] Thus, Egypt has been forced to look for those resources outside from one or more of the superpowers, from oil-rich Arab countries on the governmental level, and from remittances from hundreds of thousands of expatriate Egyptians (some sources estimate these at two million) in the Arab world. However, in order to ensure access to these vitally needed material resources, Egypt has felt the urge and the necessity to play a highly active and visible role based on its critically important geostrategic location and large pool of manpower (which is a debilitating *economic* liability but an obvious *military* asset) on a variety of levels, both global and regional. (Nasser defined these levels as the three circles: Arab, African and Islamic.) In fact, there can be little or no argument as to the assumption that it is only the combination of its geostrategic importance with the determined effort to utilize it via an active foreign policy backed by a huge military establishment (which it can ill afford) that has enabled Egypt to escape the fate of say, a Bangladesh: abject poverty made hopeless by the inability to attract resources to effect fundamental change.

Hence the critical, perennial Egyptian dilemma, "the dialectics of poverty and power": in order to harness outside resources, an active, vigorous foreign policy has to be pursued in a conflict-torn area full of potential enemies, and in order to play such a role Egypt must maintain a military force and engage in danger-fraught conflicts out of all proportion to its resources. (By contrast, the Saudi dilemma is "the dialectics of wealth and weakness.") This dilemma is at the heart of Egypt's security policy, from which the Sadat initiative attempted to signal a way out. Our analysis will address itself to this dilemma and to other factors on three levels: interstate functions (global and regional), primarily military functions (forces and doctrines), and intrastate functions (political, social, economic, and technological).

Assumptions about the International System

The early thinking of the postrevolutionary regime in Egypt was strongly colored by the struggle to put an end to the British military presence in the Suez Canal area. In fact, this was perceived to be the first pressing national task to which all political forces were committed. This commitment was enhanced by the strong residue of resentment against the British—and to a lesser extent, the French—for their role in first bringing Egypt under European colonial control. Moreover, the European powers were perceived to be interfering constantly in the political thicket of semiindependence and to have the ambition to continue to maintain bases in Egypt and elsewhere in the Arab world, while attempting to put down independence movements in the Arab countries. All this was coupled with the Cold War rhetoric coming out of John Foster Dulles's United States, according to which the resented British and French were to be considered as part of the "Free World," led by the United States. Although culturally very much Western in orientation, Nasser and his fellow Free Officers initially were obsessed with this general resentment factor. Their views were later reinforced by the 1956 Suez War, the French attempt to crush the nationalist movement in Algeria, and the repeated wars with Israel in which invariably Egypt found Israel armed by one or more of the Western powers. Some very ill-thought-out diplomatic moves, such as the establishment of the Baghdad Pact in 1955, merely served to reinforce then prevailing Egyptian perceptions.

The conclusion drawn from all this was a perceived need to lessen and eventually totally eliminate Egypt's dependence on the West for arms, to overcome the British presence once and for all, and to acquire a stable and reliable source of armaments. Such a source had to supply weapons on relatively convenient economic terms in large quantities and of high quality, unrelated to restrictions linked to the balance of power with Israel or considerations having to do with America's European allies. This was realized in the famous Egyptian-Soviet (via Czechoslovakia as a proxy) arms deal in 1955, and from then on fairly consistently well into the 1970s.[5]

This perceptible pro-Soviet shift lacked almost entirely an ideological dimension. Rather, it was a pragmatic attempt to swing the pendulum from one pole where Egypt was perceived to have been overly and unacceptably dependent, toward the other where support and resources seemed to be offered on more acceptable terms. Obviously, this had a great deal to do with the perception of the global system as essentially bipolar and as one in which the nonaligned—which happened to have an economic strategic value to the two great powers in their global competition—had a great deal of room to maneuver, particularly in alliance with other uncommitted states. This was to be an alliance of the uncommitted who wanted to make the structure of the international system permissive versus the committed superpowers who seemed to want to make the structure constrained. This was perceived to be particularly true as far as the United States was concerned. Hence Egypt's very important role in developing the concept of nonalignment from the Bandung conference on. For Egypt, a leading role in the nonaligned world along with Yugoslavia, India, Indonesia, Ghana, and others became an increasingly important component of the national identity card, along with Nasser's famous three circles.[6]

Nasser's policy shrewdly exploited the possibilities inherent in extracting resources from two global superpowers competing for the favor of a semidominant regional power maneuvering between them. Nasser had no illusions that nonalignment would create a new world order in which some balance between the superpowers combined with the moral force of the Third World and the close ideological affinity of its countries or the close personal relations between its leaders would lead to stability and security. The Egyptian perception was that military force was still to be predominantly important in regional security, and that in effect superpowers would not be impressed very much by regional powers that lacked military force and thus could be of little service. In the Egyptian mind nonalignment was a pragmatic, practical, and adroit way both to enhance national military power and to utilize its potential on the global scene; it was never considered a substitute for security by way of a strong national defense. Moreover, precisely because of the inevitability of outside arms, nonalignment was necessary to diversify sources and options.

From the Egyptian point of view, this active, rather anti-Western and pro-Soviet policy of nonalignment worked for a long time, at least until the aftermath of the 1967 war with Israel. Only when this version of nonalignment seemed to outlive its usefulness did perceptions change substantially. A combination of circumstances underlined the shift. The obvious failure of Soviet arms and doctrines in 1967 and later Soviet diplomacy in 1973 to prevent the losses to Israel or to effect Egypt's recovery, the Soviet Union's lack of leverage over the traditional military adversary, disillusionment with Soviet technology now perceived to be inferior to that of the West, and the heavy-handed and cumbersome behavior of the Soviet military personnel in Egypt all played their role. Equally important were the increasingly obvious disintegration of the leadership of the original third-world nations, the constraints on traditional policies of nonalignment when the United States seemingly lost interest in courting Egypt from 1968 to 1973, the *embourgeoisement* of the regime and the resulting anxiety over Soviet-supported radicalism in Africa and the Middle East, particularly in the overly Soviet-Cuban supported adventures in Angola, Ethiopia, Zaire (at least in the Egyptian view), South Yemen, and Afghanistan. This was further reinforced by the rise of an anti-Soviet Islam, the increasing dependence on anti-Soviet oil-rich regimes, and the need to attract Western investment in the liberal phase of the Sadat regime.

The most important single factor in fact, something of a filter variable, is really generational. The starting point for Nasser in 1952 was a heavy dependence on the British, for Sadat in 1970 it was a heavy dependence on the Soviets.[7] Thus, if nonalignment for Nasser honestly meant a strong pro-Soviet shift, for Sadat it meant a strong pro-American orientation. And just as Nasser personally resented the British, so Sadat personally resented the Russians. Most important, just as Nasser overcommitted Egypt to the Soviet Union in the late 1960s, so Sadat may have overcommitted the country to the United States in the early 1980s. The pendulum has completed a full swing, but it is unlikely to rest because pragmatic reasons for further swings keep appearing; generational corrections of course are by definition likely to continue; the environment is always dynamic.

The one thing that has remained truly constant throughout all this abundance of change is Egypt's commitment to a strong defense capability and the pursuit of its national interest in an international environment that its own dynamic policy must keep as permissive as possible, so as to enable Egypt to cope effectively with threats posed to it mostly by regional[8] and, to a lesser extent, domestic forces.

Definition of Threats to Regime and Nation

Although Egypt has common boundaries with only three countries, Libya, the Sudan, and Israel, its national-security policy identifies a multitude of actual and potential threats and a number of corresponding national objectives to be supported by the use or threat of military force. At this point we ought to note that in Egypt since 1952 little distinction exists between threats to the nation and threats to the regime, as the identification of the two in the mind of the policymaking elite is exceedingly strong. Moreover, the strong nationalist flavor of the regime, coupled with the long tradition of a highly centralized state populated by a rather high-density—and therefore easily controlled—homogenous population has reinforced the tendency to blur the conceptual boundaries between regime and nation, both centering around the majesty of the Egyptian state, a well-established heritage from time immemorial.

The most obvious perceived threat has been that of Israel, against which Egypt has fought five major wars and countless skirmishes since 1948. One war, 1948-1949, was fought in the framework of a grand Arab coalition, one, 1967, in a triple alliance, and one, 1973, in cooperation with Syria. On two occasions, however, Egypt had to fight alone, 1956 and 1969-1970, in the former case of course having had to confront an Anglo-French invasion at the same time. Although the initial Egyptian involvement with Israel was on the level of Egypt's involvement with, and commitment to, the Arab nationalist cause, Egypt has traditionally borne the brunt of the burden. This meant not only suffering by far the most painful human, material, and territorial losses, but also having had to rely principally and most exclusively on its own military power. Egyptians know that in addition to being left all by themselves on two occasions, in 1948-1949 the Arab coalition was poorly coordinated and little inter-Arab military cooperation was really evident; in 1967 the battle in the Sinai was by and large over before Jordan and Syria acted, the latter, notwithstanding its fiery rhetoric, making practically no strategic contribution to relieving the pressure on the Egyptian front. Only in 1973 did Egypt get real help from Syria in the opening days of the war, with good results, but even this came to an end when the Syrian attack was contained, and Israel again managed to concentrate its counteroffensive on the Egyptian front. Characteristically, the Egyptian-Syrian axis soon fell apart, and the war was terminated by Egypt—and the superpowers—when the situation on its own crumbling front demanded this.[9]

In addition to the simple and conspicuous, although rather deceptive, facts that Israel has on three occasions taken a part or almost all of the Sinai in 1949, 1956, and 1967, demonstrated in 1969-1970 virtual freedom of movement in the skies over Cairo, and managed in the later stages of the 1973 war to cross the Suez Canal and get within sixty miles of Cairo, three salient components of Israel's strategy have been perceived by Egypt as particularly threatening.[10] One is the general stress on mobility, logistics, and a blitzkrieg capability; the second is the doctrine of quickly transferring the war to enemy territory and concentrating *there* on the strongest adversary—this had invariably meant Egypt; and third is the Israeli attempt to maintain a balance of power against any conceivable combination of Arab armies, which in the Egyptian view has meant Israeli superiority vis-à-vis Egypt, particularly since conceivable combinations of Arab armies have thus far existed merely on paper.

In the early stages of the revolutionary regime a very real target was the liberation of the Suez Canal zone from British occupation by conventional or guerrilla forces, if necessary, and later its defense against the British and the French—which indeed became necessary in 1956. This threat later receded to the background, but it strongly influenced Egyptian strategic thinking for several years.

Threats to the revolutionary, and post-revolutionary, regime have been perceived at various times as: (a) a reactionary backlash backed by Western powers and conservative Arab states; (b) a possible military counter-coup; (c) subversion by agents of competing revolutionary regimes; (d) the penetration of the party apparatus by the military in a possible take-over attempt, perhaps backed by the Soviets (May 1971); (e) disaffection and mass riots, as in January 1977, in the wake of socioeconomic problems and other blatant failures undermining the legitimacy of the regime; (f) Marxist and leftist elements backed by various outside forces; and (g) Islamic elements organized in both secret societies and a mass movement, possibly backed by Libyan and other external patrons. Practically all of these threats have necessitated the allocation of military resources and the deployment of forces.

Recently, a threat has developed from the West, with the evolution of Libyan policy toward an adventurous, unpredictable, and distinctly anti-Egyptian posture, culminating on a number of occasions in serious armed clashes. At the same time, Egypt has had a long-standing interest in protecting its southern flank, the Sudan, the origin of its all-important water supply. Egypt has had a policy of extensive cooperation with the Sudan on security matters and has on a number of occasions extended aid crucial to the survival of the friendly Sudanese regime. In 1979-1980, Egypt reportedly deployed about 50,000 troops there in two armored and three infantry brigades.

The defense of the Suez Canal is perceived by Egypt as necessitating a naval presence and capability in the Red Sea, stretching to the Straits of Bab al Mandeb, on the correct assumption that control of these straits can lead to bottling up all traffic in the Red Sea, thus making the Suez Canal virtually useless. Hence Egypt's strong interest in that area, including Somalia on the African side of the straits. In 1973 Egypt successfully conducted a naval blockade against Israel's southern seaway by controlling these very straits.[11]

Egypt's active policy of leadership in the Arab world since 1955 notwithstanding, the visible gradual decline of this role in the past decade has necessitated not only the widespread use of military aid as a means of inter-Arab policy, but also an outright military capacity to support friendly regimes in remote places, if necessary by direct, massive military presence. During the Egyptian-Syrian Union of 1958-1961, Egypt had to maintain a substantial force level in Syria, and during the Yemen War of 1962-1967 as many as 80,000 Egyptian troops were tied down in Yemen in active and burdensome warfare, stretching Egyptian logistics to the limit. At present, Egypt has an obvious interest in maintaining the friendly regime in Oman in the Persian Gulf, one of its very few supporters left in the Arab world.

Finally, Egypt has been a traditional African power,[12] a role that it finds increasingly attractive as its problems on the inter-Arab level multiply. This has meant not only an active role in Afro-Arab military cooperation, but also a direct military participation in areas such as the security of the regime in Zaire, both in the framework of UN forces as well as in other multilateral frameworks. Recently, with the increase in Soviet- and Cuban-backed radical activity in African countries of interest to Egypt and with the Libyan invasion of Chad, a capability to contribute to the containment of such radical activity has become increasingly important to Egypt both as inherent interest as well as a demonstration of the fact that Egypt is a significant asset to Western interests and security in the region.

Strategies and Policies of Alignment
and Communication

Following an initial short period of internal consolidation and a successful effort to put an end to the British military presence in the Suez Canal zone, the revolutionary regime embarked upon an active campaign to build up an Egyptian role in foreign policy that would be congruent with the necessary response to the perceived series of threats.[13] Between 1955 and 1961 this meant an active role in the nonaligned movement aimed at enhancing Egypt's freedom to maneuver between the superpowers as well as to strengthen the Egyptian cause via-à-vis Israel. Even more important, Egypt appeared for the first time as the institutionalized leader of Arab nationalism, participating in various inter-Arab collective-security arrangements—none of which proved very helpful—both multilateral and bilateral; Syria, which was intended to be the nucleus of a critically important eastern front against Israel, was an especially important partner. In this period, Egypt seriously pursued the ideal of Arab unity as the merging of sovereignties and the creation of powerful, new entities. On one occasion this ideal was indeed realized: during the union with Syria in the years 1958-1961. Egypt attempted in this period to put itself into the unchallenged position of the *core* of all conceivable Arab combinations and to preempt all possible anti-Egyptian alignments in the region.[14] Egypt definitely succeeded in preventing the Baghdad Pact from dominating Arab security. Its success in forcing an evacuation of the Anglo-French as well as the Israeli forces from the Suez and the Sinai in 1956 seemed to vindicate the Nasserist version of nonalignment, particularly since it was the Soviet-U.S. pressure on the three parties that brought about their withdrawal, thus enabling Nasser to claim a political victory.

After the unhappy dissolution of the Egyptian-Syrian union in 1961, the ideal of practical Arab unity began to be postponed to the indefinite future. The Arab world split into ideological blocs, with Egypt leading the socialist-radical group of countries, which incessantly quarreled among themselves in the framework of what Malcolm Kerr has called "the Arab Cold War."[15] Efforts at bilateral defense agreements continued, and the Egyptian-Syrian as well as the Egyptian-Jordanian treaties were in effect realized under Egyptian overall command. However, the tripartite alliance proved to be singularly ineffective in the 1967 war. All the while, Egypt's ideological commitments led to alienation and dangerous confrontation with Saudi Arabia, obviously one of the most important emerging Arab power centers, and they also caused the Egyptian intervention in the incessant fighting in Yemen, tying down some 70,000 Egyptian troops at the time of the 1967 war.

In the wake of the 1967 defeat, a reassessment took place in Cairo. A much less ideological and more pragmatic style began to emerge during the late Nasser period, and this of course accelerated in the Sadat regime. A reconciliation took place with Saudi Arabia; the Yemen war came to an end; and the idea of collective Arab security receded more and more to the background. The need to recover the territory lost to Israel on honorable terms emerged as the *leitmotif* of Egyptian diplomatic as well as strategic thinking. However, this was very difficult because of the obviously excessive reliance on the Soviet Union in the wake of the 1967 defeat, which necessitated, and brought into being, a massive Soviet effort in rehabilitating and rearming the Egyptian armed forces. This difficulty was exacerbated by the concomitant alienation between Egypt and the United States at a time when the latter progressively replaced France as Israel's main supplier of arms as well as its most important diplomatic support and the enhanced strategic strength of post-1967 Israel. The 1969-1970 "War of Attrition" eventually evolved into even greater dependence on Soviet strategic support particularly as far as air defense was concerned. Although this war prompted rather extensive diplomatic activity, it lacked a sense of urgency and danger and thus failed to break the territorial stalemate.

The realization of this state of affairs, along with the disappointingly minor contribution made by the other Arab countries during the War of Attrition heavily influenced Egyptian strategic and diplomatic thinking. The result was close cooperation with Saudi Arabia—whose contribution in utilizing the oil weapon in 1973 was immense—and the emergence of a limited but within its scope very effective Egyptian-Syrian military axis, which in 1973 created for the first time, if even for only a few days, a viable eastern front, and yielded impressive strategic results. Paradoxically, this was accompanied by a gradual loosening of ties with the Soviet Union precisely at the time when Soviet military aid proved to be most effective, and a parallel *rapprochement* with the United States had already begun; in fact, closer ties had started on a more limited scale even before the 1973 war. The rapprochement was intended at one and the same time to restore more freedom of movement for Egypt and to isolate Israel as much as possible, using American leverage over it in order to gain concessions.

After 1973, the trend accelerated; Egypt attempted to translate rapidly the advantages gained in the October war to the language of territorial gains through a diplomatic process under American auspices. The disengagement agreement in 1974 and the interim settlement in 1975 set the tone, the latter in particular demonstrating the new state of affairs: an Egypt-first policy, territorial gains and diplomatic concessions, an increasing American role accompanied by growing alienation from the Soviet Union, and a policy of building a viable coalition of Arab countries, with priority to Saudi Arabia, backing the diplomatic road to resolving the Arab-Israeli dispute. This new approach takes place in a context of close cooperation with the United States and the effort to ensure a continued flow of resources both from the United States and the oil-rich Gulf states.[16] The difficulties emerging after the 1975 interim agreement foreshadowed what was to come after the 1977 Sadat initiative.

The 1977 initiative and the resulting peace treaty with Israel clearly constituted a watershed. Syria, which had been consulted, objected vehemently. Saudi Arabia, which had been consulted on just about every other major decision of the Sadat regime, was apparently left out of this one and resented it; its initial policy of fence-sitting gradually turned into open and surprisingly active hostility. Jordan, which could have played a crucial role in joining in, with particular reference to the Palestinian question, stayed out. Egypt became increasingly isolated in the Arab world, on account of its perceived separate peace policy as well as its inability to deliver on the Palestinian issue. Noteworthy support came at times only from Morocco, the Sudan, and Oman, and in the latter, Egyptian military aid played a role. The shah's friendly regime in Iran was overthrown; the confrontation with Libya became worse—it had already erupted into armed conflict in 1977; the radicalization of South Yemen became more and more obvious; inter-Arab plans to finance an Egyptian-based arms industry were shelved; and the level of Arab financial support was drastically reduced. Moreover, the region-wide perception of a stronger Soviet impingement on the periphery and American weakness as revealed in Iran and Afghanistan did not make a very close Egyptian-American relationship so attractive. Nonetheless, Sadat stuck with his policy, and he became a strong proponent of building an American military capability based on the Kenya-Somalia-Oman axis. In fact, he offered Egyptian facilities for U.S. forces and just about volunteered to be the U.S. policeman in the area. If the Carter doctrine does materialize in the form of an enhanced U.S. military presence in the Middle East, and if it manages to encourage a number of central powers in the region to participate in this framework, perhaps Sadat's policy will have been vindicated.

In the meantime, the peace treaty with Israel has greatly improved Egypt's strategic position and has released several key units from duty on the Suez-Red Sea front for duty on the Libyan frontier, in the Sudan, and possibly in Oman. Talk about Egyptian-Israeli military cooperation is premature, however; only the future outcomes of the treaty and the still uncertain realignment of the Arab world, coupled with questions to be resolved in regard to the emerging U.S. role in regional security will create a context in which such a future possibility can be fruitfully analyzed.

It is noteworthy that throughout the numerous twists and turns of Egypt's alliances, alignments, and partnerships, a highly centralized control over an extensive system of communications and propaganda—radio, television, newspapers, magazines, public speeches, gatherings and demonstrations, plays, films, and books—has enabled the regime to justify its policies, to counter outside propaganda, and to mobilize support. Notwithstanding, for example, Egypt's recent isolation in the Arab world, and the many weaknesses and vulnerable areas in Egyptian society, coupled with extensive diverse contacts with the Arab world, Arab opponents have not been able to penetrate Egypt's political structure to a very significant extent.

**Military Doctrines, Force Levels,
and Weapons Systems**

The active foreign policy of the Nasser regime and the high priority it gave to military considerations from about 1955 on soon led to substantial increases in military strength. The old, small, British-equipped and -trained force gave way to a large, Soviet-equipped and -trained military establishment. This increase obviously accompanied the growing regional involvement of Egypt, the escalation in the conflict with Israel, and the rising costs of the more sophisticated weapons systems. Defense spending rose to 6 percent of the GNP, then to 11-12 percent by 1965-1967, reaching 20 percent by 1970, and rising well into the twenties in the 1970s. Although there has been a decrease in real terms in defense spending in the past two or three years, in the late 1970s it was still over 20 percent of the GNP, over $2.8 billion in 1978-1979. (The 1979-1980 figure is apparently smaller, around $2.2 billion. If correct, this figure signifies very substantial relief.)

The multitude of strategic threats and targets has been reflected in the complexity and diversity of the Egyptian armed forces. For instance, Egypt has spent considerable resources in maintaining a large navy, by regional standards, which may have been necessary for its role as a regional power. However, given the nature of the arena, this naval force has yielded relatively meager results. Although overwhelmingly stronger than Israel at sea, Egypt has not been able to accomplish much strategically by the use of naval forces, except for the prestige of sinking the Israeli destroyer Eilath after the 1967 war and the participation in the successful blockade of the Straits of Bab al Mandab in 1973, for which a large naval force was not really necessary, given the access to the straits from friendly states in the area as well as their distance from Israel. Israeli control of the skies over the relevant parts of the Mediterranean has more than offset Egypt's naval advantages, and by the 1973 war the speed and maneuverability of Israel's missile boats actually put the Egyptian navy very much on the defensive. Yet it may be that as long as Egypt has ambitions to have a possible presence in Somalia or Yemen, this naval power makes sense. It includes such traditional vessels as twelve submarines, five destroyers, two escorts, and twelve submarine chasers. Still, naval strategy has not yielded very impressive benefits so far.

The Egyptian air force by 1967 reached 470 combat aircraft, all of them Soviet-made. This meant almost a 2.5:1 superiority over Israel, and a 1.5:1 superiority over the other relevant (competing) Arab countries. This force also included 30 TU-16s and 40 IL-28s, acquired relatively early in the Middle Eastern arms race. These gave Egypt a theoretical capability to strike at population and industrial centers in Israel, which Egypt completely failed to do in the 1967 war. Nor did the strategic capabilities of the Egyptian air force play a decisive role in the Yemen war. Nonetheless, contrary to many popular misconceptions, the Egyptian air force did plan a significant offensive role for itself in June 1967, which failed to materialize mainly because of the success of the Israeli attack on the Egyptian airfields in the first few hours of the war.[17] The 1967 war also demonstrated the poor integration of the air force and the air-defense system, the poor serviceability of aircraft, and the other glaring weaknesses in the human and organizational structure.

During the 1969-1970 War of Attrition, the inferiority of the air force became more and more obvious, not only in tactical dogfights, but especially in the strategic inability to prevent the Israeli air force from functioning as a flying artillery over the Suez Canal, as well as to penetrate deeply into Egypt's industrial heartland and to demonstrate its freedom of movement in the skies over Cairo. In the absence of more advanced Soviet aircraft available to Egypt, a direct Soviet role in Egypt's air defense evolved, eventually creating a dense system of surface-to-air missiles that began to show its effectiveness in the dying days of the War of Attrition. This system eventually proved to be crucial in enabling the Egyptian army to cross the Suez Canal in October 1973, by which time the air defense command was rather well integrated with the army. This new system severely hindered the Israeli air force until the last stages of the war. In the 1973 war, Egyptian planes did carry out numerous offensive missions against Israeli bases and forces in the Sinai and played a respectable, although not very decisive, role in the initial attack. The planes were kept in hardened storage bunkers, substantially resolving the problem of vulnerability to surprise aerial attack. The introduction of SCUD surface-to-surface missiles, as well as the KELT air-to-surface missiles created a potential strategic threat to Israel's heartland, and this created a virtual balance of terror sparing both countries' hinterlands in 1973.

Strategically, and in every other respect, the bulk of Egypt's power is in its large land forces, which include two armored divisions, three mechanized infantry divisions, and five infantry divisions. In addition to these ten divisions, there are three independent armored brigades, seven independent infantry brigades, two airmobile and two paratroop brigades, as well as smaller commando forces. In 1973 this force included over 2200 pieces of artillery, a decisive margin over Israel, almost 3000 armored-personnel carriers, and almost 2500 tanks. Until the Yom Kippur war and to a lesser extent, its forerunner, the War of Attrition the large force suffered from debilitating doctrinal weaknesses. Obviously, neither the skirmishes on the Libyan border nor the essentially antiguerrilla warfare in the remote, mountainous terrain in Yemen are good indicators of Egyptian military doctrine, which must be judged by and large on the basis of the various wars against Israel.

This doctrine appears throughout most of the period since the mid-1950s as almost uncritical adoption of Soviet military principles developed on the huge land mass and the relatively cold climate of Eastern and Central Europe, where the time element is far from essential. Following the Soviet doctrine, Egyptian forces were normally deployed in specified areas in the Sinai, mostly dug in along a tier of three major lines spread in depth of several miles each. Such areas contained large forces of infantry, armor, and artillery. This doctrine was based also on Egypt's ability to maintain a large standing army as well as an overwhelming concentration of firepower, two areas in which it could hopelessly outclass Israel. On the other hand, the resulting machinery was slow, cumbersome, highly visible, and insufficiently mobile. Given the need to move into—and inside—the logistically difficult, barren Sinai desert, under conditions of high visibility and almost ubiquitous Israeli air superiority, the results in 1956 and 1967 were disastrous, particularly in light of the element of surprise; this was also true of the British-French attack in 1956.

After 1967, the Sinai desert lost its function as a visible buffer zone. In the later stages of the War of Attrition, Israel progressively lost its aerial freedom of movement, and with the Russians more or less resolving the problem of defending the hinterland, the superior numbers and firepower of the Egyptian forces along the Canal, coupled with more stress on offensive initiative by small but more mobile units, began to tell and indicated a significant advance in Egyptian strategy. By 1973 this improvement was congruent with a combination of very favorable circumstances almost uniquely clustered. For the first time, Egypt had the element of surprise; it had an overwhelming quantitative advantage; the Canal-crossing operation had been superbly prepared and supplied by suitable Soviet equipment; a second front was actively functioning; the Soviet resupply lift in the air and sea began rapidly; and in general the Soviet doctrine was applied under the optimal circumstances of a quick stroke of mass strategic attack and then tactical defense under a dense antiaircraft and antitank missile umbrella. As long as the original circumstances lasted, the successful Egyptian performance also endured; in the later stages a combination of Israel's crossing of the Suez Canal, a stalemate on the eastern front, and a gradual regaining of Israel's aerial freedom of movement again left the relatively immobile Egyptian forces outmaneuvered, clinging to their diminishing missile umbrellas; eventually, the Third Army was encircled. However, by then the time element dictated by the superpowers began to play the dominant role.

Thus, it is difficult to identify a clear and persistent Egyptian doctrine. There are no salient definitions of a casus belli on either front. There is no precise definition of an acceptable balance of power with either Israel or a combination of other regional powers in either qualitative or quantitative terms, although there is a general attempt to have a quantitative advantage over Israel in forces as well as weapons systems—with the ratios changing numerous times—coupled with an effort to achieve the highest possible quality, certainly balancing everything Israel received; in 1956 this resulted in such a clear prospect of overall Egyptian superiority as to trigger an essentially preventive war on Israel's part. To the extent that there is a doctrine, it is a rather rigid and uncritical adoption of the Soviet model, well into the 1970s.[18] Moreover, the doctrine had to take into account that in addition to the forces fighting Israel, substantial reserves had to be maintained on the Libyan border, for internal security and for various inter-Arab and African commitments.

Egypt recovered from the huge losses of the 1973 war much more slowly than either Israel or Syria, and in three key categories—tanks and fighters and bombers—has still not managed to get back to the 1973 levels. In 1975 General Muhammed Ali Fahmy, later to become chief of staff, suggested an analysis of three main lessons from the 1973 war: (a) increased importance of surface-to-air systems, along with the intensification of the battle for air superiority; (b) increased importance of infantry; and (c) diminished importance of the tank.[19] He added also improved command and control systems as well as a stronger emphasis on surface-to-surface missiles. Indeed, Egypt's recovery program reflects this analysis; however, it has been decisively hindered by the rift with the Soviet Union and the radical reduction of supplies from the traditional source of the past generation.

Although Egypt began to diversify its key weapons systems in the early 1970s with the acquisition of Mirage III and Mirage F-1 jets from France, through Saudi Arabia and Kuwait, as well as negotiating for the British-French Jaguar strike-attack aircraft, a substantial rebuilding of the forces, compensating them for 1973 losses, could only be accomplished through one of the superpowers.

In 1976, Sadat complained in the Egyptian parliament that the Soviet Union had refused to resupply Egypt, and he bluntly predicted that in a couple of years Egypt's Soviet arms would become "junk"; the parliament then abrogated the treaty of friendship with the Soviets. Israel's chief of military intelligence, General Jeral Sagi, estimates that Egypt in fact did lose its regular supplies from the Soviet Union around January 1974, although it has managed to acquire spare parts and some weapons systems through Romania, China, and North Korea.[20] In June 1975, Sadat met President Ford in Salzburg and complained about the "drought" in Soviet weapons. A few months later, the United States began to supply Egypt with communications equipment, vehicles, and C-130 transport planes. By May 1977, further similar items were added and several groups of Egyptian officers began training in the United States. In February 1978 Egypt was promised fifty F-5E jets, and when in the wake of the December 1978 Camp David agreements the Saudis withdrew their promise to pay for these, the U.S. administration announced its intention to replace them with thirty-five Phantom fighter-bombers. Apparently, during the Camp David conference secret talks were held on Egypt's military needs. Later the United States sent Defense Secretary Harold Brown and other high Pentagon officials to Cairo.

According to Egypt, the result was a huge new U.S.-Egypt arms deal worth over $2 billion—some Israeli sources speak about $3.5 billion—to be delivered from mid-1981 on, including in the initial stages of 40 F-16 jets and 250 M-60 tanks as well as armored personnel carriers and Hawk surface-to-air missiles.[21] Although subject to congressional approval, this deal is rather likely to evolve into a full-fledged American effort to resupply Egypt in every important category. Egypt's defense minister, Gen. Kamal Hassan Ali, estimated the cost at $4-6 billion over five years and revealed that talks along such lines were under way with the United States.[22] In all probability, this signified a full transition from an army based on Soviet weapons to one based on their U.S. counterparts. The doctrinal consequences are yet to be revealed, but they will undoubtedly be significant.

Human, Material, and Technological Resources and Constraints

Notwithstanding many obviously beneficial spillover effects on various civilian sectors, the burden of maintaining the huge military establishment in Egypt has been staggering. A country with Egypt's economic weaknesses is simply unable to sustain armed forces of this size. This is particularly true in times when acquiring new, sophisticated, and expensive weapons systems raises an immediate need for concentrated, long-term investments from funds Egypt does not possess.[23] As a result, at various times massive foreign underwriting of military development has been necessary, creating dangerous processes of indebtedness and dependence. At one point this meant mortgaging half of Egypt's staple cotton exports to the Communist countries; on other occasions this meant that the Gulf states had to underwrite military expenditures to the point where Egypt was almost to become a Saudi-Kuwaiti mercenary. At present, it means an excessive direct dependence on the United States. The political implications of such heavy dependence—at a time when Egypt has lost the maneuverability originally envisaged in the concept of nonalignment—are evident. The resulting constraints and dilemmas are equally obvious: for one, is it really worthwhile to expand military strength to enhance the capacity to deal with outside threats when the inevitable dependence thus created generates more threats and seriously undermines the freedom to deal with the original ones?[24]

Failing, at least until the recent peace treaty, to create a situation in which by political means a reduction in threats would have meant the sufficiency of a much less expensive military force, Egypt has made efforts to be self-sufficient in several key security fields. An attempt was made to develop an indigenous industry producing jet combat aircraft, but this failed. The effort to build missiles with the cooperation of German scientists also came to naught. Until late 1978 serious progress was made in building an inter-Arab, mainly Saudi-financed, arms industry on Egyptian soil, planning at first to assemble French Mirage 2000 fighters and British Lynx helicopters, but the Saudi withdrawal of financing in the wake of the Camp David agreements apparently landed a mortal blow to this project. Recent U.S. advice to Egypt has been to transform these facilities to the production of spare parts for Western arms, but this too necessitates huge investments not readily available.

In general, the weaknesses of Egyptian technology have been a most powerful military constraint. The infrastructure has been frequently unable to absorb sophisticated technology, resulting in poor maintenance, underutilization, and low combat readiness in several critical areas especially as far as the air force is concerned, at times leading to quick deterioration and depreciation of highly sophisticated equipment. This difficulty that so blatantly puts Egypt at a severe disadvantage versus Israel has now been compounded by the introduction and utilization of at least three major technologies simultaneously in the crucial area of combat aircraft, where the maintenance of Soviet equipment, which is still the backbone of the force, was made so problematic by the absence of adequate spare parts, must be accompanied by the maintenance of entirely different French planes, as well as by progressively larger numbers of extremely complex and, again, significantly different U.S. systems. These problems are virtually endless and a tremendous effort is required to overcome them.

On the positive side, Egypt has achieved virtual self-sufficiency in the production of ammunition, a notable accomplishment.[25] Also, the 1973 war showed that when complex technological operations are broken down into large numbers of simple units with which lengthy, intensive, and relatively inexpensive training is possible, excellent results can be accomplished. Building and replacing the bridges over the Suez Canal, utilizing wire-guided antitank missiles by masses of infantry, and operating a variety of antiaircraft missiles on various levels in an integrated system on a massive scale conclusively showed the optimal—and realistic—adoption of suitable technology to the prevailing conditions in Egypt.

Egypt maintains a large standing army, necessitating mass conscription. Given Egypt's population and economic conditions, there is no quantitative problem as far as manpower is concerned. This does mean, on the other hand, that the bulk of the force has been a poorly educated peasant army, rather ill-suited to the necessities of modern warfare. The revolutionary regime made much of the effort to build a "new Egyptian man," and in fact by 1973 it was obvious that even the masses of the peasants had mastered the basic skills of mass, infantry-carried missile technology or, rather, technique. Still, the increasingly high level of sophistication needed for the technology and administration incorporated in modern warfare has made it imperative at least from the post-1967 era on to attract to the armed forces more educated, mostly middle-class elements. Some of this was evident by 1973, particularly in the Third Army. Nonetheless, the imminent arrival of still more complex Western weapons systems has drastically emphasized the imperative need for more skilled manpower.

Normally, service in the Egyptian army lasts three years for conscripts, but only a year and a half for high-school graduates and a year for college graduates. Egyptian sources estimate that by doubling the duration of service of the educated manpower, it will constitute as much as 15 percent of the conscript force. The Egyptian government has been seriously considering the possibility of treating a second-year duty by college graduates as a volunteer-professional service in terms of pay and perquisites, thus creating attractive inducements and preempting some resistance for doubling the length of conscription. If implemented, such a step may be an indication of at least some movement toward a more compact but technologically more advanced military force better suited to the demands of contemporary warfare.

**The Domestic Scene: Political Forces, the Military
Establishment, and the Regime's Objectives**

Postrevolutionary Egypt started out as a military regime in which real power was concentrated for many years in the original group of revolutionary officers, the Revolutionary Command Council, under Nasser's undisputed leadership. This was an extraordinarily cohesive military junta. Its task was made easier by Nasser's charisma, by the long dual tradition of strong, centralized rule and a clear sense of national identity, by the rising prestige of Egypt in the region and the world, by the obvious cooptation of virtually all middle-class elements into the regime, and by an extensive network of vocal propaganda organs already mentioned. Egypt has had one of the few military regimes in the Third World that did not suffer subsequent coups d'etat. It has had only two presidents in the past twenty-six years, the second being a member of the original junta.

Although the regime has now evolved into a postmilitary, significantly civilianized phase in which parliamentary procedures, elections, and parties again play a central role in political life, the respected, highly visible, and privileged position of the military has never been challenged. The officer corps, once virtually outsiders in Egyptian society, have become prestigious members of the ruling elite, on the higher level, and the prosperous upper middle class, as well as the broader technocratic stratum so important to the backbone of the regime. Although badly hurt by inflation, the officer corps realizes that it receives a very high priority in the distribution of national resources and is likely to continue to do so in the foreseeable future regardless of the vagaries of foreign policy. The military also enjoy a highly visible role in national symbolism, in celebrations, parades, and other public occasions. It is noteworthy that on such occasions the president appears in military uniform.

Throughout the years, the regime has been very sensitive to the needs and feelings of the officer corps. Only on one occasion, in the wake of the 1967 debacle, did tension arise in "civil"-military relations; even then, however, Nasser first blamed himself, then through his resignation whipped up mass support, assured a massive infusion of new resources to the military, via the Soviet resupply effort, and only then proceeded cautiously to purge the upper level of the military, carefully distinguishing it from the army as such, which was not blamed but was rather presented as a victim of negligence, incompetence, or treachery. The image of the army as the symbol of national unity and revolutionary values has been carefully and systematically nourished in the state-controlled media.

Selection of the top echelon of the officer corps was coordinated with loyalties to the regime and the president. Trusted men, *ahl al thiqqa*, are normally implanted in every unit. There is a tendency to consult with top military men on important decisions. Sadat flew to Jerusalem after a visit to headquarters of the Second Army, demonstrating the support of the military for his peace initiative. Political education in the military explains and justifies the regime's objectives, strategies, and tactics. All the while, the new, postrevolutionary officer corps have increasingly accepted the role of a professional, nonpolitical military force loyal to the regime and its values, although most Egyptians as well as numerous outside observers assume, apparently quite correctly, that the military continue to constitute the ultimate veto group on crucial policy questions should the regime falter in the future.

The president, himself a military man, is the commander-in-chief. However, he delegates running the affairs of state on a daily basis to a prime minister, normally a nonmilitary technocrat, who concentrates on economics or diplomacy or both. (In emergencies the president assumes the Prime Ministership as well.) The prime minister usually takes the blame for the inevitable mishaps and routine difficulties of everyday life in the country, while the president remains the symbol of authority and legitimacy, making the key policy decisions; every so often prime ministers change and cabinets are reshuffled. The president controls the military via the minister of defense, always a senior general, the chief of staff, and recently through the senior vice-president—the heir apparent, the ex-commander of the air force. At certain times, a delicate balance is created between these officers who represent different elements in the military, and at times one is clearly regarded as the representative of the military in government.[26] The president also personally assures the appointment of loyal officers as commanders of the three armies, the commander of the air force, and the chief of intelligence. Although the reshuffling of top officers is at times surprisingly rapid, not much evidence of resulting strain has been discernible. Beyond all this, a conscious and consistent effort has been made to keep the military out of controversial and sensitive issue areas; the one exception, the involvement of the military in suppressing the January 1977 riots following cutbacks in basic subsidies, not only strengthened civilian rule by alerting decision makers to the possible dangers of a politicized army, thus inducing them to prevent the recurrence of such situations, but also demonstrated the loyalty of the military in an embarrassing moment of dangerous disorder.[27]

Recently, political life has been much less restricted. Until Sadat's liberalization, virtually all political groups were coopted into the ruling party, were carefully surveyed by the security apparatus, and were certainly in no position to challenge the basic security objectives and policies of the regime. In the initial stages of liberalization, debate tended to focus around daily socioeconomic problems and criticisms of administrative performance rather than around operations of security or foreign policy. In the past two years or so the emergence of a far less restricted multiparty competition and increased freedom of speech have been accompanied by clear signs of dissent from Sadat's rapid pace of peacemaking with Israel and the rising alienation from the Arab countries. Thus far, this dissent has been neither too vocal nor very widespread, and it has not been perceived as a threat to a strong consensus based on an overwhelming majority of all relevant political forces and strata of the population backing the regime's post-1977 policies. It remains to be seen how the regime will handle more massive and visible dissent if the peace process grinds to a halt over the Palestinian stalemate, while the expectations for socioeconomic progress are frustrated. On the whole, however, the regime's ability so far to marshal overall support from the military establishment as well as the overwhelming majority of civilians on both the elite and mass levels under delicate circumstances of rapid and at times puzzling political twists and turns has been nothing less than impressive.

Conclusions

The picture that emerges from this analysis of the various security functions is that of a country acutely conscious of security problems, which perceives a multitude of threats mostly on the regional level, which spends a huge proportion of its scare resources on maintaining a large military establishment commensurate with the perceived magnitude of the numerous threats, and which constantly shifts its orientation in search of a more satisfactory regional and international alignment suitable to its own security requirements—which are aggravated by a dire shortage of badly needed resources.

The centrality of security, strategic factors, and military considerations in national politics is striking. In the Egyptian case, there is practically no support for any thesis arguing the decline of military force as a major variable in international relations, although the combination of imminent poverty, large population, and a central geostrategic location in the heart of a conflict-ridden area may be rather exceptional. On the other hand, the Egyptian case seems to indicate that a large military establishment and its resulting economic burden do not have to hinder a conflict-resolution orientation. In a way, the contrary may be the case: the Egyptian military have certainly been no more—and it seems that, on the whole, even less—hawkish than most civilian political forces in the country.

An intriguing question relates to the remarkable continuity of control amidst rapid strategic and political change. Although a good deal of this may have to do with Egyptian political culture, the evolution of the postmilitary regime is also a relevant variable. Only a comparative study with other cases can reveal to what extent the evolution of such regimes enhances legitimacy, generates possibilities of a more open society, and creates a more pragmatic orientation in foreign policy. Of course, Egypt had one of the first military regimes in Africa or Asia, and it is also one of the first to evolve to the next stage. Its foreign policy has also changed more frequently and more sharply than that of almost any other country in the Third World. Still, it constitutes a useful case for comparison; at times it is an extreme case, cautioning against hasty generalizations one way or another.

Recently, two themes seem most dominant in Egyptian security policy. The first is the persistent quest for a regional order that would create an acceptable territorial status quo with a commensurate opportunity for domestic progress under conditions of relative stability and freedom from immediate threats to security. In this framework, it is striking that Egypt has found it so obviously necessary to assign a dominant role to an outside superpower in conflict resolution and in maintaining an acceptable regional balance of power. In this respect, recent Egyptian perceptions strongly link global developments to regional security, much more so than its traditional regional leading role would indicate.

The second dominant theme is the surprisingly broad range of political options open to counter the multitude of threats. This creates a great deal of fluidity, for better or for worse. Although at one time this may have been an attractive fact of life for the Egyptian regime, at a later stage, more oriented toward stability and domestic development, this has evidently brought about a strongly perceived need to reduce the number of threats and to deal with some more intensively at the expense of others, even at the price of major concessions. In other words, the tendency is to streamline policy and develop a more compact strategy, one that is more consistent, more systematic, less extensive and demanding in commitment and resources. This involves a series of radical changes in relation to erstwhile adversaries and allies alike. The magnitude of change in the half-decade or so following the 1973 war, and the analytical difficulty in grasping it indicates the need for some concept of *realigning diplomacy* or *critical strategic move* rather analogous to the concepts of *critical* or *realigning* election used in comparative politics. This may be a fruitful way of organizing analysis of discontinuities in the relevance, relative weight, and interrelationship of the various levels of security decisionmaking.

Needless to say, having witnessed such dramatic transformations in Egyptian security policy, we have no reason to expect that the present version will endure unchanged for very long. The rate and direction of change will probably be determined by: (a) the concrete benefits that Egypt will be able to derive from the peace treaty with Israel; (b) the evolving relationship with the United States as the country's main source of military supplies; (c) the post-Iran and post-Afghanistan role of the Reagan administration in Middle Eastern security; (d) the nature of the changes in the regional system in the wake of the Iranian revolution; (e) a possible transition of the regional arms race to a nuclear phase; and (f) the continued evolution of the postmilitary regime in Egypt under the shadow of persistent, and mounting, socioeconomic difficulties and pressures.

Identifying the six rather general likely sources of future change is not much of a prediction, nor is it intended to be one. Much like the general analytical framework of security functions, it helps focus attention on possible processes of change by linking together pertinent global, regional, and domestic variables in a coherent, policy-oriented context. At this stage of the development of relevant theory, more explicit hypotheses simply cannot be introduced with much confidence. Only one thing can be argued with certainty: notwithstanding the scholarly arguments of a good many analysts (who tend to explain, for example, the Sadat initiative as an Egyptian attempt to break away altogether from military considerations in the Arab-Israeli conflict, rather than as an original effort to build a new relationship precisely reflecting the military realities of that conflict), politics, in the minds of the Egyptian elite, is indeed about power, and military force definitely continues to be a constantly important, central component of power.

Notes

1. These data are taken from International Institute for Strategic Studies (IISS) *The Military Balance 1978-1979* (London, 1978), pp. 36-37.

2. This point is developed in detail in Gabriel Ben-Dor, "Civilianization of Military Regimes in the Arab World," *Armed Forces and Society* 1 (May 1975).

3. See John Waterbury, "Egypt: The Wages of Dependency," in *The Middle East: Oil, Conflict and Hope*, ed. Abraham L. Udovitch (Lexington, Mass.: Lexington Books, D.C. Heath and Company, 1966), p. 292 and the sources there cited.

4. Recent discoveries of oil in Egypt, and the return of the oil fields in the Sinai improve the situation, but do not alter the fundamental argument.

5. A great many misconceptions seem to abound on this point. For the most authoritative account see Uri Ra'anan, *The U.S.S.R. Arms the Third World* (Cambridge, Mass.: MIT Press, 1969).

6. See G.A. Nasser, "The Egyptian Revolution," *Foreign Affairs* 33 (January, 1955):199-211.

7. See the instructive comparative analysis in Shimon Shamir, "Nasser and Sadat, 1967-1973, Approaches to the Crisis," in *From June to October: The Middle East Between 1967 and 1973*, eds. R. Rabinovich and H. Shaked (New Brunswick, N.J.: Transaction, 1978), pp. 189-218.

8. As the termination of every Egyptian-Israeli war has demonstrated, global constraints have become increasingly dominant in coping with

regional threats. To this extent, global policies and regional-security doctrines had to be closely integrated (as they were in the 1973 war).

9. For further information on this important point, see Gabriel Ben-Dor, "Inter-Arab Relations and the Arab-Israeli Conflict," *Jerusalem Journal of International Relations* 1 (Summer 1976).

10. For details, see Michael Handel, *Israel's Political-Military Doctrine*, Occasional Paper no. 30 (Cambridge, Mass., Harvard University, Center for International Affairs, July 1973).

11. See Mordechai Abir, "Sharm al-Sheikh-Bab al-Mandeb: The Strategic Balance and Israel's Southern Approaches," Jerusalem Papers on Peace Problem, no. 5, March 1974.

12. Cf. Tareq Ismael, *The U.A.R. in Africa* (Evanston, Ill.: Northwestern University, Press, 1971).

13. Because of the highly centralized nature of the regime, the domestic aspect of the dimensions of security policy is of little importance; the most intriguing aspect of inter-state communication, namely the use of deception and surprise as in 1973, has been literally analyzed to death in literature and there is little of interest to add.

14. See Y. Evron and Y. Bar Simantov, "Coalitions in the Arab World," *Jerusalem Journal of International Relations*, 1 (Winter 1975).

15. Malcolm Kerr, *The Arab Cold War* (London: Oxford University Press, 1971).

16. In this context, cooperation with (and aid from) prerevolutionary Iran was an important cornerstone of Egypt's regional policy.

17. See Israel Defense Forces, Air Force Intelligence, *Egyptian Attack Orders Against Israel*, June 1967.

18. The almost total lack of Soviet experience in desert warfare is obvious. This is clearly evident also in the cold-weather oriented Soviet equipment, which was *not* adapted by the Egyptians to the radically different climate and terrain in the Middle East.

19. *Aviation Week*, 14 July 1975, pp. 14-15.

20. Interview in *Maariv*, 12 December 1979.

21. As reported in Cairo's authoritative newspaper *Al-Ahram*, 21 February 1980.

22. *Associated Press* report, 25 February 1980. Israeli sources mention 85 F-16 jets and about 1000 M-60 tanks.

23. See Geoffrey Kemp, *Arms and Security: The Egypt-Israeli Case*, Adelphi Paper No. 52 (London, 1968).

24. This is a demonstration of the tension inherent in the "dialectics of poverty and power," as mentioned earlier.

25. This is the estimate of Israel's chief of military intelligence in an interview in *Maariv*, 12 December 1979.

26. Such appears to be the case with Vice-President Hosni Mubarak.

However, caution should be exercised in this regard, as a former seeming heir apparent, former Defense Minister Gamasi, was suddenly removed shortly after the Sadat initiative.

27. For the formidable potential of the emerging anti-Egyptian forces, see for instance Amos Perlmutter, "A New Rejectionism," *Foreign Policy* (Spring 1979):165-181.

10 Israel

Bernard Reich

Israel is a small state with an unusual preoccupation with security. The preeminent concern of Israeli policymakers and Israelis in general is with national survival and security as a result of its conflict with its Arab neighbors and its geostrategic situation. In the first thirty-two years of its existence it fought five wars with the Arab states and still remains technically, if not actually, at war with all but Egypt. Israel spends a major portion of its budget and GNP on defense and defense-related items and has a sizable standing army and easily mobilized reserve force. Its military power is substantial but not unlimited, constrained by its own economy and by international factors. Its military is civilian controlled, and retired officers play an important but limited role in politics. The policy that results from these factors is unusual and instructive in dealing with the security policies of developing states because Israel is a special case. Israel's security policy has had a remarkable general consistency over time, a result of the continuity of the Arab threat, the predominance of Mapai in the political system until 1977, David Ben-Gurion's dominance of the defense establishment during a formative fifteen-year period, and the general success of the policies and the high quality of the Israel Defense Forces (IDF) during much of Israel's history.

The Nature and Definition of the Threat

Israel's overriding concerns with national survival and security are imperatives deriving from the conflict with its Arab neighbors. Israel is perhaps unique among states in having hostile neighbors on all borders—with the exception, since 1979, of Egypt. This central concern dominates, directly or indirectly, all aspects of Israeli life, and it has prevailed since 1948 when its declaration of independence was greeted by an invasion of hostile Arab armies dedicated to the destruction of the fledgling state. The Holocaust, Arab hostility during the Mandate period, five wars, countless skirmishes and terrorist attacks, and incessant, vituperative rhetoric against the state have all left their mark on Israel's national psyche and perceptions, but have not led to a comprehensive, permanent, and meaningful peace.

Israelis have a clear and unequivocal view of Arab hostility that has been modified only by the actions of President Sadat of Egypt in the period since 1977.[1] To Israelis the threat is real and constant. The Arab world's aggressive intent is further "confirmed" by its unwillingness to join in the process initiated by Sadat and by its reiteration and amplification of the 1967 Khartoum Arab summit formula, which spoke of "no peace with Israel, no recognition of Israel, no negotiations with it, and insistence on the rights of the Palestinian people." At the Baghdad conferences in 1978 and 1979 and at subsequent meetings the Arab states took a strong line against the Sadat initiative. Consistent Arab refusals of Israeli suggestions over the years to negotiate an end to the conflict were seen as part of the overall Arab opposition to the state.

The threat is not seen as an aberration of history but rather as its latest, and continuing, manifestation. Israel reads its history as the most recent phase of four thousand years of Jewish history and remembers it as replete with episodes of persecution and conquest. Israelis recall clashes with outside military forces seeking to overrun their country and defeat and enslave their people. They recollect the exile of the Jews from their homeland—Israel—and the creation of the diaspora. Nineteenth-century European anti-Semitism (when Jews became the scapegoat for the failings of society in much of Europe even when they did not often participate in the mainstream decision-making structures and processes) led to the founding in 1897 in Basel, Switzerland, of political Zionism, which argued that Jews could avoid anti-Semitism by creating a state in which they would govern themselves.

Israelis believe that the primary historical lessons of the Holocaust are that there are those who seek the destruction of the Jews, and that Jews should not depend on the guarantees or efforts of others for their safety. Thus Israel must depend on its own defense capability to ensure its survival and protect its people.

Israel's historical perspective is further influenced by Arab hostility as manifested during and since the British Mandate of Palestine. At the outset, hostility emanated from a small section of the Arab community, but it spread over time, and political tension between the communities became a permanent feature of life in Palestine. This led to a series of anti-Jewish acts by the Arab community that became progressively more severe and included disturbances and massacres as well as more extensive actions. Israelis argue that for more than half a century Arabs opposed the establishment of an independent Jewish state and, after Israel's independence, continued to focus on "driving Israel into the sea."[2] President Sadat of Egypt has noted that for thirty years there was a wall between Israel and the Arab states and an Arab refusal to accept Israel in the region. Israel was isolated and rejected by the Arab world.[3] Despite the beginnings of change associated with the Sadat initiative, Israel's perspective is still conditioned by a vivid view of Arab hostility as the latest manifestation of a centuries-old trend of history.[4]

Israel's position is also affected by its isolation. Israelis seeking to leave their country, for whatever purpose, can do so only by air or by sea, since they are not permitted to enter or cross the territory of neighboring states (with the exception, now, of Egypt) as a result of the Arab boycott and nonacceptance of Israel. This geographical isolation is compounded by the lack of an alliance system and the fact that, partly by Israel's choice, no state is formally committed to come to Israel's defense or provide support in the event of war.[5] In none of the five wars it fought between 1948 and 1981 (1948-1949, 1956, 1967, 1969-1970, 1973) was Israel joined in combat by another state—with the minor exception of the British and French role in 1956, which occurred after the primary Israeli effort in Sinai and did not significantly affect Israeli successes—and no state is obligated to do so in the event of future hostilities. In addition, Israel's diplomatic relationships have declined in number since the June 1967 war, especially as a result of the substantial ruptures with the states of black Africa at the time of the October 1973 war, and it has been repeatedly condemned in the United Nations and other international organizations by lopsided votes in recent years.

Israel's vulnerability is affected by its geographical setting. The frontiers that existed prior to the June 1967 war were vulnerable to enemy attack and made the defense of population centers difficult.[6] The distance between Israel's Mediterranean coast and enemy military installations in the West Bank, which included the coastal corridor between the main port city of Haifa and the commercial center of Tel Aviv, was often less than ten miles. At its widest point, near the Negev town of Dimona, Israel's territory was only sixty-five miles wide. In most locations there were no major natural defense barriers to the advance of enemy forces. Israel's population centers, particularly its three major cities of Jerusalem, Tel Aviv, and Haifa, and main air bases were within a few hours advance by enemy ground forces, and many were within enemy artillery range. This helped to generate a perception of vulnerability that has been important in shaping Israel's view of the significance of the occupied territories—that Israel must not return to the vulnerability created by the pre-June 1967 war frontiers.[7]

For Israel, this combination of its historical-psychological perspective, antisemitism, geographic and political-military isolation, and vulnerability to enemy attack has conditioned the formulation of its security policies.

In its assessment of the threat Israel relates its security to a broader concern for its self-identity and its ultimate purpose within the broader international system. Israel sees itself as having a number of interrelated requirements: the prevention of threats to its independence and territorial integrity, its need to preserve its Jewish character, and its role as protector of persecuted Jews everywhere; the latter helps to explain such legislation as the Law of the Return, which allows Jews to immigrate to Israel and become citizens virtually at will. Israelis also seem to believe that if Israel loses this opportunity no Jewish state will ever again exist, with all that implies for the survival of world Jewry.

Although Israel sees the threat as having broad consequences, it sees the source of the threat, in real terms, as more limited in scope. The threat is essentially confined to the Arab world and is not extraregional in nature. In a strict military sense the focal point has been the "confrontation" Arab states—essentially those sharing a common frontier with Israel plus Iraq (and, since 1973, Saudi Arabia because of its oil reserves and production and its substantial earnings of petrodollars), although the definition is flexible and has varied over time both in Israel and the Arab world—but the other Arab entities are included in the broader conception of the enemy. After all, they have been allied with the participant states in the Arab League and other institutions, have participated in Arab summit meeting's decisions against Israel, have joined in the general chorus of anti-Israel rhetoric, and have provided some of the wherewithal for, and occasionally participated in, the wars, terrorist acts, and other anti-Israel military and paramilitary actions undertaken by the confrontation states.[8]

Although Israel has been concerned about Soviet actions and potential roles, neither the Soviet Union nor other enemies have been at the center of planning or conceptional elements. The potential of a broad Soviet threat has been seen as something to be dealt with by the United States and the West, not by Israel alone. At another level of analysis, there is also no perceived threat to the regime at home, other than an earlier notion (more or less in the period 1948-1966) that the Arab population of Israel constituted a security risk, rather than a threat. Although some Israelis continue to be concerned about the country's Arab population, it is not a focal point of military concern. Similarly, Israel's military has never been seen as a threat to the regime and there never has been consideration of a possible military coup, other than a brief rumor at the time of the June 1967 war, despite the centrality, size, popularity, special position, and budgetary expenditure of the army.

Military Structure, Military Doctrine, and Weapons Systems

The Israel Defense Forces (or Zahal)[9] have their roots and origins not only in the security forces and organizations of the Yishuv, the Jewish community in Palestine prior to independence, but also in Jewish history, particularly Jewish defense units established in Eastern Europe and Russia. Haganah (Defense) was established in the 1920s as an underground defense organization within the Yishuv, and in 1941 the Haganah created a commando or striking force, the Palmach (a full-time military force of volunteers, something of a professional and elite unit), which later provided a large proportion of the senior officers of the IDF. Alternative military groups were created under the Mandate, especially the IZL (Irgun Tzevai Leumi, National Military Organization, or Etzel), and LEHI (LHY, Fighters for the Freedom of Israel, or Stern Group: Lohamei Herut Yisrael)—but after independence the various military groups were brought together as the IDF.

The prime minister and the cabinet exercise ultimate control over the Israel Defense Forces and the minister of defense is the cabinet officer charged with responsibility for security. The Defense Forces of Israel are unified and presided over by the chief of the General Staff, who is also commander of the army. The exact relationship between these elements is not clearly defined and has varied over time and with the nature of the individuals—and personalities—involved in these positions.[10] The General Staff, composed of a general-staff branch and branches for intelligence, manpower, logistics, planning, and the headquarters of the air force and navy, directs the activities and operations of the various commands of the IDF. The IDF is divided into territorial or regional commands, as well as commands for the navy, air force, and armored corps.

Israel has developed an impressive body of fundamental principles[11] and concepts (political-military in nature) on which it bases its security policy, although it has no known published, formal national-security doctrine.[12] This has drawn on foreign sources but is largely an Israeli creation. The foundations for Israel's concept of national security were laid by David Ben-Gurion, Israel's first prime minister and minister of defense, and one of the founders of the state. They have been modified and updated, particularly as a result of the June 1967 War and the consequent Israeli occupation of sizeable amounts of Arab territory.

A number of assumptions concerning the nature of the threat and raison d'être of the state undergird the military doctrine. Israel's purpose is seen in a broad sense in its existence as a Jewish state whose survival helps to ensure the future of the Jewish people in addition to the survival of Israel and Israelis. Israel continues to see the Arab-Israeli conflict in stark terms—it is a war of survival, a fight for existence, in the face of the Arab call for the destruction of the state. The unremitting hostility of its Arab neighbors is the central element in Israel's calculations. Given that factor it must take into account the asymmetry of its situation vis-à-vis the Arabs, its numerical inferiority ("few against many"), the territorial and resource disparity, and the political influence of its enemy. It plans for, and must be prepared for, the worst-case scenario of a combined and coordinated Arab attack. This leads to several significant conclusions concerning the nature of the conflict and war with the Arabs.

Israel realizes it cannot achieve quantitative superiority and thus seeks to ensure a qualitative edge over its rivals. Highly trained personnel with strong personal motivation are equipped with the most sophisticated and advanced weapons systems; they are the core of the Israeli answer to the overwhelming superiority of Arab numbers. Israel also seeks to minimize losses and reduce expenditures in all encounters to decrease the financial and personal drains of warfare in a small and relatively poor system. To accomplish this, principles such as short wars and extensive use of advanced weaponry come into play. Israel believes that an Arab victory would be final and would result in the destruction of the state with all that that implies for Israel and world Jewry.[13] Should Israel win additional victories they, like past achievements, could never be final and definite decisions, given Arab numerical superiority. But it must win wars and battles, destroy enemy forces, and inflict heavy losses on the Arabs, and it believes that such decisive temporary victories might have a deterrent effect.

In building its military power Israel must exploit fully all its national resources (manpower, equipment, and vehicles) both in time of peace and in time of war.[14] There is a constant need for readiness and alert. The importance of an early-warning system, especially intelligence concerning enemy intentions and actions, is clear in a system that must secure mobilization of its forces to meet a military threat. Intelligence must be prepared for all eventualities at all times and must provide sufficient warning time to permit efficient and rapid mobilization of Israel's reserve forces. Because of this there is flexibility in the organization of the IDF in order to allow integration of reservists. This means the establishment of a small standing army and a larger readily mobilized reserve force (by comparison with the large standing armies of the Arab states). The ground forces could be militia, but the intelligence corps, the air force, and the navy must be standing forces.[15]

Since Israel in its 1949-1967 frontiers had no strategic depth[16]—and this was essential for security—artificial depth was created by means of area defense (including the use of settlements as fighting positions in wartime) and by carrying the war to enemy territory as quickly as possible. In combat the IDF must deal with the most dangerous enemy and strongest opponent first. This typically led to an Israeli focus on Egypt and the southern front, although in the 1973 war Israeli concerns about Syria dictated a modification of this perspective. Israel must strike the first blow as a preemptive strike (1967) or a preventive war (1956), take and keep the initiative, and dictate the terms of battle. Again, in 1973, the problem of transferring combat operations to enemy territory was partly obviated by the fact that Israel already occupied substantial amounts of enemy territory, which provided a strategic advantage (despite a tactical disadvantage of longer interior lines), since the fighting could take place in those territories rather than in pre-1967 Israel or in the remaining territory of the Arab enemy. It must stress and utilize fast, mobile attacks. Substantial flexibility is granted to field commanders in direct-combat contact with the enemy to permit innovation. The need to achieve a quick victory and ensure that the Arabs lose the war is a result of the anticipated intervention of the great powers or the United

Nations, the need to avoid high casualty levels, and Israel's economic difficulty in maintaining mobilization of its civilian sector over an extended period.

The problems of strategic depth and long borders were altered with the acquisition of substantial Arab territory during the June 1967 war, and, as a result of this and changes in weaponry and costs, there were modifications in Israel's doctrine and the growing acceptance of a defensive approach. The expanded lines allowed for a more normal life at home and alternative war options, including the possibility of not preempting Arab attacks in future wars. Although other factors were involved, the strategic depth and alternative options available to Israel in 1973 helped to influence the prime minister's decision not to launch a preemptive strike against Egypt and Syria and to absorb the first strike but nevertheless allowed Israel to respond and prosecute the war successfully.

After 1967 the concept of defensible or secure borders became important elements of Israel's vocabulary and affected its subsequent political-military planning.[17] Israel thought in terms of constructing settlements in the occupied territories to serve security purposes, much as the frontier settlements in pre-1967 Israel had served to enhance the defense capability of the state. Between 1967 and 1977 the Israeli government approached the problems of settlement in the West Bank and elsewhere primarily in terms of the concepts and phraseology of security needs. The Labor governments of that period seemed to believe that settlements established in strategically important areas essentially devoid of Arab inhabitants, for example, along the Jordan River, would help to ensure the security of the state. Not all strategic thinkers, however, regarded such settlements as serving that need or as the most effective means of so doing, but the security argument, combined with other factors, dominated.

In its response to the Arab threat Israel has created an impressive military establishment relative to its population, size, and resources, although not all elements have been equally developed. At different times different military components have been given priority for funding and for weapons systems, an interesting example being the substantial increase in the navy's budget after the 1973 war. In general, however, considerations of short wars and the need for decisive action and flexibility and mobility in combat have led Israel to focus on its air force and armored corps in structuring its forces. Both are regarded as essential, and neither can perform the required tasks alone.[18]

Israel's air force has been seen from abroad as its most colorful and effective fighting element. Despite its inferiority in numbers to the forces of the Arab states, the Israeli air force has been indisputably superior at least since the 1967 war when it virtually eliminated the Egyptian air force from the conflict in the first few hours of combat, assuring Israeli air superiority and decisively influencing the pace and nature of the ground conflict in the Sinai zone with Egypt. During the 1969-1970 War of Attrition, Israeli air superiority became more obvious in both air-to-air combat and in its unique function as flying artillery (partly to offset the superior firepower of Egypt) across the Suez Canal against Egyptian west-bank installations. In the later phases of that conflict in January 1970 it took on the task of deep-penetration raids into the heartland of Egypt's population and commercial centers. It was also in the War of Attrition that Israeli airmen came into direct conflict with Soviet pilots who were flying air-defense missions for Egypt and managed to best them in combat. But, it was also at this time that the IDF reinforced the Bar-Lev line along the Suez Canal to protect its positions against Egyptian artillery shelling and sent commandos across the Canal to attack Egyptian positions.

The War of Attrition was a major step in Egypt's development, with Soviet assistance, of the substantial missile-defense system along the west bank of the Suez Canal that was so important to the Egyptian war effort in 1973.[19] The surface-to-air missile system was indispensable to the Egyptian crossing of the Suez Canal and was responsible for reducing the effectiveness of the Israeli air force in ground support in the opening days and through much of the October 1973 war. Eventually Israel penetrated into Egypt proper but primarily through the actions of ground forces that had made their way across the canal in a surprise attack and destroyed various missile emplacements.

Israel's ground forces are the largest and the central element of the IDF. Its role has varied with modifications in Israel's military doctrine, but the armor corps has received much attention for its highly flexible, and ultimately decisive, operations in Sinai in 1956, 1967, and 1973.

The IDF has, from the beginning and even before the founding of the state, sought to achieve the essential military strength and to acquire the wherewithal to meet the identified threat and provide for the defense of the state. This has generated a continuous effort to secure military equipment and to have the necessary quantities and quality of material to ensure the country's defense. As a result, a substantial proportion of the GNP and the budget have been allocated to defense and defense-related expenditures and the development of a substantial defense-production capability.[20]

The equipment available to the IDF is of various types, quality, and generations. At the beginning the equipment was little more than a motley assortment drawn from any available source for a force with multiple backgrounds and little organized and formal training, except for some individuals and some locally trained units. The escalation of the conflict after Israel's War of Independence and the increasing sophistication of weapons systems led to growing weapons expenditures. Subsequently, equipment has come from several foreign suppliers including, most prominently, the

United States, France, England, and West Germany. The IDF also has a significant quantity of Soviet equipment, most of which was captured in combat in 1967[21] and subsequently refurbished.

Despite the development of a substantial military establishment with much of the latest and most sophisticated military equipment, the IDF has limited its ability to act primarily in response to specific threats from the Arab world. It has projected its power into Lebanon and has played a role in Jordan and, in battle, has struck in Egypt and Syria. But other than the July 1976 raid on Entebbe, Uganda, to secure the release of hostages, it has not employed force beyond its own limited geographic area, because of political decisions rather than inherent limits in forces or equipment. Its military-assistance programs, now mostly in limbo, have involved limited training of foreign personnel most of which has taken place in Israel, primarily the training of parachute units. Some advisers have served abroad on a very limited scale and mostly in connection with specific and limited tasks, including some military sales.

Other than the sale of military equipment and the transfer to third parties of some matériel acquired from other powers, including Soviet military and ancillary equipment captured from the Arab states, Israel's ability to influence worldwide military or security developments is limited. It has not been able to help finance other states' military acquisitions; has not had long-range military action or shows of force or other symbolic uses of power beyond its immediate area. But there are substantial rumors concerning Israel's support of various minority groups in neighboring states and beyond, in order to reduce those states' ability to join in the Arab effort against Israel and to make a point concerning survival of beleaguered minorities. Israel was involved with the Biafran revolt in Nigeria and supports the Christian forces of Major Haddad in South Lebanon as well as the militias in the north. It reportedly has also helped the Kurds in Iraq[22] and the Southern Sudanese against the Arab-Muslim dominated northern-based government. It has also been active in counterterrorism in Europe and elsewhere.

Israel's desire to acquire conventional weapons for its defense and security is affected by its views concerning nuclear proliferation. Israel's official position continues to be that it will not be the first to introduce nuclear weapons into the region, but it has continually refused to adhere to the nuclear nonproliferation treaty. In 1980 it modified its position by proposing, at the United Nations, that a conference of Middle Eastern states write a treaty barring the production and use of nuclear weapons in the region. The general consensus of knowledgeable analysts suggests that Israel has the ingredients to produce and deliver a nuclear weapon—some believe it already has nuclear devices— and that such a capability has been a focal point of Israeli activity for some time.[23]

Israel's nuclear ambiguity is regarded as a strategic asset, serving as a deterrent to Arab adventurism while not necessarily goading Arab nuclear development. This argument does, however, have an alternative side, which suggests that it stimulates Arab nuclear activity. The ambiguity has been one of the factors, albeit a minor one, in the arguments for increased conventional United States military supply to Israel as a means of reducing the prospects for nuclear development and deployment. Israel has not utilized this argument on a public level and it appears unlikely on an explicit private level. Israel might decide to reveal the existence of its nuclear weapons should it deem that necessary to maintain or rectify the regional balance of power or to increase its deterrent strength vis-à-vis the Arab states. This would be a distinct possibility if an Arab state acquired an overt nuclear-weapons capability.[24] Iraq's nuclear program proved sufficiently threatening to trigger the Israeli destruction of Iraq's nuclear facility. Israel is likely to act as decisively against other threats to its security from nuclear proliferation spreading to the Arab states.

The existence, real or supposed, of an Israeli nuclear capability has not apparently affected conventional military doctrine, or force posture. If Israel has assigned an actual or potential role to that capability, it must be seen in terms of an ultimate doomsday weapon, that is, a weapon to be used in the event of the possible or prospective downfall of the state because of hostile enemy actions; however, the possibility of use of tactical nuclear weapons should not be ruled out. In the event that the state was about to be destroyed it might make sense to threaten the destruction of major Arab population or resource centers, and one could speculate on such targets as the Aswan Dam on the Nile, the Suez Canal, and cities such as Cairo, Alexandria, Damascus, and Baghdad in this extreme instance. Short of that form of speculation, there is no identified role for nuclear weaponry in the openly expressed Israeli military doctrine except insofar as the uncertainty of the nuclear weapons' existence has a deterrent effect on Arab military-political action and behavior.

Alliances and Security

From the outset Israel's approach to alliances with other states has been marked by ambivalence. Its isolation in the Middle East and the Arab threat have suggested a need for positive relationships with other members of the international community as a means of meeting security and related needs. Israel sees itself compelled to elicit the support of at least one Western power for weapons supply and to deter Soviet participation in conflict on the side of the Arabs. Since 1967 the United States increasingly has been identified as this power.[25] But, Israel believes in self-reliance and has demonstrated wariness of dependence on others. Skepticism regarding the security value of international or great-power guarantees is voiced by Israelis representing all points on the political spectrum.[26] Despite these limitations Israel has sought friendly ties with major powers and small states alike.

At independence, some of Israel's leaders thought in terms of a policy of neutrality and nonalignment and saw the potential for support from both superpowers, although a large number realized that Israel's long-term interests lay with the West. They viewed Soviet and American support for Israel and the competition between the two as auguring well for the new state. The United Nations was seen as a benign and positive element, having been a significant factor in the birth of the new state. But as early as 1950 Israel lost its ability to play off the superpowers against one another. Israel became increasingly linked with the West, and its relationship with the Soviet Union deteriorated as the Soviets apparently became convinced that the Arab states were a more likely and significant prize. From then on Israel's sources of political, military, and economic aid were to be found only in the West.

In Israel, the succession of ruling elites all seemed to have similar perspectives on the nature of the international system and varied primarily in the strength rather than the direction of their convictions. This pragmatic and ideological perspective prevented Israel from following a strategy similar to some of its neighbors of playing off the superpowers one against the other to secure economic and military aid. Israel has been by necessity and ideology increasingly Western oriented, and this has led to, at best, cool relations with the Soviet Union and the Eastern-bloc states, rather than a nonaligned stand.

In the broader international system Israel has not been a major regional-military factor nor has it been involved in a central way in the functions of international organizations or blocs. Israel is not a member of any regional organization, belongs to no voting bloc in the United Nations, and is not a part of any informal grouping of states in the international arena. This has been a result of its relations with the Arab states, their boycott of Israel, and their international political influence in the form of boycotts, U.S. votes, and oil-supply politics and other instruments of power usable to convince other states of the righteousness of their position. To a significant degree, Israel is isolated in the regional and international systems.

Israel is not now, or has it ever been, allied by treaty to any other state. No state is formally committed to come to its defense in the event of attack. There is no formal mutual-security pact, no Soviet-style treaty of friendship and cooperation. There have been implicit or quasi alliances—first with France and then with the United States and, in the instance of the 1956 Suez war, a temporary alignment with England and France. These relationships have been seen as valuable and useful but all have been viewed as having limitations.

The credibility of the ally and of the alliance has been viewed differently at various times. The arrangement with Britain and France was for a short duration and had a particular and limited set of objectives: the reduction of Egyptian power; the desire to remove Nasser as a credible force affecting the revolts against France in North Africa; the security of the Suez Canal; and the threat to Israel of newly acquired Egyptian military capability. But it failed to change the regional or international structure. Nasser emerged from the encounter with increased prestige, if not power, and the British and French roles in the region were substantially reduced, if not formally terminated. Israel gained a respite from Arab threats in a practical sense and something of a reputation as a military force, which may have had a deterrent value over the ensuing decade.

The tacit alliance with France that lasted from the mid-1950s until after the June 1967 war (although its quality suffered after Algeria's independence in 1962) was more of a marriage of convenience, with mutual benefits derived by the participants, than a full-fledged alliance.[27] It provided Israel with substantial military equipment and technological, including nuclear, assistance. but the decline of the relationship under de Gaulle in the period 1967-1969 contributed to Israel's negative perceptions concerning the reliability of allies.

Israel's multifaceted relationship with the United States is the major exception to its go-it-alone posture, although it retains important relations with states in Western Europe. Israel's special and complex relationship with the United States, revolving around a broadly conceived ideological factor and based on substantial positive perception and sentiment evident in public opinion and official statements and manifest in political-diplomatic support and military and economic assistance,[28] has not been enshrined in a legally binding commitment joining the two states in a formal alliance or requiring the United States to take up arms automatically on Israel's behalf. Although the idea of a treaty guarantee has been raised on several occasions, the prevailing sentiment appears to be that such a treaty is neither necessary nor desirable. Despite the substantial links that have developed, the widespread belief in the existence of a commitment, and the assurances contained in the 1975 Sinai II agreements and memoranda, the exact nature, form, and content of the United States commitment to Israel remains imprecise.[29] It has been generally assumed that the United States would come to Israel's assistance should it be gravely threatened. However, there is no concrete evidence to support this view, and the exact nature of the American role in the event of such a situation remains in some doubt, especially in light of growing Soviet capabilities. Instead, Presidents Reagan, Ford and Carter, like Presidents Truman, Eisenhower, Kennedy, Johnson, and before them, Nixon, have reaffirmed American "interest and concern in supporting the political independence and territorial integrity" of Middle Eastern states. The presidential statements affirm that the United States stands ready to ensure the independence and integrity of Israel, along with other states in the Middle East, although there is no binding legal requirement to do so and the actions essential to the attainment of these ends in specific situations remain imprecise.

Undergirding the relationship is a general agreement on broad policy goals, such as Israel's existence, security, and well-being. Despite this general agreement, noncongruence of policy on specific issues has derived from a difference of perspective and overall policy environments. After the 1967 war there was a divergence on technique as well as discord on specific issues such as the appropriate form of response to Arab terrorism, the value of great-power efforts in the resolution of the conflict, and required military supplies. There were also clashes concerning the status of Jerusalem, the extent of Israeli withdrawal from occupied territories, the increase in Israeli settlements there, and the role of the Palestinians (and the Palestine Liberation Organization-PLO) in the quest for Arab-Israeli peace. The increase in Israeli dependence on the United States and the areas of policy discord suggest possible reemployment of various forms of pressure utilized previously including the withholding of economic aid (as in the mid-1950s), military-aid decision and delivery slowdowns since 1967 (especially the slow response to Israeli requests during the 1973 war), joining in United Nations censures, moral suasion, private and open presidential letters, and similar devices. This raises questions concerning the reliability of the United States.

The United States is today an indispensable, if not fully dependable, ally.[30] Witness the Reagan administration's temporary embargo of F-16 jets in the wake of Israeli attacks against Iraq and Lebanon. It provides Israel, through one form or another, with economic (governmental and private), technical, military, political, diplomatic, and moral support. It is seen as the ultimate resource against the Soviet Union; it is the source of Israel's sophisticated military hardware; it is central to the Arab-Israeli peace process. But, although there is this positive relationship there is also the Israeli reluctance, bred of history, to abdicate security to another party's judgment and action, particularly in light of the U.S.' role in Iran and in response to the Soviet invasion of Afghanistan. Israel will continue to view its own perceptions of threat and security as controlling.

Human, Material, and Technological Resources and Constraints

Israel's security policy is constrained by its limited natural-resource base and small population. Israel does not possess the raw materials necessary for its military industry nor those that might generate financial resources or leverage abroad. Its population of four million, three million of whom are Jews, compounds the difficulty. Israel has seen the threat as substantial and, therefore, despite these limitations, it has embarked on a wide range of activities that it believes are essential to its security.

Arms acquisition has involved purchases from foreign sources and production by Israel. It has the benefit of providing access to modern and sophisticated equipment of all types—including those that Israel cannot produce—but this has increased Israel's debt and its dependence. At the same time Israel has increasingly sought to produce, coproduce, and sometimes develop equipment on its own, in part as a means of guaranteeing supply and reducing defense costs and external debt and of earning foreign exchange through sales.

Foreign-arms acquisition has been a necessary element of Israeli policy from the outset, but the foreign-debt burden was relatively small until after the 1967 war and the increased purchases of sophisticated and expensive equipment from the United States. The 1973 war compounded the problem because of the substantial losses and expenditure during the conflict and because of the increased costs of the newer equipment that was acquired in its wake. That led, in particular, to a heavy and direct dependence on the United States with all that that implied for security and political decision-making. The foreign debt burden is high and likely to remain substantial, and some analysts suggest it may grow.[31] Increasingly the size of the debt is a constraint on policy and on the ability of the IDF to acquire and utilize weaponry given Israel's resource base.

An indigenous military industry has been an element of security planning since independence, and considerable resources have been invested in it with uneven results.[32] Its basic shortcoming has been resources, both natural and financial. There is also the problem of economies of scale and the difficulties posed by the enormous start-up costs involved in the development and production of a sophisticated weapons system. Israel seems to have overcome many of the technological problems that plagued the industry in earlier years. Its infrastructure has been relatively well suited to the advanced technology of a sophisticated armaments industry.

Despite the constraints, Israel's industry has achieved important results. It produces a wide range of high-quality and advanced weapons and related defense items and is an exporter ranking only after the major powers.

Israel Aircraft Industry (IAI) is the centerpiece of the armaments industry.[33] It has grown rapidly from a company of less than one hundred employees when founded to more than twenty thousand by 1980. It has a wide range of products, some produced under license, including aircraft such as the Fouga-Magister, ammunition, armor, radar/sonar and gyroscopes, and it produces some indigenous products such as the Kfir jet aircraft and the ship-to-ship Gabriel missile.[34] Israel's indigenous defense-manufacturing capability includes military and civil aircraft, surface-to-surface antishipping missiles, air-to-air missiles, patrol boats, combat vehicles, tanks, howitzers, mortars, grenades, radar systems, communication and navigation systems, industrial and shipborne monitoring and control systems, medical electronics, microelectronics, computers and computerized communications systems, fire-control systems, security systems, air- and ground-crew equipment, ground-support equipment, microwave components, and small arms.[35]

A major challenge appears to be limited export capability. Israel has sold a range of products to a number of customers—including West Germany, Indonesia, South Africa, Singapore, Taiwan, Chile, Ecuador, Mexico, Honduras, and Guatemala—but has been constrained by United States limitations placed on products (such as the Kfir jet) that have American components,[36] by a self-imposed limitation concerning the political ideology of some prospective customers, and by the Arab-imposed boycott that threatens states that deal with Israel, as well as by the technical limitations of some of Israel's products.

Israel's military exports have earned a substantial amount of foreign exchange, although the precise levels remain classified.[37] Export sales of the Gabriel surface-to-surface missile, the first operational sea-to-sea missile in the Western world, have earned hundreds of millions of dollars, and it has been purchased by South Africa and Argentina among others. Israel's arms exports have involved several dozen states ranging from small third-world countries to West European NATO allies of the United States and include Latin America and the United States.

Despite its significant accomplishments in this area, Israel remains dependent on the United States for many sophisticated weapons systems and for some of the advanced components of its indigenous products, a condition that is not likely to be altered in the near future. And it remains dependent on other states for critical raw materials.

Israel's main human-resource problem is the overall size of its population. With less than four million citizens Israel is at a substantial disadvantage when compared with its far more numerous neighbors. To deal with this problem it has devised a special system of reserve service and of rapid mobilization. Because of its small population Israel relies on a relatively small standing force and a large number of reserve units that can be quickly mobilized and still fight with a high level of efficiency. But this creates an additional burden for Israelis. The financial costs of defense reflected in substantial budgetary allocations are compounded by the heavy burdens on manpower. In personal terms the contribution is virtually universal; young men and women (with some exemptions on religious and other grounds) serve in the IDF upon reaching the required age, and many former servicemen are called to fulfill reserve obligations each year.

Israel's security posture is aided by the existence of what is generally regarded as a high-quality intelligence service.[38] Despite the "failure" of Israeli intelligence at the time of the October 1973 war, its capabilities are significant and its results have been remarkable. It has benefitted from the high level of education and diverse backgrounds of its people—including substantial immigration from the Arab world. In addition to its own capabilities Israel has had close and beneficial links with the intelligence operations of other states, particularly France and the United States. There are continued linkages with the latter and exchanges between the two states in some areas. But unlike many developing states Israel is not dependent on the data (except, perhaps, in particular instances, for specialized data from electronics and satellite sources) or analysis of these other services but rather relies on its own gathering and analysis activities.

Security, the IDF, and Domestic Politics

The IDF is unique in the Middle East in that it does not, as an entity, play a role in politics, despite its size, budget, and importance. Individual officers and men, and indeed senior commanders, have played important roles, but they have done so as individuals when not on active service and without the backing of the military as an institution. The IDF plays the role of the traditional army—the defense of the state—and performs its tasks in an apolitical fashion.

The domestic scene has been an important element in the formulation and execution of Israel's security policy. Israel benefits and suffers from its being a democratic system with a parliamentary form of government subject to public criticism and the often less than total agreement of its parliament and population. Although Israel has had some twenty governments since independence, the regime has remained relatively stable. The government was controlled by the Labor party (in various incarnations) between 1948 and 1977 and by the Likud bloc since then. Even with the change in coalitions after the 1977 election the primary concern and central focus of government activity remained the security of the state. The centrality of security and the need for a strong and effective IDF, in which virtually all participate at some point, in some way, has not been questioned within the mainstream of Israeli life and politics. The highly visible and respected position of the military has not been challenged.

The respect of the people and the government for the military has prevented the purges often associated with the militaries of developing states and has led to the phenomenon of leading general officers and some of lower rank having a stature and prestige of a sufficient level for them individually to establish themselves as important political figures—somewhat like Eisenhower in the United States.

The elite of Israel's Defense Forces have not raised doubts concerning, and have shown a continued confidence in, the political system, although there are occasional complaints about some of the individuals who run it and their political views and perspectives. Civilians continue to control the military and do so by virtue of their dominant positions within the Israeli system, not because they control the military itself.[39] The officer corps as a unit has not, and probably could not, become closely aligned with one political faction or party. The highly developed and sophisticated nature of the political system and its several institutions and the complex and often bewildering array of political and quasi-political institutions would make it extremely difficult for the army to play an independent political role and seek to seize power through political means and institutions and procedures. The close identification of the Israeli leadership with the development of the state significantly reduces the ability of the army, even if cohesive on this point, to claim that the political leaders had betrayed the state and therefore had to be replaced by military coup or similar device.

The political ambitions of senior Israeli officers have been somewhat restricted, although there seems to be a growing tendency for postcareer political roles as was seen among senior officers in the periods following the 1967 and 1973 wars. Relatively few senior officers have joined political parties. Those who have become involved in politics seem to wish to take advantage of their military accomplishments, charismatic appeal, or established prestige. They have joined various parties representing diverse political views and ideologies. Retired military officers seem to concentrate their talents in other realms, particularly business and industry, and some have become a part of the bureaucratic machinery of the country. In fact, the system has been able to absorb with relatively little disruption virtually all of the retiring senior officers and in most cases in positions of some responsibility that take advantage of their administrative and organizational talents and skills developed in the IDF.

Military men have played a key role in political life only after their retirement. Conspicuous examples are Generals Moshe Dayan, Yigal Allon, Yitzhak Rabin, Yigael Yadin, Ezer Weizman, and Haim Bar Lev. They have attained position and power through their use of and within the political system and by joining political parties, not by their utilization of the military in opposition to the system. Their military reputations and popular prestige enhanced their chances for, but did not ensure, significant political careers. Active-duty officers may not play a political role while serving in the IDF.

Contributing to the limited role of the Israeli army in politics and the prospects that this assessment will continue to be accurate is the very nature of the IDF, which is so different from its counterparts in other states of the nondeveloped world. The IDF is an army of small standing size with a sizeable reserve. Its officer corps and its manpower reserve are clearly integrated in society. There is little in the way of a separate barracks mentality. Permanent service is limited to a relatively small group of men. No separate ideology or political life can be easily created. Israel's army is part of its society—its manpower and political concepts and its ideology are a part of the Israeli national life-style—and not a separate unit seeing itself in opposition to the civilians who control it. Thus, despite the extraordinary role and performance of the military in Israel, civilian rule over the military has persisted.

The pattern for civil-military relations in Israel was established at independence when David Ben-Gurion as prime minister assumed the defense portfolio. He asserted the authority of the government and assured the consolidation of the several underground military forces under the IDF and, ultimately, the ministry of defense. Ben-Gurion early set the pattern for the IDF with his view that the army should be small and professional with a large reserve and serve as something of a nation-building instrument through education, integration, agricultural activity, and youth activity. Ben-Gurion also sought to ensure the creation of a national depoliticized army —despite strong opposition—by combining the disparate concepts and structures of the Haganah, Palmach, and IZL.

Civil-military relations have not been a serious problem. Despite strong military participation in Israeli life, decisions are made at the political level. The minister of defense controls the defense establishment, usually with a firm hand. Of those who have served in that capacity only Moshe Dayan and Ezer Weizman, and, now, Ariel Sharon were senior military officers. On the other hand the chief of staff and often, too, the director of military intelligence (DMI), sometimes accompanied by other officers have participated in cabinet meetings and meetings of such bodies as the Ministerial Committee on Security Affairs, pointing up further the significance of security issues. The advice of senior military officers is sought on all security-related matters. It is the DMI who provides the government with political-military intelligence. The criterion of loyalty to the regime or the leader has not been central to the decision-making process by which senior military positions are filled or retained. Competence and skill have been the major factors involved in the determinations of senior positions in the IDF. To a great extent the military had been insulated from politics in Israel.

Although Israel is a political system characterized by high levels of political participation and political intensity relatively unknown in developing states and by a wide diversity of views on most political issues, national-security considerations have been the subject of a wide and remarkable consensus that seems to pervade Israel's political factions and population despite disparate political ideologies and contending politicians.

Security is and is likely to remain the central theme of Israeli life. It is pervasive. All Israelis have a direct and intimate stake in those aspects of Israeli society that relate to this issue. Constant focus on this theme has bred a population with a particular awareness of military issues and a special competence to deal with its manifestations. Because Israelis believe that their survival is ultimately at stake they are not prepared to leave defense issues to the concern of a group of "whiz kids," military professionals, or elected politicians. Until and unless a just, lasting, and comprehensive peace with all its Arab neighbors is achieved, security for Israel will continue to be at the center of thought, contemplation, policy, and action.

Notes

1. The Israeli perception of danger has been articulated on numerous occasions by many of its decision makers. Moshe Dayan stated it quite forcefully as early as 1955 when he wrote: "There is no other state . . . whose very right to existence is so persistently challenged by all its contiguous neighbors." Major-General Moshe Dayan, "Israel's Border and Security Problems," *Foreign Affairs* 33 (January 1955):250. A decade later then Chief of Staff Yitzhak Rabin noted: "The [Arab] aim . . . is the destruction of the State of Israel." Text of address to the Engineers' Club in Tel Aviv on 24 December 1965 (mimeographed), p. 7. See also Y. Harkabi, *Arab Attitudes to Israel* (Jerusalem: Keter, 1972), p. 37, on the Arab aim of "politicide," the murder of the Jewish state. Egypt's decision to establish peace and to normalize relations with Israel is an important factor in Israeli security thinking. But, there are numerous Israelis who wonder about the long-term commitment of Egypt to peace. Some have suggested the possibility of a reversal of the Egyptian role at various identified points in the future. Yitzhak Rabin gave voice to some of these concerns when he addressed Israel's security problems in the 1980s with the suggestion that: "At the end of three years of peace with Israel, Egypt may renew its alliance with Syria—at a time when Israel will have withdrawn from the whole of Sinai. If this situation were to materialize, the possibility of a combined Arab offensive directed against the very existence of Israel cannot be discounted." Yitzhak Rabin, "Israel's Defense Problems in the Eighties," *Ma'arachot,* October 1979, page 20.

2. For elaboration of this position see Yehoshafat Harkabi, *Arab Attitudes to Israel* (Jerusalem: Israel Universities Press, 1972); *Palestinians and Israel* (Jerusalem: Keter, 1974); and Y. Harkabi, *Arab Strategies and Israel's Response* (New York: Free Press, 1977).

3. See his speech to the Knesset, *The New York Times,* 21 November 1977.

4. For a description of this phenomenon, see interview with Arie Eliav, one of Israel's leading and most articulate doves, in *Worldview* 21 (January-February 1978):8.

5. In general, Israel has not sought formal alliances in the belief that such dependence would not be to its advantage and that the spilling of foreign blood might lead to a cooling of relations with the state whose soldiers were affected.

6. On the military vulnerability of the 1967 lines see Yigal Allon, "Israel: The Case for Defensible Borders," *Foreign Affairs* 55 (October 1976): especially 41-42. See also Steven J. Rosen, *Military Geography and the Military Balance in the Arab-Israel Conflict.* Jerusalem Papers on Peace Problems, no. 21, (Jerusalem: The Hebrew University, 1977).

7. Despite the value of the occupied territories to Israel, it must be recalled that Israel did not go to war with the intention of occupying territory but rather to defend itself against enemy threats. Its decision in 1967 to annex only East Jerusalem reflects this factor.

8. Numerous skirmishes and cross-border incidents have involved Egypt, Jordan, Syria, Lebanon, and the Palestinians. The five wars between Israel and the Arabs have all involved Egypt. In the War of Independence (1948-1949) Egypt was joined by Syria, Jordan, Lebanon, and Iraq, and there was general Arab League collaboration. In the June 1967 war Syria and Jordan played major roles while other Arab states contributed to the effort. In the War of Attrition (1969-1970) Soviet air and missile assistance supported the Egyptian effort. In the 1973 war, Syria was the second major participant, although there was widespread, if often token, Arab action against Israel.

9. For a general overview of the IDF, its background and development, see Edward Luttwak and Dan Horowitz, *The Israeli Army* (New York: Harper and Row, 1975). An indispensable source for the study of Israel's security and defense problems and policies is *A Lexicon of Israel's Defense* (Hebrew), eds. Zeev Schiff and Eitan Haber (Israel: Zmora, Bitan, Modan, 1976).

10. See chapter 3 of the report of the Agranat Commission, the blue-ribbon Israeli commission of inquiry established after the October 1973 war to investigate Israel's preparedness for the conflict.

11. Readers interested in pursuing the subject of Israeli military doctrine further may find the following sources useful: Michael I. Handel, *Israel's Political-Military Doctrine* (Cambridge, Mass.: Harvard University Center for International Affairs, July 1973); and Dan Horowitz, "The Israeli Concept of National Security and the Prospects of Peace in the Middle East," in *Dynamics of a Conflict: A Re-examination of the Arab-Israeli Conflict,* ed. Gabriel Sheffer (Atlantic Highlands, N.J.: Humanities Press, 1975), pp. 235-275.

12. Dan Horowitz has pointed out that "Israel has never had an authoritative security doctrine, one which had institutional approval and was set out in a clear and orderly fashion." See Horowitz, "The Israeli Concept of National Security," p. 255.

13. For supporting commentary, see the remarks ot Zeev Schiff, military analyst for *Haaretz* and Israel's foremost commentator on defense matters, in "The New Balance of Power," *Midstream* 22 (January 1976):9.

14. See Major General Israel Tal, "Israel's Defense Doctrine: Background and Dynamics," *Military Review* 58 (March 1978):24.

15. Ibid.

16. A recent and important discussion of this subject may be found in Major General (Res.) Aharon Yariv, "Strategic Depth," *The Jerusalem Quarterly,* 17 (Fall 1980), pp. 3-12.

17. See Tal, "Israel's Defense Doctrine," pp. 30-31. For further discussion of the defensible borders factor see Dan Horowitz, *Israel's Concept of Defensible Borders,* Jerusalem Papers on Peace Problems No. 16 (Jerusalem: Hebrew University, 1975). The role of borders in Israel's security thinking and its evolution over time is well illustrated by Major General Moshe Dayan, "Israel's Border and Security Problems," *Foreign Affairs* 33 (January 1955):250-267; and Yigal Allon, "Israel: The Case for Defensible Borders," *Foreign Affairs* 55 (October 1976):38-53.

18. See Tal, "Israel's Defense Doctrine," p. 37.

19. See *Proceedings of the International Symposium on the 1973 October War, Cairo, 27-31 October 1975,* vol. 1, *Military Sector* (Cairo, 1976); and Hassan El Badri, Taha El Magdoub, and Mohammed Dia El Din Zohdy, *The Ramadan War, 1973,* rev. ed. (New York: Hippocrene Books, 1978).

20. According to information provided by the Israeli Ministry of Finance and the Israeli embassy, Washington, D.C., Israel's defense expenditures reached 40.7 percent of the GNP in FY 1973. In FY 1974 it was 30.2 percent; in FY 1975, 33.6 percent; in FY 1976, 36.2 percent; in FY 1977, 30.5 percent; and 27.1 percent in FY 1978. On defense expenditure, see also Paul Rivlin, "The Burden of Israel's Defence," *Survival* 20 (July-August 1978):146-154.

21. Soviet-built T54 and T55 tanks captured by Israel during the 1967 war were modified and subsequently incorporated into the Israeli armored corps and played a role in battles. Disclosures of Major General Avraham Adan, *Jerusalem Post* and *Washington Evening Star,* 23 October 1972.

22. On 29 September 1980 Prime Minister Menachem Begin said Israel "provided arms and instructors to train Kurdish fighters." See also *The New York Times,* 30 September 1980.

23. Robert Harkavy has summed up much of the thinking concerning Israel's nuclear potential. "Spectre of a Middle Eastern Holocaust: The Strategic and Diplomatic Implications of the Israeli Nuclear Weapons Program," University of Denver, Graduate School of International Studies, Monograph Series in World Affairs, 14, Book 4, 1977, p. 19. On the origins and development of the Israeli program see Fuad Jabber, *Israel and Nuclear Weapons: Present Option and Future Strategies* (London: Chatto & Windus for the International Institute for Strategic Studies, 1971).

24. In recent years Israel has been increasingly concerned about Iraq's acquisition of a nuclear capability and, therefore, French nuclear assistance to Iraq. See *The Jerusalem Post,* International Edition, 20-26 July 1980; and *Washington Post,* 20 July 1980. In June, 1981, Israel bombed and destroyed Iraq's nuclear reactor near Baghdad.

25. The need of Israel to rely on the United States to deter a Soviet role in the region is central. It was perhaps best expressed by Shimon Peres in the *Jerusalem Post,* 9 September 1971.

26. Prime Minister Golda Meir summarized this view in "Israel in Search of Lasting Peace," *Foreign Affairs* 51 (April 1973):454. See also Shimon Peres, "A Strategy For Peace in the Middle East," *Foreign Affairs* 58 (Spring 1980):891.

27. See Sylvia K. Crosbie, *A Tacit Alliance: France and Israel from Suez to the Six Day War* (Princeton, N.J.: Princeton University Press, 1974).

28. In its dealings with the United States, Israel has a substantial advantage obained from the role in the United States decision-making process played by the American Jewish community.

29. Sinai II (and particularly the United States-Israeli memoranda) tended to formalize, codify, and articulate many of the implicit assumptions of the special relationship and provided for a substantial amount of specific support for Israel on a wide range of issues. The United States and Israel agreed that "in view of the long-standing United States commitment to the survival and security of Israel" the United States "will in the event of such threat consult promptly with the Government of Israel with respect to what support, diplomatic or otherwise, or assistance it can lend to Israel in accordance with its constitutional practices." U.S. Senate Committee on Foreign Relations Press Release No. 16, 3 October 1975. This was to reassure Israel of United States support against a Soviet'threat—the pledged response was similar to that contained in the treaties establishing the main United States alliance systems. The United States also provided additional assurances on the questions of military and economic assistance and on energy (that is, oil) supply.

30. Yitzhak Rabin states this case in *Ma'arachot,* October 1979, p. 19.

31. Israel's foreign debt and debt-service payments grew substantially over the decade of the 1970s. At the end of 1971 its debt was $3.4 billion, but that figure reached $10.4 billion at the end of 1977. The debt-service payments rose from $505 million in 1971 to $1.275 million in 1977. This represented a per capita debt of $2,900 in 1977, up from $1,100 in 1972 and $515 in 1967. Although the absolute level of debt is high, the burden of debt is not as large as it might appear because of the long-term structure and soft nature of much of the debt. For further details, see U.S. Congress, Joint Economic Committee, *The Political Economy of the Middle East: 1973-78* (Washington, D.C.: U.S. Government Printing Office, 1980), p. 147.

32. Relatively little has been published about Israel's arms industry. An interesting discussion of its origins and early development by former Deputy Minister and later Minister of Defense Shimon Peres may be found in *David's Sling* (London: Weidenfeld and Nicolson, 1970), especially pp. 109-136. See also Michael Moodie, "Defense Industries in the Third World: Problems and Promises," in *Arms Transfers in the Modern World,* eds. Stephanie G. Neuman and Robert E. Harkavy (New York: Praeger, 1979), pp. 294-312, and the sources cited by Moodie.

33. See Sheldon Kirshner, "Report of Israel's Budding Arms Industry," *New Outlook* 16 (September 1973):43-49. See also *The New York Times,* 7 January 1973. See also *ibid.,* 24 August 1981, "Arms Are a Crucial Export for Israel."

34. In an unusual statement a Defense Ministry spokesman said on 25 January 1977: "Israel's total export of military equipment is a little more than 300 million dollars, of which not more than 250 million dollars is of a military nature, and the rest is equipment adapted for civilian use." Israel, Prime Minister's Office, Government Press Office, Press Bulletin, 25 January 1977, p. 1. See also *The New York Times,* 12 January 1976.

35. Although details are rarely published, occasional reports on Israel's weapons industry do appear in the press. See, for example, on the Reshef patrol boat, *The New York Times* and *Washington Post,* 5 February 1973; *Jerusalem Post Magazine,* 9 February 1973, pp. 7 and 10. On the Galil assault rifle see: *The New York Times,* 22 March 1973 and 15 April 1973; *Washington Post,* 20 March 1973; and *Haaretz,* 19 March 1973. See also *The New York Times,* 15 January 1977.

36. The Kfir jet has become symbolic of the problem. The plane is powered by General Electric J79 jet engines. The United States can veto the sale of the aircraft to third countries and the president of the United States has done so in the case of Ecuador.

37. On the Gabriel missile, see *Jerusalem Post,* 31 January 1972.

38. On Israel's intelligence activities in general see Dennis Eisenberg, Uri Dan, and Eli Landau, *The Mossad: Israel's Secret Intelligence Service—Inside Stories* (New York and London: Paddington Press, 1978). See also *Christian Science Monitor,* 26 September 1980, p. 14.

39. On the general nature of civil-military relations see Amos Perlmutter, *Military and Politics in Israel: Nation-Building and Role Expansion* (London: Frank Cass, 1969); and Amos Perlmutter, *Politics and the Military in Israel 1967-1977* (London: Frank Cass, 1978).

11 Iraq

John F. Devlin

This chapter assesses the security interests and policies followed by most Iraqi governments, including the monarchy and the republican governments that followed it in 1958. Particular attention is given the Baath regime that has governed Iraq since 1968.

Iraq is a new state formed after World War I out of the debris of the Ottoman Empire, of which it had comprised three provinces for several centuries. As a new state it has had to establish its own identity. Although several of its enduring military security interests—pan-Arab nationalism, the Israeli question—have roots in the past, they have by and large appeared in the lifetime of people now living. Other concerns—border problems, friction between Iranian and Arab, ethnic discontent—are older, but are now problems for Baghdad, not the Ottoman capital of Istanbul.

Of fundamental importance to an understanding of Iraq's security outlook is an appreciation of the central position that the military establishment has occupied since the inception of the Iraqi state. The army dates from 6 January 1921, before Faisal was named king by Britain and before the League of Nations assigned the mandate for Iraq to Great Britain. The military establishment has been deeply involved in the politics of the country through *coups d'etat*, direct rule, and as the ultimate prop for civilian governments ruling a country in which wholehearted support for the government of the time has been rare and in which the concept of loyal opposition is scarcely known. Its officers have considered the army to be an embodiment of the national spirit, with a right to be a part of the political process. The army dominated Iraq from 1936 to 1941, overthrew the monarchy in 1958, ruled for nine of the next ten years, and was used by the currently ruling Baath Party as its instrument to seize power in 1968. The Baath regime has put the armed forces under party control, but it is a virtual certainty that they will at some time again assume a direct political role.

Iraq and the International System

Iraq's place in the international system, both as it is and as Iraqis perceive it, is a major determinant of the country's security policy. Determining the country's dimensions was a major issue in the early years; the northern part of the country was not definitively acquired until 1926. Defending borders

227

from tribal raids was a problem in the 1930s. Iraq was under British Mandatory tutelage until 1932, and British connections with the monarch and Nuri Said, who was prime minister at various times, assured British influence on Iraqi affairs thereafter until 1958. Iraq's principal resource, oil, was extracted, exported, and marketed by a group of major international oil companies until the industry was nationalized in the early 1970s.

Within the Middle Eastern region, Iraq has been a contender for influence and leadership. Never acknowledged by its neighbors as preeminent, Baghdad has dueled with Cairo for influence in Syria, has consistently sought to extend its influence in the Persian Gulf, and has endeavored to be a leader among Arab states. It has had harmonious relations with Turkey since the 1930s. With its other non-Arab neighbor, Iran, relations have been marked by dispute, barring a few years in the 1930s, the 1950s, and the 1975-1978 period. The two have differed over borders, the Kurdish issue, and influence in the Gulf. Each has a part of its people with rather special links to the other: the Shia Muslim 55 percent of Iraqis who look to their co-religionists in Iran and the Arabic-speaking population in Iran's oil-producing province of Khuzistan whose tribal and ethnic ties run west into Iraq.

Iraqi governments since the monarchy, and especially the ruling Baath regime, have seen their surroundings as constraining and their country as beset by enemies. The opposition to the monarchy—and to the politicians who supported it—that grew during the 1950s derived largely from what the opposition saw as the subservience of Iraq's leaders to foreign influence. Nuri Said's refusal to take measures against Britain in 1956 when it joined France and Israel in attacking Egypt made revolution inevitable. External support for the Kurds in their struggle for autonomy from 1961 until Iran closed its borders to such support in 1975 was, for the Iraqis, evidence that foreign powers were continuing to intervene in Iraq's domestic affairs. So were efforts at various times in the past quarter century by other Arab states, chiefly Egypt and Syria, to limit Iraq's influence in Arab councils.

The consequence has been an Iraqi determination to be independent. As Iraq's President Saddam Hussein has noted: "Our absolute independence in internal, external and Arab policies and non-interference in the affairs of either party are the basis for our friendship with the Soviet Union."[1] He also said: "Iraq is an exception, . . . (to the prevailing phenomenon that small states are either subservient to or agents of the super powers), since it is its own master and deals with all states (equally)."[2] This determination to be as free of susceptibility to external pressure as possible shows clearly in Iraq's oil policy. Geography has placed Iraq so that all its petroleum exports must cross the territory of other states or go through the Straits of Hormuz, long under the guns of the shah of Iran's navy. The oldest route, and long the only one, a pipeline across Syria, was closed at Syrian initiative in 1956 and in 1966-1967. In 1973 Syria unilaterally doubled the transit fee. Beginning in the 1970s the Baghdad regime undertook major, expensive projects with the goal of having alternative routes for oil exports. There are now three: the original system across Syria, a three-year old pipeline running through Turkish territory to the Mediterranean, and a pair of major loading terminals in the Persian Gulf. In addition, an internal pipeline running north and south permits up to a million barrels per day of oil from northern fields to be exported through the Gulf or a similar quantity from the southern fields through the pipelines to the Mediterranean. In normal times, either the Turkish or Syrian pipeline plus the Gulf outlet permit Iraq to export about all the oil that its facilities can produce.

Oil production and exports might seem far removed from security policy, but in fact oil revenues provide the vast bulk of Iraq's income, over $25 billion a year at today's prices, until the war with Iran severely damaged oil export installations. Oil production and the revenues from its export are the basis of Iraq's security policy. They provide the funds to buy military equipment. Iraq has no heavy industry and no arms-manufacturing capability. Iraq's security policy and its raising of armed forces that it has used or threatened to use have taken into account the vital importance of ensuring that its oil can be sold in foreign markets. Since the overthrow of the monarchy, Iraqi governments have worked to take control of the oil industry away from foreign companies. The current Baath regime completed the nationalization process in the mid-1970s and controls oil affairs from exploration through marketing of crude by means of state-run establishments.

The goals that Iraq pursues by military means, by the use or threat of force, are several:

domestic security, including maintenance of the regime in power and subordination of ethnic groups (primarily Kurds) to central-government control

maintaining integrity of the country's borders

extension of influence over the Arab states of the Gulf

opposing the existence of Israel, assisting Arab states in hostilities with Israel, supporting a Palestinian entity

promoting Arab political movements compatible with its Baath-socialist philosophy

Staying in power has often been the governments' prime security policy. This has been carried out by screening of armed-forces personnel for loyalty to the regime and by extensive use of internal-security services. The number of *coups d'etat* indicates a certain lack of success in this policy over the

years. The present regime has a well-developed party organization throughout the armed forces and has kept them out of politics for the past ten years.

Maintaining control over its own population has been a task with which
successive Iraqi governments have struggled. About one-fifth of Iraq's
population is composed of Kurds, a non-Arabic people who inhabit contiguous mountain areas in Iran and Turkey as well as in Iraq. Traditionally
unreceptive to rule from Baghdad, Kurds rose against the central government in the 1920s, 1930s, and 1940s. Under Mulla Mustafa Barzani a new
round began in 1961, and for some years the bulk of northeastern Iraq—save
for major cities and main roads—was out of government control. The Iraqi
army typically would make some advances in summer only to fall back in
winter. Turkey forbade the use of its territory to the Kurdish dissidents but
Iran provided safe haven, supplied materiél, and permitted other states to
do the same.

The Baathist regime arranged a cease-fire in early 1970; in the ensuing
years efforts were made to accommodate Baghdad's desire for control and
the Kurds' for autonomy. In the end the two sides were not to agree, partly
because the Kurds wanted the northern oil-producing area included in the
autonomous area and the government would not hear of it. In the new
fighting that began in 1974, an enlarged and better-equipped Iraqi army kept
fighting into the winter and drove Kurdish forces, now heavily dependent on
wheeled transport and external supply, back toward the Iranian border.
Iranian-Iraqi clashes occurred, and the leaders of each country, concerned
that a serious outbreak of fighting might damage their respective oil facilities,
signed an agreement in March 1975 that snuffed out the Kurdish rebellion.
Iraq later asserted that it was running low on munitions and needed to end
the fighting. Under the agreement, the shah stopped allowing arms to reach
the Kurds. In return, Iraq agreed to share the Shatt al-Arab, the waterway
that divides the two in the south, with Iran. It had long been under Iraqi
sovereignty, and the larger of Iraq's ports, Basrah, is situated on it.

This agreement ushered in four years of unaccustomed quiet in Iranian-
Iraqi relations. The two countries had not engaged in major hostilities since
the early 1800s, but relations between them have been marked by quarrels
over reciprocal borders, by sanctuary extended to exiled political opponents, by support for each others' dissidents, and by disagreement over
the numbers and residence status of Iranians in Iraq. (The most important
religious sites of Shia Muslims are Karbala and Najaf in Iraq, and Iranians
go there in large numbers for study and pilgrimage.) With the fall of the
shah, relations between the two states went back to normal, perhaps even
worse than normal. The Iranian radio began to urge Iraq's Shia Muslims to
overthrow the Baath regime, and Iraq began to send arms to Iranian
minority groups. Iraq's purpose in extending support to such groups was
not to promote the breakup of Iran. Such a development would not be good

for Iraq because it would set a bad example for Iraq's own Kurds and Shias. Rather, Baghdad hoped to get rid of the Khomeini government and to see a regime less inimical to Iraq's interests take office in Teheran.

Iraq's decision to raise the level of hostilities in September 1980 by invading Iran follows logically, if not wisely, on Baghdad's policy of using force to advance its interests. The 1975 agreement with Iran had succeeded in stopping the Kurdish rebellion but at the cost to Iraq of sharing the Shatt al-Arab waterway with Iran. Iraqi leaders, believing Iran to be vulnerable, struck for two broad reasons: one, to regain control of the Shatt and, two, to administer a shock to the Iranian Islamic regime that would discredit Ayatollah Khomeini and bring about changes in Iran's government and policies. Khomeini's incitement to Iraqis to rise against the Baath gave great concern to the leaders in Baghdad, who have repressed domestic opponents with great rigor over the past twelve years. However, President Saddam Hussein and his associates miscalculated Iran's military competence and will to resist. Although Iraqi forces have had the upper hand, the two sides are moving into a situation of stalemate.

From its neighbors to the south, Iraq perceives no threats in a military sense, but Iraq does have ambitions that may be advanced by force, the threat of force, or assistance to political groups. Successive Iraqi regimes have viewed neighboring Kuwait as rightfully a part of Iraq. Baghdad claimed it in 1938, urged that it join the short-lived federation of Jordan and Iraq (1958), and claimed it again in 1961. Fear that Prime Minister Qasim intended to use force led to British and, later, Arab forces being sent to Kuwait's aid in 1961. In the years since Iraq has recognized Kuwait, but it has also pressed for the cession of territory, chiefly uninhabited islands, Warbah and Bubiyan, fronting on the channel to Umm Qasr, the newer of Iraq's sea outlets. Iraqi pressure involved the use of military units, and this led to border shooting incidents. For a time in the late 1970s, Iraq occupied some areas on Kuwait's side of the border.

The smaller states farther down the Gulf have for years been objects of Iraq's interest. Baghdad has extended support to local Baathist movements, which by definition are opposed to government by ruling families. For a time, it urged the formation of a Gulf states' security organization, in which it hoped to have a prominent role. In recent years it has been active in Organization of Arab Petroleum Exporting Countries (OAPEC) economic projects in the Gulf.

Central to Iraq's military strategic concerns is the Arab-Israeli issue. Iraqi forces fought in Palestine in 1948-1949; Iraq refused to sign an armistice agreement with Israel. It sent forces in 1967 (which stayed on in Jordan until 1970) and in 1973 to the Syrian front. The scale of hostilities has risen with each round. Iraq still refuses to recognize Israel. It has not accepted UN resolutions 242 and 338, which implicitly recognize Israel's existence. It supports maximalist Palestinian demands and sponsors its own Palestine organization, the Arab Liberation Front. And it led Arab opposition to the Camp David agreements and the subsequent Egyptian-Israeli treaty.

Although it has supported Syria in the latter's contest with Israel, Iraq in a broader sense looks on Syria as an impediment to its interests, barring access to the Mediterranean and opposing the spread of Iraqi influence westward. Modern Iraq has wanted a regime in Syria that would be amenable to its interests, and Syrians today, as in the past, resist Iraqi pretensions to a superior status. The competition has a sharper edge now because each country is ruled by men who regard themselves and their own Baath party as the legitimate offspring of the original Baath. The competition has surfaced in recent years in the tumult of Palestinian politics. Iraq supported the maximalist Palestinian groups with arms and, for a time, with small forces. Men were sent to Lebanon in 1976. These ostensibly volunteer forces sided with the Palestinian elements that opposed Syrian intervention on behalf of the Christian Maronites in that country. Once Syria fell out with the Maronite forces and reconstituted an association with the Palestinians, Iraq did not need to be as actively involved, and the volunteers were withdrawn.

The policy goals previously discussed above have provided reasons for expansion of the Iraqi armed forces. A number of other factors have also contributed. One was the availability of materiel. Baghdad had, in the years following the overthrow of the monarchy, turned from its traditional source of arms, Great Britain, to the Soviet Union. The latter was willing to provide arms in some quantity. First deliveries were made in 1958, and as time passed the armed forces came to be almost exclusively equipped with Soviet materiel. The 1967 Arab-Israeli war showed the Iraqis that there were serious limitations on their capability to move forces expeditiously. Their troops did not reach the front in time to join in the fighting. Moreover, Iraqi troops were not having notable success against the Kurds in the 1960s. There were political reasons for some of these deficiencies; military participation in politics and changes of government had left insufficient time for officers to develop professional skills. Dismissals were frequent; political acceptability was more important than fighting ability.

To the east, the shah's military-expansion program markedly increased Iran's ability to project power beyond its borders by the end of the 1960s. This program took a quantum jump in the early 1970s, when U.S. policy permitted the shah to purchase virtually anything he could pay for. Vastly increased oil revenues after 1973 increased the scope of Iran's military buying. The shah stated that it was Iran's intention to establish and maintain military superiority in the Gulf after the withdrawal of British forces from the area. Such Iranian military strength concerned the Iraqis.

For the above reasons, a military expansion program was begun and has continued. It wrought startling increases in the size, amount of equipment, and capability—insofar as that can be measured—of Iraq's armed forces. In the October 1973 Arab-Israeli war, Iraqi units reached the Syrian front in time to join in the fighting. Increased numbers, firepower, and mobility enabled the Iraqi army to push the Kurds back closer to the borders in the winter of 1974-1975, setting the stage for the March 1975 agreement with Iran. Expansion continued through the 1970s. Table 11-1 outlines the growth of Iraqi military power. It is worth noting that Iraq has also acquired about a thousand tank transporters.

Security Policymaking Process

The factors that bear on specific security decisions are hidden in secrecy. Military policy is not a subject for public discussion in Iraq, nor for that matter is any policy. The Baath regime is authoritarian; power resides in the governing body of the Baath party, the Regional Command. This body of twenty-one members, which with the addition of one officer also constitutes the Revolutionary Command Council (RCC), is the executive organ of government. It legislates by decree, and on occasion its members serve on tribunals trying persons accused of crimes against the state. Among its members some are more powerful than others, and the man who holds the posts of president and chairman of the RCC in addition to that of secretary of the Regional Command, Saddam Hussein, is clearly the boss. During the eleven years that he was second to now-retired Ahmad Hasan Bakr, Saddam

Table 11-1
Iraqi Armed Forces

	1967	1973	1979
Total	82,000	101,800	222,000
Military expenditure	—	$338 million	$2 billion
Army			
Men	70,000	90,000	190,000
Tanks	600	1,065	1,900
Artillery (75-152 mm)	—	700	800
Navy			
Missileboats	—	3	12
Torpedoboats	—	12	10
Air Force			
Bomber	—	8	22
Fighter/Interceptor ground attack	—	216	305

Source: International Institute for Strategic Studies, *The Military Balance, 1968-1969,* pp. 43-44; *1973-1974,* pp. 32-33; and *1979-1980,* p. 40 (London, 1968, 1973, 1979).

gradually expanded his power in a sort of slow-motion succession as Bakr's health gradually failed.

Decisions on military purchases, on expansion, and on security policy are made by this body or by certain of its members. The framework within which those decisions are made is that of the goals previously listed. And although Iraq's position in regard to hostility toward Israel, say, is frequently repeated, there is no evidence to indicate what weight various factors have in the Baath leaders' deliberations. Certain military purchases may become known when the arms arrive or are paraded. In most cases, and certainly in the case of military and security matters, there is no public discussion before a government policy is announced. For example, the Baath regime's decision to increase the level of hostilities with Iran from border clashes to invasion was forecast only a few days before in a speech by the president. Such differences of view as may exist within the RCC/Regional Command come to notice when members are expelled. No such expulsions have been tied to military policy.

The role of the press, radio, and television in Iraq is to explain and support government policy. The government employs a variety of rationales to explain its security policies to its own people and to those abroad. Its policies and actions with respect to the Israeli issue and to Arab affairs generally are presented in a pan-Arab framework, with the government saying that Iraq is acting for the benefit of all Arabs. Israel is portrayed as an agent of imperialism, and antiimperialism is a constant element in Iraq's explanations of its security policy. The language it uses to justify the war with Iran and even Baghdad's earlier military activity along the border appeals to long-standing Iranian-Arab differences. In addition, Ayatollah Khomeini's regime typically is portrayed as acting against the true interests of Islam.

Although security policy is not discussed publicly, certain aspects of it can be inferred from what Iraq has been doing. The Baath regime has aspirations for a leading role in the Arab world. (The party is pan-Arab in ideology and has affiliates in many Arab states.) A strong military establishment gives weight to Baghdad's policies. It is likely therefore that the Iraqi armed forces will continue to grow in size and capability, certainly as long as those of certain other regional states continue to do so. Iraq will want to be able to at least keep pace with and preferably to improve its military position vis-à-vis Israel. It will want to have armed forces at least as large as Syria's. It will want to be able to exert influence in the Gulf.

These desiderata will for some time be overshadowed by war with Iran. A large part of the Iraqi armed force is tied up in that fighting. Iraq's first priority must be to prosecute that war or, in the event of an armistice or cease-fire, to be prepared for a resumption. Continued growth in the size and strength of its armed forces seems certain. As in the past, Iraq will remain dependent on external sources for its armaments.

In the last few years, there has been some publicity about Iraq's nuclear intentions. The public discussion is possible because Western nations are building Iraq's nuclear facilities, and Baghdad cannot enforce secrecy as it does domestically. France, Iraq's principal source of nuclear expertise and equipment, has trained Iraqi scientists and undertook to build a seventy-megawatt reactor and to supply the enriched uranium to fuel it. Sabotage to major components of the reactor during the construction in France in 1979 set back the schedule. The reactor was slated to go into operation in the early 1980s, but the Israeli air attack in June 1981 did heavy damage to the installation. Iraq is negotiating for reconstruction; terms have not yet been agreed on. Under the original agreements, Iraq would have acquired the basic items of nuclear technology that could lead in time to the development of an explosive device.

As for intentions, Iraq signed the nuclear nonproliferation treaty, and its official position is that it intends to use nuclear expertise and facilities for peaceful purposes. But the same facilities can be used to develop weapons. And, in the wake of the Israeli raid, Iraqi President Saddam Hussein called on Muslim states to work together to produce a nuclear bomb.[3] If Iraq decides to try to build weapons, the development will be as secret as Iraq can make it. In any event, Iraqi possession of nuclear explosives lies some time in the future, and the development of nuclear weapons is even further distant. It is entirely plausible, even likely, that the Baghdad regime intends at the least to put itself in a position to make nuclear explosives if it sees a need.[4]

Internal Security and Civil-Military Relations

Civilian-military relations are as obscured as is the development of national security policy. Although the Baath party came to power in 1968 with military support, in the following years it established party control over the military establishment. Former President Bakr's position as a respected military officer helped this process. A party apparatus already existed in the armed forces, and it was quickly expanded throughout them; political activity within those forces has been limited to the Baath. It is fair to estimate that many if not most military officers are Baathists, that they see their ambitions helped by such membership. Indeed, one observer states that party membership is compulsory for regular officers.[5] But whether the party apparatus in the military, the general staff, or selected senior officers express the desires and views of the armed forces to the political leaders is simply not known. That the political leaders are alert to keep the armed forces contented is evidenced by the pay raises granted to the military at times of domestic crisis, for example, after a major party shake-up and a score of executions in mid-1979.

The regime's view of the correct posture for the military services was succinctly put by Saddam Hussein some years ago, "the Armed Forces . . . report to and implement the orders of the Party with faith and enthusiasm."[6] As far as external affairs are concerned, security policies that the Baath regime and most of its predecessors have followed have received broad support in the country and from the military. The exception was the old regime's close ties to the West, previously cited. Anti-Israeli feeling is strong and so is antipathy to Iran, at least among the Sunni Arabs who have provided modern Iraq with most of its political leaders and military officers. Domestically, regimes in Baghdad, whether monarchy, military clique, or Baath party, have asserted a claim to run the entire country, with little or no power adhering to the provinces. The military establishment has supported this claim. Even when the army was doing poorly against the Kurds there were few who counseled awarding autonomy to them.

One area of security policy that Iraqi governments do not have to worry about is that of financial resources. Up until 1974 this was not the case. Disputes between Iraq and the oil companies beginning in 1961 held production down, and prices of crude oil were relatively low. In 1973 military and security allocations were some $338 million. In 1979 they were $2 billion. Iraq, since the big oil price increases of 1973, and even more in the last few years, has had the financial resources to spend what it wanted on the military establishment without restricting economic or social programs for lack of money. Constraints on military growth are found in other areas. Because it must obtain arms from abroad, Iraq is dependent on the willingness of such countries as the Soviet Union and France to sell weapons. This is a theoretical rather than a practical constraint, although the Soviet Union has occasionally held up shipments. Much more important is the limited trained manpower. The government has been increasing training for some years. A year or so ago it inaugurated a compulsory adult-literacy program. These efforts will bear fruit in time, but manpower limitations will compel choices for many years. The doubling in size of the armed forces between 1973 and 1979 undoubtedly pulled many into the services who would otherwise have contributed to the civilian economy.

Iraq's military and security doctrines have not been laid out systematically by the country's leaders. The following description and analysis therefore is extrapolated from what the country has done to meet threats or to advance its interests. It has, as all countries able to would, used its military force to maintain the integrity of its borders. In the 1920s this effort was chiefly in the southwestern desert where tribes from central Arabia would attempt to raid the settled areas along the Euphrates River. Then, and in later years, troubles along the border with Iran occupied the attention of Iraq's armed forces. The border, established by treaty in the nineteenth century, demarcated in 1913-1914, and reaffirmed by treaty in 1937, was artificial to the people living near it. Incursions to help friends to flee punitive expeditions were common, and these provided opportunities for each government to use such events as excuses for poking at one another. Iraq's border with Turkey has been for the most part untroubled since the northern third of Iraq, the Ottoman province of Mosul, became part of Iraq by treaty with Turkey in 1926. For the eight years prior to that a bitter dispute over the area had been fought with diplomacy and guns.

The difficulties of establishing control over a population that had long rejected any central authority beset the new Iraqi state and its British mentors from the beginning. In the southern half of the country, where the 55 percent of Iraqis who are Shia Muslims live, tribal uprisings were eliminated as a serious threat by World War II. In the Kurdish areas, a sense of separateness in language and culture, dislike of rule by non-Kurds, and the self-determination doctrine in the air at the end of World War I led immediately to efforts at separation and subsequently to struggles for autonomy. The last eruption lasted from 1961, with interruptions, until 1975. The continuity and scale of armed objection to one or another aspect of government from Baghdad has contributed greatly to a philosophy that successive regimes in Iraq have held. Put simply—and no doubt over-simplified—it is that the government in Baghdad should hold and exercise all power in the country. Provinces are run by officials appointed from Baghdad.[7] To make this system work, physical control is paramount; only when order is maintained can proper administration follow. This has meant that the Iraqi armed forces have been employed in maintaining domestic security as a major element of their mission. That element is at least as important as defending borders. Over the years, far more Iraqi soldiers have seen action fighting their fellow countrymen than have fought external enemies although current Iranian-Iraqi hostilities may well change that balance.

The philosophy and the domestic mission are complicated by the role that the armed forces have played in the political life of Iraq. The officer corps, a thoroughly politicized body, has frequently believed that the political leadership has been inadequate in its governance or its foreign policy. The monarchy depended on the military and was overthrown by military officers who believed that it had failed to support important Arab interests. Military involvement in politics continued after that. One expert has counted "at least ten coups and attempted coups, and two armed rebellions" since 1958.[8] The most recent attempt at a coup by military force was in 1973. The Baath party has maintained control over the military since. One element of that control was provided by Ahmad Hasan Bakr, president until mid-1979, a respected military officer who was among the group of officers that plotted the overthrow of the monarchy. Whether the civilian Baath regime will continue to keep the military under control is a question for the future. The leaders have placed a trusted officer, a close relative of Saddam Hussein, in the post of minister of defense and continue to treat the officer corps well in terms of pay and perquisites.

Governments in Baghdad have raised military forces according to their means and needs. Those needs have changed in the past thirty years. Domestically, the southern, Shia, half of the country has required little military attention since the late 1930s. But the Kurdish area took on a new dimension in the 1960s. Prior to that time, divisions among the Kurds had kept them from combining against the Baghdad government, and the army typically had to deal with only one district or tribe at a time. Moreover, it often could play one tribe off against another. During the 1960s, the Kurdish rebellion grew to include a clear majority of Kurds and spread over almost all Iraqi Kurdistan. Instead of the brigade or two used in the typical operation of the 1930s and 1940s, the Iraqi army had eight brigades in the field against the Kurds in 1963 and six divisions in 1974.[9]

Until after World War II, Iraq's armed forces were used only for domestic security and defense of the country's integrity. Indeed, they were not designed or equipped to do much more. But since then their field of action has broadened, keeping pace with Iraq's broadening interests in the Arab world. The major element in this broadening has been the Arab-Israeli conflict. Iraqi concern at Iran's military buildup and its own desire to project power down the Persian Gulf are more recent developments.

Externally, the scale of military activity with respect to Israel has grown over the years, and Iraq, although not a state bordering on Israel, has cast itself as a major element on the eastern front. In 1948, Iraqi troops took over a section of the West Bank/Samaria and held the area until the armistice agreements between Jordan and Israel in April 1949, at which time the Iraqi contingent had grown to 19,000 troops that were withdrawn and replaced by elements of the Arab Legion.[10]

Iraq had put its forces under Egyptian command a few days before the "Six Day War" broke out in June 1967. An Iraqi unit fought in Sinai. Iraq also dispatched a division-sized force to the Syrian-Jordanian front, but it did not participate in the fighting. Iraqi forces remained in the area for some years; they were concentrated in eastern Jordan where they stayed until 1970.[11] During this period, Baghdad used these forces as a channel for arms to Palestinian fedayeen groups. During the fighting of 1970, when the Jordanian army cleared Palestinian guerrillas out of Amman, Iraq stayed aloof. Its leaders apparently felt that a reasonably stable Jordan between Iraq and Israel was desirable at that period, when their domestic position had not been fully secured. This posture later led to bitter recriminations between Iraq and the major Palestinian organizations.

In 1973, although there was no advance warning to Iraq of the planned Syrian-Egyptian attack, Iraq showed substantial improvements over 1967 in its ability to move forces to the eastern front and have them arrive in condition to enter combat. Despite strained relations with Syria, Iraq's leaders continue to assert that they are ready to send forces to aid Syria in the event of new conflict with Israel.

Iraq continues to stress that its armed forces exist to defend Arab land. Saddam Hussein said in a February 1980 speech, "We will not be satisfied with the defense of the soil and honor of Iraq alone, we should prepare ourselves to defend the Arab nation's honor, principles, unity and pan-Arab struggle."[12] Iraq advocates a military solution to the Arabs' quarrel with Israel. Because it is not an immediate neighbor of Israel, Iraq must work with and through those states that do border Israel. This circumstance cuts two ways. Iraq is militantly hostile to Israel, but it cannot initiate hostilities with Israel. It can only respond, as it did in 1973, to events brought about by others. And those others, Israel's Arab neighbors, wary of the military might of Israel, follow a far less intransigent line than Iraq does, thus in practice limiting the effectiveness of Iraq's tough posture. Syria and Jordan, by acceding to UN Resolutions 242 and 338, acknowledge Israel's right to exist; Iraq does not. Even among the Palestinians Iraq's backing of those holding the most extreme views limits its influence, for those Palestinians are in a minority.

In its policy toward Arab world issues, and toward other Arab states, Iraq has limited occasion for the open use of military force. As with any proposition, there is an exception; Iraq has employed military units to establish claims to small amounts of territory—a few square miles—that Kuwait considers to be its own. It continues to press a claim for control of two uninhabited islands fronting the channel to Iraq's new port of Umm Qasr. Many Iraqis feel that Kuwait should properly be part of Iraq. But Baghdad is constrained from an attempt to seize it militarily, because such action would bring Iraq the enmity of the rest of the Arab world. Arabs have fought Arabs frequently in the past three decades, but the extinction of an existing recognized Arab League state or even the seizure of territory from such a state by another would not be tolerated. It lies outside the bounds of acceptable political behavior. And Iraq itself has recently adopted and publicly advocated that all other Arab states adopt a declaration "Banning any Arab state from resorting to force against any other Arab state . . . "[13]

There are more subtle and less direct ways of encouraging the emergence of regimes compatible with Iraq's ideology open to Baghdad. Some are political, for example, the training of political cadres or the sponsoring of Baath organizations in other states; some are economic. Neither type directly concerns us here. But the existence of a large well-equipped military establishment gives certain power to Baghdad in these political endeavors. In addition, Iraq has provided military equipment and training to other Arabs. Most notable in this regard has been such help to certain

Palestinian guerrilla organizations. It has also donated funds to be used for military purposes to North Yemen.

Iraq and the Persian Gulf

It is in the Gulf that the political utility and the limitations of Iraqi military power are to be seen. Iran's military buildup during the last dozen years of the shah's regime concerned the smaller Arab states of the Gulf. It is fair to say that the rulers of these states did not really expect the shah to invade them; indeed, the rulers understood that he was ready to come to their aid should they ask for it. But memories are long in that area; Iran had once ruled both sides of the Gulf, and the shah was quite clear in asserting an Iranian right to maintain the security of the Gulf as Iran defined that security. Iraq, though sponsoring a political-economic system not in harmony with that of the Gulf rulers, was an Arab state. Until 1975 it was at odds with Iran. As it began in the mid-1970s to come out of a self-imposed isolation, it found other Gulf states willing to cooperate with it on a number of issues. But when Iraq in 1975 urged the establishment of a formal Gulf security organization, the others balked. That would tie them too closely in a sensitive area to a state that was not completely in harmony with them. And it might have antagonized Iran unnecessarily. Iraq has since dropped its advocacy of a Gulf security organization in favor of bilateral ties with the several states. It now portrays itself as an Arab champion against the threat of Iranian expansionism. Its growing navy will be a physical reminder to the other Gulf states of Iraqi military power.

But while its role as Arab champion will in a way advance Iraq's security interests among the Arab states of the Gulf, the war will have effects directly relevant to other aspects of Iraq's military-security policy. A great increase in Iraqi-Iranian antipathy has already occurred. Whatever the outcome of this war, there is sure in time to be a sequel most likely started by the loser. Until some cease-fire arrangement is made, Iraqi oil exports through the Gulf will not resume. Even full restoration of oil exports through the pipelines to the Mediterranean, which are less vulnerable to Iranian attack, would amount to less than half the total prewar volume, and the larger of those lines crosses hostile Syria. In brief, although the availability of multiple export routes permitted Iraq to employ major military force against a perceived threat—and may or may not succeed for a time in reducing that threat—its concentration on Iran has weakened its capacity to deal with other interests. Baghdad will have to guard persistently against an Iran seeking revenge; it will be that much less a factor in the Arab-Israeli military balance. Syria is also in a position to affect the export of Iraqi oil.

Iran has been considered in Baghdad to be a surrogate of the United States. The latter has not been a popular country with regimes in Iraq since the overthrow of the Iraqi monarchy in 1958. The reasons may be simply stated. The United States—and Great Britain—supported the monarchy. The United States has been Israel's strongest and most consistent supporter. The United States and Great Britain involved Iraq in an alliance, the Baghdad Pact, directed against the Soviet Union. U.S.- and British-owned oil companies held the major share of oil concessions under the monarchy, and efforts begun under Qasim in 1960 to change in Iraq's favor the terms under which oil was extracted and exported made little headway, due in Baghdad's view to obstructionism on the part of the companies. All these factors combined to turn Iraq after 1958 in the direction of the Soviet Union for military aid and support.

Alignment Patterns

Association with the Soviet Union is one of Iraq's alignment strategies as alignment with the West had been before 1958. Its other alignment strategies for the most part deal with Iraq in its role as an Arab state, particularly in the Arab confrontation with Israel. The two types of alignment have not in practice been completely separate, but for analytical purposes they will be discussed separately here. Soviet arms supplies began in 1958 and have continued in subsequent years with major new agreements from time to time.[14] This is an area where a major shift in Iraqi policy occurred as compared to the monarchical period.

Iraq's association with the Soviet Union and its reliance on that country for arms and on it and its East European associates for a variety of technical and economic services has not been trouble free. It has become entangled with the domestic fortunes of the Communist party of Iraq, which has on several occasions over the past twenty years attempted to play a larger role in the Iraqi state than the regime in power has been willing to grant. Vigorous repression of Iraqi Communists (for example in 1963) and repression of the Kurds (1974) has soured military as well as political relationships with the Soviet Union and occasioned slowdowns in delivery of materiél.[15] But this is an area where revolutionary Iraq's determination to avoid subservience to any outside power leads Baghdad to follow its self-interests. Militarily, the relationship is one-sided; the Soviet Union gets no base rights, automatic use of facilities, or the like. Transit for aircraft and occasional port calls are the extent of Soviet access. Iraq pays for the weapons it buys.

Iraqi-Soviet relations were closest in the early 1970s, a period when the Baath regime was working to ensure its control of the country. Iraq was, by the choice of its regime, isolated from the mainstream of Arab politics, engaged in a struggle with the oil companies, and only in a temporary truce with the Kurdish dissidents. A series of agreements culminated in a Treaty of Friendship and Cooperation on 9 April 1972. Although not a military treaty, Article 9 states: "In the interests of the security of both countries the high contracting parties will continue to develop cooperation in the strengthening of their defense capabilities."

The treaty has now run more than half its fifteen years, and Iraq's security relations with the Soviet Union, though still important to Baghdad, have grown less intimate. Iraq has made major purchases of military aircraft from France and buys military equipment from other European states. An alternate source of arms lends flexibility to Iraqi security policy, a flexibility that Baghdad appreciates the more following the Soviet invasion of Afghanistan. For the relationship that has existed between the governments of Iraq and the Soviet Union since 1958 has never been as close as that between the monarchy and Great Britain until 1958. The latter two shared a view of the Middle East and believed that their mutual interests were linked. From Baghdad's point of view, Iraqi and Soviet congruence of interests is extensive but by no means all-encompassing.

In the years since 1958, Iraqi alignments within the Arab world have revolved around two issues: antagonism to Israel and opposition to "imperialist" efforts to reimpose control and influence. As noted earlier, Iraq has participated in a number of joint military commands. Typically, such joint commands involving Arab forces are more political than military in effect, because they rarely allow true command authority to the ostensible leading state, nor remain in effect long enough for effective arrangements to develop. Nonetheless, participation in such arrangements has been a consistent element of Iraq's policy.

The antiimperialist efforts are, nowadays, more political than military, since there has in fact been only one Western military action in the region in the past twenty years, that is, the British movement of forces to Kuwait in 1961 in response to a perceived military threat from Iraq. Iraq's attempts at a formal security agreement among the Gulf states have not been welcomed, and after some years Baghdad dropped the attempt. After first refusing to participate in the Steadfastness and Confrontation Front formed to rally those opposed to Egyptian President Sadat's initiative in going to Jerusalem, Iraq later changed course. It called, directed, and profited from a meeting of Arab states held in Baghdad in November 1978, marshaling opposition to the Camp David agreements and increasing the acceptability of its government in other capitals. Most recently it has promoted a charter to regulate relations among Arab states. It calls on them to reject foreign bases, fighting one another, and the use of their forces on behalf of a non-Arab state, and it calls for solidarity against foreign aggressions.

Conclusions

What lessons can one draw from this analysis of the security policy of a state that craves independence but is limited in fulfilling that desire by geography, by size, and by the historic necessity of acquiring all its military equipment from abroad? First, that such a state will choose to rely more on a particular great power for its military needs rather than trying to balance its military and security relations among two or more states. With major change in government, the principal source of arms may also change. The principal source of arms has influence over Iraq. At the same time the supplier's own felt need for association with the recipient and the latter's potential options for changing alliances give Iraq opportunities to use the relationship for its own ends. To receive arms is not to be subject to the supplier's control. A second lesson is that fundamental security policies are dictated by basic circumstances, by deeply and widely held popular views much more than by the personal views of a leader or leadership group. Thus, Iraq's first priority for sixty years has been to establish and maintain Baghdad's authority over the entire country. Its second has been to defend borders. The third is to play an Arab role, espousing unity at times but always Arab solidarity in the face of enemies, especially Israel and more recently Iran. The fourth, growing increasingly important as other neighboring states have grown in power and ambition, has been to ensure that at least some of the oil on which it depends for existence as well as for military supplies will be able to reach market.

There is a slight tension between the two lessons. Clearly the appearance in 1958 of a leadership holding a fundamentally different ideology than its predecessor caused a change in the major power that Iraq has chosen to rely on. This is a basic security policy. However, a majority of politically articulate Iraqis were not in agreement with the monarchy's close ties to the United States and Great Britain. And, even though it is tempering its reliance on the Soviet Union, Iraq is still far closer to it than to the Western European states with which it has mutually beneficial ties.

Iraq's large armed forces, whether they level off or continue to grow in size, give Baghdad some tools for use in promoting its interests. They allowed it to turn to war as the instrument to force Iran to restore territory surrendered in 1975 and, Baghdad hoped, to topple Khomeini. Armed forces a quarter-million strong would permit it, if peace with Iran is achieved, to deploy forces along western borders, halfway to the eastern front with Israel and therefore able to join hostilities more quickly in any future conflict.[16] Iraq's enlarged forces far outnumber the combined forces of the Arab Gulf states. Their existence, and especially the growing Iraqi navy, must be considered by riparian states in the future, even if Baghdad never even threatens to use its navy.

Iraq has responded to an international system that it has seen as threatening by creating large armed forces. For some years it stretched its resources and limited nonmilitary spending to do so; since 1974 such financial limits have been unnecessary. A centralized, authoritarian government has made choices and decisions; it has commanded support. Its alignment strategies, force levels, and doctrine have been appropriate to the threats it has perceived. It regards the application—or the potential for use—of military power essential to its domestic security, to its Arab role, and to its relations with foreign states.

Notes

1. *Saddam Hussein on Current Events in Iraq* (London: Longmans, 1977), p. 67, interview with foreign and Arab journalists, 8 April 1974.

2. Iraqi News Agency (Baghdad), 3 January 1980, Foreign Broadcast Information Service (FBIS), reporting remarks by President Saddam Hussein on 2 January. Similar language occurs frequently in the regime's statements.

3. *The Economist*, 22 August 1981, p. 31.

4. See *Washington Post*, 7 April 1979 and 30 July 1980, and *Christian Science Monitor*, 24 April 1979. *The Economist*, 28 July 1980, asserts, "Iraq hopes to have atomic weapons."

5. Claudia Wright, "Iraq," *Atlantic Monthly*, April 1979, p. 26.

6. *Hussein on Current Events*, p. 78.

7. Rulers in Baghdad have represented the Sunni element, some 25 percent of the population, but even those from the subordinate groups—Kurds and Shias—who have joined or been coopted into the system under monarchy, military, or Baath have accepted the philosophy.

8. Phebe Marr, "The Political Elite in Iraq," in *Political Elites in the Middle East*, ed. George Lenczowski (Washington: American Enterprise Institute, 1975), p. 125.

9. Uriel Dann, *Iraq Under Qassem* (New York: Praeger, 1969), p. 340; and *Daily Telegraph* (London), 13 November 1974, cited in *The Kurds* (London: Minority Rights Group, 1975), p. 20. Casualties were heavy: 16,000 soldiers killed and wounded in 1974-1975 according to Saddam Hussein. Iraqi News Agency (Baghdad), 6 March 1979 (FBIS).

10. John Bagot Glubb, *A Soldier With the Arabs* (London: Hodder & Stoughton, 1957), pp. 227 and 237. Nadav Safran, *From War to War* (New York: Pegasus, 1969), p. 237, gives the number as 6,000 to 7,000.

11. Edgar O'Ballance, *The Third Arab-Israeli War* (Hamdon: Archer Books, 1972), pp. 178-179.

12. Saddam Hussein, speech, 8 February 1980, Baghdad, Voice of the Masses, 8 February 1980 (FBIS).

13. Ibid.

14. Details may be found in Roger F. Pajak, *Soviet Arms Aid in the Middle East* (Washington: Center for Strategic & International Studies, 1976), pp. 28-36.

15. Ibid., pp. 29 and 34.

16. There are occasional tidbits in Arab information media indicating that the Iraqis may be doing something along this line. Cf. Doha, Qatar News Agency, 4 July 1979 (FBIS).

12 Iran

Ann T. Schulz

Iran's security inevitably is framed within the context of superpower politics. Iran's strategic geographic position helped to guarantee its nominal independence in the past. It also linked the country's domestic political stability to international power politics. A history of great-power intervention in domestic political crises has left Iranian rulers highly sensitive to external threats, while a domestic environment relatively poor in nonoil resources and an ethnically heterogeneous population diminishes their ability to respond to those threats. If power in the contemporary international system is more diffuse, it is not apparent in Iranian security policy.

The gap between the threat of great-power intervention and Iran's ability to defend itself is characteristic of developing countries and affects the security policies adopted by Iranian leaders, posing the difficult question of whether Iran's security can be enhanced by working within the bipolar international system, associated as it is with intervention. If not, what are the implications of the alternative of self-reliance for Iran's security in light of recurrent domestic conflict and military vulnerability?

The ruling Islamic Revolutionary Council's response to this choice is different from the shah's. Ayatollah Khomeini and his followers are attempting to withdraw from superpower politics and offer a revitalized Islamic society as the basis for security. This doctrine, along with the contrary views of the monarchy, illustrate two alternative approaches to the security dilemmas faced by third-world leaders in the contemporary international system. They also are the parameters for Iran's security policies, barring a leftist takeover in the foreseeable future.

Iran in a Bipolar World

Iran's Islamic revolution was a watershed for security policy. The security policies that the shah pursued were closely identified with the structure of his Western-oriented regime. Iran's Islamic leadership makes radically different assumptions about the nature of government and about Iran's position within the existing international order. They also govern a fragile state with an unresponsive civilian bureaucracy, an uncertain military, and persistent ethnic rebellions—characteristics of postrevolutionary regimes throughout history.

Iran's Islamic regime shares the monarchy's preoccupation with superpower intervention and Iran's vulnerability. History provides ample justification for their defensive orientation. The first Iranian revolution (1906-1907) led to a period of domestic instability and to Russian and British military intervention. In the course of World War I and again in World War II, Iran's northern provinces were occupied by Soviet troops, while British troops were stationed throughout central and southern Iran.

Iranian regime elites of every ideological persuasion attribute domestic political conflict to the interference of outside powers. The shah emphasized the dangers of Soviet intervention in regional and domestic politics ("red imperialism") and concluded that by working within the bipolar system, Iran could develop sufficient military power to defend itself against Iraq and India, which he conceived to be the Soviet Union's local surrogates. Within Iran, rapid modernization would eliminate the threat of communism and of the "black imperialism" of the clergy.

U.S. involvement in the 1953 ouster of Premier Mohammed Mossadegh, by contrast, convinced Muslim politicians that relations with any of the major military-industrial powers were inimical to Iran's security. Khomeini and his followers see the role of a true Islamic government to be protecting the economic and spiritual well-being of the Moslem community and "defending the Moslems and the *Mustazafeen* (disinherited) of the world."[1] In Khomeini's writings, imperialism is the root cause of economic injustice. Khomeini's treatise *Islamic Government* contains several references to the Western exploitation of Iran:

> They want our minerals, they want to open our markets for their goods and capital. This is why we find the lackey governments obstruct the industrialization of the country, being content at times with assembly plants and nothing else . . . (They wish to) plunder whatever they want without any opposition or any obstruction.[2]

According to documents published during the monarchy by the *Mujaheddin,* a Muslim underground organization, the shah allowed Iran to be drawn into the Western industrial system, destroying Iran's Islamic values and leading to the impoverishment of the Muslim peoples.[3] The *Mujaheddin* argued that Iran's economic relations with the Soviet Union and Eastern Europe were not "positive nationalism" (the shah's term) but were a politically-motivated distraction from Iran's increasing economic dependence upon the United States. Balancing Iran's economic relations with the two superpowers could only disguise the fundamental opposition between the industrialized, secular states and the Islamic world. The superpowers depicted Islam as a backward theology, Khomeini wrote, while, in reality, modernization was the root cause of poverty: "(In) the villages and the rural areas (of the shah's Iran) you will hardly find a single clinic in every 100 or 200 villages!"[4]

The shah, too, was suspicious of the superpowers, particularly of the sincerity of their avowed commitments to Iranian security. During the last years of his rule, he spoke more frequently of the decline of the Western democracies. When President Johnson withdrew U.S. military support from Pakistan during the 1965 Indo-Pakistan war, the shah saw it as evidence that the United States was not seriously committed to the Central Treaty Organization (CENTO) alliance. After the dismemberment of Pakistan in 1971, the Shah renewed his determination to make Iran into a "second-order power," a country with a regional military capability that would make Iran the guarantor of its own security in the Persian Gulf and, later, on the Indian subcontinent.

What distinguished the shah's mistrust of the United States from that of Khomeini was the shah's acceptance of the existing international order as providing an environment within which Iran could become more powerful. By contrast, Iran's present Islamic leadership sees the existing international order as illegitimate. An Indian writer, Girilal Jain, contrasts the Islamic revival in Iran, which totally rejects Western culture and the political values associated with it, and Indian nationalism, which combines a desire for independence with a belief in the universality of certain human values.[5]

The cultural and political exclusiveness of Iran's Islamic regime precludes full participation in international organizations like the United Nations, which many Iranians see as dominated by the interests of the superpowers. In keeping with this outlook, Iran rejected the authority of the International Court of Justice and the Security Council to intervene in the 1980 U.S.-hostage crisis. Khomeini reminds his followers of the Shi'ite's responsibility to rebel against injustice, which proscribes cooperation with "godless" powers for any reason. He specifically warns Muslims not to refer "to the tyrannical authorities and their judiciary agencies. Whoever refers to them is seeking the judgement of the false god which God has ordered us to disavow."[6]

This hostile view of the existing international system includes regional politics. Many Muslim leaders, like Khomeini, see Middle Eastern history as a continuing confrontation between Europe and Muslim Asia. To Khomeini and his followers the shah's de facto alliance with Israel was the clearest example of the corruption of the monarchy's Western orientation. Even during the shah's repressive regime, clergy preached angry sermons against the Israeli connection. In Khomeini's words, "They (the shah's regime) purchase the Phantom aircraft so that the Israelis may be trained on them. Considering that Israel is in a state of war with the Muslims, then whoever helps and supports it is in turn in a state of war with the Muslims."[7] As soon as the Islamic regime took power, it severed diplomatic relations with Israel

and formalized a long-standing relationship between the Palestine Liberation Organization (PLO) and the revolutionary leadership. It was later to
rescind this policy and clandestinely purchase arms from Israel for use in its
war with Iraq.

Iran's religious leadership also is hostile toward the country's Arab
neighbors. Khomeini rejects the possibility of reaching political accom-
modations with regional states as long as they are governed by secular
regimes. His repeated calls for Shi'ite Iraqis to rise up against the secular
Baath government in Baghdad helped to precipitate the outbreak of war in
September 1980. Iraq's Baathist government relies upon the loyalty of a
Sunni minority within a majority Shi'ite population that is particularly
receptive to Khomeini's religious appeals.

The differences between the monarchy and the Islamic republic over
regional politics are primarily ideological. The existence of secular governments pose a threat to Islam. Khomeini would like to bring about the "unity
of the Muslim world against imperialism," but doubts that that will
materialize in the face of Arab nationalism, Marxism, and established
(secular) governments.[8] The leaders of the Arab states have responded to
Iran's Islamic regime in kind. Even before the 1980 war, Iraq gave military
support to the Kurdish and Arab insurrections against the government in
Teheran. During the monarchy, hostilities between Iran and the Arab states
never were very far from the surface. The shah ordered Iranian troops to
occupy three Arab islands in the Persian Gulf in 1971 and lent military support to the Kurdish rebellion in Iraq throughout the early 1970s. At the
same time, he initiated a series of diplomatic efforts in 1974 and 1975, concluding a settlement with Iraq over the disputed Shatt al-Arab boundary
and an end to Iran's support for the Kurds and, on Iran's eastern border, an
agreement with Afghan President Daoud regulating the movement of tribal
insurgents into Pakistan.

Danger Is Everywhere

The pervasive sense of threat to Iran's security coming from all sides ("tous
azimuts") was a cornerstone of the shah's security doctrine.[9] It applies
equally to the views of Iran's religious leaders. A pervasive anxiety toward
the superpowers, their neighbors, and minorities within the country is a permanent feature of Iranian security policy. The shah saw the three threats
as merging into a pincer movement with the Soviet Union trying to subvert
his regime through surrogate states, Iraq on the west and India and
Afghanistan to the east. India and Iraq signed mutual-friendship treaties
with the Soviet Union in 1971 and 1972 respectively and were arming
themselves largely, though not exclusively, with Soviet weapons. On Iran's

eastern borders, the Soviet Union could exploit ethnic insurrection and the continuing Indo-Pakistani conflict. In western Iran, Iraq potentially had leverage over the Arab population of Khuzistan province and the Kurds.

After the revolution, the centrifugal forces of ethnic politics heightened Iranian leaders' fears of superpower intervention through neighboring states. Iran is an ethnic state. For centuries, a Persian and Turkic (Azerbaijani) coalition formed the core of the civilian and military bureaucracies, respectively.[10] The coalition held together briefly after the revolution, when former Prime Minister Mehdi Bazargan and other Azerbaijani Turks joined the new government.

As Khomeini consolidated his hold on the Revolutionary Council, however, he alienated Ayatollah Shariatmadari, the symbolic leader of the Azerbaijan-based Moslem People's Republican party. The split between the two leaders developed during the summer of 1979 when the constitution was being drafted. At issue was how much authority the *faghih* (supreme religious leader) would have over parliament and what powers Teheran would exercise over the provinces.

Historically, Azerbaijani's have defended constitutionalism. What the shah chose to depict as a wholly Soviet-inspired separatist movement following World War II also contained the seeds of the 1978 protest against the shah's absolute rule and in support of the constitution. In a repetition of the shah's tactics, Khomeini linked the Azerbaijanis' continuing protest against his rule to outside interference, with the United States in this case, and reacted forcefully. Late in 1979, Shariatmadari was under house arrest in Qom and Khomeini's version of the constitution was approved.

The regime's fears of outside interference stem from its recognition that domestic ethnic conflict is fueled by the movement of supplies and personnel across Iran's highly penetrable borders. The monarchy was concerned about Baluchi insurrection in the southeast. And indeed gun-running had occurred regularly from the Arabian Sea northward through Zahedan, Birjand, and across Khorassan to anti-shah guerrillas on the Caspian littoral. In 1973, Iraq was implicated in the gun-running when a cache of Soviet arms, apparently destined for the Baluchis, was discovered in the Iraqi embassy in Islamabad, Pakistan.[11] Iran's Islamic leaders have voiced similar complaints that U.S. arms are being funneled from Iraq to ethnic dissidents in western Iran.

Protecting Iran's eastern borders is a matter of ensuring the stability of the Pakistani state. Pakistan's future looked grim to the shah, following the separation of Bangladesh in 1971, when Iran "suddenly saw military divisions crossing international borders, the dismemberment of Pakistan, and the mass media applaud."[12] In 1973, Iran's ambassador to Pakistan, Manuchehr Zilli, announced that Pakistan's integrity was vital to Iran's security. By 1975, the shah and President Bhutto had consolidated their diplomatic approaches to regional politics. President Bhutto traveled to the United States in May and declared that the Indochina wars had ended the U.S. military role in South Asia. Four months later, the shah announced his intent to block firmly any separatist movement in Pakistan.[13]

The Islamic regime's position on the security of Iran's eastern borders is somewhat less clear, partly because its own fragility precludes making military commitments to Pakistan. Overall, Iran's policy is a passive nationalistic defense against Soviet and U.S. encroachment rather than one of active involvement in regional security. Hashemi Rafsanjani, a right-wing member of the Revolutionary Council, declared that Iran did not give up its ties with the United States in order to create new ones with the Soviet Union.[14] Problems in Iranian Baluchistan have been blamed on U.S. subversion.[15] At the same time, the Revolutionary Council has made formal protests to the Soviets against the Afghan invasion. The first protest note, delivered by Foreign Minister Ghotbzadeh in January 1980, complained that the Soviet invasion interfered with Iran's efforts to "remove itself from imperialist and international Zionist domination."[16] Although Afghan rebels were bitter about the lack of material support from Iran for their battle against Soviet troops and questioned Khomeini's commitment to Muslim unity, Iran's borders remained open to refugees and rebel forces.[17] The foreign minister also joined a three-man international delegation sent by the Islamic Conference in July 1980 to mediate the Afghan civil war and lay the groundwork for Soviet troop withdrawals.

The greatest similarity between the security concerns of the monarchy and the Islamic regime is a deep-rooted suspicion of superpower collusion, a suspicion that occasionally borders on paranoia and that is particularly evident in their interpretations of events in the eastern region. At the turn of the century, Russia and Britain agreed to partition Iran into spheres of influence, and Iranian leaders are convinced that this experience could be repeated. The 1978 coup that replaced Afghan President Daoud with Mohammed Taraki and the 1979 Soviet invasion were thought to have been supported by the United States. Eventually the Soviet Union would gain access to the Indian Ocean through Baluchistan, while the United States would counter the Soviet advance by taking over the Gulf and Iran's oil fields.[18]

Iran's economic dependence on the Gulf intensifies Iranian sensitivity to superpower intervention in the western region, a vulnerability amply demonstrated by the 1980 war with Iraq. According to the shah, the radical guerilla forces operating on the Arabian Peninsula posed a long-term threat to the security of the Gulf. The security of Iran's oil fields against attack by Iraq rested upon mutual-destruction capabilities. However, the shah doubted that the traditional Gulf sheikdoms could defend themselves against Soviet-backed radical movements. He continually urged their Arab leaders to join into a mutual-defense arrangement with Iran. The defense pact that the Shah envisioned never emerged, because the Gulf states were equally suspicious of Iran's intentions.

Khomeini's regime also is preoccupied with the weakness of the traditional Gulf regimes. His objective is to replace them with Muslim regimes that would support his radical offensive against the secular Western superpowers. Under the Islamic regime, Iran continued to hold the strategic islands in the Strait of Hormuz that it had occupied since 1971, despite Iraqi demands that they be returned to the United Arab Emirates.

Iran's clerical leaders, like the shah, saw the necessity of maintaining an Iranian presence in the Gulf. In the southern Gulf, the shah's fears of radical movements were replaced by the Muslim leaders' fear of U.S. intervention in response to the Soviet invasion of Afghanistan or to the hostage crisis. Iranian leaders used their naval presence at the Strait as a bargaining lever in the 1980 war to deter outside intervention. Two Soviet resupply ships bound for Iraq did, in fact, turn away at the entrance to the Strait in the early weeks of the war.

The Islamic Republic's secular officials saw the security of Iran's oil fields and shipping lanes as guaranteed by superpower competition. The Republic's defense minister, Mustafa Ali Chamran (killed in the Iranian-Iraqi War), held the view that Iran would be protected from attack by one of the superpowers because each would check the other and equilibrium would be established.[19] More limited threats from regional states, in Chamran's view, would be met with a traditional military response. The clerical leadership remained suspicious of the military establishment, although it concurred about the nature of the threats to Iranian security.

Military Doctrine

The shah's conception of a Soviet pincer movement and the Muslim leaders' emphasis upon superpower interference in regional affairs both acknowledge the need for a security doctrine appropriate to Iran's clear vulnerability. Without a credible military response, the shah gambled on a U.S. nuclear umbrella, while maintaining limited economic and military relations with the Soviet Union. In response to lesser threats he enunciated three concepts of Iran's defense posture: (1) Iran as a second-order power, "guardian of the Gulf;" (2) Iran as a major power, a "fifth power" in a postbipolar world; and, (3) Iran as a counterinsurgency state.

The present regime is too unstable to project a consistent military doctrine. Defense Minister Chamran spoke of a two-way nuclear umbrella, a contemporary formulation of the buffer state between a great-power stand-off. His clerical overseers in the ministry object to any kind of reliance on the superpowers, even a negative one of balancing their power.

With a nuclear umbrella, according to Chamran, the Islamic Republic's armed forces would strive to combine "Israeli efficiency with the righteousness of Cromwell's new model army of 17th century England."[20] Chamran led the revolutionary guards (Pasadaran) in action against the Kurds after the revolution and outspokenly criticized the present army's "lethargy and cowardice." The clerical position is still more antimilitary than Chamran's, placing its emphasis on a politicized militia.

Well before the 1978 revolution, clerical politicians described the army as having a religious role, not a state one. Most of Iran's Shi'ite leadership has resided outside Iran in other Shi'ite areas, primarily Iraq, and have family connections throughout the Middle East. They believe the Islamic community to be the only legitimate political entity. By example, in 1955, following continued pressure from the clergy against secular reforms, the shah courted their support by directing an army attack on the (non-Muslim) Baha'i center in Teheran. Following the attack, Ayatollah Behbehani congratulated the shah and praised the army as the *artesh-e Islam* (army of Islam).[21] In the months preceding the 1978 revolution, however, the shah's religious opposition had made significant inroads into the rank and file of the shah's armed forces.

The views of former President Bani-Sadr are in fact more in line with those of the shah, who saw Iran's military capabilities as those of a second-order power that ultimately would have to provide its own security against regional threats. The war with Iraq lent credence to Bani-Sadr's position, although the second-order power concept and Iran's role as Gulf policeman was identified with the requirements of U.S. security in the region. For both the shah and the present regime the linchpin of the security of the Gulf was Iran's ability to protect its oil fields and refineries from attack by Iraq and to secure its oil shipments through the Strait of Hormuz against attack by radical insurgents on the Arabian Peninsula.

Iran's war with Iraq brought the latter's military forces within a few miles of the partially destroyed Abadan refinery, reducing oil exports from 4 million barrels a day to an estimated 1.3 million barrels a day. The physical proximity of Iraqi forces had earlier led the shah to adopt a "mutual value deterrence plan," according to which the Iranian air force would destroy Iraq's oil fields if Khuzistan were attacked. The Islamic regime's attempt to implement this plan met with only moderate success.

That scenario was precisely what did occur in the 1980 war. The lack of strategic depth reduced the ability of both sides to initiate adequate defensive measures against incoming air strikes, and heavy losses were sustained to oil and industrial facilities. Iranian territory also was lost. During the first year of the Islamic Republic, clerical control over the military demanded the effective abandonment of the mutual-deterrence doctrine. Continued purges of the officer corps and the deterioration of relations with the United States placed the Iranian military in a position of serious inferiority, vis-à-vis that of Iraq. The most immediate obstacles to continuing the shah's active Gulf policies were materiél and expertise. Chamran admitted in March 1980 that the sophisticated aircraft demanded for an active Gulf defense are "too difficult for us to maintain."[22] Iranian naval craft continued to patrol near the Strait against guerilla attacks on civilian shipping. But the navy, like the air force, was seriously weakened by the lack of spare parts and technicians. Foreign technicians had manned Iran's surface-to-air missiles during the 1975 Kurdish war; they could not be used in 1980.

After the 1973 oil-price increases quadrupled Iran's oil revenues, the shah formulated a more ambitious projection of Iranian security. In conjunction with Iran's new financial power and its future industrial potential, the country would become a "fifth power." Advanced military equipment purchased during the 1970s was expected to serve as a trip-wire against Soviet attack a decade later and to give the navy greater strategic depth in the Indian Ocean against threats from intermediate powers and revolutionary forces. To accompany the militarization efforts, the shah's "wider co-prosperity sphere" was to make Iran's oil revenues available to capital-hungry industrialized and industrializing countries, particularly to India and Egypt, the major powers in the region, and to U.S. allies in other parts of the world. Their financial dependence was to ensure their support for Iranian interests.

Ironically, the potential of this strategy was realized only after the revolution had deposed the shah, when Japan and the European Economic Community (EEC) countries found it difficult to support the United States in the hostage crisis. Its value is acknowledged in the Muslim leaders' references to the oil dependency of the West. At the same time, however, Iran's economic and financial ties with the West are being loosened in favor of Eastern Europe and the developing world. The regime's early decision to cancel advanced-weapons imports confirmed the demise of the fifth-power military doctrine.

A "people's army" and an inward-looking view of Iranian security took precedence over the more ambitious plans of the previous regime. A scorched-earth policy was the shah's last defense against Soviet invasion.[23] Iran's Islamic leaders made popular resistance the first line of defense against superior military power. This politically motivated doctrine eventually spelled Iran's defeats in the 1980 battles for Khuzistan. The concept of a people's army was introduced by the guerilla organizations of the Left that supported Khomeini during the revolution. The first public mention of such an army was at a rally of the Marxist *Cherikha-ye Feda-ye Khalq* in Teheran, which by 1981 was in active opposition to the regime. It was quickly adopted by the Muslim leadership as representing the Islamic community in arms, replacing the shah's army.

Abbas Zamani (Abu Sharif), commander of the Pasadaran and member of the Amal group that spent several years fighting with Shi'ite irregulars in Lebanon, details the Pasadaran's functions as follows: (1) eliminate the remnants of the monarchy; (2) maintain internal and border security following the collapse of the police, gendarmerie, and army; (3) preserve the security of sensitive centers in the country and of political personalities; (4) protect army and police installations; (5) promote Islamic culture and ideology; (6) carry out development projects in rural areas.[24] The wide-ranging mission that Zamani spells out reflects the fragility of the postrevolutionary state in the face of ethnic rebellions and groups demanding a more secular and open politics. Conflict between Zamani (on behalf of the state) and clerical politicians from the Islamic Republican party (on behalf of the regime) over recurrent clerical intervention in the Pasdaran finally led to Zamani's threatened resignation in the summer of 1980. Simultaneous threats of political dissension, military collapse, and the continuing insecurity of Iran's borders prevented the consolidation of a security policy for the republic. The absence of a clear policy and command structure was a serious liability to Iran during the war with Iraq.

Military Organization and Capabilities

Counterinsurgency

The shah relied upon the military for internal and border security. A growing airborne counterinsurgency capability was based upon earlier experiences with antitribal warfare and upon U.S. counterinsurgency doctrines. Two organizations were created during the 1960s for counterinsurgency operations: the Army Airborne brigade, centered in Isfahan, and the Special Forces, modeled after the U.S. Special Forces and trained at Shiraz and at Fort Bragg, North Carolina.

The loyalty of its counterinsurgency troops is vital to any Iranian regime. The shah chose to create the two new units rather than to rely upon the Gendarmerie, an organization that dated from the previous Qajar dynasty. The Gendarmerie had primary responsibility for tribal affairs, antinarcotics activities, border security, and rural justice. However, the late Prime Minister Mossadegh, the shah's most powerful rival until Khomeini, had favored the Gendarmerie over the army and after the shah's successful coup against the Mossadegh government, he appointed his trusted army commanders to head the Gendarmerie and kept its ranks small. Its lack of weaponry and troops made it impossible for it to carry out military action without support from the Special Forces and Ground Forces' artillery.

The shah's Army Airborne, by contrast, was placed under General Manuchehr Khosrowdad and given a virtually unlimited budget for buying sophisticated weapons. The Airborne troops provided support for Iran's intervention in the Oman civil war, where they opposed the Dhofar insurgents. However, their successes were limited and they were circulated every three months to forestall domestic opposition to the intervention.

Technology is one remnant of the shah's counterinsurgency policies in the Islamic Republic. Sophisticated weaponry like advanced helicopters are valued for their ability to overcome the physical isolation and lack of roads in provincial Iran. In 1974, Iranian helicopters were sent into action against Baluchi insurrectionists in Pakistan and Iran. After the revolution, helicopters were used regularly against Kurdish rebels, and the Bell Cobra UH-1J gunships gave close-air-support in Khuzistan during the war with Iraq. Despite the absence of U.S. technicians, the difficult maintenance requirements for the helicopter fleet were met sufficiently to put them into action to a limited extent.

Personnel caused more political problems for clerical politicians than did technology, particularly for carrying out internal-security functions. Because the Army Airborne and the Special Forces were closely identified with the shah and the United States, the Islamic leadership was quick to replace them. General Khosrowdad was executed in the early months after the revolution. In total, approximately 8,000 officers were purged from the military, most of them with U.S. training. Many were called back when the war broke out.

More trusted by the clerical members of the regime, the Pasadaran led counterinsurgency operations against ethnic insurrections in Kurdistan, Azerbaijan, and Khuzistan and dominated the ground war with Iraq. In December 1979, the Pasadaran commander announced that relations between troops and the army and ministry of defense "still are cold. It (the Iranian Army) belongs to the defunct regime and has a royalist organizational setup."[25] Five months later, the ease with which U.S. aircraft penetrated Iranian territory in the aborted hostage rescue attempt brought complaints from the clergy about the reliability of the traditional military organizations.

Traditional state military organizations have a political handicap in counterinsurgency operations. Neither the shah nor Iran's Muslim rulers have wanted to set "the State" against "the people" by using the army against ethnic insurrectionists. The Islamic leadership's efforts to politicize the Pasadaran link it still more closely with the Persian, Shi'ite regime.

The shah was more successful in countering minority opposition through political cooptation. For example, he appointed Kurds to many of the top civilian and military posts in that region of the country. He staffed the Special Forces with Baluchis and ordered the army to train and arm

Kurdish fighters during their 1970-1975 war with Iraq. Ironically, the shah's policies contributed to the politicization of minority-government relations and to the postrevolution ethnic rebellions. The Kurds' demand that locally-controlled police replace the Pasadaran is a case in point. It is central to their strategy of gaining control over the security apparatus in Kurdistan and derives from the period of cooptation under the shah.

Guarding the Gulf

Beyond Iran's borders, the backbone of the shah's regional-security doctrine was the air force, committed to the defense of Iran against Iraq and to the security of Pakistan against India. In 1978, Iran's planes outnumbered those of Iraq four to three. The Imperial Iranian Air Force was run for many years by the late General Khatemi, a brother-in-law of the shah, who like military leaders in other third-world countries, showed a distinct preference for sophisticated warplanes. He purchased combat aircraft like the Grumman F-14 Tomcat, competitive with MiG-25s and equipped with Phoenix air-to-air missiles. F-16s were on order when the revolution overtook events.

Iran's naval forces dominated the Gulf. Iraq had alternative overland oil routes and chose not to compete with Iran's naval buildup. The shah also intended to build a deep-water navy, including an antisubmarine capability. Prior to the revolution, four Spruance-class destroyers were on order, and construction was begun on a major naval base at Chahbahar, near the Pakistan border.

The projection of Iran's naval capabilities into the Indian Ocean was, in part, a response to India's growing power. India's naval successes in the 1971 war with Pakistan and its explosion of a nuclear device in 1974 encouraged the shah to think in terms of a military capability comparable to India's. By the time of the revolution, Iran was even considered to be a potential nuclear power despite the fact that Iran had signed the 1979 Nonproliferation treaty and had obligated itself to abide by International Atomic Energy Authority safeguards.[26]

Although the shah believed that a diverse military capability eventually would render Iran less dependent upon the existing nuclear powers, the Republic's clerical leaders oppose sophisticated-weapons imports because of the dependencies they create. The capable performance of Iranian pilots during the 1980 war was indicative of U.S. training successes. But the costs of the shah's arms build-up included the presence of American trainers and technicians, the accompanying dependence upon U.S. production decisions,[27] and conflict with Washington over use of the weapons as in Iran's continuing efforts to supply Pakistan with arms.

Washington's leverage over arms supplies was evidenced in the hostage crisis. The arms boycott was supported by the Western allies of the United States. It affected high-technology weaponry more than it did ammunition, which had been accumulated in Iran for years. When the war with Iraq broke out, at least three-fourths of Iran's combat planes were grounded for lack of spare parts and maintenance personnel.[28] The weapons had been removed from Iran's F-14s immediately after the revolution, rendering them useful only for early-warning and air-control radar platforms. Meanwhile, Czechoslovakia, North Korea, Libya, Syria, and Israel have furnished supplies for Iran's military forces.

Iran's military capabilities have been limited by domestic political conflict as much as by weapons dependence. At times, regime security has determined military policy more than has national or state security. The shah used his Imperial Guard, armed with tanks and armored-personnel carriers, to protect his throne against potential army coups. He also insisted that all communications among his officers be channeled through the palace and forbade armored units from traveling more than 200 kilometers in one year. His suspicion of military loyalty prevented the Army Airborne brigade from carrying out regular exercises with the pilots who were to transport them in war. The absence of coordination was evidenced in the war with Iraq and was a result of this history as well as of revolutionary chaos.

Even the shah's billions of dollars of expenditures on arms did not give Iran an extraregional military capability. Before the revolution, Iran was the pacesetter in an arms race with Iraq, but the Islamic regime has ended that. Iran's military growth during the early 1970s was more rapid even than that of India, the dominant military power in Southwest Asia. But India always possessed far more soldiers, more heavy ships, and more aircraft than did Iran. Furthermore, India was able to build, repair, and fly its own military aircraft, while the shah imported Pakistani pilots to fly U.S. equipment.

Militarily, upon the shah's departure, Iran was a guardian of the Gulf, not a fifth power. This reality was acknowledged before the Islamic regime took power when Prime Minister Bakhtiar began to cancel Iran's strategic-weapons orders. The Islamic regime confirmed Bakhtiar's projection of a more limited military posture for Iran. In the aftermath of the revolution, guardianship of the Gulf has been reduced to a capacity to wage guerilla wars of attrition.

Communicating Military Intentions

Iranian leaders confront a politically intolerable dilemma. The gap between Iran's military capabilities and those of its most likely adversaries has a notable effect upon the ways in which national-security policies are communicated internally and abroad. The extent of Iran's dependence upon external powers is minimized while superpower interference in regional and domestic conflicts is exaggerated. Indirect military challenges to Iran's security from the superpowers are met by political maneuvers, chiefly procrastination, while the extent of Iran's military involvement in actual regional conflict is underplayed.

One of the shah's clearest messages regarding Iran's intentions was his belief that regional instability could be attributed to Soviet interference. India and Iraq were the Soviet Union's willing clients. That message served to elicit support from the United States. In congressional testimony given in 1975, then Undersecretary of State Joseph Sisco pointed out that "Iran sees a close arms relationship between the Soviet Union and India . . . and he (the shah) is concerned about the access routes for his oil."[29]

At the same time, the shah optimistically described closer economic links with India as a way of ending superpower intervention in the region. In 1969, before the Soviet Union-India Friendship Treaty, the shah issued a joint statement with Indira Gandhi to the effect that "The two leaders affirm that the preservation of peace and stability in the Persian Gulf is the exclusive responsibility of the littoral states and there should be no interference by outside powers."[30]

The shah backed up these overtures to regional cooperation with military threats after the arms buildup was well underway: "They (the Indians) profess that they have only peaceful intentions and I would like to believe that . . ."[31] Similarly, "we do not want Iran to procure nuclear weapons just for the sake of having them. But I tell you quite frankly that Iran will have to acquire atomic bombs if every upstart in the region gets them."[32]

Khomeini and his supporters have courted Indian trade and support but have made no overtures to the superpowers. When the Soviet ambassador to Teheran made public his government's offer to come to Iran's aid in the hostage crisis, Iranian diplomats throughout the Middle East asked their Soviet counterparts *not to repeat* that offer. Defense Minister Chamran's statement that Iran was relying on a two-way nuclear umbrella, similarly, made in an interview with foreign newsmen, was for external, not domestic, consumption.

Thus far, the Islamic regime also is unwilling to communicate anything other than hostile intentions toward the Gulf states, far different from the shah's carrot-and-stick approach to regional security. Officials in the Islamic regime who earlier fought alongside Shi'ite irregulars in Lebanon have adopted the language and outlook of the Palestinian revolutionary in contrast to that of the established statesman. The war with Iraq produced a clear distinction between Iran's radical supporters (the PLO, Syria, Libya, and Algeria) and a relatively new Iraq-Jordan coalition.

The shah's relations with Iraq were far from smooth. Iranian military vessels showed the flag in the Shatt al-Arab[33] and the army and the Gendarmerie lent military support to Kurdish rebels against the Baghdad government, but the shah was careful not to provoke an all-out war with Iraq. Officials in his government always described Iranian involvement in the Kurdish war as occasional defensive actions to protect Iran's borders and to ensure the safety of Kurdish "refugees."

Despite the fact that in 1975 the shah's maneuvers succeeded in bringing about a rapprochement with Iraq, several highly informed Iranians were critical of his approach to regional security. Shahram Chubin, a former member of the Institute for International Political and Economic Studies of Teheran, described the shah's foreign policy as "Bismarckian," a policy of "restraining, reassuring, and entangling the fractious states of the subcontinent (that) needs a 'fine-tuned' diplomacy."[34] The shah's reactions to events in the region were too erratic to support a *pax Iran* that would depend on Iran's ability to make reliable commitments to neighboring states. Realistic policy assessments were obstructed by the shah's inability to tolerate criticism and uncertainty, a posture that the Islamic regime also has assumed.

That posture is a function of Iran's position in an unstable region and its endemic military weakness, dramatically exacerbated by domestic political conflicts since the revolution. The shah's immediate reaction to the 1973 coup in Afghanistan by the late President Daoud was to cite it as an instance of Soviet imperialism. A year later, the shah changed his approach, seeing an opportunity to settle a long-standing dispute with Afghanistan over water rights and to open a rail link from Kandahar to the Indian Ocean port of Bandar Abbas. In order to facilitate the reconciliation, *Keyhan* newspaper editor Amir Taheri assumed responsibility for the shah's initial "overreaction," assuring a group of foreign defense analysts that "policymakers (the shah) had not been concerned about the coup, they had everything ironed out."[35] Ultimately, Iran was unable to do anything about the Soviet invasion of Afghanistan, and Iran's leaders were confronted by doubts about their credibility. Khomeini's claims that his regime would spread the Islamic revolution to Iraq, Saudi Arabia, and the United Arab Emirates (UAE) was equally incredible given the state of Iran's military preparedness.

The Economics of Defense

The shah's attempts to close the credibility gap through his armament program overextended Iran's economic capabilities just as it overburdened its political system. Iran's industrial capability is limited, and poverty in the country is extensive. Iran's defense budgets under the shah amounted to more than thirty percent of government spending, while in 1975, the year of greatest growth in the defense budget, Iran ranked 85th in literacy and 106th in infant mortality in the world.[36] The pressing needs of the civilian economy turned defense budgets into a target for the monarch's opponents.

Iran was at a particular disadvantage when the shah became involved in the South Asian security region, where he confronted Pakistan and India, with their far more advanced industrial establishments. With the benefit of protective legislation, Iran's industrial sector grew at an annual rate approaching fifteen percent between 1965 and 1975. However, production increases were largely in consumer goods, not in heavy industry.[37] Modern plants make up only a small portion of the industrial sector as a whole; most industrial workers are employed in small-scale, artisan enterprises. Iran's arms-manufacturing capacity is limited to small arms, military clothing, and minor tank-repair operations.

By 1976, inflation overtook spending. The shah complained that rising prices would severely limit Iran's military expansion, the navy in particular. "Given the loss of oil revenues and the increased unit cost of those (Spruance) destroyers, I could no longer afford the six destroyers we had originally planned to purchase." According to the shah, the price increases jeopardized the entire Chahbahar naval base.[38]

The burden of defense expenditures on Iran's development budget provoked a serious conflict within the cabinet, one of the few to surface during the shah's rule. Nonoil exports had not increased sufficiently during the 1970s to encourage optimism about the economy's future. Government planners wanted to improve nonoil export production, whereas the shah's critics argued that arms purchases should be limited immediately. His response was to champion both approaches. In 1977, roughly one-third of Iran's import bill was for arms; the remaining two-thirds was for capital and consumer goods.[39] The 1976-1977 defense budget showed a marked decline in growth over the record of previous years. From a high growth rate of 189 percent in 1974-1975, the 1976-1977 budget increased only 7.7 percent.[40]

After the revolution, the economy slowed to a near standstill. Military expenditures were reduced still further. Officials in the new regime announced that they intended to shift resources to Iran's stagnating agricultural sector, to provide more rural amenities, and to work on making the small-scale industrial sector self-sufficient. For the time being, the priorities of the civilian economy held sway.

The Constraints of Neutrality

The most effective constraints upon Iran's security policy in the future are domestic conflict, limited military and industrial capabilities (drastically reduced by the Iran-Iraq war), and the Islamic regime's posture toward its neighbors. Pressure from the Iranian left initially pushed the Islamic regime toward increasing isolation and self-reliance. This retreat, coupled with the regime's lack of confidence in the military and its reluctance to depend upon the superpowers for military equipment, rendered the regional political situation highly unstable and, in fact, provoked the war.

Iran's revolution illustrates two characteristics of the bipolar world. The permeable states of the third world face endemic regional-security threats. These potential conflicts outlast specific political regimes and are partially independent of superpower politics. Developing countries that have the potential to exercise power at the regional level pursue security policies that are distinct from those of the superpowers.

On the other hand, although the industrial states no longer are ideologically and economically omnipotent as they once were, the security policies of the developing states still bear the imprint of the bipolar system if only in their rejection of it. The continuing de facto power of the industrial states is affirmed by their dominance in weapons production. Weapons supplies, in turn, influence military training and doctrine even to the point of delineating strategic regions on the basis of superpower alliances. The availability of arms on the international market make armaments programs possible, but they often undermine a delicate political consensus in the recipient country.

Iran's Islamic leaders are reacting to the earlier process of militarization by reducing and politicizing their security objectives. A product of necessity, the politicization of security doctrine may be the most characteristic response to the more diffuse international system. According to Iran's new regime, advanced strategic weapons are not important for countering the most central threat to Iranian security: domestic conflicts and border violations. Iran's military vulnerabilities, the dominant clerical ideology, and worsening ethnic and ideologically motivated violence have led to the acceptance of counterinsurgency strategies as the most appropriate response to insecurity. These strategies suit the Muslim leaders in their effort to eliminate domestic challenges to the religious regime following the ouster of President Bani-Sadr. Meanwhile, Iran's capabilities cannot be extended further unless it returns to the bipolar system or reaches settlement with its neighbors.

Throughout the Middle East Islamic revivalism is on the rise, and the established governments in the region are extremely sensitive to its revolutionary potential. The shah was equally hostile to Muslim politics and adopted an accomodating stance toward neighboring states; Iran's successor regime has been riding with the Islamic revival. Its belligerent approach toward the Arab states elicited equally strong reactions and was risky in view of Iran's diminishing economic and military power. Should the military conflict with neighboring Arab states bring the Soviet Union or the

United States to their defense, the shah's fear of a pincer movement will be realized by Iran's Islamic regime. For Islamic Iran, self-reliance almost certainly means defensive isolation as a truncated buffer state between Soviet-dominated Afghanistan and a Western-dominated Arabian Peninsula.

Notes

1. Note from Foreign Minister Sadegh Ghotbzadeh to the Soviet government, quoted in the *Boston Sunday Globe,* 13 January 1980.

2. Ayatollah Ruhollah Khomeini, "Islamic Government," p. 9.

3. "The Aryamehr Steel Mill and the Aryamehr Agriculture Shareholders' Organization;" (Persian), *Mujaheddin-e Khalq,* 1 (1974).

4. Khomeini, "Islamic Government," p. 55.

5. Girilal Jain, "Islamic Revivalism and Oil," *Times of India,* December 19, 1979.

6. Khomeini, "Islamic Government," p. 41.

7. Ibid., p. 55.

8. Cheryl Benard and Zalmay Khalilzad, "Secularization, Industrialization, and Khomeini's Islamic Republic," *Political Science Quarterly* (Summer 1979):229-241.

9. Shahram Chubin, "Iran's Foreign Policy, 1960-1976: An Overview," in *Twentieth Century Iran,* ed. Hossein Amirsadeghi (New York: Holmes and Meier, 1977), p. 215.

10. John Mason Smith, "Turanian Nomadism and Iranian Politics," *Iranian Studies* 11 (1978):57-82; Michael Weisskopf, "Regionalism Seen as New Phase in Iran's Revolution," *Washington Post,* 11 January 1980.

11. *Newsweek,* 21 May 1973, p. 44.

12. Shahram Chubin, "Iran: Between the Arab West and the Asian East," *Survival* 16 (July/August, 1974):172-182.

13. Rouhollah Ramazani, *Iran's Foreign Policy 1941-1973* (Charlottesville: University of Virginia, 1975), p. 434; Ann Schulz and Onkar Marwah, "New Regions for Old: Iran, Pakistan, India," Working Paper 86, Comparative/International Studies Section, International Studies Association, 1976.

14. *Washington Post,* 12 April 1980.

15. *Iran Times* (Washington, D.C.), 28 December 1979.

16. *Boston Sunday Globe,* 13 January 1980.

17. *Washington Post,* 8 January 1980.

18. *Boston Sunday Globe,* 13 January 1980.

19. *Washington Post,* 21 March 1980.

20. Ibid.

21. Shahrough Akhavi, *Religion and Politics in Contemporary Iran:*

Clergy-State Relations in the Pahlavi Period (Albany: State University Press of New York, 1980), p. 77.

22. *Washington Post,* 21 March 1980.

23. Fereydoun Hoveyda, *The Fall of the Shah of Iran* (New York: Simon and Schuster, 1980).

24. *Merip Reports* 86 (March/April 1980):28, reproducing an interview with Abbas Zamani from *As Safir* (Beirut), 1 December 1979.

25. Ibid.

26. Anne Hessing Cahn, "Determinants of the Nuclear Option: The Case of Iran," in *Nuclear Proliferation and the Near-Nuclear Countries,* eds. Onkar Marwah and Ann Schulz (Cambridge, Mass.: Ballinger, 1975), p. 186.

27. Michael Klare, "America's White Collar Mercenaries," *Inquiry,* 16 October 1978.

28. *Washington Post,* 19 April 1980.

29. U.S. House of Representatives, Committee on International Relations, *The Persian Gulf, 1975: The Continuing Debate on Arms Sales,* Hearings before the Subcommittee on Investigations, 10 June-29 July 1975, Washington, p. 27.

30. Quoted in Rouhollah K. Ramazani, *Iran's Foreign Policy 1941-1973: A Study of Foreign Policy in Modernizing Nations* (Charlottesville: University Press of Virginia, 1975), p. 416.

31. *Kayhan International* (Teheran), 4 October 1974.

32. *Kayhan International* (Teheran), 20 September 1975.

33. Ramazani, *Iran's Foreign Policy,* p. 417.

34. Chubin, "Iran's Foreign Policy 1960-1976," p. 211.

35. Amir Taheri, "Policies of Iran in the Persian Gulf Region," in *The Persian Gulf and the Indian Ocean in International Politics,* Abbas Amirie ed. (Teheran: Institute for International Political and Economic Studies, 1975), p. 267.

36. Nicole Ball and Milton Leitenberg, "The Iranian Domestic Crisis: Foreign Policy Making and Foreign Policy Goals of the United States," *Journal of South Asian and Middle Eastern Studies* 2 (Spring 1979):41.

37. Fred Halliday, "Iran: The Economic Contradictions," *MERIP Reports* 69 (July-August 1978):11.

38. Alvin J. Cottrell and James E. Dougherty, *Iran's Quest for Security: U.S. Arms Transfers and the Nuclear Option* (Cambridge, Mass.: Institute for Foreign Policy Analysis, Inc., 1977), p. 25.

39. Dan Morgan and Walter Pincus, "Iran's Ambitions Fed U.S. Strategists, Weaponeers," *Washington Post,* 13 January 1980; Ann Schulz, "Arms, Aid, and the U.S. Presence in the Middle East," *Current History,* July-August, 1979, p. 15; Kenneth J. Rothwell, "International Trade of the

Middle East, North Africa, and West Asia and the 'New International Economic Order,'" Speech delivered at Mexico City, January 1979.

40. Robert Graham, *The Illusion of Power* (New York: St. Martins Press, 1978), p. 243.

13 Syria

Itamar Rabinovich

In 1945 Syria won independence. It was a weak and fragmented state whose boundaries, semiparliamentary regime, and small army were legacies of the French mandate. The first thirty-five years of Syrian independence were marked by domestic and external violence. The Syrian army was the first in the post-World War II Arab world to intervene in politics. The army's continued intervention has led to its present domination of Syrian political life. Syria also participated in three full-fledged wars and two wars of attrition with Israel, invaded the territory of two of its Arab neighbors (Jordan and Lebanon), and as a rule has had hostile or tense relations along all its frontiers. In the course of these years the Syrian army has grown into a large and sophisticated military machine.

Three factors endow Syria's security policy with particular interest and significance: (1) The Syrian military's unique formula for the domination of an apparently civilian political system—a formula already partially applied in a somewhat modified form in Iraq; (2) the complex interplay of domestic, regional, and international factors that have shaped Syria's security policy; and (3) the actual and doctrinal changes that Syria's security policy underwent in the 1970s. In the mid-1970s, following a few years of unprecedented domestic stability, the Baath regime of Hafiz al-Assad formulated a new security policy that carried with it a shift of emphasis from the two traditional tasks of the Syrian army—support of the regime and implementation of Syria's policy in the Arab-Israeli conflict—to a newly defined one: Syria's quest for regional leadership. In November 1975, after five years in power, the Assad regime indeed appeared stable and secure. Its involvement in the conflict with Israel remained deep, but the struggle was now perceived and couched in terms of a new regional policy. This was the immediate backdrop to the first full-fledged employment—in Lebanon—of the Syrian army as the instrument of an interventionist policy. This policy contributed more than any other single factor to the outbreak of the crisis that now besets the Assad regime and has forced the Syrian army to revert to the maintenance of the regime as its primary task. Syria in the 1970s and early 1980s thus offers an excellent case for the study of the security policy of a developing nation as a dynamic process paced by the interplay among the various functions of security policy simultaneously at work.

267

The Domestic Political Role of the Syrian Army

The intervention and participation of the Syrian army in politics began soon after independence and has been a permanent feature of the Syrian republic's political history.[1] Three sets of relationships have been involved: (1) the army and the civilian government of the day; (2) sectors and factions in the army; and (3) the regime and the broader political system.

The development of the Syrian army's political role unfolded in three successive stages. The first period spanning the years 1945-1963, was characterized by the antagonism between a civilian regime, dominated by the leadership of the national movement, and an army that developed out of the local troops created by the French mandatory government. By the end of the period the sharp distinction between social and political elites of the earlier years of independence had blurred. Military intervention and participation in Syrian politics during this period took the form of coups d'etat, military dictatorships, shared military and civilian rule, and indirect military rule. None of these modalities succeeded in institutionalizing the political role of the Syrian army or in stabilizing Syrian politics.

In the second period, from 1963 to 1970, the Baath, partly by design and partly through trial and error, devised a unique formula for regulating civil-military relations that was based on a symbolic alliance between the group dominating the Syrian army and the new leadership of the Baath party. The military were the dominant element in this partnership, and their supremacy was accepted by the civilian party. Still, the partnership was genuine in that the civilian party's participation was deemed vital for the regime's stability and smooth functioning. The army's political and policy-making roles were formalized through the military organization of the Baath party, whose representatives participated in party congresses and commands.

The Baath regime was less successful in two other respects. Factional strife, which manifested itself most significantly in the conflict between generals Salah Jadid and Hafiz al-Assad (1967-1970), continued within the ranks of the Baathist officers. Second, although the regime dominated the army, thus ensuring its control of the country, it could not make itself acceptable to the urban Sunni (Muslim Orthodox) population. This sector of the population refused to accept the legitimacy of a regime most of whose leaders originated in rural and minority communities, particularly the Alawi community.

Having seized full power in Syria in November 1970, Hafiz al-Assad decided to retain the pattern of civil-military relations that had come to characterize and distinguish the Syrian Baath regime. But in this third period from 1970 to 1977 he also introduced reforms and changes that were designed to remove the difficulties that had interfered with the regime's stability during the latter part of the 1960s;[2] the regime was organized on a dual basis. The core of the regime consisted of Assad and his coterie, most of them army officers along with some party functionaries. This group (1) controlled the army, the party, and the governmental machinery; (2) with the president, made all the major military and civilian decisions, and (3) operated the formal structure of the regime that was to mask its military and partisan bias and to legitimize its rule.

The army's loyalty and support were guaranteed through a series of mechanisms: an elaborate series of security and intelligence services, a network of loyal officers (largely drawn from the Alawi community) who were carefully placed in all battle formations and sensitive units, and a close control of all units placed near the capital or engaged in internal security. Of particular interest and significance in this context are the Defense companies, a force commanded by the president's brother. The force began as a rather small unit charged with the protection of air force bases against takeover attempts. In time it developed into an elite force equivalent to an army division and supplied with the best weapon systems and equipment. Its functions are to protect the regime and to engage in military and security missions of particular importance and sensitivity.

Special attention was paid to the latent tension between the professional nonpartisan officer corps of the Syrian army and the politicized Baathist officers. Such tensions had appeared before 1970, but the danger from the regime's point of view became more acute with the expansion of the army and the efforts to improve its professional standards. Minister of Defense Mustafa Talas discussed the ideological and conceptual levels of the problem in 1972 in an article published in the People's Army (the army's journal):

> . . . I should state simply: the ideological army is the army believing in the people's ideology . . . and with regard to our Syrian Arab army that ideology is . . . the ideology of the Arab Socialist Ba'th Party and nothing else. . . . The March 8 [1963] Revolution transformed the Syrian army from a traditional army to an ideological one, believing in the people's ideology which is represented in the principles and goals of the Arab Socialist Ba'th Party . . . but here the matter became somewhat confused . . . some might think that the army became a partisan army . . . none whatsoever . . . it merely became an ideological army . . . since not all the officers, NCOs and soldiers of the Syrian Arab army have joined the Arab Socialist Ba'th Party while all of them do believe in the party's goals and ideology. . . .[3]

Talas and his colleagues must have realized that this was an idealized rather than a realistic description of the mood and proclivities of the non-Baathist officers in the Syrian army. Their loyalty and contentment were to be achieved through several strategies. First, a political directorate was established in the Syrian army in 1971 that was distinct from the military organization of the Baath party. Its importance was underlined by the fact that General Abd al-Ghani Ibrahim, a very senior officer and at that time a member of Hafiz al-Assad's coterie, was placed at its head. Its task was to supervise political activity and indoctrination in the Syrian army. Among other things it directed a network of agents *(muwajihun siasiyyun)* charged with the political and ideological education of the army as well as with the raising of individual standards of discipline and devotion.[4]

Second, a special sensitivity to the importance of public opinion, inside the army and in all sectors of Syrian society, has characterized the political system of Hafiz al-Assad since the first days of his regime. Major operations and turning points, such as the October 1973 war with Israel, the signing of the disengagement agreement in June 1974, and the invasion of Lebanon in June 1976, were all preceded by elaborate campaigns designed to maximize public support for them, particularly within the army.

Third, the development and expansion of the Syrian army and the procurement of the latest Soviet weapons—in addition to their intrinsic importance—have been perceived by the Assad regime as an effective means of satisfying the professional and personal aspirations of the officer corps. Still, the military buildup in Syria should be seen primarily in the context of the Arab-Israeli conflict.

Syria's Regional Environments: Policy Objectives, Threats and Opportunities

The external threats and opportunities that have shaped Syria's security policy, have originated by and large in its immediate environment.

Syria's regional policies since independence have been concerned with three sets of intertwined relationships: inter-Arab relations, a series of bilateral relations with neighboring and nearby states, and the Arab-Israeli conflict.

The cardinal fact affecting these sets of relations during the twenty-five years of Syrian independence was the fragmentation and frailty of the Syrian state. The system of inter-Arab relations has been, particularly up to the late 1960s, conducive to interventionism. The doctrine of pan-Arab nationalism holds that all Arab states created by the peace settlement of 1918-1921 are artificial and illegitimate and should be submerged in a greater Arab national state. It also legitimizes the intervention of one Arab state or group in the affairs of another to the extent that such intervention is, or is perceived as, designed to promote the cause of Arab unity. In practice this meant that all efforts by ambitious or revisionist rulers, states, or parties to alter the map of the region were couched in terms of Arab unionist policies.[5]

Syria, a weak state with a political elite committed to pan-Arab nationalism and situated at the center of the Eastern Arab world, was a natural target for the expansionist and interventionist policies of other states. In the 1940s and the 1950s the major challenge to Syria's independence was provided by the Hashemite regimes of Jordan and Iraq. After the break-up of the United Arab Republic (the Syro-Egyptian union of 1958-1961), it was Nasser's Egypt that offered the major challenge to Syrian independence and sovereignty. As a rule, though, direct military pressure was not applied in this "struggle for Syria."[6] Instead, influence was bought and acquired in the Syrian political system and in the ranks of the Syrian officer corps. It is only since 1970 that military force has been employed (against Jordan and Lebanon) or threatened (by Syria and Iraq) in Syria's relations with its Arab neighbors.

Although these relationships are part of the system of inter-Arab relations and are affected by the general trends of that system, they can also be viewed as a set of bilateral relationships between neighboring countries. Syria's invasion of Jordan in 1970 was primarily concerned with an all-Arab issue—the war between the Hashemite regime and the PLO—but Syria's 1976 invasion of Lebanon and the concentration of Syrian and Iraqi troops along the Syrian-Iraqi border in 1975 were primarily grounded in bilateral issues.

Of Syria's two non-Arab neighbors, Turkey has had the lesser impact on Syria's security policy. Syria lays an irridentist claim to the region of Alexandretta which Turkey annexed in 1939, but no Syrian leader has seriously believed in the possibility of regaining that region. In the 1950s, with Turkey a member of NATO and the Baghdad Pact and Syria drifting into the Soviet orbit, the possibility of a Turkish (or Iraqi) invasion of Syria was seriously feared in Damascus. Since then relations between Syria and Turkey have tended to be tense but far from the threshold of active hostility.

Syria's involvement in the Arab-Israeli conflict, on the other hand, has been of an entirely different nature.

Syria and the Arab-Israeli Conflict

Politically Syria played a crucial role in inciting the Arab-Israeli conflict prior to the June 1967 war, and prior to that war it was a minor military actor.[7] Its armed forces were small and their professional standing was diminished by the political upheavals of the 1950s and 1960s. Two considerations explain the discrepancy between Syria's military and political roles in the Arab-Israeli conflict in the initial period. First, successive Syrian governmental declarations to the contrary notwithstanding, Syria did not seriously entertain the notion of war waged by itself alone against Israel. War with Israel was seen as an all-Arab affair with Egypt providing the bulk of the Arab military effort.

Second, military engagements with Israel took the form of border skirmishes and sabotage activities where the topographical advantages afforded
by the Golan Heights and well-equipped Syrian artillery enabled the Syrian
army to contend successfully with Israel. Changes in Israeli strategy, particularly the employment of the Israeli air force for border skirmishes after
November 1964, altered this situation by the spring of 1967. Syria's strategy
in the Arab-Israeli conflict during the mid- and late-1960s was formalized
into the doctrine of the Popular War of Liberation.[8]

The low performance of the Syrian army in June 1967 and the loss of
the Golan Heights introduced several important changes in Syria's military
and political standing in the Arab-Israeli conflict. The Baath regime was
confronted with a permanent challenge: the need to regain part of the
national territory lost in the war in circumstances that many in Syria regarded
as shameful. Syria lost the geographic advantages offered by the Golan
Heights and was thus exposed to the danger of an Israeli offensive toward
Damascus in case of war. The issue of Arab military cooperation in a war
against Israel was now couched in new terms. Egypt, Syria, and Jordan, the
three Arab states that had lost territory to Israel in 1967, cooperated in
exerting political and military pressure in order to regain it (the "War of
Attrition" of 1968-1970). They were also implicitly allied in a comprehen
sive war designed to achieve the same result. But the political foundations
for the Egyptian-Syrian military coalition that launched the October 1973
war could only be laid after Assad's rise to power in November 1970.[9]

The Syrian army was primarily organized around the prospect of war
with Israel in the Golan Heights (to be initiated by Syria) or in southern
Syria (to be initiated by Israel or to develop out of a war of attrition). The
nature of the terrain, the composition of the Israeli army, and the Soviet
military doctrine affected the Syrian army's development. By 1980 the
buildup process brought the Syrian army to impressive levels.[10]

Syria's decision to launch the October 1973 war was based on a number
of premises and assumptions: (1) military coordination with Egypt; (2) an
expectation that Syria could overrun the Golan Heights and consolidate her
hold over them through a Soviet-initiated Security Council resolution
decreeing a cease-fire; (3) Soviet military resupply during and soon after the
war; (4) active support by other Arab armies; and (5) a realization that for
Egypt the war was part of a broader strategy that included the prospect of a
political settlement but an expectation that with a territorial-military
achievement at hand the political differences between Syria and Egypt
would become meaningless.

The Syrian assumptions were only in part justified. The Syrian army
overran much of the Golan Heights during the first hours of the war and the
Soviet sea- and air-lift was swift and efficient. Israel—surprised, its military
machine out of gear and engaged in a two-front war—was hard put to

mount a counteroffensive in the Golan Heights. Once that was launched, Israel directed its major efforts against Syria before turning to the Sinai.

This development exposed the limits of Syria's strategic coordination and cooperation with Egypt and the Soviet Union. Military coordination with Egypt was practically limited to the simultaneous launching of the war. Later, the Syrians complained that there was no Egyptian effort to reduce the pressure on Syria during the Israeli counterattack on the Golan Heights. The Soviet Union, in deference to Egypt rather than to Syria, did not press for a cease-fire until 22 October. As a result the Israelis had sufficient time to re-capture the Golan Heights and additional Syrian territory further north ("the salient"), which placed Damascus within the range of Israeli field artillery.

Syria did receive effective support from two Arab neighbors that had not been advised about its war plans. Jordan dispatched one armored brigade and Iraq sent an even larger force to southern Syria. Both were instrumental in preventing Israel from inflicting a defeat on the Syrian army heavier than that which had been accomplished. Syria was quite comfortable with the continued presence of Jordanian troops on its territory, a foreshadowing of the Syrian-Jordanian rapprochement. But the Iraqi military presence was awkward because of the continued conflict between the two rival Baath regimes. The Iraqis then decided to recall their troops from Syria as a protest against Syria's acceptance of the 22 October cease-fire. The possibility of their return to the Syrian front was discussed several times during the next seven years, but the political difficulties remained insurmountable.

This state of affairs had manifold consequences for Syria's security policy. Syria joined the "peace process"—the U.S.-inspired effort to resolve or at least regulate the Arab-Israeli conflict. It signed a "Disengage-ment Agreement" with Israel in June 1974 and considered the possibility of further interim agreements. This policy was formalized in 1975 when a Baath party congress endorsed the notion of a phased settlement for the Arab-Israeli conflict. Yet Syria continued to have reservations about the process of a settlement and more particularly to the junior position assigned it by Egypt as the senior but unreliable partner. Nor could the possibility of another war with Israel be ruled out—even in the short run—should the efforts to arrive at a political settlement fail. Syria thus continued to face the problem of having to prepare for the eventuality of a war while in a state of undue dependence on Egypt.[11]

A New Regional Policy

It was against this background that the Assad regime began in 1974 to develop a new regional policy that aimed at establishing an autonomous power base in Syria in the eastern Arab world. Politically, Syria sought to extend its influence over Jordan, Lebanon, and the PLO. Syria, thus, was to be the leader of a regional bloc, negotiate with both Moscow and Washington from a position of strength, and hold the key to a resolution of the Arab-Israeli conflict.

Syria's enlarged regional policy also had important military and security aspects. The expanding Syrian army was an important foundation of Syria's enhanced stature. Egypt was caught in the transitional phase in which it had lost the Soviet source of supply and was not yet receiving substantial U.S. military aid. Syria, on the other hand, was being supplied generously by the Soviet Union, which sought to demonstrate the benefits accruing to loyal Soviet clients.[12]

Syria also tried to build an eastern front based on cooperation among Syria, Jordan, Lebanon, and Iraq. With Iraqi participation these states could launch war against Israel even without Egyptian participation. But even if Iraq were to stand aloof, there were important advantages to be gained from Syrian military coordination with Jordan and Lebanon. Jordan possessed a significant army and could take part in a potential war with Israel by opening another front, by reinforcing the Syrian front (as it did in 1973), and by blocking an Israeli effort to outflank the main line of Syrian defense with an offensive through northern Jordan. In fact, in the spring and summer of 1975, when Syrian troops were dispatched to the Iraqi border, the Jordanian army reinforced the Syrian front against the possibility of an Israeli attack.

Lebanon's military importance for Syria derives from its territory rather than its army. Syrian military planners have always worried that Israel might use the Beqa Valley (a much better route than northern Jordan) in order to bypass the Syrian army and threaten Damascus. This did not happen in 1973 but with the impressive buildup of the Syrian order of battle the temptation for Israel to resort to this option in the future grew considerably. As a second step, the deployment of Syrian or other Arab forces along the Lebanese-Israeli border could serve to alter the military balance in the eastern front.

The major obstacle to the formation of an eastern front in the 1970s was the continued rivalry between the Iraqi and Syrian Baath regimes. Disagreements over such issues as their respective shares in the water of the Euphrates and the transit of Iraqi oil and goods through Syrian territory compounded the political antagonism and policy differences between the two regimes. In 1975 Syrian authorities pushed toward a confrontation with Iraq to forestall what was perceived to be its eventual regional superiority. With the temporary Iraqi-Iranian mending of fences and the quelling of the Kurdish rebellion, the large Iraqi army could soon be directed as an instrument of pressure and intervention against Syria. In 1975 Syria still possessed an advantage that enabled her to force a confrontation just short of a military conflict, which ended in a Syrian political victory.

This victory added momentum to Syria's new regional policy and inspired her leaders with a sense of confidence. Thus, in November 1975 the Syrian minister of information enumerated to an American correspondent the qualifications that enabled his country to replace Egypt as the leader of the Arab world. Rather than emphasize Damascus's historic role in Arab civilization and Hafiz al-Assad's leadership, the minister dwelt on Syria's newly acquired military strength and political influence. "Syria," he said, "has increasing support and confidence of other Arab states, excellent international relations with East and West, a population united behind the regime and a professional army of 150,000 with the latest Soviet weapons; it is the largest Arab army after Egypt."[13]

Despite the reference to the size and importance of the army the accent of Syrian policy at that time was more political than military. It was Syria's intervention in the Lebanese civil war that shifted the focus of Syria's regional policy to military issues.

The Syrian Army as an Instrument of an Interventionist Foreign Policy

The Lebanese civil war (April 1975-October 1976) was fought between two broad coalitions: a predominantly Christian coalition seeking to maintain the status quo and a predominantly Muslim and Palestinian coalition seeking to alter it.[14] Syria's policy toward the war and the crisis of which the war was a part has gone through four phases.

From April 1975-December 1975, Syria's intervention in the war was indirect, limited, and muted. Syria supported the revisionist coalition and gave it some military aid but also maintained contacts with the members of the rival coalition. Syria's dilemma could be defined in the following terms: although Syria was interested in further change in Lebanon and in further enhancement of its position there, it was fully aware of the risks inherent in the Lebanese situation. A clear-cut victory of the revisionists could lead to American or Israeli intervention, to a war with Israel, or to Iraqi or other undesirable radical influence.

In January 1976, Syria was forced to make a decision and intervene directly in the war, first by dispatching Palestinian units of the Syrian army, then by staging two massive invasions. The objectives of Syria's intervention underwent two radical changes during the period from January to October 1976. Although its intervention in January was apparently on the side of the revisionist coalition, Syria was determined to impose a compromise settlement. This was made clear to the United States, whose tacit agreement was given to the Syrian move. The Syrian attempt at effecting a compromise was accepted by the Christian militias as the best solution available under the circumstances but rejected by the revisionist coalition as offering them too little and as being likely to guarantee Syrian domination. In the face of this challenge to his Lebanese policy, Assad decided to change allies. He used the army to support the Christian militias against his former Arab partners.

The agreements that terminated the civil war recognized Syria's hegemony in Lebanon and assigned a formal role to the Syrian army in the guise of the Arab Deterrent Force. During the next three years, from October 1976 to January 1980, the Assad regime sought to consolidate and institutionalize Syria's position in Lebanon. Most of its difficulties were of a political nature, but during most of 1978 it clashed militarily with the Christian militias without being able to defeat them.

Primarily because of domestic problems in the winter of 1980, the Assad regime pulled some of its army units from Lebanon to quash the semi-rebellion in northern Syria. Syrian troops were taken from Beirut and the coastal plain and deployed in the Beqa Valley, thus implementing the traditional Syrian goal of defending the flank of Syria's main line along the Israeli front. Developments in 1980, however, exacerbated a problem that had originated in earlier years. South Lebanon became an area of escalating clashes between Israel and the PLO. Whenever a major Israeli operation was staged, the pressure on Syria to intervene, even at the risk of incurring significant losses, was dramatically increased.

At various points in 1976 and 1977 Syria's intervention in Lebanon seemed to be the high point of the Assad regime's success, and it may yet appear to be so from a future vantage point. From the present perspective the balance of the military intervention is clearly negative. Syria still has a predominant position in Lebanon and occupies a territory of great strategic importance, but the intervention in Lebanon was the catalyst that triggered the current sustained domestic crisis in Syria and has also significantly diminished Syria's military and political options in the Arab-Israeli conflict. The constraints and factors that have hampered President Assad's policy in Lebanon are of general interest. The Syrian army was ill-prepared for the tasks it had to perform in Lebanon. The Syrian army was developed primarily with a view to a war in Israel in which masses of infantry, armor, artillery, and the air force were to play the chief role. The major test of the Syrian army in the Lebanese civil war was the invasion of 1 June 1976, which took place in a mountainous area and in which the Syrian army failed in its initial mission. Nor did the Syrian army perform well in the urban fighting against the Christian militias in 1978. Furthermore, the Syrian leadership has been alarmed by the political consequences of the army's exposure to the open political atmosphere of Lebanon.[15]

A fragmented polity like Syria was not able to establish its hegemony over a weaker and smaller polity across its border. Assad's policy in Lebanon was perceived by the Sunni majority in Syria as a sectarian alliance between Alawis and Christians against fellow Muslims in Lebanon. Together with the economic costs of the intervention in Lebanon and the internecine bickerings it produced in the ranks of the Baathist military, this led to the outbreak in 1977 of the domestic crisis that has continued to the present.

Regional and international pressures limited Syria's freedom to maneuver in Lebanon both militarily and politically. Egypt and Iraq were hostile to Syria's presence in Lebanon; Saudi Arabia vetoed Syria's decision to crush the PLO; and Israel supported the Christian militias and would not permit Syria to cross a "red line" in South Lebanon. Internationally, the direction of Syrian policy in Lebanon in 1976 put the Soviet-Syrian relationship to its severest test.

The International Context of
Syria's Security Policy

During the 1970s Syria launched one war (October 1973) and two military interventions (the Jordanian civil war of 1970 and the Lebanese civil war of 1976). The Syrian invasion of Jordan in September 1970 was primarily prompted by considerations of Syria's domestic and Arab policy, but in the broader scheme of things Syria served as a Soviet proxy in a Soviet-American confrontation. Eventually, the United States balanced the Soviet Union, Israel neutralized the Syrian air force, and Jordan defeated the invading Syrian column. The defeat exacerbated the conflict between the Assad and Jadid factions and led to Assad's seizure of power in November 1970.

The international context in which the October 1973 war was launched and fought was far more complicated. For President Sadat the war was part of a comprehensive strategy based on a political alliance with Saudi Arabia and oriented primarily toward the United States. Syria was Egypt's military ally but not a full partner to the war's political planning. Syria's own planning was focused on the Soviet Union—the power that was aware of Syria's plan to go to war and was to resupply the Syrian army to guarantee a cease-fire at the time desired by Syria or possibly, to deter Israel from approaching Damascus in case of a total Syrian defeat.

The circumstances and results of the October 1973 war altered this political context. The Soviet Union disappointed the Assad regime twice—by failing to arrange a cease-fire when requested and then by arranging one without notifying Damascus—while the United States appeared as the power that dominated political developments in the Middle East and possessed the key to Israeli withdrawals. A Syrian-American dialogue opened in 1973 with Syria seeking to diversify its policies and options while keeping its military relationship with the Soviet Union.

The Syrian-American dialogue reached its zenith in 1975-1976 on the eve and during Syria's military intervention in the Lebanese civil war. This was the first military operation launched by the Baath regime that had an American political orientation. American endorsement was necessary since Lebanon had been considered a pro-Western country and in order to assure Israeli complicity with Syria's intervention in an eventual invasion of Lebanon.[16] The Soviet Union, on the other hand, grew progressively more critical of the direction of Syria's policy in Lebanon. The disagreements and lack of coordination were fully demonstrated when Prime Minister Alexei Kosygin, upon arrival in Damascus on 1 June 1976, was confronted with the fait accompli of the Syrian invasion of Lebanon.[17]

But in 1977 Syria lost the ability to maneuver between the Soviet Union and the United States and reverted to a clear-cut Soviet orientation. Militarily, the Soviet-Syrian relationship since 1977 has focused on the Arab-Israeli conflict. The Soviet Union has supplied the Syrian army generously in order to redress the Syrian-Israeli military balance that has been affected by the Egyptian-Israeli peace. But it has remained a moot point whether the Soviet Union has agreed to extend to Syria an explicit security guarantee to be applied in the eventuality of another Syrian-Israeli war.

The issue has not been clarified by the signing of a Treaty of Friendship and Cooperation between the Soviet Union and Syria in October 1980. Throughout the 1970s it had been the Soviet Union that wanted to sign a treaty with Syria like the ones signed with Egypt and Iraq in 1971 and 1972 while Assad insisted on preserving the appearance as well as the essence of Syria's independence. By 1980 the roles had been reversed. Assad now wanted the treaty in order to enhance the credibility of his regime, to increase the Soviet Union's commitment to Syria's security, and to confirm the Soviet Union's willingness to extend military aid. The treaty was signed after several months of negotiations in which these issues must have been discussed. Still, it is couched in general terms and its text offers no indication of a change in the security relationship between Moscow and Damascus.

Current Perspectives

This analysis of Syria's security policy during the past few years has served to show the interplay of the chief determinants of that policy, the changes in their relative importance, and the resulting policy fluctuations.[18] The dominant threat to the regime is now domestic, and the Syrian army has in 1980 been deployed and engaged in quashing the domestic opposition. This has hampered the regime's ability to pursue its objectives in the two spheres with which Syria's security policy was concerned during the past decade—the Arab-Israeli conflict and Lebanon. This trend of development was reinforced by the Egyptian-Israeli peace, which, in the Syrian view, has removed Egypt, for the time being, from the ranks of the Arab states committed to participate in a possible new war with Israel, thus altering the Arab-Israeli military balance. In the present circumstances the distinction between threats and opportunities presented by Syria's regional environment is not at all clear. The Syrian Baath regime is distinctly afraid of an Israeli-initiated war but does not rule out the possibility of participating in a Arab coalition that would initiate such a war. With the other aspects of its regional policy checked, the issue of another potential Arab-Israeli war dominates Syria's current thinking on matters of security policy. In this context three elements are of particular importance. First, there is Syrian interest in military cooperation with other Arab states. Syria's efforts to organize an effective anti-Sadat front that would obstruct Egypt's Israeli policy and force her to return to the Arab camp have so far met with little success. Egypt may yet in future years change its present policy but Syria would have a very limited influence on such a decision; however, Damascus cannot count on Egypt in its strategic planning. In a similar vein, the Syrian-Jordanian military and political alliance of the mid-1970s lost much of its value by the end of the decade. Syria suspects that Jordan might join Egypt at some convenient point, but the major irritant in the Jordanian-Syrian relationship is the presence on Jordanian soil of Muslim Brethren, the chief opposition to the Syrian Baath regime.

Syria's relations with Jordan were further aggravated in 1980 when Jordan substituted a new alliance with Iraq for the virtually defunct Syrian alliance. When the Iraqi-Iranian war broke out, Syria and Jordan found themselves on opposite sides with Syria supporting Iran and Jordan supporting Iraq.

The key to a significant reinforcement of Syria's military capabilities lies in a genuine Syrian-Iraqi rapprochement. This was attempted several times in the 1970s, the most recent attempt having begun in October 1978 (in the aftermath of the Camp David accords) and collapsed in July 1979. The Syrian-Iraqi polemics of the last few years afford an insight into the military and political aspects of the cooperation they have sought to establish. Iraq's rulers have suspected all along that Syria is ultimately interested in joining the political option championed by Egypt. It therefore insisted that an Iraqi reinforcement of the Syrian front be linked to irreversible political guarantees provided by Syria. This has been unacceptable to a Syrian regime determined to keep all of its options. Furthermore, the prospect of large Iraqi units stationed near Damascus and taking their orders from a hostile regime is clearly unattractive to the Assad regime. Although a change in the Syrian-Iraqi relationship remains theoretically possible its prospects were made more remote than ever by the Iranian-Iraqi war. This war has had a dual effect on the Syrian-Iraqi relationship. The course and apparent outcome of the war are likely to keep the Iraqi army pinned down to the country's eastern border for a long time. Iraq's ability to contribute troops for the formation of an effective eastern front against Israel has been diminished. Also, Syria's support of Iran in its war with Iraq has further embittered the Syrian-Iraqi relationship and has affected their capability for military cooperation at least in the near future. At the same time, Iraq's preoccupation with Iran and the apparent decline in its military and political standing have served to reduce the Iraqi pressure on Syria.

Another possibility is the further buildup and development of the Syrian army to a point that would seriously reduce Syria's dependence on military cooperation with other Arab states. This option is limited by manpower and by economic and political constraints. There is a shortage of manpower, particularly trained and technically oriented personnel who are also needed in the civil sector's development projects. Syria's military buildup has in recent years been financed primarily by Arab oil-producing states whose assistance cannot be guaranteed. Finally, the exacerbation of the antagonism between regime and populace and the appearance of serious disagreements in the ranks of the Syrian army are likely to reduce its rapid growth capacity. Nor have Syria's resources been significantly influenced by the nominal union with Libya in September 1980. The union is in fact a limited political alliance. In agreeing to it Assad was primarily motivated by the quest for legitimacy and by expectations of Libyan financial aid. So far, though, there is no evidence of Libyan willingness to increase economic aid to Syria in any significant fashion.

The diminishing prospects of effective military cooperation with Arab states increase the importance of the Soviet Union as Syria's superpower patron, the source of military procurement and instruction, and potential guarantor. The renewed Soviet-Syrian rapprochement of the past two years has been underlined by the severance of the tenuous Syrian-American dialogue of the mid-1970s. Yet, the Soviet-Syrian relationship is ridden with ambiguities. The Syrian government cannot be certain of the extent of Soviet involvement on Syria's side in case of another war. The Soviet Union, having supplied Syria with Scud missiles and advanced airplanes, has no assurance that Syria will not escalate the Arab-Israeli conflict beyond the point desirable to the Soviets at any given time. The text of the Soviet-Syrian treaty as well as a number of press reports suggest the possibility of a secret annex to the treaty that deals with these aspects of the two states' relationship. But in the absence of any concrete information the issue will remain vague until clarified by authoritative evidence or the course of events.

Syria's security policy is, thus, as the result of the combined effect of these interlocking developments, in a state of immobilism. A radical change in one of the political spheres that affect this policy most profoundly—the domestic political situation, Syria's relations with the major Arab states, and the superpower rivalry in the region—will have to take place before new prospects open for the security policy of Syria.

Notes

1. See Gordon Torrey, *Syrian Politics and the Military* (Columbus, Ohio: Ohio State University Press, 1964); George M. Haddad, *Revolution and Military Rule in the Middle East, Vol. II* (New York: Robert Speller and Sons, 1971); John Devlin, *The Ba'th Party* (Stanford, Calif.: The Hoover Institution Press, 1976), chapter 16; and Itamar Rabinovich, *Syria under the Ba'th 1963-1966* (Jerusalem: Israel Universities Press and New York: The Halsted Press, 1973).

2. See the chapters on Syria in Colin Legum, Haim Shaked, and Daniel Dishon, eds., *Middle East Contemporary Survey,* vols. I, II, and III (New York: Holmes and Meier, 1978, 1979, 1980).

3. *Jaysh al-Sha'b* (The People's Army), 17 March 1972. See also the speech by President Assad during a visit to army units on 30 March 1973, in which he expounded similar ideas; Radio Damascus, 30 March 1972.

4. Jaysh al-Sha'b, 17 March 1972.

5. See P.J. Vatikiotis, "Inter-Arab Relations," in *The Middle East: Oil, Conflict and Hope,* ed. A.L. Udovitch (Lexington, Mass.: Lexington Books, D.C. Heath and Company, 1976), pp. 145-180.

6. Patrick Seale, *The Struggle for Syria* (London: Oxford University Press, 1965).

7. For a survey of Syria's policy in the conflict see Itamar Rabinovich, "Syria, Israel and the Palestine Question, 1945-1977," in *The Wiener Library Bulletin,* 31, New Series, nos. 47/48, 1978, pp. 135-141.

8. See Daniel Dishon, ed., *Middle East Record, 1967* (Jerusalem: Israel Universities Press, 1971), pp. 159-160.

9. See Itamar Rabinovich, "Continuity and Change in the Ba'th Regime in Syria," in eds. Itamar Rabinovich and Haim Shaked, *From June to October* (New Brunswick, N.J.: Transaction Books, 1977), pp. 219-228.

10. Land forces numbering 2-3 armored divisions, 3 mechanized divisions, 3 independent infantry brigades, 3 paratrooper and special forces brigades; the air force consisting of 480 airplanes (100 high-quality fighters, 100 medium-quality fighters, 280 interceptors), 105 helicopters, 17 trans-

port planes and supplied with 20 airfields, 40 runways; the navy equipped with 2 frigates, 14 missile boats, 8 torpedo boats, 3 minesweepers, 1 patrol boat; plus the following major weapon systems and ground forces: 2,800 tanks (100 high-quality, 1,550 medium quality, 250 low quality), 1,500 armored personnel carriers, 2,200 artillery pieces, 12 Scud ground missile launchers, 1,200 antitank missile launchers, 170-180 ground-to-air missile launchers. The data are based on studies conducted by the Center for Strategic Studies at Tel Aviv University, particularly Brigadier-General Y. Raviv, *The Arab-Israeli Military Balance after the Egyptian-Israeli Peace Treaty* (Tel Aviv: Tel Aviv University, 1979).

11. Itamar Rabinovich, "Phases in Syria's Policy in the Arab-Israeli Conflict," in Aloupha Hareven and Yehiam Padan, eds. *Between War and Settlement* (Tel Aviv: Zmora, Bitan, Modan, Publishers, 1976), pp. 41-54.

12. Galia Golan and Itamar Rabinovich, "The Soviet Union and Syria: The Limits of Cooperation," in Ya'acov Ro'i, ed., *The Limits of Power* (London: Croom Helm, 1979), pp. 213-231.

13. Associated Press dispatch from Damascus, 21 November 1975.

14. For studies of the Lebanese civil war, Syria's policy, and the military aspects of the crisis, see P. Edward Haley and Lewis W. Snider, *Lebanon in Crisis* (Syracuse, N.Y.: Syracuse University Press, 1979).

15. Syria's military campaigns in Lebanon were analyzed in a number of studies published in *Ma'arachot,* the Israeli military journal. See, for instance, Lieut. Col. Danny, "The Syrian Invasion of Lebanon, Military Moves as a Political Instrument," June 1977, pp. 7-14.

16. Details of the Syrian-American coordination can be found in John Bulloch, *Death of a Country* (London: Weidenfeld and Nicolson, 1977), pp. 107-108, and William B. Quandt, *Decade of Decisions* (Berkeley, Calif.: University of California, 1977), pp. 282-283.

17. See Golan and Rabinovich, "The Soviet Union and Syria."

18. See Legum, Haim Shaked, and Dishon, "Middle East Contemporary Survey."

Part IV
Africa

14 Nigeria

John M. Ostheimer and
Gary J. Buckley

Nigerian national-security policy derives from a complex set of rapidly evolving relationships between historical circumstances and present conditions. The country's international outlook has been strongly affected by its growing potential to act as a force in the international arena. A number of nonwhite former colonies share similar expectations toward the West and toward the communist world. What sets Nigeria apart from other African states, and from most of the larger, non-Western group, is its growing capacity for action. No other country on the African continent comes close to Nigeria's ninety million people. Of course, as with all African countries except Somalia, nationhood did not follow automatically from independence. But even the diversities in Nigeria's population offer some advantages: its many different ethnic groups represent potential bridges to the continent's welter of cultures.

Nigeria accounts for more wealth than all other black African states combined. Its gross domestic product of $30 billion was likely to surpass South Africa's in the early 1980s. Beyond sheer size, Nigeria's economy is bolstered by high-quality oil reserves. In just twenty years, the country has become the world's seventh-ranking oil producer. Such sudden revenue offers great flexibility to a government; 70 percent of the population remains traditionally rural and agrarian, and the government, with a $15 billion budget, has wide latitude to shape future development.

Nigeria's economic and political fragility limits its competence in international and regional matters. As the 1980s begin, that competence seems relatively high. The return to civilian rule proceeds as well as can be expected, and oil revenues continue, although unevenly depending on world supply and demand. One must recall, however, that similar predictions based on the favorable appearance of Nigeria's political outlook at the time of independence, two decades ago, were notoriously premature.

The rapid evolution of Nigeria's political system has deeply affected its national-security policies. During the First Republic (1960-1966), the moderate-conservative politicians in charge of foreign policy did *not* articulate a military-force-related role in African affairs. They saw their country as a mediator between the extremist pan-African nationalism of Ghana's Nkrumah and the cautious, sovereignty-guarding stance of Malawi's Banda or Ivory Coast's Houphouet-Boigny. Good relations with Israel were established, showing the lack of pan-Islamic consciousness even from a government dominated by the Muslim northerners. Their view of the communist world was essentially negative. They were ambivalent toward the West. On the one hand, First Republic politicians were products of Western education and values, and they understandably revered the technology and material accomplishments of the West. On the other, they detested the racial prejudice and political domination of the recently concluded colonial era. On the whole, the First Republic established a more notable record in foreign policy than in most domestic matters. Nigeria hosted key, formative Organization of African Unity (OAU) meetings as well as the 1965 Commonwealth conference on Rhodesia's Unilateral Declaration of Independence (UDI), and it sent troops as part of the UN mission in the Congo.

The civil war (1967-1970) significantly weakened this pro-Western orientation. Nigerians learned that communist states could be counted on for certain types of help, while Western democracies were fickle: their governments would take a stand only to be undermined by significant groups of citizens. Most notably, the turmoil and civil war propelled the army to political power, destroying the First Republic and the Western constitutional heritage. Finally, the first significant oil revenues coincided with the war, allowing Nigeria a measure of real and psychological independence from Great Britain.

Throughout the 1970s, Nigerian policies regarding national defense and security have reflected the orientations of the military elite, first the Yakubu Gowon regime (1967-1975), then the more aggressive attitudes of Murtallah Mohammed and, after his assassination, Olusegun Obasanjo. Particularly after the Vietnam war left center stage, Africa became a center of ideological and ethnic struggle, with violent conflicts in the Horn, Portuguese territories, the Spanish Sahara, Chad, Zimbabwe, Namibia, the Southern Zairian borders, the Central African lake regions, and elsewhere. These crises served to constantly remind the Nigerian regimes of the fragility of politics on their continent. They can have few illusions left about Africa's stability.

Finally, the return to civilian rule in 1979 has brought politicians back into apparent primacy in national-security policy. During the election campaign, the five political parties offered policies that varied little from those of the military governments of the 1970s. This calls into question the magnitude of the changes since 1960, for the leaders of all five new parties were First Republic politicians. The victor, Shehu Shagari of the Nigerian Peoples Party (NPP), will probably prove somewhat more cautious than his military predecessors, though his campaign stressed issues similar to theirs. The NPP regime will probably try to mediate any African disputes in such a way that African solutions are stressed, will continue to support southern African liberation movements against white rule, and will strive to promote the consciousness and confidence of black peoples throughout the world.

Of course, the limits of its own pace of nation-building and development may divert Nigeria from the most significant of its goals in foreign and national-security policy. Also, it remains to be proven that the military will really submit to civilian control over such matters. These limits may in fact be quite severe and unpredictable.

Assumptions about the International System

Nigerians share a typically "African" perspective toward the world, dominated by concern that the future should not resemble the past. Through African eyes, every manner of indignity—political, economic, and worst of all, racial—has been heaped upon the continent by outsiders. Contemporary African disorganization is perceived as a function, in part, of the colonial experience. The partition of Africa in the nineteenth century created some fifty entities that were advantageous to the colonialists but are unnatural and only questionably viable as independent units in the modern world. Nigerian leaders share an acute awareness of these ironies of history. But the reaction of most African leaders, including the Nigerians, is predictably human. They intend to defend the integrity of the sovereign but anachronistic products of colonialism that they have inherited in any way they can.

The Western world is still viewed with deep hostility as the source of colonialism, still seen as a threatening and highly racist force. Of course African elites are in different stages of psychological liberation from colonial ties. Some are still closely linked to their former tutors, particularly France, whereas others have more totally severed the colonial umbilical cord. It should be recalled that, except for Algeria, Portugal's territories, and southern Africa, Africa's new states were freed by discussions and constitutional deliberations. Nigeria, for example, did not have to win independence through a war of liberation, the sort of process that galvanizes a people, settling doubts about their own identity and creating the state of mind we call nationhood. One typical result of this was a postindependence period of strong orientation toward Britain that would probably have lasted longer had Nigeria's civil war not shown the dangers of relying on the former metropole.[1] Nigeria's elites still show the ambivalence of hating the West, on the one hand, and being its product, on the other.

More specifically, like other Africans, Nigerians view the West as an interventionist force, envious of raw materials that they once controlled directly, who now conspire to dominate through economic power or political intrigue. The Nigerians are no doubt constantly reminded of these potential "neocolonialist" intrusions by the sometimes quite open statements Westerners make about the significance of Africa's raw materials.

These increasingly sophisticated Nigerian evaluations of West and East are balanced by a heightened sense of competence and mission regarding the continent of Africa and tempered by the type of modern society that is evolving there. On the former point, oil revenues give the country a measure of economic strength rare on the continent, and Nigeria's self-image is further elevated by the size and experience of its army, one of the few in the world to win a recent military victory. Nigerian reactions to this growing competence demonstrate a sort of coming of age in the country's national-security policies. At present, Nigeria's national-security priority is continental and regional. The Foreign Policy Review Board, headed by the executive secretary of the Economic Commission for Africa, Adebayo Adedeji, has recommended such a reorientation in terms of personnel as well as policy. The most crucial posts, requiring the most competent diplomats, are no longer to be Paris and London, but rather African capitals. The most important remnant of colonialism-racism is the nearest one, South Africa, and the formation of a military African High Command to coordinate defense plans and, if necessary, the ouster by force of white domination has become a key goal.

Finally, Nigeria's growing modern sector shows the ambivalence of its attitudes toward the outside world. While distrusting the West's historical role, it is rushing to emulate the Western, particularly American, style. The Nigerian political economy is quite "American" in such values as entrepreneurship and lack of central direction, and it is increasingly tied to the West through cross- and multinational corporate structures. These realities tend to give official Nigerian complaints about the actions of "imperialists" a somewhat hollow ring.

Specific Perceived Threats and National-Security Policies

Perhaps the clearest statements pertaining to the specific threats that challenge Nigeria, and to how these are perceived and prioritized by that country's leadership, are those of General Obasanjo of 29 June 1976 and of President Shehu Shagari in his October 1979 inaugural address. Obasanjo's five pillars of Nigerian policy, which were presumably stated in order of priority, group proximal concerns first, then widen to more general goals:[2]

1. defense of Nigerian sovereignty, independence, and territorial integrity
2. creation of necessary economic and political conditions in Africa and throughout the world that will foster national self-reliance and rapid economic development
3. promotion of equality and self-reliance in Africa and the rest of the developing world

4. promotion of social justice and human dignity everywhere, particularly for black people
5. commitment to the United Nations and to world peace and international security

Summarizing these aims, it seems that the first deals with Nigeria, the middle three with Africa and the black world, and the last with general world peace. During his presidential campaign, Shehu Shagari described his party's foreign-policy program as "neither East nor West, neither Capitalist nor Socialist." Later, in his inaugural address, Shagari specifically mentioned two key goals: nonalignment with world power blocs and continuing efforts to fight South African racism. One must assume that the goal of Nigerian sovereignty and territorial integrity was so obvious that he did not need to state it. Furthermore, given the political instabilities of the past, one must also assume that anyone governing Nigeria, civilian or military, will be likely to make national-security policy decisions that are indirectly designed in part to keep the regime in power, promote the domestic economic prosperity so crucial to political legitimacy, and even appeal to crucial domestic ethnic or regional interests. In other words, the interplay between "national-security" policies and domestic policies may be more significant, more a matter of Nigeria's very survival, than with more established countries.

These goals are strongly interwoven. Nigeria's civil-war experience taught that though the seeds of disintegration may germinate from within the complex social fabric of the country, forces both within and outside Africa are quick to become involved. The Biafran revolt lured support first from non-African powers whose motives, as usual, had little to do with the real problem. The Soviets had chosen the Federal government side because they saw a chance to plant a foot in the door of a Western client state. China came to the Biafran side probably to embarrass the Soviets. France's support for Biafra most likely stemmed from a combination of the specific potential for economic gains derived by widening its sphere of influence in resource-rich parts of Africa and its age-old compulsion to be on whatever side opposes the Anglo-Saxons.

Eventually a few African states defied the dominant view on the continent that supporting Biafra was a dangerous precedent in a political setting where nearly all countries have their own centrifugal trends. Tanzania's motives no doubt differed from those of francophone Ivory Coast. But regardless of their individual reasoning, the impact of their decisions must have been to shake Nigerian faith in the protections that the OAU charter purports to offer. Recognizing their fragility in the early 1960s as individual states, the black African leaders, with Nigeria's Prime Minister Sir Abubakar Balewa playing a key role, thought they had forged a continental agreement that placed interference in each other's internal affairs at the top of their list of proscriptions.

In practice, it is not so easy to define when one country is meddling in another's domestic problems—or simply acting on behalf of humanitarian ends, as the Tanzanians insisted. If Nigeria has indeed solved its own disruptive internal problems through the sequential impacts of civil war and constitutional change, then it is now entering an era to be marked by its own decisions about whether to intervene in the problems of neighboring states. To date, the Nigerians have not articulated a clear doctrine in this regard. But Nigeria's involvement in Chadian politics offers some indication of the types of opportunities and of the regional power's responses to them. For years, Nigeria's northeastern neighbor has been divided by civil war between Saharan, Muslim northerners, backed off and on by Libya, and groups of Christian and pagan southerners who took power under a post-colonial—but pro-French—setting. By the late 1970s, Chad's political cauldron featured nine political groupings and gave little hope of resolution. Finally, in 1979, Nigeria sent a force of 850 troops to Chad's capitol, Ndjamena, in hopes of influencing events toward an African solution. Libya, France, and other outsiders were asked to end their involvement. The Nigerian efforts failed at first; their peacemaking force was asked to leave by a provisional government the Nigerians had helped install, but which then accused the Nigerians of excluding some Chadian factions from participating. After a fourth conference on the matter was held in Lagos, a solution appeared in the form of a transitional government to be followed by free elections. The French force of 2500 was withdrawn as a prelude to anticipated elections. This solution, however, was negated by Libya, which intervened militarily in Chad and by early 1981 had established control over the northern half of the country, much to Nigeria's chagrin and opposition.

The Libyan intervention was an embarrassment to Nigeria. Lagos had encouraged an internal political solution in Chad and implicitly consented to increased Libyan participation in bringing the civil war to a close. Nigerian expectations, however, did not extend to a Libyan military intervention. The Lagos government was thus outflanked by its own policy. The Libyans had temporarily ended the conflict in favor of President Goukouni but had done so by extending their military influence in northern Africa. The threat posed by Libya to neighboring black African states challenged Nigeria's emerging claim to regional dominance and as an arbiter in the region. At this writing, it is not clear how Nigeria will deal with the Libyan invasion. It has presently confined its opposition to diplomatic efforts with other black African states which call for Libyan withdrawal. Whether it will assume a greater military role for the Chadian problem remains to be seen.

Future events will show whether the Chad exercise can serve as an example of Nigeria's potential as a regional peacemaker. Chad's problems are particularly intractable. And not far beyond these immediate borders lie Ghana, Congo, and numerous other future targets for Nigeria's role as regional problem-solver.

Despite the Libyan challenge, black African countries are unlikely to compete with Nigeria for regional or even continental dominance. Some are likely to look to Nigeria for assistance and protection. Some of these states are physically large but are held back either by small populations or pitiful economies. Those that possess any ideological intensity and sense of mission tend to be both small and poor. Perhaps the closest serious competition comes from Zaire. But Zaire's armed forces total only a quarter of Nigeria's, and the country struggles with a $3 billion debt and volatile copper-export prices.

On a continental level, the specter of racism in southern Africa dominates Nigerian attentions. In spite of the distance, Nigerians perceive the South African threat as very real.[3] Racist regimes are seen as aggressive forces. Throughout the two decades of black African independence, Portugal, Rhodesia, and the South African Republic have been connected with a number of "counterrevolutionary" activities north of their borders; for example, the South Africans supported the enemies of the Popular Movement for the Liberation of Angola (MPLA) and Portugal's secret police are usually held responsible for assassinating Eduardo Mondlane of the Front for the Liberation of Mozambique (FELIMO). Thus, Nigerians assume that the remaining white regime, South Africa, will take advantage of any excuse to destabilize the more significant black states. The conjecture during the late 1970s about a South African nuclear capability caused particularly nervous reactions.[4]

This principal continental threat is a major reason for vigorous Nigerian support for the concept of an African High Command (AHC). The AHC concept comes about as close to a doctrine for liberating blacks in South Africa as any the Nigerians have articulated. It is *not*, at this stage, very specific. Most Nigerian leaders readily admit that their army is in no condition to initiate a military solution to South African racism. They fully recognize the military superiority of South Africa. But the widely shared attitude is that if white control has not ended by that future time when Nigeria *has* developed the economic strength and military prowess to do something about it, then Nigeria *will* lead the armed struggle. It remains to be seen how near that time is, objectively speaking. It is also difficult to imagine anything happening soon, given the introspective, almost hedonistic, society of contemporary Nigeria.

It is virtually impossible to separate Nigeria's view of the world beyond Africa from her perception of continental affairs. Nigerians see the Western countries as more or less willing conspirators with white rule in South Africa. The 1979 U.S. Senate vote to ignore the embargo of Zimbabwe is the type of event that confirms their suspicion.

Force Levels and Weapons Systems

Although the experience of the civil war generated a powerful thrust toward military expenditure and expansion of men under arms, Nigeria has consistently spent between 2 and 5 percent of GNP on military resources over the past decade. This exceeds the proportions expended by all her adjacent neighbors with the exception of Chad. In actual money terms, however, Nigeria's military outlays dwarf those of her neighbors.

Nigeria's military can be described basically as light infantry, with total armed forces around 125,000-150,000. Although certainly the largest military force in black Africa and one of the few with combat experience, the primary emphasis is unquestionably on home defense. For example, Nigeria has as many engineering brigades as artillery brigades (four of each). However, considering the low state of military preparedness of its immediate neighbors, Nigeria possesses all the military force it needs at the present time as long as defense is used as the criterion.

Immediately after independence Nigeria continued to rely upon Great Britain for direct military assistance. For example, in 1960 approximately 75 percent of the officers of the Nigerian armed forces were seconded from the British Army. The last British officers did not depart until 1966, after military-training programs for Nigerian personnel had been created in a number of other countries. As part of its attempt to maintain some sort of neutrality in East-West disputes, Nigeria accepted assistance from a wide assortment of states: Great Britain, Canada, Australia, Pakistan, Israel, Ethiopia, and the United States.

The military coups and the civil-war era were a major watershed in Nigerian military affairs. Between 1966 and 1970, Nigeria's armed forces grew from approximately 8,500 to 250,000 as a result of these events and created a body of experienced officers and men, permitting extensive mobility within the senior ranks and commands.

In 1980, the "light-infantry" designation given to the Nigerian army described a force of four combat divisions totaling approximately 130,000. For weapons available to the fighting forces, Nigeria deployed fifty Scorpion light tanks plus an assortment of scout cars, armored personnel carriers, and other armored vehicles (Saracen, Saladin, Ferret, Fox, and AML). Such relatively light weapons would prove more than adequate for civil disturbances such as those at Kano in 1980, or small skirmishes in the bush, but against a well-armed and determined foe they would not be able to generate much firepower.

Recently it was reported that Nigeria has purchased more than one hundred Soviet T-55 main battle tanks—although it is unknown whether they were purchased from the Soviet Union or a third party.[5] If this report is correct, these tanks provide for a significant boost in firepower with their 100-mm guns. The acquisition of more powerful armor could also signal a more professional, and particularly a more external, role for the Nigerian armed forces. An American military mission, paid for by the Nigerian government, is working to upgrade the professional competence of the army. Situated as it is at the hub of a growing trans-African highway system, Nigeria may well have in mind the development of a peacekeeping role for trouble spots beyond her borders.

A country with a coastline of merely 530 miles undoubtedly does not require an extensive naval establishment. But if that country's foreign exchange depends more and more upon the shipment of oil and the importation of key commodities, some level of naval power becomes necessary to protect ports, pumping facilities, docks, berths, and storage reservoirs. The present Nigerian navy (6,000 personnel) is composed of one frigate, three corvettes, and eight large patrol boats. All of these craft serve something of a coast-guard function. These craft can easily intercept smugglers, waterborne commandos, and the like, but they would not be effective against larger naval vessels. In the last five years, however, Nigeria has embarked on an ambitious program of naval expansion. This has included the placing of orders for a 2,000-ton frigate (German) and six guided-missile fast attack boats (three German and three French). All these vessels will carry either Otomat or Exocet antiship missiles. These craft will give Nigeria an enormous firepower to ship-size ratio, and their acquisition conveys the clear impression that Nigeria is interested in greatly improving its ability to maintain coastal defense as well as to protect its sealanes.[6]

Beyond this newly acquired role for the Nigerian navy is yet another facet of naval development. Nigeria has four roll-on roll-off (ro-ro) Tank Landing Ships (LST) on order. These ships can handle armored cars and medium tanks and are undoubtedly intended to give Nigeria an amphibious-assault-force capability. When these ships are combined with its growing air mobility, Nigeria will then be able to project armed force a considerable distance.[7]

The Nigerian air force (approximately 7,000 personnel) is presently equipped to act only in limited air-support and interdiction roles. With twenty-one interceptor aircraft (three aging MiG-17s and eighteen MiG-21 MFs), there is little else it can do. Furthermore the Nigerian air force has suffered from poor maintenance of its existing jet aircraft as well as Soviet reluctance in supplying spare parts. This situation has caused operational limitations for an already limited force. And although these craft may appear ominous compared to the air forces of neighboring Chad, Niger, Dahomey, or Cameroon, they are small compared to the forces available to South

Africa. On the other hand, Nigeria's forces would be more able to obtain base privileges closer to South Africa than would the reverse be true.

Air mobility is one area where Nigeria is making rapid strides. Two transport squadrons of six C-130 Hercules aircraft (range 4,000 miles) have been added to its air force. These aircraft are capable of carrying up to either 90 fully equipped combat troops or several small military vehicles or artillery pieces. In addition, Nigeria has ordered six CH-47C helicopters from the United States, each craft capable of carrying up to forty combat troops. The addition of such aircraft along with amphibious-assault naval craft indicates that Nigeria is in search of a larger regional-defense role than it has heretofore adopted.

Finally, it is interesting to note that Nigeria has recently ordered twelve Alpha Jet FGA aircraft for delivery in 1981-1982. The Alpha Jet is useful for training, reconnaissance, and light ground support. This French-German craft was undoubtedly sought to move away from dependency upon Soviet aircraft. There seems little doubt that Nigeria has deliberately set out to diversify its sources for arms to reduce supply vulnerabilities. In fact Nigeria's growing interest in a regional-defense capability, its increasing industrial potential, and its interest in more sophisticated weaponry point to Nigeria as the future "India" of Africa.[8]

Communication and Implementation Strategies

We have examined Nigeria's assumptions about the state of the world, its strategic response, and its military capabilities. But presumably Nigeria would prefer to accomplish its goals short of force. What is it doing specifically to implement policies and to give clear signals that might avoid the sort of misunderstandings that lead to armed conflict?

At the most visible level of analysis, treaty arrangements can indicate the types of formal commitments that bind a country to military action. The history of Nigeria's experience with defense pacts illustrates the country's movement over a twenty-year period away from attachment to the West and toward a more nonaligned, Africa-oriented strategic role.

The final stages of constitutional negotiation with Britain included an Anglo-Nigerian defense agreement. When this pact was revealed in February 1960, a heated debate ensued between government and opposition politicians, particularly Obafemi Awolowo.[9] The pact provided for transit rights and tropical training facilities for British forces on Nigerian territory, which naturally struck the opposition as vestigial colonial influence. The pact was abrogated in 1962, but the First Republic remained solidly committed to the British until it disintegrated. With this heritage, even the idea of a formal defense pact in which Nigeria is not clearly dominant may still leave a bad taste.

The contemporary concept of the African High Command (AHC) comes closer to a formal defense agreement than anything since the Anglo-Nigerian pact. Nigerians talk in romantic terms about the idea; they seem confident of African states' ability to build a multinational defense structure. This may be a function of their unspoken confidence that Nigeria would play a key, even dominant, role, and that the AHC would carry out strategic goals to which Nigeria was committed. Smaller African countries may be far less eager for an AHC: they might have difficulty forgetting the past political role the Nigerian army has played in his own country's domestic politics.

The firmest base on which to build cooperation for defensive security purposes is general trust and understanding among black African states. Nigeria has been working toward that goal during the past decade by contributing (some say more than $50 million) to southern African liberation movements, by peacemaking initiatives in Chad and southern Zaire, by working diligently within the OAU, and, more locally, through the construction of Economic Community of West African States (ECOWAS), an economic grouping of West African states. Nigeria has been a chief promoter of ECOWAS, taking the view that gradual, functional development of trade and commercial ties, leading to broader relationships, will result in firmer eventual unity. It will not be easy, however, to extend ECOWAS into topics closer to defense and security. Francophone states, like Senegal and Ivory Coast, both of which allow resident units of French troops, might well pull out. The other members, Benin, Togo, Guinea, and Ghana, would be more enthusiastic, but Guinea at least is surrounded by the two pro-French states. Nevertheless, an ECOWAS defense committee already exists, and the organization's resilience thus far does show potential for expansion into political and security areas.

In its dealings with world powers, Nigeria's growing economic strength indicates several new alternatives. Nigeria has surpassed South Africa as the primary African trading partner of the United States. This has led to politically inspired threats against supply of the major product involved—oil. In 1979, when the U.S. Senate tilted heavily against further commitment to the UN embargo against "Zimbabwe-Rhodesia," Nigeria let it be known that senators should consider America's need for Nigerian oil before they voted, and subsequently the debate became much more of an even contest as a number of senators changed their position toward going along with the UN embargo. The same potential exists for Nigerian relations with other major powers. Nigeria now ranks as the premier African trading partner for both France and Britain.

Of course, these trade relationships are two-edged swords: half of Nigeria's oil production goes to the United States and given periods of temporary oversupply, such as 1974 and 1980-1981, Nigeria will be the vulnerable partner. Unlike the Saudis, who can tolerate fluctuations with ease, Nigeria *must* have steady oil revenues in order to keep pace with development needs.

Naturally, the Nigerians would prefer to obtain their goals through constructive diplomacy. In this respect, casual observers might be tempted to accuse Nigeria of playing the Cold War game, but it really had little choice in the matter. Soviet assistance proved invaluable during the civil war, when British and American military help was paralyzed by debate within both countries. Richard Nixon had made the Johnson administration's support for the Federal Nigerian government a campaign issue. Thus Nigeria entered the 1970s with Soviet arms and military advisors plus a full complement of nonmilitary Communist connections. The Soviets supplied MiG fighters and Ilyushin bombers, encouraging Egypt to send pilots. Also, with Soviet encouragement, the Czechs sent Nigeria Delphin L-29 jet fighters and other arms until Alexander Dubcek ended such aid in May 1968. But one impact of the Soviet tanks was the renewal of that arms source for Nigeria's Federal government.[10] At no time, however, did Nigeria become a Soviet satellite: it constantly reminded visitors that genuine Soviet commitment to Nigerian development would be measured by economic and technical, as well as military, aid.[11] Growing frustrations over the quality of that aid and the arrogance of Soviet personnel led Nigeria to slash Soviet programs in 1978. Sixteen hundred Soviet advisors were sent home.

U.S.-Nigerian relations improved rapidly after the 1976 election. The new relationship was characterized by UN Ambassador Andrew Young's initiatives and by visits exchanged between President Carter and General Olusegun Obasanjo. But this relationship has been tempered by the U.S. failure in Nigerian eyes to take concrete steps to end South African racism. The Nigerians know well that South African public relations in the United States works hard to convince Americans that South Africa is Christian and anticommunist and that it deserves support. Through initiatives such as the Nigerian-American Bilateral Commission, Nigeria hopes to counter this propaganda with a greater understanding of the black African position.[12] However, although many U.S. Africanists—official and unofficial—may realize that the best buffers against Soviet, Cuban, and other unfriendly influences in Africa are strong, independently minded, and domestically successful African regimes, too many powerful Americans retain a perception of Africa that fits the traditional Cold War framework. Nigerian diplomatic and informative efforts face an uphill struggle, and the concept of a unified continental defense structure, together with the threat of continued oil diplomacy, must be held in ready reserve.

Constraints on Nigerian Security Forces from
Economic and Technological Underdevelopment

Nigeria's economic base looks impressive at first glance. The comparatively young population numbers about ninety million. Educational levels are improving. The resource base is solid. Agricultural potential is shown by the many years Nigeria relied on agriculture both for domestic consumption and export. Iron-ore reserves are substantial, with three major sites currently producing. Coal, long a major source of industrial energy, is still available. And of course Nigeria has profited greatly from oil, which is not only abundant but also comparatively clean (low in sulphur). In short, Nigeria appears to have the economic base to classify as a significant regional power.

But this encouraging picture is misleading for several reasons. Population growth is menacingly high at 3.7 percent annually, while the agricultural sector has fallen behind so badly that Nigeria has become a net food importer.[13] Even the cash-crop sector has decayed through civil war and neglect so that Nigeria now imports palm oil. Recent government pronouncements indicate growing resolve to reemphasize agriculture, but the country's commitment to these stated goals must be evaluated within the context of the remarkable degree of free-market spontaneity that is being allowed to prevail.

Industrialization is crucial to Nigeria's future capacity for economic development and also for its role as regional power. Though rich in petroleum, the country currently lacks refining capacity and imports fuel. Also, the shortage of dock space at Lagos, the only port with international capacity, means that refined fuel often has to be off-loaded and transshipped from Dakar or Cotonou. Thus, ironically, shortages of gasoline develop in a country earning, by 1980, $15 billion a year from crude oil.[14]

As the previous discussion suggests, Nigeria's economy is fragile and vulnerable. Furthermore, not even oil has been a blessing in every sense. An ethic of quick wealth has encouraged imports that have nearly consumed oil earnings. Foreign-exchange reserves drew down from $5.6 billion in 1975 to $1.9 billion in 1978. Big pay hikes in 1975 had contributed to some of the more frivolous imports.

Federal-government revenues, increasingly based on oil, quadrupled between 1975-1976 and 1979-1980, while real economic growth progressed at about 8 percent annually. Meanwhile, defense expenditures have remained relatively constant at between 2 and 5 percent of GNP. Although this still allows for overall expansion in a growing economy, the military expenditures have generally gone for pay and benefits and not for military hardware. Increased income from sales of crude oil will allow for increased government expenditure on sophisticated weaponry as well as diversion of resources for the creation of a small, domestic military-industrial potential. At the present time the bulk of military goods and equipment are purchased from abroad. An exception is the small-arms plant at Kaduna. Also, the Leyland and Steyr assembly plants give Nigeria capacity to produce military Land Rovers and armored personnel carriers. In addition, there are hints that Nigeria may obtain help from Brazil or India to develop an aircraft industry that would have military potential, and a new naval shipyard has been started in Lagos.[15] But further increases in military-industrial potential will require much greater expenditure of resources and effort and sacrifices in other sectors.

Obviously, Nigeria has the economic potential to be a significant regional power. Besides working toward greater military self-sufficiency, it must diversify into import-substitution areas, rebuild the agricultural sector to replace imports and broaden exports, control population, and develop human resources. Nigeria is fast becoming a land of severe contrasts. Too few are prospering: too many remain on the outside, looking in. Twenty years ago Nigeria was a typical (though huge) underdeveloped country, dependent on primary product exports, tied to European industrial economies, with 90 percent illiteracy and rare modern health care. Now much of that picture has changed, but greater efforts will be necessary before Nigeria will have the technological and economic capacity for an extensive role in broader regional defense.

Domestic Political Factors

The current Nigerian leadership is certainly more Africa-oriented, independent, and assertive in its national-security goals than twenty years ago. Ironically, however, along with this growing sense of purpose has come an increasing set of constraints from the domestic political arena.

The general Nigerian public is far more literate now than twenty years ago (25 percent compared to 10 percent). There are now thirteen universities, and the National Union of Nigerian Students (NUNS) is increasingly vocal and rather radical. For example, NUNS urged Obasanjo not to visit the United States. In addition, many thousands are studying abroad, including approximately twenty thousand in the United States. Newspaper readership has expanded, and a Nigerian regime today can reach more of the public with explanations of foreign-policy problems and requests for mass support. Of course, it is tempting to use foreign issues to divert public attention away from domestic problems. The military regime may have used ECOWAS for that purpose. The competitive ethics of Nigerian democratic political traditions should offer some control over this temptation. As the population becomes more sophisticated about world issues the diversity of reactions may be a greater problem. To some extent this is already true, and Nigerian society is not unified enough to prevent this tendency from being widespread.

The ethnic differences between Nigerians that previously caused turmoil and civil war have by no means disappeared. The Nigerians have chosen to rely on constitutional structures as a way to mute the effects of an ethnically diverse prenational society. The new federal constitution is almost a copy of the U.S. system. A popularly elected president and an independent judiciary supply centripetal force, while the bicameral legislature should allow representation of Nigeria's diversities. Separation of powers is rigorous, both vertically between states and federal, and horizontally within the federal government. Furthermore, political parties must demonstrate multi-ethnic membership and constituencies and espouse nationally oriented programs. Politicians are constrained by a web of disclosure-type provisions from developing the sort of contacts that will revive the ethnicity and corruption that strangled the First Republic. The Nigerians hope these new constitutional measures will hold their Second Republic together. If they succeed, however, it will be *in spite of* the wide-open style that dominates Nigeria's political economy.

Extragovernmental institutions are not as prolific and significant as in fully developed polities, but a variety of political interest groups do exist to influence decisions concerning Nigeria's role in the world. The press proved to be a factor during the 1970s. Traditions of vigorous political journalism persist in spite of partial government ownership and occasional censorship. Though they were wary of criticizing the military regime's foreign policies, journalists who follow world affairs were quick during the past decade to attack facets of Nigeria's policymaking machinery. They were critical of mixups in the External Affairs ministry and in overseas posts that embarrassed the government during Obasanjo's 1979 travels. Also, they criticized poor services for unofficial Nigerians abroad. Students, for example, had trouble receiving tuition expenses and obtaining visas. Under the new constitution, however, the press has not been guaranteed complete freedom, one of the few ways in which the new Nigerian system does not follow the U.S. model. On the contrary, the press is specifically required to support the Constitution. Furthermore, one wonders how far the military—or the civilian regime wishing to stay on the good side of the soldiers—will allow the press to criticize policies advocated by the military.

Perhaps the most important extragovernmental elite concerned with national-security affairs is the academic community. The Foreign Policy Review Board formed in 1978 to comment on Nigeria's regional and world policies includes strong academic input. The board recommended that African affairs be emphasized and that a National Advisory Council on foreign policy be formed to encourage communication between government policymakers and concerned groups in the private sector.

Another organization, the Nigerian Institute for International Affairs (NIIA), headed by the academic, Bolaji Akinyemi, has also established an influential role in policymaking. The military regime maintained good rapport with the intellectuals of NIIA perhaps because Akinyemi's group agreed with the military's more assertive role for Nigeria. The academics had criticized the First Republic's hesitancy. Also, even more pertinent, they agree with the cautious pace of demobilization that the army prescribed. Akinyemi has argued that Nigeria needs to keep a strong infantry to guarantee military credibility. Thus, unlike so many other countries, dominant sectors of Nigeria's intelligentsia do not disagree fundamentally with the military over national-security goals and tactics.

The national-security policies offered by the new political parties must now also be considered. Ironically, the 1979 campaign produced five national parties with personnel similar to those who dominated the First Republic. Also, national-security issues were not significant during the election, reflecting the weakness of Nigeria's neighbors as well as the preoccupation with enjoying the fruits of development. The parties' views were quite similar and were remarkably close to those of the military. Shehu Shagari's National Peoples Party, the victor, was probably the most conservative of the five in overall philosophy, but by the next election in 1983 a new set of faces may emerge to replace the "men of the 60s." Perhaps they will be more innovative in foreign affairs. But new ideas may not be the only requirement for a new direction in national-security policy. The present regime will be hampered by the lack of a strong majority: the 1979 election left Shagari's NPP with only 168 of 444 seats in the House of Representatives and 36 of 95 in the Senate. Shagari will have to be careful not to give opposition elements any issues around which to coalesce. The faces may change in 1983, but the parties' perceived need to concentrate on domestic issues and to preserve slim majorities through coalition may *not* change. Nigeria reminds one of the United States in some ways; such a large, diverse, and in many ways individualistic society can be hard to galvanize for coherent national-security policies backed up by palpable national will. Nigerians are busy with their own individual prospects. Their relations with the outer world may well take on a reactive rather than anticipatory flavor.

Of course, an analysis of domestic political factors must consider the political role of the military. Murtalla Mohammed and his successor, Obasanjo, took power in part because the civil-war government of Yakubu Gowon seemed to be drifting away from the goal of return to civilian rule. Indeed, the presence of corruption and the fear of too rapid demobilization served as arguments for keeping the military in power. But Gowon's successors stuck rigorously to the schedule of returning Nigeria to civilian rule in 1979, and they were no doubt sincere in realizing that a military organization cannot substitute as a government forever.[16] They were perhaps chagrined to see only familiar faces from the First Republic emerge as national party leaders. During the transitional period of August and September 1979, however, Obasanjo consulted almost daily with President-elect Shagari, who seems to have earned the confidence of the military.

It is inevitable, however, that in case of any real conflict over national-security goals, or over the role and strength of the military itself, a force with the ruling experience of Nigeria's army will be sorely tempted to intervene. Military intervention in Nigeria took the form that S. E. Finer has called "direct," as opposed to indirect, dual, or quasi civilian. This form of past intervention might mean that it is more difficult for Nigeria's soldiers to retire to the barracks. Demobilization is the most crucial issue, and a decade after the war military leaders still stress the need to show gratitude to the troops for their service in holding the country together. Even so, demobilization has progressed from 230,000 down to fewer than 150,000 in the past five years, which is no small accomplishment.

In spite of incentives for them to be political, army leaders seem determined to abide by their promises. Obasanjo did not just withdraw to the barracks. He and all high-level officers holding political responsibilities retired from the military altogether on or about 1 October 1979. According to Obasanjo, "We are putting everything we have into the transition to insure that when the military goes back to the barracks they remain in the barracks."[17] Thus, there seems little question that the military wishes to be out of politics. The problem is whether they will be forced to reenter because the politicians have failed. No clear indication of the real civil-military relationship will be available until it is genuinely tested by events.

Evaluating the military's future political role is made even more difficult by the threat of insurrection from lower ranks, a prospect that must worry both Nigeria's officers and politicians. The successes of Flight Lieutenant Jerry Rawlings in Ghana and Master Sergeant Samuel Doe in Liberia may not be replicable within a larger, more diverse force such as Nigeria's, but the possibility does exist.

A final domestic political constraint involves the quality of the decision-making machinery in national security-foreign policy issues. The new constitution has separated the National Defense Council (defense policy) from the National Security Council (foreign policy). This approach has been criticized on the grounds that the two functions need to be closely coordinated. Perhaps the appointment of an executive official in the president's office to work for coordination would solve this problem, which may be even worse than it appears on paper because of a personal antagonism between the two academics who direct these councils.

The most significant potential constraint limiting Nigerian options and threatening its security remains the absence of political legitimacy. Nigeria's first priority must be to construct a successful economic and social order. If it fails, specific interest groups may become disruptive, and ethnic pressures may again destabilize the system. Ethnicity may never again be as direct a factor as it was during the First Republic when, for example, the Western Regional Government maintained its own office in London. But it remains the most important indirect variable affecting security and other policy areas.

Conclusion

Nigerian attempts to guarantee its own national security under the new federal republic will depend largely on the domestic political, social, and economic constraints the new regime faces and on how well it copes with them. Unlike most of the other case studies considered here, Nigeria faces a greater challenge in making its own system work than in controlling threats to its security from outside. It is quite possible that efforts directed toward internal reconciliation and development may divert Nigeria's elites from all but the most immediate foreign threats. Success in forging a stable popular government will be as important as anything the outside world can do in defining Nigeria's role within its region and beyond it. Nigeria is so big that if it develops into a genuine nation-state, it will automatically be a force to be reckoned with. But if its domestic unity dissolves, the most impressive regime-intentions will count for little.

Africa today has the distinction of being one of the least militarized third-world areas, while at the same time being one of the most rapidly militarizing. Perhaps because of the relatively low level of military sales to sub-Saharan African states in the past, weapons purchases on that continent have increased dramatically over the past several years. In Nigeria's case, the continent's military power vacuum presents a variety of dangers from outside the continent and from within. Nigeria's path toward the status of regional military power will be arduous and fraught with dangers, not the least of which is failure to overcome the duality that divides stated policy goals from the undisciplined rush by Nigerians toward the "good life." Developing Nigerian nationalism will be tempered, as long as the present wide-open economic style prevails, by the international contacts and the strong profit motivation of the country's developing economic elite.

Notes

1. For a comprehensive review of this period, see John J. Stremlau, *The International Politics of the Nigerian Civil War, 1967-70* (Princeton: Princeton University Press, 1977).

2. *Times International* (Lagos), 31 July 1978; also the text of General Obasanjo's July 1978 OAU speech in *Africa Currents* 12 (Autumn-Winter 1978-1979).

3. See T. Danjuma's speech, *Times International* (Lagos), 4 September 1978.

4. *Daily Times* (Lagos), 22 March 1979.

5. Robert D'A Henderson, "Perspectives on Nigerian Defense Policy in the 1970s," Unpublished paper (February 1980), p. 12. Permission to cite given by author.

6. Ibid., p. 13.

7. Ibid., pp. 16-18.

8. Ibid., p. 21.

9. Gordon J. Idang, "The Politics of Nigerian Foreign Policy: The Ratification and Renunciation of the Anglo-Nigerian Defense Agreement," *African Studies Review* 13 (September 1970):227-252.

10. John de St. Jorre. *The Brother's War: Biafra and Nigeria* (Boston: Houghton-Mifflin, 1972), p. 182.

11. *Daily Times* (Lagos), 11 January 1979.

12. *Times International* (Lagos), 4 September 1978.

13. Kalu A. K. Ogwu, "Time for a Meaningful Population Policy," *Daily Times* (Lagos), 31 March 1979; and Andrew Marciniak, "Forecasting Nigeria's Population: 154 Million Mouths in 2000," *Daily Times* (Lagos), 15 February 1979.

14. *Daily Times* (Lagos), 16 January 1979.

15. Henderson, "Perspectives," pp. 7-8.

16. "Nigeria: 'Fair Play' Elections Run Late," *Africa Confidential* 20 (11 April 1979).

17. *Africa Report* 24 (July-August 1979):47.

15 South Africa

Timothy M. Shaw
and *Lee Dowdy*

White South Africa is a nation on the defensive. The world has changed significantly since apartheid was declared and developed immediately after World War II; racial and economic inequalities are less acceptable now than when the Afrikaner Nationalist party formalized its hold on state power in South Africa in 1948. The uninterrupted political dominance of the Afrikaner nation over the last thirty years has enabled it to articulate and advance domestic, foreign, and strategic policies based on racial separateness (and dominance)—apartheid. Given the challenge that such white minority rule generates almost everywhere, South African policy in these three areas has remained remarkably coherent and comprehensive. Sam Nolutshungu's perceptive comment on the character of the country's foreign relations applies equally well to its defense strategy: "South African international activity has been little more than the extension of its internal conflict—a struggle to make the world safe for apartheid."[1]

However, the world of the 1980s is much less safe for apartheid than that of the 1950s and becoming increasingly so. Indeed, the formal declaration of apartheid in South Africa coincided with the beginnings of formal decolonization in the rest of the British Empire. The defensiveness of the South African leadership has intensified as decolonization has spread—as the wind of change has moved southward through Africa—so that the "white tribe" is more isolated today than ever. It is on the retreat at all levels, global, continental, regional, and national, as it is subjected to U.N. sanctions, excluded from Western alliances, shunned by African associations, and targeted by domestic guerrillas. The reconsideration of "separate development" at the beginning of this decade is a belated and partial response to this multifaceted challenge. Issues of strategic and security policy are more urgent and pervasive as the regime attempts to salvage, if not to save, apartheid.

Questions of defense are intimately and integrally related to any reformulation or redefinition of apartheid. And just as the challenges to the white government derive from all levels, so responses have implications at each interrelated level. As the chief of the defense force argued in 1977, "Every activity of the state must be seen and understood as a function of total war."[2] The retreat of the regime has meant that as it came to be excluded and shunned at the global, continental, and regional levels in both diplomatic and strategic issue areas, so it has come to concentrate its attention at the subregional and national levels; hence the current "constellation of states" proposal designed to bring together "bantustans" (native homelands), "South Africa," and the smaller states of the area in an economic-cum-security system. With the demise of South Africa's *cordon sanitaire* in the second half of the 1970s, apartheid can no longer be defended in depth, but only along and within South Africa's own borders; thus the strategic and related political reassessment as the 1980s open.

Robert Mugabe's electoral victory in neighboring Zimbabwe in February 1980 marks the latest turning point in regional affairs, with profound implications for South Africa's security, foreign, and economic policies; earlier milestones of similar import since 1948 were the Sharpeville massacre in 1960 and the 1974 Portuguese coup. Both of the earlier instances were followed by related events—departure from the Commonwealth and the beginning of a military buildup in 1961 and intervention in Angola and the Soweto riots in 1975 and 1976. It is too early to judge the full ramifications of ongoing changes in Zimbabwe, but they clearly bode ill for traditional South African attempts to establish forward security lines despite a stubborn holding of the line in Namibia (South West Africa). Each of these three periods–1948 to 1960, 1960 to 1974, and 1974 to 1980—is marked by different challenges to Pretoria and different, if consistent, responses. But together the periods also reveal an ineluctable trend toward international isolation and an inward-looking orientation; that is, toward a growing defensiveness.

The tactical and territorial retreat away from involvement in subcontinental affairs has been the result of the white nation's unwillingness to retreat in terms of ideology and political economy. The perpetuation of apartheid has also kept the white nation (now less than 20 percent of the total population) out of touch with the realities of life for most nonwhite South Africans and with the depth of their frustrations. So, simultaneous with growing international isolation, the ruling race has become more isolated and threatened at home, just at the time when it has come to need a secure *laager* to which to return.

Settler Nation in the World System:
From Partner to Pariah

Until the early 1950s, South Africa's defense had largely consisted of participation in imperial and Western strategic alliances. Despite the ambivalence of some Afrikaners in World War II, the white government and its troops had been actively involved on the side of the Allies, and Prime Minister Smuts was a leading figure in discussions about the postwar world: the United Nations and European reconstruction. However, the colonial powers, Britain and France, soon began to distance themselves from South Africa in terms of continental African defense and despite the bilateral Anglo-South African Simonstown Agreement in 1955 South Africa was unable to join any of the containment alliances established during the cold war. Yet, given historic links with Europe, especially with Britain, the South African authorities remained confident that their strategic interests would continue to coincide with those of, and so be supported by, the West. Despite a growing coolness and the absence of formal alliance links, South Africa's level and pattern of defense expenditure reflected such established assumptions. Defense spending was low in the 1950s—between 1 percent and 2 percent of the GNP—and major purchases were limited to Centurion tanks and Sabre aircraft for possible use, in collaboration with Commonwealth forces, in the Middle East, and two destroyers, for Pretoria's part in the defense of the Cape Route.

So, until 1960, despite the gradual dissociation of the Allies, South Africa's strategic posture was essentially Eurocentric and anticommunist, in tacit association with the Western powers in the cold war. Any threat emanating from Africa, especially black-nationalist movements, was treated as part of this global "Communist threat." As Robert Jaster comments:

> . . . an over-riding objective of the Malan and Strijdom governments was to keep radical black nationalism from spilling southwards over South Africa's borders and infecting her non-white population. To this end they adopted a three-pronged strategy. First, the government determined that in the event of war against communism, the enemy must be engaged as far away as possible from South Africa. Second, the leadership attempted to become involved in a formal western defence alliance. Third, the government tried to commit the western powers to the defence of Africa.[3]

The governments that preceded Prime Minister Hendrik Verwoerd's government were successful in keeping communism at bay, but they were unsuccessful in maintaining a close association with the West. Indeed, after having been a valued wartime ally, South Africa was becoming a postwar pariah as apartheid measures were relentlessly implemented. But even after 1960, when it was clear that Africa and the West were changing and that South Africa was increasingly isolated, policy was still oriented toward Europe.

Despite the increasing official distance between Pretoria and the Atlantic capitals, South Africa could take some comfort in the fact that unofficial transnational linkages were multiplying. The South African economy developed rapidly after World War II in terms of both mineral extraction and local manufacturing, partially aided by increased demand and price increases prompted by the Korean and Vietnam Wars. Western multinational corporations, many of which had already become established in South Africa, rapidly increased their investments and operations. The global trend toward multilateralization was apparent in the South African market: American and German, then French and Japanese, companies challenged Britain's dominance of external trade and internal production.[4] Even if Western embassies were ambivalent about their links with the South African regime, Western companies were less cautious. The latters' concern was the growing involvement of the South African state in the marketplace, involving both local regulations and partial nationalization through state corporations. However, profit margins were so generous that multinational corporations continued to increase their activities in Africa's major consumer market and mineral production throughout the 1950s.

Sharpeville changed both external and internal perceptions and led to a dramatic shift in South African strategic doctrines and policies. As Robert Jaster notes: "The years 1960-63 were a watershed for South African defence policy. Strategic judgments and decisions made in that period led to a new defence posture, which remained essentially unchanged until the mid-1970s."[5] Basically, this posture was one of greater self-reliance because of increasing Western alienation and a shift to regional priorities. As South Africa became an independent republic, so it reluctantly but realistically recognized that it could not expect a close defense relationship with the West; it had to begin to defend its interests in southern Africa on its own.

From Sharpeville to "Outward Movement"

In South Africa, the 1960s opened with Sharpeville: a black rising against the intensification of apartheid with a police over-reaction leaving 67 dead and 186 wounded. The contradictory pressures of the 1950s had come to a head: the racism of Afrikaner nationalism versus the populist demand for decolonization and African nationalism. "Communism" was no longer considered a distant problem; from the viewpoint of Prime Minister Hendrik Verwoerd and his white supporters, it was now inside and outside South Africa's own borders. Moreover, South Africa was increasingly alone in confronting this particular threat; it had to leave the Commonwealth in 1961.

The regime responded to Sharpeville by increasing police controls, legislating further harsh security laws, and augmenting overall defense expenditures. The rapid rise in military spending—from 1 percent of the GNP at the beginning of the decade to 2.6 percent at its end and rising to 5.5 percent in the mid-1970s led to a considerable improvement in the short-term security situation. The process of arming the South African Defence Force (SADF) and maximizing recruitment into the Permanent and Active Citizens' Forces continued through the 1960s and into the first part of the

1970s. Manpower (white) rather than finance was the major constraint despite the extension of the period of conscription for all white males from one to two years. The number of national servicemen trained each year jumped quickly from 2,000 in 1960 to 12,000 in 1962 and to 20,000 in 1964, but it has rarely risen above 25,000 since then because of minimal increases in the number of available white youths.[6]

The process of providing the expanding SADF with more modern and sophisticated equipment had two purposes. First, it was designed to create an independent and effective military capability so that South Africa could face a variety of internal, regional, and global challenges, including sanctions. But second, paradoxically, it was also intended to enhance the regime's value to the West in its continuing quest for association with the Atlantic Alliance. Ironically, however, as the domestic threat was contained at the beginning of the 1960s, so South Africa's ostensible need for such association receded. Nevertheless, for a combination of social, political, and strategic reasons, each Afrikaner leader has tried sporadically by a variety of means to revive South Africa's wartime intimacy with the Allies.

In the 1960s, South Africa began to create truly independent military forces for land, sea, and air defense as well as to construct a more or less independent armaments industry to supply them. The former goal was designed to reassure white citizens and Western corporations that their property was safe as well as to provide for national security; the latter was intended to advance Afrikaner and state capitalism so that South Africa was less dependent on Western investment and technology. Both were expressions of Afrikaner nationalism in its determination to maintain its identity and affluence; but the armed forces were directed against African nationalism, whereas the armaments industry was directed against multinational corporations as well as against the prospect of Western arms embargoes. Both policies served to enhance the security of the regime; by the middle of the seventies it appeared to be more secure politically, strategically, and economically because of its response to Sharpeville. But this security was somewhat brittle and short-term, as the pressures that caused the first expression of African anger had only been contained, not treated. Indeed, apartheid structures and strictures were intensified in response to the regime's fears and isolation.

In the decade of the 1960s, South Africa invested more than $830 million on new weapons, an increasing proportion of which was spent locally as the national armaments industry grew and as international arms embargoes reduced the number of external suppliers. Although the navy was augmented with three Daphne-class submarines from France and two refitted helicopter-carrying destroyers, and although the air force received Mirage jets and a range of helicopters and jet trainers, ground defense received the highest priority, particularly at the beginning of the 1970s. One perceptive analyst summarizes the strategic thinking of this period:

The landward defence share of the budget rose from 17 percent in 1969 to 25 percent in 1972 and 31 percent a year later. This rapid rise reflected mainly the expansion and upgrading of the army which was begun in 1968-69 and carried out over several years. The "protracted war of low intensity" in which South Africa was engaged led the army, in the early 1970s, to review its tactical doctrine in order to adapt it better to local conditions. This review pointed to an ever-increasing need for mobility and striking power and more extensive training to a higher standard.[7]

Once the potential repercussions of Sharpeville had been contained and military modernization was underway, the defense effort remained quite consistent from the early 1960s into the early 1970s at something over 2 percent of the GNP: between $ 280-400 million. The level of actual expenditure rose in proportion to the GNP, which increased by 140 percent in the decade of the 1960s, one of the highest rates anywhere in the world for the period, along with that of Japan: between 5 and 10 percent per annum. As Jaster comments on this period: "defense cannot have been an excessive burden on the economy."[8]

In the decade 1964 to 1974 South Africa's economic "miracle," combined with relative political tranquillity after Sharpeville and before Soweto, provided a breathing space not only for military reequipment and training but also for foreign-policy initiatives, with their clear strategic implications. Under Prime Minister B. Johannes Vorster, South Africa's essentially reactive foreign policy underwent a transformation. The combination of Western distance, U.N. censure, and third-world opposition led to a foreign- as well as strategic-policy reassessment: South Africa was determined to be no longer a passive suitor of the Western alliance. Instead, it proceeded to transform itself into a leading African power, one that would dominate the region and might thereby become more attractive to Western interests. But the priority would be regional defense, not global role, a reversal of earlier postwar policy rankings.

South Africa successfully resisted the first round of decolonization in West Africa. But as the process spread toward southern Africa, it became more tolerant and attempted to turn the independence of Botswana, Lesotho, Swaziland (BLS), and Malawi to advantage. Having failed to incorporate them earlier, it now advocated continental dialogue and regional cooperation. The ambiguities of white-settler nationalism, however, were apparent in Pretoria's simultaneous encouragement of Ian Smith's Unilateral Declaration of Independence (UDI) in Rhodesia. Nevertheless, South Africa's "outward movement" in the late-1960s did represent an innovative attempt to combine economic and political links with black African states, especially neighbors, with economic and strategic association with the white-ruled territories of Angola, Mozambique, and Rhodesia: coprosperity sphere and *cordon sanitaire,* respectively. But this careful balance between white and black regimes and among political, economic, and strategic interests—essential in South African eyes to the vestigial remains of its relationship with the West—was shattered by dramatic regional and global changes in the mid-1970s: the anti-colonial *coup d'état* in Portugal and the jump in the price of oil leading to political change regionally and economic disruption globally. Only South Africa's earlier rearmament enabled it to deal simultaneously with regional change (Mozambique and Angola) and national challenge (Soweto) as well as with international inflation and recession (resulting, incidentally, in a high price for gold as well as for oil).

The Loss of Lisbon and Salisbury: Retreat to the Laager

The April 1974 Lisbon coup marked the beginning of the ongoing transformation of southern Africa from a settler-dominated region into a subsystem of the rest of black Africa. This process has undermined South African and Western assumptions about the stability of the region and necessitated a further reassessment of South Africa's foreign and security policies. The six years from April 1974 through the Angolan civil war and Soweto disturbances to Robert Mugabe's electoral victory in Zimbabwe in February 1980 were traumatic ones for the Afrikaner government and people, leading from regional dominance to defensiveness and culminating in an unwillingness to accept the terms of U.N. initiatives over its own colony of Namibia. Kenneth Adelman offers several reasons for this dramatic shift in politico-strategic assumptions and postures:

> Why South Africa has slipped from being one of the continent's most stable nations to its most defiant one, threatened both from within and without, is due to a host of factors: the rise to power of the Marxist black regimes in the former "buffer zones" of Angola and Mozambique; South Africa's ill-conceived and ill-fated intervention in the Angolan civil war; the large-scale Soweto riots of 1976; the international outcry against possible intentions to test nuclear weapons in the summer of 1977; the death of Steve Biko and the subsequent inquiry into police treatment of political prisoners; the crackdown of dissident groups . . . and the reaction thereto (UN mandatory arms embargo and US withdrawal of naval and commercial attaches); as well as the advent of black rule in Rhodesia . . .[9]

The swiftly changing and generally adverse circumstances of the middle and late 1970s led to reappraisal of the regional policy of dialogue. The successor policy, détente consisted of coexistence with an economically dependent, albeit radical, Frelimo government in Mozambique and encouragement of a transition away from settler rule in Rhodesia. "The essence of the policy," as Jaster observes, "was that South Africa should assert vigorous leadership in regional affairs and should win the cooperation of black African states—conservative states in particular—in order to bring stability to the area and to prevent the further spread of radicalism and chaos.[10] But the combined failures of the August 1975 Victoria Falls talks over Rhodesia and the August 1975 to January 1976 involvement in Angola signified the end of regional détente and a retreat back into the *laager*, even if there are lingering hopes that the *laager* will be somewhat broader than white South Africa alone.

Some of those hopes for a broader *laager*—or, at least, for a friendly buffer area athwart one approach to the *laager*—rest with the ultimate status of Namibia, under South African administration since 1920 when it was constituted a League of Nations mandate. But ever since 1966, Pretoria's rule has been challenged by the U.N. General Assembly and contested through armed insurgency by the South West Africa People's Organization (SWAPO), operating principally from guerrilla bases in neighboring Angola.

The deep incursions of South African forces into Angola during the civil war in that country and their subsequent slow withdrawal to the south in early 1976 led to an unprecedented buildup of South African military forces in Namibia, variously estimated at 15,000 to 45,000 men.[11] The logistical bases established by Pretoria for support of the Angola operations were transformed into staging areas for vigorous counterinsurgency measures against SWAPO as well as a forward defense line for the South African *laager*.

Since a Western-powers initiative in 1977, Pretoria has been negotiating intermittently—and ambivalently—over the future of the territory. The Afrikaner government has been sustaining a two-track policy of discussing an internationally sponsored settlement, while at the same time keeping open the option of an internal settlement resulting in a Namibian government favorably disposed toward South African interests. Fearing a SWAPO victory if free and open Namibian elections are held under U.N. auspices, the Pretoria leadership has skillfully obstructed efforts in that direction for over three years. Meanwhile its sponsorship of elections in Namibia was predictably boycotted by SWAPO. The resulting Namibian government, in an effort to win domestic support and foreign acceptance, has ironically undertaken liberalizing measures that have substantially begun to alter the face of apartheid, going well beyond the token reforms in South Africa itself.

Some of the most recent South African intransigence, respecting internationally sponsored and sanctioned Namibian elections, can be explained as an attempt to buy time—both to await the Reagan administration's Africa policy and to allow the Botha government itself to stand for reelection without the onus of having sold out to "Marxist terrorists" or international pressure tactics. The presence of several thousand South African troops in forward defensive positions gaining valuable counterinsurgency experience is, arguably, well serving Pretoria's security interests. There are also drawbacks: the economic burden, the casualties, and the difficulties of fighting a guerrilla war with a high proportion of conscripts whose training and morale are less than optimal.

While South African defense forces were battling the "Communist onslaught" hundreds of miles from their white homeland on the northern border of Namibia, the Afrikaner government was suddenly confronted by violent challenge inside the "white redoubt" itself: the Soweto riots of June 1976, the most serious domestic African resistance of the century. Youthful black resistance was encouraged by the Mozambique revolution and by white South Africa's perceived defeat in Angola. Soweto took considerably more time to contain than Sharpeville had. Despite its origins in the opposition to the use of Afrikaans in black schools, it became a symbol of black alienation, determination, and anger. It not only revealed the difficulties the authorities had in restoring internal order; it also displayed the new courage that the black community had acquired in the aftermath of the Portuguese coup: the South African state could not be isolated and insulated forever. Moreover, refugees from Soweto swelled the ranks of supporters of banned black opposition parties in exile as well as the pool of potential guerrilla fighters ready to slip back across the border between black- and white-ruled Africa.

The major liberation movement in South Africa, the seventy-five-year-old African National Congress (ANC), is the center of a powerful transnational coalition of nationalist parties, regional and continental African allies, and global supporters, mainly socialist states and parties.[12] Its primary goal remains the overthrow of racist rule. Given the denial of the parliamentary option, it has been forced to strive for this end through guerrilla struggle as well as through the use of political and diplomatic methods. With the borders of Botswana, Mozambique, and Zimbabwe now open to it, the ANC can infiltrate exiled South Africans back into the country without the risks of going through a *cordon sanitaire.* It also maintains links with major internal institutions, such as *Inkatha,* the Zulu-based party of Chief Gatsha Buthelezi, the Azanian People's Organization (AZAPO), and the Soweto Civic Association (SCA).

Since 1975, the number and scale of guerrilla attacks have increased to include raids on police stations, railroad lines, and major installations such as SASOL 1 and 2 (oil-from-coal plants). In return, South Africa has not only extended its cross-border raids from Angola and Zambia (against SWAPO) into Mozambique (against ANC), it has also cleared border areas and accelerated counterinsurgency training and exercises. But the post-Soweto black exodus into exile, either for safety or for training, continues out of South Africa.

Although the South African army has engaged organized guerrilla units outside the Republic's border and remains the first line of defense against conventional land attacks,[13] the task of countering internal urban and rural terrorism has fallen largely to South African policemen and commandos working in cooperation with the intelligence-gathering and special-operations organization, the Department of National Security (DONS), formerly BOSS (Bureau of State Security). Commando units comprise officers and men who have completed two years of compulsory service and are discharging their eight-year reserve obligation. In general, the more senior officers and noncommissioned officers are volunteers. The units are located in more than two hundred cities, towns, villages, and industrial complexes throughout the country. They are lightly armed, intimately familiar with their turf, and high-spirited in the tradition of Boer homestead defenders. Some commando units have volunteered for service on the borders and, after special training, have been so employed.[14]

During the last two years naval reservists in Citizen Force units have been assigned to help with internal-security tasks, specifically to defend harbor and port installations against sabotage and landward attack.[15] Indeed, the navy's Permanent Force is itself to a large degree in counterinsurgency operations. It searches for men and material being infiltrated from the north along each coast. South African naval vessels spend much more time on harbor protection and coastal defense than they do patrolling Cape sea routes, a role reflected in the navy's continuing purchase of fast patrol craft.[16]

In sum, the Afrikaners' response in the late seventies to the demise of détente regionally and the appearance of black unrest internally has been the familiar one of repression of almost all forms of opposition and acceleration of the bantustan policy by forcing "independence" onto the black homelands. Most recently, it has attempted to formulate a regional policy that explicitly ties strategic issues to the bantustans: the "constellation of states" proposal. Although there are some indications to the contrary—such as the "multiracial" Presidential Council in place of the Senate and some revisions to *petit apartheid* in terms of domestic, labor, and sports legislation—the underlying trend is toward defensiveness, a continued retreat into the *laager*. As Jaster argues,

The years 1975-79 witnessed the cumulative militarization of South African society. Although South Africa's leaders have denied that this has occurred, the evidence is persuasive. It includes:

A dramatic change in the perceived threat and in South Africa's response to it;

Sharp increases in defense spending and a rise in the defense share of the budget and GNP;

An enlarged military "presence" in South African life;
The growing role and involvement of the military in policy-making;
A broad mobilization of the population.[17]

This movement toward the establishment of a garrison state has been facilitated by the prior development in the 1960s of military manpower, indigenous arms production, and weapons stockpiling and modernization. It requires, however, continued economic expansion, white political support, and black social passivity. Given changes in regional and global affairs since the mid-1970s—especially decolonization and recession, respectively—these conditions may not be present over the next twenty years.

As discussed below, white military leadership seems to recognize its tenuous situation to a greater degree than do some Afrikaner politicians or Anglophone entrepreneurs. For the SADF has already mobilized its personnel base into the maximum readiness attainable in "peacetime": 86,000 troops, 66,000 of which are conscripts in the Permanent Force; 71,000 of these are in the army (6,000 white men, 3,000 black and colored regulars, 2,000 white women, and 60,000 conscripts), 10,000 in the air force (4,000 conscripts), and 5,000 in the navy (2,000 conscripts); in addition there are 35,500 policemen (19,500 white and 16,000 nonwhite). The Citizen Force of reservists who serve several days a year for eight years has 120,000 in the army, 25,000 in the air force, and 10,000 in the navy. There are also 110,000 in the Commandos, a white, paramilitary citizen group whose members train for twenty days each year. The International Institute for Strategic Studies estimates South Africa's total mobilizable strength at 404,500.[18]

"Total Strategy": Military in Politics

As the 1970s gave way to the 1980s, as Samora Machel's guerrilla victory in Mozambique was followed by Robert Mugabe's electoral triumph in Zimbabwe, so the white South African nation has come to feel very isolated and alienated from prevailing regional and global trends. The lenses through which it views the world, including its own burgeoning and restive black population, were formed in the 1950s; communism and bipolarity are still the major features of its conceptual map, at least in its populist version.

The white community, in defensive mood, is determined to save its identity and property, its distinctive way of life. As Adelman observes,

Faced with worldwide condemnation, but determined to survive at all costs, the South African government has assumed a posture of defiance and adopted a carefully formulated "grand strategy" to assure that survival. In this sense, South Africa offers a classic example of a threatened state approaching problems from a strategic, rather than tactical perspective, as well as a state whose foreign and security policy is directly derived and driven by domestic considerations.[19]

These ineluctable moves toward a "fortress South Africa," a tightly defined and regulated national *laager,* are related to two salient and interrelated characteristics of contemporary South African political culture that are likely to be features of the politico-strategic debate over policy for the rest of this century: factionalism and militarism.

First, dating back to Vorster's original outward-looking stance of dialogue, the Afrikaners have been divided into *verligte* (reformist) and *verkrampte* (hard-line) factions. The *verligtes,* products of South Africa's post-war "quiet revolution," are modernized professional Afrikaners who recognize the need for change and welcome modest reform internally and limited cooperation regionally. By contrast, the *verkramptes* are resistant to such an evolution, preferring fundamentalist doctrine and the persistence of strict apartheid. *Verkramptes* in the Nationalist party, the *Broederbond,* the Dutch Reformed Church, and other central Afrikaner institutions have consistently opposed and diluted any *verligte* initiatives.

Second, and related to the *verligte-verkrampte* dispute, the SADF, especially since Angola, has become increasingly involved in governmental decision making. Reflecting the growing strategic content in all aspects of South African life, military personnel and priorities have played a growing part in decision making. In general, given their worldly professionalism and their ominous intelligence reports, most top military leaders espouse *verligte* rather than *verkrampte* positions. Senior officers appreciate that African nationalism cannot be defeated by military might or means alone. As Gwendolen Carter notes, "It is commonly said that the Defense Force view of security is that twenty per cent is involved in meeting external dangers but that eighty per cent of South Africa's security problems lies inside its border. The Defense Force feels it can easily handle external dangers, such as they presently are, but that serious internal disruptions would be another and far more dangerous matter."[20]

The military shares the predisposition of the *verligtes* to deal with South Africa's security problems in depth in two ways: first, to confront the enemy outside rather than inside South Africa's borders and, second, to treat the roots of unrest—apartheid—rather than merely the symptoms. They have encouraged moves toward a general reassessment of policy following the traumatic changes of the second half of the 1970s: "Peering out of the *laager* into a hostile world the Afrikaners have fashioned their total strategy encompassing military, economic, political, and diplomatic dimensions."[21]

There appear to be two major strategic strands in this policy for the 1980s in addition to reform of some apartheid structures (for example, permitting black trade unions): first, military officers in the cabinet and the prime minister's office and, second, a security dimension to the latest regional "constellation of states" proposal.[22] The military's involvement in national decision making has two central aspects. First, in 1980, the commander of the SADF, General Magnus Malan, was brought into the cabinet to succeed his friend and confidant, Pieter Botha, as defense minister. Second, SADF officers are continuously involved in Botha's revived, reorganized, and strengthened prime minister's department. This central secretariat services a set of working groups and cabinet-level committees, "of which the most important is the resurrected statutory State Security Council (created in 1972), a body with the conveniently open-ended function of 'formulation of national policy and strategy in relation to the security of the Republic'."[23]

Although the military has a harsh image throughout southern Africa and is feared and resented by South Africa's black population, it may be quite moderate in domestic political affairs even if prepared to hit hard in regional military conflicts. Its *verligte* orientation is a function of its awareness that counterinsurgency tactics are rarely victorious without simultaneous social change; hence its advocacy of "total strategy." As Chester Crocker points out in his plea for constructive American engagement in bringing change to South Africa: "Malan, Botha and their colleagues were in fact the first Afrikaner nationalists to articulate the view that the military's purpose is to buy time for political solutions that would expand domestic support and permit expanded black military recruitment. They were also the first to state publicly that defense depends on avoiding domestic disaffection—as several prominent black leaders have pointed out."[24] There are now coloreds and Indians in the navy and black troops in the "Namibian" and bantustan armies, but white South African officers remain very much in charge of such units. More important, though, than reform inside the military is the military's encouragement of reform in the rest of the country.[25]

The pragmatism displayed by SADF officers may be more out of necessity than preference. For the challenges facing the regime are Olympian; the tensions of decades of racism combined with the contradictions of the bantustan policy and expectations stimulated by regional change all point toward an impossible agenda. The amount of pressure is indicated by the degree of reform already outlined by the Botha regime. But although this outrages the *verkramptes,* it is quite insufficient to engender black political support. Therefore, the military remains preoccupied about the prospects of simultaneous internal and external attacks as the white nation is in a minority position at home as well as abroad. As Adelman suggests, "South African military planners perceive three types of possible threat: insurrection from within, guerrila actions on the border, and conventional attack from outside."[26] What they seek to avoid at all costs is a situation in which these three threats are combined simultaneously, an increasingly likely prospect now that the border of white southern Africa is at the Limpopo River rather than the Zambezi. Hence the frequent cross-border land and air raids on guerrilla bases in Angola, Zambia, and now Mozambique. Hence, also, military advocacy of the constellation idea—an economic and security grouping centered on South Africa with the small black states of the region, plus the "independent" homelands—an attempt to recreate earlier schemes for regional detente and coprosperity.

Many commentators have pointed to a crisis in Afrikanerdom as the 1980s open,[27] one that undermines the basic assumptions and assertions of apartheid, one that has strategic as well as social, political, and economic dimensions, and one about which military leaders are uncomfortable as white power is confronted by indefatigable black resistance.[28] Cracks in the edifice of apartheid combined with regular and angry black outbursts despite continuing repression leave the government with a deteriorating situation over time. Internal reformism and regionalism may prove to be less effective and less realistic than earlier schemes. Indeed, Jaster suggests of the latter that the regime may have simply "wanted to confer an aura of grand strategy and larger purpose on a policy which, in fact, was based on narrow, pragmatic self-interest."[29]

Anticipating Sanctions: National Defense Industry

As already indicated, the Afrikaner regime developed its own armaments industry after World War II for two reasons. First, it recognized the prospects of disruptions in external arms supplies either because of the Western powers' disapproval of apartheid or because of U.N.-imposed arms embargoes. Second, it saw the creation of a national armaments capability as one way to rectify the historic Afrikaans-English-speaking imbalance in terms of ownership of industry. Furthermore, the development of such a military-industrial complex would serve to enhance South Africa's general technological capacity. As Lewis Gann and Peter Duignan claim,

> The defense complex, including ARMSCOR [Arms Corporation of South Africa Limited] with its subsidiary arms factories, is one of the country's most advanced technical organizations, one that is engaged in manufacturing, operating and maintaining a wide range of highly sophisticated equipment. About 45% of defense expenditures goes to internal development . . . South Africa's industrial infrastructure enabled the country to emphasize self-sufficiency in arms production and improvement in its ability to withstand foreign economic pressures . . .[30]

South Africa's defense and strategic industries have developed their capabilities in three areas in particular: conventional arms, nuclear weapons, and indigenous energy production.

The country is increasingly independent in the supply of a range of conventional armaments: land-based equipment, aircraft and missiles, and now naval craft. The development of local manufacturing provided the base for an armaments industry. The Iron & Steel Corporation (ISCOR) and African Explosives and Chemical Industries (AECI) have supplied the basic ingredients for arms and ammunition manufacture, which has been organized by ARMSCOR with its nine nationalized subsidiaries and 1,200 defense subcontractors. South Africa now makes it own rifles, guns, and ammunition. It also produces Eland armored cars (1,600 now in service) and Hippo and Rhino personnel carriers (500), mainly under license from France. And with Israeli assistance it has modernized its 250 Centurion tanks, adding impregnable Chobham-type armor from its own sophisticated steel industry.[31]

South Africa's air force is now supplied with fighters, helicopters, and missiles by the local Atlas aircraft factory. Its previous reliance on aging British-produced aircraft—Shackletons (7), Canberras (6), Buccaneers (6), and Wasp helicopters (11)—has been superseded by assembly of Mirage jets (100), Alouette (67), Super Frelon (15), and Puma (40) helicopters, and Cactus (18) missiles under French license. Impala (200) jet and Bosbok (20) and Kudu (20) turbo-prop trainers are built under Italian license. Atlas is also increasingly capable of producing the avionics as well as jet engines and airframes for this range of aircraft and missiles.[32]

Finally, the navy has begun to commission locally produced fast-attack craft, having relied previously on British frigates and French submarines. It already has six Israeli-designed fast-attack craft (Minister Reshef) with another six Ministers on order. All these craft are equipped with Scorpion (Gabriel) surface-to-surface missiles.[33]

Simultaneous with the development of an antiguerrilla capability, South Africa appears to have prepared itself for a go-it-alone situation with a nuclear deterrent and indigenous energy sources; the latter include both enriched uranium for nuclear-power generation and oil-from-coal plants. South Africa's nuclear developments are controversial both because of their weapons proliferation considerations and also because of the alleged roles-intended or not-of outside powers in uranium enrichment and weapons-delivery techniques (Canada, Israel, West Germany, and the United States).

South Africa's mineral cornucopia includes extensive uranium deposits. Uranium oxide has been mined in both the Transvaal and Namibia (Rossing) for several years, as a byproduct of South Africa's gold industry. Its major mining conglomerates, Anglo-American Corporation and Rio-Tinto Zinc, have extracted low-grade uranium (South Africa has the world's third-largest deposits) as an adjunct to the mining of high-grade gold.

Abetted by South Africa's long-established (1949) Atomic Energy Board, the country has developed a partially independent nuclear-research capability, centered on laboratories at Pelindaba. There its first research reactor—South African Fundamental Atomic Research Reactor (SAFARI-1)—has been in operation since 1965 with the second, Pelinduna Zero, going critical in 1967.

South Africa's Nuclear Fuels Corporation (NUFCOR) produces uranium concentrate for the domestic and international markets, especially for Great Britain and other Western states. NUFCOR has become, according to Zdenek Cervenka and Barbara Rogers, "the largest single uranium supply company in the world,"[34] a central link in the five-country uranium cartel that has included Australian, British, Canadian, and U.S. firms. Using and refining the West German Becker jet-nozzle technique for uranium enrichment, South Africa has developed its own enrichment plant at Valindaba, though whether it presently produces weapons-grade U-235 is not known. For the last few years its Uranium Enrichment Corporation (UCOR) has had an operational enrichment facility enabling it to produce apparently at below-world-level prices. French contractors are already building the country's first nuclear-power station, Koeberg, north of Cape Town, which is expected to produce 1,800 MW from 1982 onward.[35]

Speculation about the nuclear potential of South Africa, a nonsignatory of the Nuclear Nonproliferation Treaty, intensified in mid-1977 and again in 1979 because of observations from Soviet and U.S. space satellites. In the first instance, in August 1977, the Soviet Union advised the Western powers that one of its reconnaissance satellites had observed South African preparations for a nuclear test in the Kalahari Desert.[36] In the second instance, in September 1979, an American Vela satellite reported a high-intensity double flash in the southern Indian Ocean, which pointed to a low-yield, high-altitude nuclear explosion. Although neither the source or the origin of the explosion has been verified, some evidence now points toward South Africa possessing nuclear capability.[37]

South Africa might have had a quite immediate nuclear potential ten years before these alleged preparations for a nuclear test. But, at least according to Jack Spence, it delayed realizing this potential lest it undermine its outward-looking policy of dialogue. Spence, a leading student of South African foreign and defense policies, argued in the mid-1970s that South Africa's "defense policy is seen as bearing directly on the Republic's capacity to gain support abroad and win friends and allies,"[38] especially in the West, but also in Africa. He predicted then that South Africa would not go nuclear within the following five years because it would not wish to jeopardize such prospects. In fact, after the mid-1970s and with the demise of détente as well as dialogue, South Africa had little to lose, given Western distance and African opposition. These unfavorable political developments may have led to a decision to operationalize its nuclear potential in the late 1970s.

Debate continues on the intentions and implications of South Africa's quest for nuclear status. Would Pretoria ever actually use the bomb? "If nuclear weapons are a last resort to defend one's self, it would be very stupid not to use it," says Deputy Defense Minister Hendrik Jacobus Coetsee.[39] Whether the minister's remark reflects government policy or is simply one man's answer to a hypothetical question, such a statement might still have a rather profound deterrent effect.

Some might argue, however, that nuclear weapons would be useless or suicidal against internal threats that are, after all, judged to be predominant in the South African security equation. It would follow, therefore, that threatening the use of such weapons would not be credible, hence nuclear weapons would constitute a questionable deterrent and have questionable utility for South Africa.

However, given their apparent siege mentality, sense of divine mission, even occasional paranoia, it does not take a very great leap of imagination to conceive of circumstances in which the Afrikaner leadership might just make the fateful decision to use the bomb, even if it meant its own destruction.

The country's probable nuclear capacity may afford South Africa a degree of diplomatic leverage over African and Western states, especially when it is subjected to moralizing criticism, since the United States, Israel, West Germany, France, and Great Britain have provided hardware, fissile materials, technology, and finance to enable South Africa to build a nuclear weapon.[40] As the Western allies have distanced themselves at the official level from South Africa's arms buildup, both conventional and nuclear, the white nation has developed links with other pariah states in the strategic as well as diplomatic and economic sectors. Relations with Israel and Taiwan have grown in the second half of the 1970s.[41] In particular, South Africa and Israel have exchanged numerous military missions with the latter providing missile and naval technology to the former, possibly in exchange for enriched uranium.

In addition to the development of its nuclear military and energy capabilities, South Africa has successfully pioneered an oil-from-coal industry. The supply (and now price) of oil has long been the white regime's Achilles heel, one that it has not yet been able to overcome fully, despite considerable effort and investment in oil and gas exploration on its own territory as well as offshore. With the overthrow of the shah of Iran, South Africa's major and most reliable source of petroleum dried up. Although it has stockpiled oil for years (now having 40 million tons or two-and-a-half years' supply in storage), since the mid-1970s it has had to buy oil at a premium on the world market while oil companies are under growing pressure to terminate their involvement with South Africa altogether.

To reduce its external energy dependence, South Africa has not only developed its coal and electricity industries, as well as its nuclear-power potential, it has also developed oil-from-coal technology and built two major plants, SASOL 1 and 2, which will provide a third of its gasoline and diesel fuel needs by the mid-1980s. Given the strategic as well as financial and symbolic importance of these plants, it was not coincidental that they were the targets of a strikingly successful guerrilla attack in June 1980.

In sum, the post-Lisbon coup and post-Soweto riots period has seen not only significantly increased military spending, but also increasing attention to and investment in a variety of defense-related industries and infrastructures: oil-from-coal and nuclear industries, and weapons-producing and high-technology infrastructures. As Jaster remarks, "Defense expenditure in the last half of the 1970s was consistent with South Africa's heightened threat perception."[42]

Conclusions

The difficulties and dilemmas confronting the white regime as the 1980s open are similar to those that faced it in each postwar decade—domestic resistance, regional opposition, and global criticism—but each of these is intensifying as the year 2000 approaches. Unless apartheid is abandoned, it is unlikely that white power will prevail over African nationalism in the long run. And even the ability to contain it until the end of the century is becoming increasingly problematic.

In the absence of options, given the exclusivity of apartheid, the militarization of the white nation continues. Robert Jaster points out: "Within the constraints imposed by apartheid, by limited white manpower and by a sometimes distorted view of the outside world, South African security policies have been increasingly flexible, tough and aggressive."[43] But because of the particular biases of South Africa policymakers and the very limited circles within which they move, and notwithstanding their self-image of toughness and self-righteousness, "South Africa's security policies . . . have been marked by a number of serious (and sometimes lasting) failures to analyse correctly the motives, capabilities, and likely actions of other countries."[44] Few alternative options are considered given the like-mindedness of senior Afrikaner decisionmakers, so stereotypes are reinforced and faulty assessments go unchallenged.

White South Africa's view of the world is still reminiscent of the 1960s rather than the 1980s: bipolarity, communist threat, and Western weakness. And, as Jaster says, so long as apartheid remains the centerpiece of the white nation's ideologies and institutions, "South Africa will have few real security options during the decade ahead. Her range of choices and her chance of success will be limited by forces that have been at work for a long time."[45] Despite changes in technologies and tactics, despite shifts southward in the border with black Africa, South Africa's security policy remains anticommunist, antinationalist, and solicitous of Western support.

Given its military and industrial capabilities, the prospects for an over-throw of white power are limited. However, socio-political pressures are relentless, and the apparent contradictions are intensifying in the ban-tustans and in the cities because of scarce land and labor and very unequal income and welfare. The specters of widespread black famine and unemploy-ment in a land of plenty cannot but increase pressures for change. As the security forces are well aware, the major source of opposition is internal rather than external, an assessment widely shared by outside analysts. Chester Crocker has written: "There is no basis for questioning the conventional military superiority of the republic in relation to any foreseeable combina-tion of independent African states."[46]

The persistence and intensification of black opposition and alienation throughout this century cannot be treated without fundamental change. Despite the apparent awareness of the regime of impending crisis, the white nation reveals a remarkable inability to abandon its ideological inheritance and devise some really new dispensation. The security threat will have to grow even further to generate sufficient pressure for such a rethinking of policy. If societal as well as military factors are included, and general global as well as particular regional conditions considered, then the prospects for such a fundamental reevaluation appear much more likely. As one analyst observes,

> Judged purely in terms of its economic and military strength and the un-doubted commitment of white South Africans to using this power to ensure their survival, the Republic's position would seem, if not impregnable, at least fairly secure. But such an evaluation fails to take into account two critical factors: South Africa's long-term dependence on powerful western economic and diplomatic backing, and the system's devastating internal contradictions. Both these factors are likely to be crucial in deciding the Republic's future, the latter in particular.[47]

Hence the relative realism and reasonableness of the SADF leadership in the white regime compared to widespread *verkrampte* views in the white nation. It is not yet clear, however, whether *verligte* definitions of the security threat will prevail: can the *laager* be defended through reform as well as through arms? Will true reform be given a chance?

The prevalent mood of uncertainty and defensiveness reflects the white nation's increasing isolation both outside and inside its territory. Although the Afrikaner nation, and perhaps whites as a group, may become more cohesive under external threats, apartheid effectively prevents a wider ap-peal to nonwhite groups. Belatedly, at the end of the 1970s, the regime made some attempt to attract colored, Indian, and black-elite support, but after decades of exclusion and alienation there is little reason why such com-munities should now turn around and help a beleaguered government.

Given the dictates of apartheid, the regime's strategic and political options are very circumscribed. They are likely to remain so until the cause of opposition is removed.

Notes

1. Sam C. Nolutshungu, *South Africa in Africa: A Study of Ideology and Foreign Policy* (New York: Africana, 1975), p. 6.

2. "South Africa" in *Africa Contemporary Record: Annual Survey and Documents, Volume 10, 1977-1978,* ed. Colin Legum (New York: Africana, 1979), p. B916.

3. Robert S. Jaster, *South Africa's Narrowing Security Options,* Adelphi Paper no. 159 (London: International Institute for Strategic Studies, 1980), p. 6.

4. See Greg Lanning with Marti Mueller, *Africa Undermined: Mining Companies and the Underdevelopment of Africa* (Harmondsworth: Pelican, 1979); and Ann Seidman and Neva Seidman Makgetla, *Outposts of Monopoly Capitalism: Southern Africa in the Changing Global Economy* (Westport, Conn.: Lawrence Hill, 1980).

5. Jaster, "South Africa's Narrowing Security Options," p. 10.

6. See Holger Jensen, "A Nation at Battle Stations," *Newsweek,* 29 September 1980, p. 19; and special section on "South Africa: Total Strategy for Total War," *Southern Africa,* 14 (January/February 1981):9-28.

7. Jaster, "South Africa's Narrowing Security Options," p. 14.

8. Ibid., p. 17.

9. Kenneth L. Adelman, "The Strategy of Defiance: South Africa," *Comparative Strategy* 1, nos. 1, 2 (1978):33-34.

10. Jaster, "South Africa's Narrowing Security Options," p. 22. Cf. Timothy M. Shaw, "Kenya and South Africa: 'Sub-Imperialist' States," Orbis 21 (Summer 1977):375-394.

11. The International Institute for Strategic Studies (IISS) *Strategic Survey, 1977* (London: IISS, 1978), p. 37. See also Nicholas Ashford, "Is Confidence Enough to Win the War in Namibia?" *The Times of London,* 17 February 1981, p. 12.

12. See Timothy M. Shaw, "International Organizations and the Politics of Southern Africa: Towards Regional Integration or Liberation?" *Journal of Southern African Studies* 3, no. 1 (1976):1-19.

13. The chances for a conventional ground attack on South Africa are rated as slight by most analysts. A conventional attack by Cuban forces out of Angola is perhaps the most possible, but even that is rated highly unlikely, particularly since South African regulars decisively defeated the Cubans when they clashed in Angola in 1975-1976. South African planners are also

concerned over periodic reports of East German and other East European troops and advisors in southern Africa.

14. Information on the Commandos is based upon Norman L. Dodd, "The South African Defence Force," *Royal United Services Institute Journal for Defence Studies* 125 (March 1980):40-41.

15. Republic of South Africa Department of Defence, *White Paper on Defence and Armaments Supply,* Pretoria, 1979.

16. With three submarines and several vessels with surface-to-surface missiles, the South African navy also provides a degree of deterrence against international intervention and blockade. Ten minesweepers give the navy some capability to keep its ports and harbors open as well.

17. Jaster, "South Africa's Narrowing Security Options," p. 27. See also William Gutteridge, "South Africa's Defence Posture," *World Today* 36 (January 1980):26-31.

18. International Institute for Strategic Studies, *The Military Balance 1980-1981* (London: IISS, 1980), pp. 54-55. All force figures, this paragraph, are from IISS. See also data in "South Africa: Total Strategy for Total War."

19. Adelman, "The Strategy of Defiance," p. 34.

20. Gwendolen M. Carter, *Which Way Is South Africa Going?* (Bloomington: Indiana University Press, 1980), p. 9.

21. Adelman, "The Strategy of Defiance," p. 35.

22. Nicholas Ashford, "South Africa's Generals in the Corridors of Power," *The Times of London,* 1 September 1980, p. 16. Cf. plans from the "Front Line States" for a "Southern African Development Coordination Community without South Africa"; see Timothy M. Shaw, "South Africa, Southern Africa and the World System," *Conference on South Africa in Southern Africa,* Pennsylvania State University (October 1980) and "South Africa: Total Strategy for Total War."

23. Chester A. Crocker, "South Africa: Strategy for Change," *Foreign Affairs* 59 (Winter 1980/81):336.

24. Ibid., p. 338.

25. Ashford, "South Africa's Generals in the Corridors of Power."

26. Adelman, "The Strategy of Defiance," p. 37.

27. See, for instance, *Southern Africa: The Continuing Crisis,* eds. Gwendolen M. Carter and Patrick O'Meara (Bloomington: Indiana University Press, 1979); R.W. Johnson, *How Long Will South Africa Survive?* (New York: Oxford University Press, 1977); and Robert I. Rotberg, *Suffer the Future: Policy Choices in Southern Africa* (Cambridge, Mass.: Harvard University Press, 1980).

28. "South Africa," p. B864.

29. Jaster, "South Africa's Narrowing Security Options," p. 33.

30. Lewis H. Gann and Peter Duigan, *South Africa: War, Revolution or Peace?* (Stanford, Calif.: Hoover Institution Press, 1978), p. 26.

31. See *The Military Balance 1980-1981*, pp. 54-55; Stockholm International Peace Research Institute (SIPRI), *World Armaments and Disarmament Yearbook, 1979* (New York: Crane, Russak, 1979), pp. 166-167 and 234-235, and "South Africa: Total Strategy for Total War."

32. Ibid.

33. Ibid.

34. Zdenek Cervenka and Barbara Rogers, *The Nuclear Axis: Secret Collaboration Between West Germany and South Africa* (New York: New York Times Books, 1978), p. 149.

35. On South Africa's nuclear development, see J.E. Spence, "The Republic of South Africa: Proliferation and the Politics of 'Outward Movement'," in *Nuclear Proliferation: Phase II,* eds. Robert M. Lawrence and Joel Larus (Lawrence: University Press of Kansas, 1974), pp. 209-238; and Ronald W. Walters, "Nuclear Collaboration with South Africa," *Objective: Justice* 11 (Spring/Summer 1979):33-37.

36. See SIPRI, *World Armaments and Disarmament Yearbook 1978,* pp. 73-79.

37. Jensen, "A Nation at Battle Stations," and "South Africa: Total Strategy for Total War."

38. Spence, "The Republic of South Africa," p. 232. See also Edouard Bustin, "South Africa's Foreign Policy Alternatives and Deterrence Needs" in *Nuclear Proliferation and the Near-Nuclear Countries,* eds. O. Marwah and A. Schulz (Cambridge, Mass.: Ballinger, 1975), pp. 205-226.

39. Jensen, "A Nation at Battle Stations."

40. Cervenka and Rogers, *The Nuclear Axis,* pp. 348-349.

41. See Robert E. Harkavy, "Pariah States and Nuclear Proliferation," *World Peace Foundation,* May 1980, pp. 33-36. Cf. Timothy M. Shaw, "Oil, Israel and the OAU: An Introduction to the Political Economy of Energy in Southern Africa," *Africa Today* 23 (January-March 1976):15-26.

42. Jaster, "South Africa's Narrowing Security Options," p. 28.

43. Ibid., p. 37

44. Ibid.

45. Jaster, "South Africa's Narrowing Security Options," p. 41. See also Michael Spicer, "Change in South Africa? P.W. Botha's Strategy and Politics," *World Today* 36 (January 1980): 32-40; and Robert I. Rotberg, "South Africa Under Botha: How Deep a Change?" *Foreign Policy* 38 (Spring 1980):126-142.

46. Chester A. Crocker, "Current and Projected Military Balances in Southern Africa" in *South Africa into the 1980s,* eds. Richard E. Bissell and Chester A. Crocker (Boulder, Colo.: Westview, 1979), p. 88. Cf. Timothy M. Shaw, "The Military Situation and the Future of Race Relations in Southern Africa" in *Africa in World Affairs: The Next Thirty*

Years, eds. Ali A. Mazrui and Hasu H. Patel (New York: Third Press, 1973), pp. 37-61.

47. "South Africa", p. B862. For other recent projections see P. Thandika Mkandawire, "Reflections on Some Future Scenarios for Southern Africa," *Journal of Southern African Affairs* 2 (October 1977):391-429; Paul Goulding and Timothy M. Shaw, "Alternative Scenarios for Africa," in *Alternative Futures for Africa,* ed. Timothy M. Shaw (Boulder, Colo.: Westview, 1981); and Timothy M. Shaw, "Southern Africa: From Detente to Deluge?," in *Year Book of World Affairs,* vol. 32 (Boulder, Colo.: Westview, 1978), pp. 117-138.

Part V
Conclusion

16 Developing States and Regional and Global Security

Edward A. Kolodziej
and *Robert E. Harkavy*

In this chapter we will try to identify some general characteristics of—and to reach some tentative conclusions about—the security policies of developing countries in three areas of concern. We will first look at some of the key determinants of the security policies of these states. Since these are too extensive in number and complexity to be discussed fully, we will focus on those that have tended to be slighted in current strategic writing. Next we will attempt to identify patterns of security policy decision making among our selected countries in an effort to see what implications they might have for regional and global security. Finally, and from a different angle of analysis, we will focus on several security processes in which these developing states are playing an increasingly important role and their impact on the outcomes of international conflict. In each of these sections we will attempt to generalize across cases and where appropriate relate these to the experiences of other emerging powers from among developing states. The three foci of the chapter parallel the division of the flow-chart of decision making and outcomes outlined in figure 1-1.

The preceding "country" chapters have provided the basis for an exploratory comparative analysis of the security policies of selected, but significant, emerging nations. In myriad ways, the analyses have indicated that they are, indeed, "emerging" as important actors in the total security system. They are abandoning previous roles as largely passive players for more assertive and independent postures. In all cases, however, there remain significant remnants of dependency regarding either economic aid and weapons acquisition or protection against regional foes, as well as the possibility of intervention from the major powers. These crosscurrents between dependence and independent initiative make the explanation of the security policies of these states more indeterminate and more elusive than those of major powers.

The introductory chapter sketched a framework for comparing and analyzing the security policies of these emerging powers. In assaying a preliminary framework for the comparative analysis, the editors were aware that the effort was fraught with many of the same traps and obstacles familiar to students in comparative politics and foreign policy.[1] Although both these latter fields of study would appear to subsume our focus, it is also evident that the lines of demarcation are necessarily blurred and that there is need for more intensive study of state security behavior. Economic and cultural policies, even sports, can be viewed as integral to security policy and politics. With the demise of laissez-faire and the inclination of states to oversee and manage all important relations between societies, almost all nations now pursue grand strategies, whatever they might be called, and correspondingly use a panoply of instruments to advance their security objectives.[2]

Even elements of foreign policy, like trade or capital flows, which were hitherto consigned to the dungeon of low politics, have security implications.[3] Our contributors even seem to suggest that where the overt level of military threat is presently low—as with Argentina or Brazil—broad issues of international economics (levels of dependency, autarky versus encouragement of foreign direct investment, free trade versus controls, and so forth tend to be abnormally prominent in overall national-security doctrines. But, even where a nation is close to the cockpits of military confrontation—Egypt or India, for example—the imperatives of poverty and economic development will often telescope security and welfare policies in a way still familiar to the guns and butter dilemmas of the United States and the Soviet Union but perhaps with a much grimmer seriousness. On the other hand, the contributors for Israel, Pakistan, and some other highly threatened states seem to find it easier to rely on a more narrowly focused construction of what constitutes national security. In short, the lines of disciplinary demarcation are difficult to define conclusively.

The discussion cannot hope to exhaust the work and analyses that yet remain if we are to develop solid, reliable, and verifiable knowledge of the security policies pursued by states that influence and determine regional and global security outcomes. It will, however, attempt to go beyond an analysis of the discrete behavior and military capabilities of individual states in order to contribute to the development of better strategic blueprints than we have now of how regional and global security processes are organized and how they operate.

The External and Internal Determinants of Security Policy: Some Comparisons

Figure 1-1 listed and schematically arrayed a variety of factors contributing to the development of security policies, involving a plethora of linked internal and external considerations. Many are quite familiar from the traditional international-relations textbook discussions of the bases for national power (Hans Morgenthau, Kenneth Organski, et al.). These focus on the military, political, economic, and geographical dimensions of power and the critical role played by diplomacy in determining a nation's security and status.[4] In recent years, of course, it has become fashionable in some scholarly circles to denigrate the importance of power politics or to discuss it only with respect to specific situations.[5] Not surprisingly, this optimistic appraisal of the role of force has little relevance for comparing the security situations of key less-developed countries (LDCs) that have been engaged in actual conflict in recent years or which are preparing for the likelihood of future hostilities. A more "traditional" analysis appears to be more appropriate in any attempt to harmonize the preceding diverse contributions.

Geopolitical Setting: Location, Population, and Resources

Location

One point stands out from our comparative analyses: the obvious importance of geography to the national-security environments of aspiring middle-range powers. During much of the postwar period, geopolitics—the application of geography to international relations—had been ignored.[6] In part this reflected a reaction against the alleged racist connotations of interwar German *geopolitik*. Other more tangible considerations also deflected attention from geopolitical analyses: the considerable obliteration of distance by modern communications and transport, the centrality of arms races where intercontinental missiles seemed to have transcended space, or the roles of vertically integrated multinational corporations in ensuring the West a flow of raw materials. More recently, however, newer trends—the need for bases from which to deploy troops to trouble-spots around the world, the growth of the Soviets' blue-water navy and long-range air-transport capability, and the close relation between geographic space and resource location in an era of growing scarcities—all have revived in a tradition linked to the writings of Halford MacKinder, Alfred Mahan, and Nicholas Spykman; hence, the now almost ubiquitous use of the term *geopolitics* in the press and in journals.

The locations of developing states relative to the lines of postwar superpower confrontation are obviously important. Many of the most heavily armed among them are roughly located along the arc around Eurasia stretching from Turkey to South Korea, first drawn by the United States at the inception of the Cold War. This arc was anticipated long ago in geopolitical theorists' discussions of "marginal rimlands" and "crush zones," which were thought to be central to ongoing or future struggles between Eurasia-based landpower and Anglo-Saxon seapower.[8] Nowadays, of course, resource location can be as important as military geography in determining strategic value, so that a Nigeria, a Zaire, an Iran, or an Abu Dhabi can become focal points of competitive activity. Then too, changes in big-power military technologies, coupled with global political trends, have resulted in the enhanced importance of small island nations deemed valuable for air staging, antisubmarine warfare, satellite tracking, or data-relay stations. In recent years this has focused attention on the alignments, sensibilities, and ideologies of even micro-states, like the Maldives and Seychelles Islands, Tonga, and Grenada, as well as on the prospects for the West's retention of Diego Garcia and Ascension Island.[9]

Still other LDCs, located astride important maritime choke points— Oman, Somalia, South Yemen, Indonesia—particularly if related to oil, also have received increased attention as strategic pawns. As these nations, along with many larger LDCs, become important *objects* of big-power attention, that attention automatically affects their security strategies. They acquire leverage for arms acquisitions, and the use of their territories becomes a quid pro quo for assistance versus regional antagonists. In many ways their vulnerability has prompted their acquisition of arms, which, in turn, has augmented their roles as determinants of their own and their region's security arrangements.

Increasingly, also, as several of the key LDCs threaten to become nascent nuclear powers—Israel, South Africa, Taiwan, India, Pakistan, Iraq—their locations, linked to the ranges of their delivery systems, become of great interest to the major powers.[10] Most are closer to the Soviet Union than to the United States. This circumstance may account partially for the Soviets' interest in halting nuclear spread. In some of these cases, a low level of minimum deterrence may be achieved vis-à-vis the Soviet Union. These new forms of threat and leverage may have application to the possibilities for Soviet intervention in regional conflicts. We may be gradually moving from a world of bilateral deterrence to multilateral deterrence in which actors at different levels of nuclear capability have varying influence on each other. But it is also one in which no one or even two actors, including the superpowers, can any longer guarantee when or how a nuclear war will be fought or what will be its outcome for their own security, for their region, or for the world.

More importantly, at least in the short run, location defines the nature and level of conventional military threats to our LDCs and hence their immediate security requirements. This involves such obvious, though often neglected, matters as the size, political character and strategic value of contiguous states (regional or superpower) and topographical features such as mountains or intervening water bodies. In these regards the variation among the states covered in this study is extreme. Some, like Nigeria and Brazil, are large states buffered on all sides by smaller and weaker ones. This condition affords them a hegemonic position, barring grand coalitions of their smaller neighbors or the menacing reach of a superpower.

As Myers points out for Brazil, however, just such a balancing regional coalition is not altogether to be ruled out; indeed, Brazilian fears of such an eventuality could trigger a self-fulfilling prophesy if Brazil reacted to such fears by expanding beyond its present frontiers. Nigeria, on the other hand, with its huge population, seems invulnerable to rival coalitions in its immediate region. The strategic position of either state might significantly change, however, if a regional rival—Argentina in Brazil's case, South Africa for Nigeria—developed nuclear capabilities.

Some other developing states, by contrast, are in very precarious situations. Their very survival is threatened by actually or potentially negative regional imbalances of force. Israel, South Africa, Pakistan, and South Korea fall by degrees into this category. These pariah states possess doubtful political leverage over other states and enjoy uncertain outside support.[11] Other states whose survival and essential national legitimacy are not seriously at issue—Vietnam, Iraq, Iran, Saudi Arabia, Syria, Egypt—are in the vortex of tension and conflict by dint of location. Some larger emerging states may also be perceived as regional hegemones (or aspire to such a status), but only so long as the lines of dominance within what they would prefer to consider strongly circumscribed, walled-off regions are conceded by others. India exerts some hegemony in South Asia as does Vietnam in Southeast Asia. They do so, however, only to the extent that surrounding and potentially more than countervailing power is conveniently ignored or, as in the case of China vis-à-vis Vietnam, neutralized by a still larger power. Iran under the shah, likewise, aspired to Persian Gulf hegemony even under the shadow of the Soviet Union. It banked on U.S. deterrent nuclear power to underwrite its regional pretentions. Iraq is now attempting to supplant the shah's former role.

On the weaker side of regional balances, some nations may be driven to dreams of a nuclear equalizer to rectify the unchangeable facts of population or weapons balances. Witness the rumors and reports emanating from Pakistan, Israel, South Africa, Taiwan, and South Korea. Others may play, wittingly or not, roles as buffer states between major powers. With reference to U.S.-Soviet-Saudi relations, Pakistan can be discussed in such admittedly elusive terms as were, earlier, Poland and Belgium. And as Cohen points out in Pakistan's case, a role as buffer state may potentially either be a source of military weakness or of diplomatic leverage.

Some states, such as Argentina, may seemingly be favored by geographic marginality in that they do not face important threats or find themselves on the front lines of major-power struggles. However, as Milenky hints for Argentina, such marginality can also paradoxically be a cause of national malaise. The resulting psychological void may tempt trouble. Indonesia is less marginal in this sense. As Lyons notes, it is an archipelagic state, defended by waters requiring more maritime than land power for protection and for force projection. However, its strategic position astride major oil and naval sea lines of communication makes it vulnerable to the designs of other states. Cuba and Taiwan are also favored by water barriers, which in each case are at the core of their security strategies.

Finally, regarding the geography of threats, the security environments of some states—Argentina, Brazil, South Korea—involve basically bilateral situations. Others—Israel, Iraq, Egypt, Vietnam, Pakistan—entail far more complex combinations. These increased possibilities of external threats and conflict are reflected in multi-tiered layers of contingency planning to respond to outside political forces. These matters have important ramifications for the sizing of military budgets, mixes between forces and services, and perceived requirements for nuclear weapons. Hence, Thomas notes that India plans for all possible military contingencies involving Pakistan, but concedes the necessity for resort to diplomacy where China is involved, that is, Soviet deterrence or U.S. restraints on China.

There is also the question, comparatively, of which of our actors under study have significant border or territorial disputes with neighbors (aside from the possibility of an ever-present temptation to expand). There is evidence to challenge the view that territoriality is passé and that territorial aggrandizement is of limited concern because evolving new norms of international law, somehow given force by the United Nations or other international bodies, regulate border conflicts.[12] A surprising number of our subject nations do have active, ongoing territorial disputes. Some are major— Israel and the Arab states over occupied territories or India and Pakistan over Kashmir. Others, including seemingly small issues, are potentially explosive, as were Teschen and Danzig a generation ago and as is now the dispute over the Shatt al Arab waterway between Iran and Iraq. Indonesia warily fends off Vietnamese designs on some islands in the South China Sea; Argentina quarrels both with Chile over the Beagle Channel and with Britain over the Falkland Islands. And numerous large LDCs—Pakistan, Nigeria, and Iran, for example—contain volatile internal ethnic-and/or religious-minority problems with cross-border implications. Iraq's Kurds and Shi'ites, the Baluchis in Iran and Pakistan, India's Muslims, Ethiopia's Ogaden Somalis—not to mention South Africa's majority blacks—are all tinder for possible explosions that could have far-reaching effects, as did once the problems within the Austro-Hungarian Empire. Brazil, meanwhile, is apparently perceived by others as still desiring to expand against poorly defined borders within a continental landmass but where problems involving mobile peoples, astride frontiers, may yet provoke armed hostilities. Some of our states—Israel, South Africa—may be considered relatively status quo powers, whereas others—the Arabs with reference to Israel, Argentina with reference to Brazil—are more legitimately characterized as revisionist states.

Population

Leaving aside for the moment current widespread assumptions about the inherent difficulties in gauging power in the contemporary world, a large population would still appear virtually a sine qua non for a nation aspiring to great, if not middle, power ranking.[13] But, Venice, Portugal, and Britain were earlier imperial maritime exceptions, and though it has recently been assumed that a closer fit had arisen between power and population, the long-range impact of technological dynamics upon that question is yet to be determined.[14]

Regarding population, our cases again vary significantly. These differences constitute wholly different classes of nations, as one moves from India with 700 million people to Israel with 3 million. India, Nigeria, Indonesia, Egypt—also beleaguered Pakistan—have large populations (though there, too, a vast range) that among other factors renders their occupation by foreign military forces nearly impossible. Egypt's population is a key element in the Middle Eastern conflict equation, a fact that cannot be ignored by Israel; India's size grants New Delhi a now seemingly irreversible advantage over a divided Pakistan. Nigeria's and Brazil's populations are important elements in support of their regional hegemonic claims. Pakistan and Argentina, with large but still inferior populations relative to their chief regional competitors, have reason to be concerned about permanent conventional military inferiority. They are prodded to consider equalizers not readily available through alliance politics. For different reasons, Israel, white South Africa, and Saudi Arabia all have populations insufficient for their perceived security requirements. In the former two cases they are apparently pursuing nuclear arms as compensation. Riyadh, instead, has chosen to rely on surrogate (effectively mercenary) forces from population-rich countries, such as Pakistan.[15]

Israel almost maximizes its population resources with its reserve system and high ratio of military expenditures to GNP. Egypt and South Korea have not followed suit even in the face of a very serious threat because of competing economic goals. Somalia's small population puts it at a serious disadvantage vis-à-vis Ethiopia. Just as Somalia attempted to take advantage of Ethiopia's temporary internal chaos in 1977-1978, so has Iraq done the same after the shah's military machine was left to wither; in both cases, the long-term population advantage is, however, likely to be telling. In some cases, however, where external threats are not currently menacing, large internal populations—Indonesia, Brazil, India, Nigeria—may constitute a burdensome control problem requiring what would otherwise be outsized military establishments. Libya, on the other hand, is seriously hampered in extending its sway over North Africa and the Middle East because its population is so small. Nor is the pool of technically trained talent large enough to take advantage of the modern military equipment bought by its oil revenues. Witness the downing of two Libyan aircraft by American jets in August 1981.

Population size, GNP, and per capita GNP are germane to an explanation of varied LDC capabilities for indigenous weapons development or production.[16] Small nations with advanced albeit small scientific establishments and relatively high per capita GNP may have advanced indigenous military-design capability (note Israel's own aircraft and missiles), but they lack the comprehensive industrial infrastructure necessary for autarkic production.[17] This forces them to rely extensively on imported components that, as demonstrated by the case of Iran, can be a point of dangerous external dependence. Some large nations with low per capita GNPs—India, Pakistan, Brazil—still have significant technological-scientific establishments. Their size can allow for elaborate weapons-production complexes once the requisite technology is in hand. Egypt, Nigeria, and Indonesia, however, have so far not arrived even at the first rung on that ladder. Iraq, meanwhile, marries a fairly significant technological infrastructure (with a medium population of over 10 million) to its ocean of oil revenues, so it is not surprising that it is considered likely to become the first Arab nuclear power despite the setback administered by Israel in destroying the Osirak reactor in June 1981.

Saudi Arabia's small population and large space create control problems and facilitate internal political upheaval. Israel's small population—and its urban concentration—is habitually cited as a potential liability in a later possible Middle Eastern nuclear balance of terror; Egypt, despite the concentration of its population in the Nile Delta, is here counted as having an advantage regarding dispersal and relative vulnerability to casualties.

Population size, extended to national pain thresholds, may determine a nation's willingness to absorb various levels of casualties, though this will depend on the situation, the political culture, and also the context in which the crisis is handled. One notes the U.S. experience in Vietnam, where such a pain threshold seems to have constituted a crucial variable, favoring a determined Hanoi. Israel has an extreme sensitivity to casualties, one perhaps yet to be matched by South Africa. Less clear are the implications for only somewhat larger Syria or Saudi Arabia. Cuba's willingness to absorb some casualties in Angola and Ethiopia for causes removed from its own immediate security needs evidences a higher pain threshold. Iraq's Hussein, on the other hand, has appeared highly sensitive to casualties in his Iranian war. He has relied on such cautious tactics as heavy and protracted artillery bombardments to wear down Iranian resistance and has eschewed direct assaults against well-defended positions.

The educational levels of a population will also contribute to its security capabilities. Israel and India appear to have developed considerable competence in maintaining and operating advanced equipment, allowing for rapid turn-around and repair of damaged systems during combat and a high-percentage rate of actually in-service equipment. These capabilities lower their vulnerability to arms embargoes during conflict. Iran and Saudi Arabia, however, appear to have developed near-total dependence on seconded U.S. personnel. Their departure in the Iranian case has been evident in the war with Iraq.[18] Information on the actual readiness status of major weapons systems in Indonesia, Egypt (reported by Lyons and Ben-Dor), and numerous other LDCs alerts us to be cautious in mechanically translating military orders of battle into combat effectiveness and staying power.

Resources

Resources also factor into our comparative analysis, both as they relate to military power (or weakness) and to a nation's strategic value to others. Regarding the latter, the importance and tempting vulnerability of oil-rich Saudi Arabia, Iraq, Iran, Nigeria, et al. needs no further elaboration. Morocco's phosphates, Zaire's copper and cobalt, South Africa's numerous metals including gold and uranium, and Guinea's bauxite are additional examples. Such seeming blessings can largely define a nation's security environment.

Resources can of course be vital sinews of war, at least insofar as the actors in question actually produce their own weapons. Most of our LDCs do not. They import finished weapons or their components from abroad, and few if any contemplate protracted conflicts where cut-offs of raw materials or food might determine outcomes. It is not clear whether this generalization will hold forever. Israel and South Africa both fear being deprived of petroleum during conflict; the same fear animates Pakistan, which, even if friendly to OPEC regimes, is very vulnerable to a naval blockade. Cuba, too, is susceptible to blockade (particularly regarding food), and so is Taiwan. Then too, some apparent aspirants to the nuclear club—Israel, Iraq, Libya, and South Korea—are dependent on others for raw uranium, and their quest may be a looming item of diplomatic calculation. Witness Libya's designs on Chad and Arab solicitation of Niger.

**Internal Politics, Societal Cleavages, and Regime Types:
Impact on National Security**

The structure of a nation's internal politics and government will of course be important to its security posture. It will also affect its perception of security threats and the international environment at large.[19] Our various chapter contributions evoke such comparisons according to types of regime (totalitarian, authoritarian, or democratic), the extent and severity of internal political cleavages (race, ethnicity, religion, class, caste, and the like), the importance of reigning ideologies, the impact of interest groups and public opinion, civil-military relations, inter-service rivalries, and bureaucratic politics. Only the surface of such matters may be touched upon in relationship to national-security strategies, but the range of possibilities provided by our sample warrants some commentary.

It would appear obvious that the lower the level of internal cohesiveness and harmony within a nation, and the higher the threat of revolution or dissidence, the more a regime's attention and resources must be devoted to internal rather than external security. One striking finding of our comparative inquiries is in fact the number of key LDCs whose ruling elites do now perceive internal-security matters as at least equally if not more worrisome than external threats and who have designed and deployed their forces accordingly. South Africa, Nigeria, Indonesia, Brazil, Argentina, and Iran surely fit such a description, while Cuba, Iraq, Egypt, Syria, and Pakistan have sufficiently serious internal problems that they require extensive attention by the military. If Israel and India—which are the closest to liberal democracies in this sample—fall outside this category, they are also not strangers to internal disaffection.

Some—Iraq, Syria, Pakistan, Nigeria, Iran, South Africa—have very serious internal ethnic and/or religious cleavages that impact significantly on national-security perspectives. Syria and Iraq, governed by rival wings of the Baath Arab Socialist party, have beleaguered ruling groups that are a distinct minority within their own countries, respectively threatened by Sunni and Shi'ite religious minorities. Iran, Pakistan, and Nigeria are complex multi-ethnic societies held together precariously despite age-old rivalries, feuds, and hatreds. Indonesia, Egypt, Argentina, and Brazil have serious internal problems that appear based more on economic-class and related ideologies than on religion or ethnicity, though here, too, Egypt's fundamentalist Muslims and Copts and Indonesia's peripheral—non-Javan—populations provide cross-cutting complications. In many of these cases not only must military forces restrain or suppress potential or actual dissidence, but there is also the question of the military's own national representativeness as an anchor of national cohesiveness. Nigeria's Muslim-dominated officers' corps, Syria's Alawite elite, Pakistan's Punjabi military caste, and Iraq's Sunni-based officers' corps (also its regionally—Takrit—concentrated elite) are all examples of asymmetric representation at upper levels that are the seeds of potentially serious internal problems. Generally, the political role of the military appears nearly omnipresent and characteristically is very important; as Lyon points out for Indonesia, there may in some cases simply be no reasonable alternative.

Cuba and Vietnam are of course Communist systems where, although the party apparat controls the army, present elites are all veterans of revolutionary wars and retain essential self-images as soldiers. Pakistan, Argentina, Brazil, and Indonesia have authoritarian military regimes, though in no case with long-established traditions. The latter four states have had recent coups in which predominantly civilian regimes were overthrown. Iraq and Syria are run by soldiers who have effected a fusion between ideologically based parties and the military, somewhat distinct from the Soviet model. Egypt, where government is headed by a military man, is seen by Ben-Dor as moving gingerly toward controlled democracy; Nigeria's former military rulers have, at least for the time being, returned to their barracks to give civilian constitutional democracy a chance. India and Israel are exceptions here again, though the latter has seen many high political posts gained by heroes from earlier wars. India's early postwar government appeared somewhat antimilitary until the Chinese assault in 1962, and it has maintained the cleanest demarcation of all between the civilian and the military with its retention of British forms. Among the Arab states, Saudi Arabia has perhaps seen the least military influence over politics, though the extended ruling family spans and transcends civil and military apparatuses.

In some cases, a blurring of traditional military and civilian functions has occurred. As Lyon demonstrates, the Indonesian military has gotten heavily involved in running nationalized business enterprises. This circumstance has made the measurement of Indonesia's defense budget more difficult. In Cuba and elsewhere, military forces are used for civic action and for nation-building; in Israel, paramilitary settlement groups have long been used for border defense and early warning.

Inter-service rivalries are of importance in many of these countries. In some cases there are well beyond the usual and expected conflicts over budgetary allocations familiar everywhere. Of course, many have geographically determined asymmetries of importance and influence, as where land-army requirements may be overriding. Yet, the Israeli navy apparently grew in prestige after the 1973 war because of its unambiguous successes. Argentina's navy has played an important role in the nation's politics because of rivalry with Brazil over the Plata estuary. However, despite Indonesia's basically seaward external-defense posture, the army has apparently retained overwhelming influence because of its crucial role in internal control. The example of pre-World War II Japan still stands, of course, as an example of how the outcomes of inter-service rivalries can determine overall national military strategies.[20]

Some of our contributions—and the contrasts portrayed by them—point to significant broad differences in cultural perspectives on war and conflict that in turn influence security policies and behavior. This is not of course the first time such a linkage has been adduced. Some analysts discern a way of war different from the Clausewitzian tradition of European security diplomacy in its emphasis on total war. Scott Boorman has provided an analysis of Chinese strategic/cultural perspectives related to the game of wei' ch'i, which emphasizes the fluidity and the interminability of conflict, an emphasis also attributed of late to Vietnamese strategy.[21] Here, one treads warily into the domain of national character (obliquely termed political culture in recent years), an area of research now usually treated as virtually off limits by Western social scientists.[22]

These cultural differences and their impact on national strategy merit further investigation. Post-shah Iran appears heavily influenced by religion, and its behavior seems significantly divorced from Western practice. Iran's recent diplomacy prior to and during its conflict with Iraq reinforces this impression. India's earlier "neutralism" under Nehru is perhaps a more familiar pacifism, reminiscent of recent Scandinavian approaches to war. Arab assumptions about a ubiquitous Israeli threat, and Nigeria's seemingly seriously held perception of a South African threat to the north of Africa may or may not also be attributed to somewhat specific cultural factors.[23] It may be difficult to identify an Indonesian, Egyptian, or Cuban way of war, but the Iran-Iraq conflict does appear to bespeak an almost nihilistic fatalism: both sides absorb enormous material damage for what would appear to be only marginal gains in a struggle that is likely to be long in light of past animosities and those reinforced by the hostilities initiated by Iraq in 1980. Do these various cultural differences suggest that deterrence as we know it may operate differently elsewhere, perhaps as well at the nuclear as at conventional levels? If so, we will need a more empirically based theory of deterrence than we now have.[24]

Security Policies of Emerging States: Implications for Regional and Global Security

The discussion has centered so far on several critical determining variables of state security that merit increased attention by practitioners and students. We turn now to an examination of some of the implications of the security policies being pursued by states for regional and global security. In looking at the broader ramifications of individual state security behavior, we will be treating these policy initiatives and responses as if they were independent variables. The preceding discussions and accumulated knowledge in security studies clearly indicate that security policy and behavior of developing states are themselves shaped by a host of factors. Nevertheless, these policies assume a life of their own as they are the causal link between the needs and preferences of a nation and its elites who articulate and execute its security policies and the external environment that is supposed to be shaped to conform to these needs and preferences. It is useful to distinguish between the general environmental factors shaping a country's security policies (Phase I of figure 1-1 of the first chapter) and the outcomes of those policies (Phase III), on the one hand, and the security policies themselves (Phase II), on the other, as a distinct level of activity. These policies act as intervening variables, linking the environment with outcomes that are of interest to security analysts and decision makers. If these policies could be simultaneously mapped for all states, we would have a better profile of regional security regimes and a better sketch of the international security system than we now have. Since there is no world government capable of asserting its will on recalcitrant states, the efforts of these states to project coercive power abroad to influence each other's behavior, are the surrogate for such a universal government. In generalizing only across a limited number of cases in terms of the dimensions of security policy developed in chapter 1, we cannot pretend to present a comprehensive picture of the security system of the world community as a whole or even in its principal parts, but such a comparative approach contributes to such a design and is worth pursuing.

Assumptions about the International System
and Threat Perception

None of the states reviewed by this book are satisfied with the regional and global security regimes of which they are a part. All find them constraining and hostile; most (perhaps with the exception of Israel and South Africa) find them illegitimate. At the most general level of analysis, what one finds is a fundamental conflict between states and their ruling elites over how their regions and the world should be organized. This proliferation of contending views, rooted in the anarchy of the international system, is itself a major source of military conflict. Religion shapes the world views of some, like Iran, and to some degree Pakistan and Israel. Interreligious differences between divergent Muslim sects disrupts Iraqi-Iranian relations. Other states are moved by secular ideologies, like the opposing Baath socialist parties in control of Syria and Iraq or communist-led Vietnam and Cuba. Race divides South Africa from its black African neighbors, and it galvanizes Nigeria to reject any international order that tolerates apartheid and to threaten diplomatic pressures and oil boycotts against any state that cooperates with Pretoria. India and Brazil, dominant states within their respective regions, much like Nigeria, identify a satisfactory order as one in which only they exercise regional hegemonic sway and enjoy enhanced global status.

Under such a competitive condition, regional and global security are fundamentally uncertain, indeterminate, and volatile. What may appear fixed and final for a state—its security aims and policies—must be viewed as essentially contingent, fluid, and changing over time since no one state or even a group of states has the power to determine the security environment to fit its image. Only an approximation can be hoped for. Whatever control that is exercised is provisional since it is under constant challenge by revolutionary, political, technological, and military forces at work within the international system.

Traditional rivalries overlay new claims to reinforce grievances against individual states and the prevailing international order. Iranian-Iraqi differences are certainly not new, but they gain in intensity and scope when religious and personal cleavages are added to long-standing quarrels over boundaries, territories, or aspirations for regional dominance. Vietnam's expansion into Cambodia and Laos is a return to old habits. What is novel is the ideological justification to rationalize and to give impetus to the extension of Vietnamese rule in Southeast Asia. In many ways, the oldest claims of all are those of Israelis who insist on regaining a place in the Middle East where their ancestors once lived. These assertions of right run contrary to no less vigorously asserted Arab claims that are mixed with attacks on Israel as a tool of Western colonialism.

The security aims of one nation are the security threats of another. Correspondingly, the security aims sought by a state are the basis on which it defines the threats to its security. Threat perceptions tend to fall into two categories that are often confused. The first refers to national or state goals, whatever the regime in power or the ideology—religious or secular—that is dominant. The Iraqi demands over Shatt al Arab or the Arab opposition to Israel's existence or its occupation of territories conquered in the Six-Day War would likely persist even if Israel's government changed or if its political constitution were radically altered. The same can be said of the India-Pakistan dispute, where a succession of Pakistani and Indian regimes have all manifested mutual hostility and fear of each other.

What is particularly characteristic of the current international-security order is the perceived threat that some political regimes, often simply because they exist, pose for other regimes of a different political persuasion, although they are physically unable to present a direct physical threat to a nation. Iran's Khomeini can apparently be assured only if the Muslim states return to theocratic rule under Shi'ite direction. Only Communist states in Cambodia and Laos will satisfy Hanoi. Similarly, Cuba's security is viewed as dependent on the export of its revolution to the Third World. The existence of socialist- or capitalist-oriented states, closely tied to the West and specifically to the United States, is considered a threat to the success of the Cuban revolution. The security of Castro's Cuba is seen to depend finally on the victory of the Moscow-led socialist camp. Nigeria, its security interests defined by racial consciousness and the experience of white colonial rule, views South Africa as a threat although Pretoria does not have the means to challenge Nigeria directly.

As noted previously, internal security also dominates the concern of many elites. Although domestic challenges to rule are often characterized by the ruling regime as externally generated, much of the military preparations of the governments of Brazil, Argentina, South Africa, and Indonesia are aimed at controlling domestic rivals. Charges of U.S. interference in Iranian affairs and competition between groups over which of them could demand more of Washington for the release of the American hostages testified to the shakiness of the Teheran government. Internal divisions are projected as external-security threats and rival factions are identified as being in collusion with foreign powers or, unwittingly, in their service. On the other hand, the ruling regime in Iraq is caught between two fires. It would prefer a more sympathetic regime in Teheran that would not incite Shi'ite Muslims against their Sunni-dominated government. On the other hand, Baghdad was checked by internal division from launching an all-out attack against Iran out of fear that large casualties might topple the Hussein regime. The Pakistani and Syrian regimes also have difficulty in distinguishing between the threats to the ruling elites and to their nations. In contrast to Israel whose security problems are exclusively external (if problems with the occupied territories are excluded), South Africa's security problems are almost totally internal, although arms shipments to dissidents and the possibility of foreign assistance in the form of Cuban advisors cannot be excluded.

What also becomes clearer from a review of the security policies of developing states is the crucial importance of the superpower balance and superpower behavior to the security objectives of these diverse states spread around the globe. Although each initially defines its security problem in regional terms, all frame those problems and the strategies that they pursue to resolve them by reference to the superpowers. This volume has emphasized the diffusion of military capabilities and the decentralization of initiative in security policy, but this accent should not obscure the pervasive reach of Moscow and Washington and their impact on the security behaviors of lesser states. The larger point is that neither the smaller nor the larger states have control of either their bilateral security struggles or of regional conflicts elsewhere that affect these regional or global contests. In one sense, Cuba and Hanoi are surrogates of Moscow, but as Robbins and Simon suggest each acts independently to achieve security aims that have not always been consistent with Moscow's timetable or interests. Neither the Iran of the shah or of Khomeini is able to do without the United States either as protector or as the object of its security concerns. Israelis agree, as Reich notes, that Israel's security depends critically on American assistance and support, yet Israel's security policies lie beyond Washington's full control.

On the other hand, Egypt has only belatedly realized that encouraging a flexible Israeli bargaining posture is likely to be achieved more readily through pressures exerted on Washington than through the search for military victory on the battlefield against Israel.

The international security system is neither bipolar nor multipolar but, paradoxically, both at once. Instability arises from the tension between them. At the nuclear level, it is predominantly bipolar, although increasing proliferation poses a long-term challenge to superpower dominance. At the subnuclear level, other states have considerable influence, accounting for the widely commented-on phenomenon of the weak manipulating the strong to do their bidding. Under these circumstances it is very difficult to maintain a stable global security system defined as the absence of hostilities or the minimization of the scope and intensity of violence if hostilities erupt. The diffusion of military capabilities and the decentralization of initiative in threatening or using these capabilities increase the chances for armed confrontations more than ever before. The superpowers view with alarm the loss of any state or its military capabilities and potential to the camp of the other. On the other hand, regional and local actors possess increasing leverage over the security behavior of the superpowers in the form of base rights, diplomatic and economic support (for example, monetary aid and oil), ideological affinity, or the military utility of their armed forces. Thus, local conflicts or changes in regime (Afghanistan, for example) threaten to draw the superpowers into a dispute and to raise the specter of a nuclear confrontation, as in the case of the Cuban missile crisis. How these emerging alignments threaten international stability will become clearer in the following discussion of arms transfers.

Military Doctrines and Strategies

Anyone looking for universally applied military doctrines propounded by the states under examination will have to look hard to find threads of commonality. Diversity appears to be more the rule than the exception. Sometimes, such doctrines may be made wholly explicit; other times they are merely implied. If explicit, as Myers demonstrates for Brazil, it may be at a very general, albeit still revealing, level, involving strictures about the relationships between military postures, economic development, and internal political cohesion; for Argentina similar doctrines may vary depending upon who is in power, since they are to reflect internal political ideologies rather than responses to external threats.

In some cases—Israel, Pakistan—geographic and demographic realities and the lessons of past wars may prompt near-formal doctrines at a mixed strategic and tactical level. Both countries must rely on rapid military mobilization and preemptive strikes, if threatened, to keep the fighting away from major-population centers located uncomfortably close to contested borders. Here, one sees short-war strategies and doctrines reminiscent of the pre-World-War I German Schlieffen doctrine and for similar reasons. For Israel, as with Germany in 1914, there is a still more specific strategic doctrine that stresses the necessity of concentrating against the strongest foe first in a two-front war; for Egypt and Syria, there is a doctrinal emphasis on taking and holding territory to allow time for external diplomatic intervention and to force Israel into attrition warfare, a mirror image of the latter's strategy. Generally, in the Arab-Israel, Iraq-Iran, and Pakistan-India contexts, changes in weapons technology and oscillations in advantage between offense and defense prompt contrasting short-war and attrition strategies. Israel's blitzkrieg preemptive doctrine, successfully applied in 1967 after a pattern first used in World War II, proved less viable after the advent of newer precision guided munitions (PGM) weaponry, particularly regarding SAMs and anti-tank missiles.

Some LDC military doctrines may appear truly indigenous, being shaped by strategic circumstances; Israel's doctrines, whatever their successes and failures, appear to fit that description. Others, however, appear to be derivative, largely borrowed from major-power mentors. Ben-Dor notes that Egypt had relied earlier on cumbersome Soviet military doctrine, stressing cautious and massive preparations before offensive operations. The uncritical adoption of Soviet methods may well have contributed to its failure to exploit its initial successes in 1973. In 1980, Iraq also appeared to adhere to Soviet doctrine, relying excessively on the attrition effect of artillery bombardments. The Hussein regime's apparent concern to minimize the domestic political impact of casualties as well as logistical constraints seem also to have played a role.

In some cases—Vietnam, Cuba—sentimental attachment to old guerrilla-war doctrines may or may not affect rational force structuring and military strategies in the altered circumstances of post anticolonial or revolutionary wars. Iranian leaders now look to guerrilla-warfare doctrine to cope with their sudden disadvantage, which appears to dictate attrition strategies. Up to the shah's demise, Iran based its regional strategy essentially on the rising technological skill of a standing professional army, overlaying the legacies of past force structuring. The hostility of elements of the officer corps to the Iranian revolution raised into serious question a strategy aiming at regional dominance and a modernized technologically advanced force structure keyed to this hegemonial objective. It is no accident that the current emphasis in Iranian thinking on revolutionary warfare corresponds to the internal political needs of segments of the revolutionary leadership to restructure the armed forces to assure their loyalty and to counter outside aggression.

The increasing sophistication of armaments in the developing world should not obscure the importance of the large land armies. These remain the backbone of most emerging military powers. Except for Israel and perhaps India, none have been able to develop their air forces or navies and to coordinate their missions with those of land forces in building a truly balanced, modern armed-service system. Manpower still weighs more heavily than machines. Machines are likely to be more important in the future. Egypt displayed impressive skill in managing the Suez crossing in the "Yom Kippur War." Iraq's attack on Iran, whatever its military shortcomings, would have been thought impossible a decade ago; also, Iran's capacity to use some of its high-technology weaponry, like jet aircraft, has surprised many foreign observers.

Until recently, solely conventional military doctrines accounted for the bulk of relevant questions regarding the strategies of our sample of LDCs. Now, however, the long relatively stable nuclear nonproliferation regime shows signs of unraveling, as Israel, South Africa, Pakistan, India, and Iraq threaten to go over the threshold, and as others—Argentina, Brazil, Libya, Taiwan, South Korea—loom menacingly in the background. It now becomes reasonable to begin to anticipate *nuclear* doctrines for emerging atomic powers in terminology heretofore reserved for the superpower nuclear balance: preemptive first strike, second-strike deterrence and pro-portional deterrence, massive retaliation or a "trip-wire," selective or escalated deterrence, launch-on-warning, deterrence by uncertainty, and MAD (mutual assured destruction).

In some cases—Israel, South Africa, Pakistan—nuclear doctrines are hinged on last-resort circumstances, where catastrophic conventional battle-field defeats are anticipated because of unredeemable quantitative im-balances. For Taiwan and South Korea, the mere threat to go nuclear is a useful item of leverage in assuring continued U.S. support, regarding ade-quate arms supplies if not also a military umbrella. India contemplates nuclear weapons both to deter China's larger nuclear force and to have a hedge against Pakistani acquisition of an equalizer. Israel apparently seeks some minimal deterrence vis-à-vis the Soviet Union as an underpinning of its deterrence against Arab conventional assaults. It may also yet come to rely heavily on a tactical-nuclear-weapons arsenal in an attempt to make credible a doctrine of escalated deterrence. If an Islamic bomb should become a reality—in Libya, Iraq, Saudi Arabia, or several Arab countries jointly—MAD may reign over the Arab-Israeli conflict, perhaps also pro-viding an umbrella for increased Arab reliance on conventional forces as both sides recognize the virtual nullification and disutility of their atomic weapons. Superpower threats of sanctions against LDC nuclear use, say in Israel or South Africa, could also prompt development of launch-on-warning doctrines in the latter or at least the use of continuous airborne patrols by nuclear-armed aircraft. Generally, in the next decade, it is likely that several new nuclear powers will emerge, all of which will face the difficult problem of harmonizing conventional- and nuclear- security doctrines. While this integration process evolves, pressures are also likely to build up for regional arms-control arrangements, similar to the nuclear weapons free zone proposed by the Israeli government to stem the introduction of nuclear weapons into the Middle East.

Announced Strategies and Coordination of Policy Instruments

Distinguishing between a state's operational and announced strategies is always difficult. Access to the security-policy process in developing states for study, when compared with the Western democracies, is obviously less readily available. The exaggerated rhetoric employed by many of the LDCs in advancing their demands or in threatening military force complicates the sorting process. Nasser's bravado helped precipitate the Six Day War. He counted on Soviet support and Western inaction to assure his blockade of Aqaba. He did not expect a preemptive Israeli strike and the quick defeat of his forces. On the other hand, India maintained a low military profile until the early 1960s that apparently encouraged attack on its interests. Its lack of preparedness, which corresponded to the neutralist, pacifist leanings of its foreign- and security-policy pronouncements, facilitated the successful Chinese offensive in 1962. The defeat inflicted by China prompted the abandonment of India's former even-handedness. Its military forces were augmented and modernized; its security ties with the Soviets were expanded as Moscow supplied advanced weapons and know-how; and its operational military posture shifted from a defense to an attack orientation. The fruits of these shifts were evident in its crushing defeat of Pakistani forces in 1971. Although it protests its defensive posture against the possibility of a resurgent Pakistan or an expanding China, it essentially pursues a hegemonic policy in South Asia keyed to its conventional military superiority over Pakistan and its possession of nuclear weapons to deter either Pakistani or Chinese attacks.

Where LDCs have shown resourcefulness is in the use of their economic resources, principally oil, in advancing their security interests. For a variety of reasons, including growing resource and monetary interdependence and the alleged, and still arguable, decline in the usability of interventionary force by major powers, small-power manipulation of international economic levers in their pursuit of security has become more frequent. This has become a *peacetime* phenomenon, and, as such, it a rather recent break with laissez-faire practices, which, a generation ago, separated security and economic domains.[25]

The OPEC states, particularly their Arab grouping, have used the oil weapon in various ways to combat Israel through embargoes and indirectly through high prices. Without the Sinai oilfields the cost of oil has become a major security dilemma for Israel. Oil diplomacy has been used to deny the United States strategic-basing access (Spain, Italy, West Germany, and so forth) usable for arms resupply to Israel. OPEC investments in the developed world, its nations' aid programs, and its nations' positions in the IMF and World Bank all have been used to pursue politico-military objectives. Increasingly, the obvious trend toward restructuring the global monetary system in the post-Bretton Woods era augurs enhanced possibilities of this sort. Witness the squabble over PLO observer status in the IMF in relation to Arab oil countries' financial donations to that institution. Nigeria's oil wealth has become an increasingly potent source of leverage vis-à-vis South Africa; the latter's gold and other resources have constituted some relatively lesser leverage in the West and the Middle East. Iraq has used various economic levers, including arms purchases and oil, to pry nuclear technology from Western Europe; earlier, the shah's Iran had attempted to force nuclear-technology transfers through its financial participation in European uranium-fuel ventures.

Resource Allocation, Public Support,
and Civil-Military Relations

However impressive the military capabilities may be of the emerging states of our study, none of them is independently able to marshal from indigenous means the economic and technological resources needed to build and maintain a modern military establishment. As the next section on alignments, alliances, and security processes indicates, these states are prompted to articulate global and regional strategies to assure needed access to military equipment and technology. Inter-state relations are thus driven by what might be called the politics of the interdependence of independence. At a national level, all of the states examined in this volume are pursuing the goal of national military and economic autarky but paradoxically the success of this effort hinges on their ability to manipulate those on whom they depend for economic, military, and technological assistance. Thus, as global and regional security become more diffuse and decentralized, the network linking states within and across regions becomes more intricate and complex, a point that will become clearer in the third section of this chapter.

What appears evident is that none of the states under discussion, with the exception perhaps of India in its early years before the 1962 war with China, have been willing to sacrifice military preparedness for economic development. Indeed, at considerable cost, they have sacrificed investment opportunities and consumer goods to maintain and continually upgrade their large military forces. Egypt spends more than 20 percent of its GNP on military expenditures; similarly, Israel, India, Pakistan, and Vietnam devoted large amounts of their small GNPs to defense. Cuba must be subsidized by the Soviet Union to maintain its extensive troop commitments abroad. The oil-rich states appear no less willing, as the shah's Iran demonstrated, to spend much of their revenues on building their military establishments at the expense of economic development and of improving the lot of their citizenry.

Arms-production facilities have received high priority in spending. Several states, like India, Brazil, and Argentina, claim that economic development will actually be spurred by advances in military technology and production. Given the drive by these countries to sell these arms, Israel and other arms-producing states (Taiwan, for example) are transforming the traditional argument of guns v. butter into the claim of butter because of guns. Military expenditures are thus viewed as a contribution to economic growth and not as a drain on national resources. A consequence of these rationalizations is to enlist the argument for economic development into the service of building larger and more sophisticated military systems.

The problem of generating public support for the nation's security policies is managed in various ways by the states of our study. As the discussion in the first part of this chapter indicates, almost all of them face critical problems of internal cohesion. Except perhaps for Egypt and Israel, the Middle East states are as much divided against themselves as against each other. Egypt has demonstrated a remarkable ability to shift orientations over time without damage to the ruling elite (which is dominated by a strong presidential figure). Israel has succeeded through democratic processes to hold its population together in confronting the Arab menace, but internal criticism is often sharp and its open system is a temptation for adversaries to manipulate. Several states, Iran most prominently, have relied on foreign threats to elicit domestic support, but in exporting revolution abroad it has ironically encouraged attack upon itself. Other weak regimes are tempted to employ the same tactics with the result that regional- and global-security politics are likely to become even more volatile.

A word should also be said about civil-military relations. In a majority of the cases discussed in this volume, the states are under direct military control. Israel, India, South Africa, Cuba, and Vietnam are exceptions although the ideological (Vietnam and Cuba) and racial (South Africa) motivations of civilian rulers often dispose them to use force more readily than regimes dominated by the military. Egypt and Nigeria appear to be emerging from tight military rule and are turning cautiously to more open processes. The others—Pakistan, Indonesia, Iraq, Syria, Brazil, and Argentina—are under firm military control. It is difficult to predict the implications of the character of a regime, whether it is military or not, on its external security behavior. More work needs to be done in this area.

Alignments and Alliances

The security environments of the LDCs under review are heavily influenced by their—and their rivals'—alliances and more informal alignments. Changing perceptions of those environments drive ever-changing new alignments. Such ties—formal, informal, implicit, or latent—may determine to the extent they are credible or operable the degree of support and protection a small state can expect in crises, particularly if it is in danger of being overrun and destroyed. Usually, a dependent nation's arms-transfer patterns will also be highly correlated with its security alignments and the closer such ties, the more likely that arms resupply (replacements, spare parts) will be assured in the event of protracted conflict.

The experiences and behavior of the countries discussed in the preceding chapters vary greatly with respect to alliance ties and arms supply. Some—Cuba and Vietnam—have close formal alliances with the Soviet Union, interlaced by arms transfers and heavy doses of economic aid. For their support the Soviets have received important basing facilities. Whereas Syria, Iraq, and India also have formal ties with Moscow, their more independent postures have resulted in a more diversified, cross-bloc arms-acquisitions pattern. This is certainly true in the Indian and Iraqi cases, less so for Damascus. It is difficult to say whether the credibility of protection afforded by the Soviet Union is correspondingly lower; that will depend on specific circumstances. Note the Soviets' hesitant support of Iraq v. Iran while offering no criticism of resupply by Czechoslovakia and North Korea. Syria, too, according to Rabinovich, has a "security guarantee" from the Soviet Union, but it is not clear whether this would be as applicable to a conflict with Iraq as with Israel.

Israel and Saudi Arabia, meanwhile, are commonly considered informal allies of the United States (the so-called Carter doctrine also applies to the latter), although the United States might one day have to choose between its clients in a direct military conflict as it was asked to do in the Greek-Turkish confrontation. The U.S. security guarantee, whose credibility often appears in question, hinges on the crucial importance of Saudi Arabian oil to the United States. Ties with Israel are more complex and rest on sentiment, perceived moral obligation, domestic political imperatives, and strategic considerations.

Some of the LDCs, of course, rely neither on formal alliances nor even on implicit security arrangements, though that does not necessarily preclude big-power support in a crisis. Nigeria seems resolutely positioned about midway between the blocs, tilting occasionally one way or the other. Neither under civilian nor military rule has it forgotten Soviet support during its civil war. South Africa, once part of the Western camp, now seems entirely cast adrift, but the importance of its resources might yet elicit Western support in a crisis. Argentina and Brazil, while still formally members of the presently moribund Rio Pact, appear moving toward neutrality and nonalignment but could probably still rely on the remnants of the Monroe Doctrine under certain circumstances. Indonesia drifts toward U.S. protection in the face of the Vietnamese threat while Pakistan, once a charter member of SEATO and CENTO, does not appear eager to revive the nearly lapsed U.S. security commitment and also slides toward a nonaligned position.

The nations most closely tied to one or the other superpower—Cuba, Vietnam, Israel—acquire virtually all of their arms from them. Some LDCs, tilting toward the West but with looser ties to the United States, split their arms purchases between U.S. and European sources. Argentina, Brazil, Saudi Arabia, and Indonesia fit this pattern. Others—Iraq, Syria, India—receive most of their arms from the Soviet Union, but some from the West, attaining some valuable leverage in the bargain. Syria, very recently, has appeared to shift back toward its former preponderant reliance on the Soviets. Under the shah Iran was on the reverse side of that pattern. Pakistan is somewhat of an anomaly. It splits its purchases between the United States, Europe, and China, in great measure because of its earlier experiences with embargoes applied by the United States and Britain, beginning with the 1965 war.

Aside, sometimes, from the most advanced and closely held items, many developing states are in a very favorable leverage position for acquiring arms, *dependencia* theories to the contrary notwithstanding. Some of the arms-importing states have the economic wherewithal and diplomatic clout to ensure almost open-ended acquisitions up to and even beyond absorption capacities. The major powers, of course, seek influence, allies, strategic access, resources, and petrodollar recycling in the bargain. Indeed, some of their customers are very heavily wooed with arms. The United States, France, Britain, and West Germany vie for Saudi markets; the Soviet Union and France for Libyan and Iraqi purchases. Sweeteners, that is nuclear reactors, are often used as bait for arms deals, a practice not visibly sidetracked by the London Suppliers' agreement on nuclear-export behavior.

In some cases, however, inherently poor leverage has resulted in difficulties in acquiring arms, and one can here speak of "reluctant" arms-supply relationships. For the most part, this applies to pariah states such as Israel, South Africa, and Taiwan, though some others—Pakistan in particular—have had similar problems. South Africa, now embargoed by all major powers—including, formally, France and Israel—is forced to rely on a combination of indigenous production, some licensed production based on earlier French technology transfers, and very likely a variety of clandestine governmental and private transactions facilitated by Pretoria's gold hoard.

Emerging powers in the developing world, aligned with one or another major power, must develop security strategies based on their evaluations of the credibility of these ties. Their experiences may impel them to deal in worst-case scenarios. In the wake of Vietnam, and in the light of the shah's demise and Taiwan's loss of recognition, many U.S. clients have come to question the reliability of U.S. commitments. American power and will to execute agreements are doubted. Soviet credibility may nowadays be stronger, but as Robbins notes, Cuba has not forgotten what was considered somewhat of an abandonment in 1962, when Moscow faced the threat of nuclear war. On the other hand, the United States did resupply Israel in 1973 after a week of denial, and the Soviets resupplied Egypt and Syria. Moscow followed suit later on Vietnam's behalf in its conflict with China. In cases where significant diplomatic counter-leverage induced caution and restraint, the United States and Great Britain embargoed Pakistan in 1965 and 1971, and the Soviets initially eschewed open resupply of Iraq in 1980.

There are some actual and nascent security alignments among the developing countries themselves, of varying importance in providing military security. Examples are the ties within the Arab League, Pakistan's alignments with Arab states such as Libya (now with a nuclear dimension) and Saudi Arabia, Indonesia's role within ASEAN (Association of South East Asian Nations) vis-à-vis Vietnam, and the earlier tie between Iran and Pakistan (note the joint suppression of Baluchi dissidence). Illustrative, too, was the virtually clandestine cooperation between Israel and the shah's Iran as well as Haile Selassie's Ethiopia.

Developing States and the International Security System: Processes and Outcomes

The nation-state perspective on which this discussion has focused should now be generalized to identify some of the implications of patterned nation-state responses for regional and global security. This marks the third phase of figure 1-1 and is divided into a discussion of security processes and outcomes. First, developing states provide or deny key resources needed by other states in pursuing their security interests. They are therefore increasingly significant actors in several critical security processes.[26] For example, they can: (1) ease or block access to territory, airspace, and sea- and air-support facilities; (2) furnish arms directly to other states from their own growing arsenals, from indigenous production, or from retransfers from other states; (3) intervene directly with their own troops or lend them to allies and clients or make them available for surrogate use by one or another of the developed states; or (4) provide needed economic resources and financing to bolster the defense efforts of other developing countries.

Security Processes and Developing States

Access to Strategic Facilities. Superpower efforts to project their nuclear and conventional forces globally have increased their requirements for an expanding list of access rights to the territory, airspace, and service facilities of developing states. These include bases for air, sea, and ground forces, overflight and landing rights, supply depots, repair facilities, training sites, command, control, and communication stations, satellite tracking and data relay complexes, and port-of-call permissions. The expansion of Soviet air- and sea-lift capacity in pursuit of regional and global security interests has generated new requirements for bases and access rights throughout the Middle East, Africa, and the Indian Ocean. The Soviet Union currently enjoys a variety of access rights to Syria, Libya, Ethiopia, South Yemen, and Angola. Aden, for example, has become a key jumping-off point in furnishing support for Cuban troops in Ethiopia and Angola. South Yemen has also been a useful ferrying point for civilian and military personnel being sent further south in Africa, including Mozambique and Tanzania. Soviet supply of Cuban forces in Africa, for example, has depended on access to these bases. Libya and Ethiopia, meanwhile, have served as forward depots for large volumes of Soviet military equipment being sent to Africa and the Middle East.

In counterpoint, the United States is seeking similar *points d'appuis,* and territorial and airspace privileges in Egypt, Oman, Kenya, and Somalia to sustain a Rapid Deployment Force in the Persian Gulf. In the past these rights might have been acquired for the taking. Nowadays, they must be negotiated with sovereign states jealous of their independence and skilled in bargaining for advantage in exchange for the strategic assets that are made available to other powers. They are able to barter for grants of arms, generous purchase arrangements, access to advanced weaponry, pledges to protect donor interests, economic and technical assistance, diplomatic support, and military-training programs, and even nuclear technology and fissionable materials. Developing states are also seeking their own access rights or are working to deny them to other developed or developing states. Cuba has moved its forces to Angola through Barbados, Guyana, Cape Verde, and Sierra Leone. Indonesia has used Sri Lanka to transfer arms to Pakistan. North Vietnam obtained staging points in Central and South Asia for Soviet arms during the Vietnam War. Iraq recently secured Jordan's consent to the use of the port at Aqaba in order to be resupplied with Soviet arms. In return, Jordan received American tanks and weapons captured from Iran and subsequently dropped its request for such equipment from the United States.

On the other hand, Iran bombed Kuwait to discourage use of that sheikdom's territory to supply Iraq. The Arab oil-producing states have put various degrees of pressure on oil-importing states to deny U.S. use of their territory, such as the Azores, to assist Israel. Somalia apparently forced the Soviet Union to make unauthorized flights over Pakistan and perhaps Egypt and the Sudan in resupplying Ethiopia because Mogadishu was able to exert influence on several Middle East states.[27] Iraq has also reportedly sought to stop the construction of American, British, and French air and naval facilities in Oman, Somalia, Kenya, Djibouti, the Seychelles, and elsewhere with blandishments and threats, but also using economic assistance and oil as inducements.

Arms Transfers. Developing states are also becoming more prominent in global arms transfers. The number of states producing arms has increased as well as the variety of materials that they are capable of supplying. The Stockholm International Peace Research Institute (SIPRI) cites thirty-one states in Africa, Asia, Latin America, and the Middle East that produce arms of some sort. Those producing heavy, complex equipment if only through licenses, have grown dramatically in little over a decade. Between 1965 and 1979, as noted in table 1-6, the number of states producing aircraft jumped from 8 to 16; missiles, from 3 to 9; armored fighting vehicles from 2 to 8; electronic equipment, from 4 to 10; and aircraft engines from 5 to 6.

Five states—China, India, Israel, South Africa, and Brazil—produce weapon systems in each of the categories listed in Table 1-6 and Brazil and Israel have risen to the level of notable arms suppliers. Their receipts are estimated to exceed $500 million. Brazilian Bandeirante troop-transport aircraft have been purchased by Gabon, Uruguay, and Chile; the Xavante ground-attack aircraft have been sold to Paraguay and Togo. France will also purchase fifty Xingu air transports in an $80 million package. Brazilian armored personnel carriers are also being used by Iraq in its war against Iran.

Similarly, Israel has sold military equipment to an increasing number of states. Kfir aircraft would have been sold to Ecuador had not the United States intervened. Israeli small arms supplied Somoza's National Guard before the Sandinista takeover in Nicaragua. Israel and Jordan have sold obsolete armored equipment to Pretoria and it would appear that Israel may have received spare parts for French systems from South Africa during the 1973 war. Meanwhile, India produces an array of potentially marketable equipment ranging from the Kiran ground-attack fighter and Marut fighter bomber to the Vijayanta tank, armored personnel carriers, and artillery pieces. It will also manufacture spare parts for the Jaguar purchased from France and Britain. South Africa has pressed its program of arms-production self-sufficiency forward. It produces missiles and Mirage fighters under French license and a host of smaller arms. A U.N. arms embargo is likely to be frustrated in the short-run by Pretoria's indigenous-production capability.

Rivaling the importance of developing states as arms producers and suppliers is their significance as conduits for arms from other states or as resuppliers of goods bought from developed states. Vietnam is accused by Washington of having sent captured American equipment to aid the El Salvador guerrillas. Somalia has sustained its war against Ethiopia by drawing on Soviet-made equipment from Egypt and Iraq while Ethiopia, formerly an American client and now a Soviet dependency, has allegedly been supplied with U.S.-origin materiél from Yugoslavia, Israel, and Libya. Ignoring Paris's remonstrances, Libya transferred French Mirage aircraft to Egypt during the 1973 war. Iran, whose military machine long relied primarily on U.S. and British equipment (but was also long supplemented by some Soviet arms), has used Libyan and Syrian retransfers of Soviet arms in its conflict with Iraq.

Dispatch of Military Personnel. Almost every one of the states covered in this volume has intervened directly in the affairs of one or more states. India intervened in the Pakistani civil war in Bangladesh. Vietnam has troops throughout the Southeast Asian peninsula. Israel has repeatedly sent its forces on raids to hit PLO camps in Lebanon. Iraq has been a participant in successive Arab-Israeli clashes. Iran under the shah sent military contingents to support the Sultan of Oman against domestic dissidents. Syria keeps troops in Lebanon. Nigerian troops have been sent on peacekeeping missions to Chad. Cuban intervention in Angola and Ethiopia has also been well publicized. South African raids in Mozambique, Zimbabwe before independence, Namibia, and Angola are well known.

Like the Cubans, the Pakistanis have become prominent as provisioners of trained military personnel capable of serving in a variety of countries under widely differing political, geographic, and climatic conditions. The advanced training, professionalism, and discipline of Pakistan's armed forces make them desirable secondaries. There are reportedly twenty-two Pakistani military missions in foreign states.[28] Sizable numbers of troops may have been or are now stationed in Jordan, Libya, Abu Dhabi, and Saudi Arabia. Approximately 10,000 Pakistani military are estimated to be serving abroad. Twice as many are reportedly earmarked for service in Saudi Arabia should the need arise.

Pakistani pilots have been engaged by France to train Arab forces on French Mirages and Pakistanis also flew and serviced Mirage aircraft for Libya and presently fly for Abu Dhabi's air force of 52 combat aircraft, including 26 Mirages.

Small states like Libya are bent on following the Pakistani and Cuban examples, although they have far fewer military-manpower resources. Libyan troops have appeared in Uganda, Chad, and Lebanon; Moroccan forces helped Zaire to repel the invasion of its Shaba province. The dispatch of Pakistani, Cuban, and Libyan troops appears to be only a harbinger of what other developing states will be in a position to emulate as their forces grow in size and capability.

Financing Foreign Military Forces. The vast amounts of funds made available to the oil-producing states have provided them sufficient surplus resources to assist the security and foreign-policy activities of other states. Saudi money supports a wide variety of military activities both of friendly and, in some cases, even rival regimes. Riyadh underwrote part of the expenses of Moroccan intervention in Zaire. It has also financed the purchase of U.S. arms for Egypt (before Camp David), Jordan, Sudan, North Yemen, Morocco, Pakistan, and Tunisia. It has balanced its support of these generally conservative regimes with funds for Somalia, Syria, and the PLO to finance their weapons acquisitions. Libya, Iraq, Kuwait, and Algeria have also lent financial assistance to selected states. Iraq reportedly contributed half a million dollars in logistical support to the Salvadoran rebels.[29] Libya and Algeria contribute arms and economic aid to the Polisario rebels opposed to Moroccan rule of the western Sahara.

The complexity of regional- and global-security support structures defies reduction into North-South or East-West polarities. In Morocco's case, for example, the Hassan II regime receives Saudi, U.S., and French assistance. The Soviet Union, while sending arms to the Polisario via Tripoli and Algiers, has also signed a $2 billion barter agreement with Rabat. Moscow strengthens the Moroccan government in its fight against the Polisario by providing knowhow and technical assistance to Morocco in exchange for phosphates. Meanwhile, the United States is Algeria's major trading partner and chief purchaser of its oil and gas and a major buyer of Libyan crude. Its payment for oil underwrites purchases of Soviet arms for the Polisario.

Developing States and the Security Outcomes

The strategic assets of developing states allow them to exercise more influence than ever before not only over the regional- and global-security processes, but also over their outcomes. They can affect and even determine which parties will prevail in a conflict between states or which group will assume power in another state. This leverage affords them greater say, moreover, over the security agendas of other states, including the saliency of issues and the timing and manner of their articulation, management, and resolution.

Influence over the Outcomes of Interstate Conflict. In the Middle East, it is apparent that neither superpower can dictate to its clients. Although Egypt and Syria received assistance from the Soviet Union in launching their Yom Kippur attack in 1973, both have resisted in different measure Soviet pressures to conform. If Syria has drifted closer to Moscow's camp in the wake of the Iran-Iraq war, Egypt remains an avowed opponent of Soviet expansionism and pursues peace initiatives, commenced at Camp David, that Moscow condemns. Iraq also attacked Iran without apparently securing Moscow's consent to use its arms.

The United States has also been unsuccessful with its clients in the Middle East. Turkey used American military equipment, contrary to American law, in invading Cyprus. The arms embargo imposed by Congress against Ankara had little effect. Washington, not Ankara, eventually backed down when Turkey closed down several United States bases and threatened not only to withdraw from NATO but also to prohibit use of Turkish territory to monitor Soviet missile development. The loss of such facilities in Iran in the wake of the Islamic revolution placed a premium on the Turkish monitoring bases.

Similarly, Israel took matters into its own hands in 1956, 1967, and 1981 without consulting the United States, when it felt its security threatened. In the Suez war it was ultimately induced to withdraw but not before it forced Washington's hand; in the Six Day War its preemptive attack and swift victory precluded Soviet or other foreign intervention; in destroying the Iraqi nuclear reactor and, later, in attacking PLO strongholds in Beirut it acted contrary to Reagan administration wishes, but still weathered Washington's temporary embargo of F16s.

In Asia, North Vietnam and India have exercised considerable influence over their respective subcontinental spheres of influence. North Vietnam conquered its rival in South Vietnam and forcibly integrated the country. Subsequently, it has extended its rule over Cambodia and Laos. In military clashes with China, its former ally, its forces have held the Chinese to a bloody draw.

India also rules over South Asia. Its defeat of Pakistan led directly to the creation of Bangladesh. Its explosion of a nuclear device and its development of a sophisticated arms industry place it in an ascendant regional position, since no other state can effectively challenge its military position.

In the spring of 1980, India signed yet another accord with the Soviet Union for arms, in the amount of $1.6 billion. India will receive MiG-23 jets and T72 tanks as well as MiG-25 reconnaissance planes. In counterpoint, New Delhi also gained approval for the purchase of enriched uranium from the United States despite congressional reservations about the peaceful aims of the Indian program and the absence of effective full-scope safeguards required by U.S. law. Both superpowers recognize India's strategic importance and appear wary of untoward moves that might jeopardize their influence with New Delhi.

Instances can also be cited where Pakistani troops have made a difference in a dispute. Pakistan's president, Mohammed Zia-ul-Haq, had earlier distinguished himself as a military advisor in Jordan, where he commanded a Pakistani brigade during the Jordanian attack against the PLO in 1970.[30]

In Latin America, Cuba plays critical regional and trans-regional roles. It has approximately 40,000 troops serving abroad in eleven countries. Its involvement in Africa is long standing, commencing with a commitment of 300-400 troops to Algeria in the Moroccan-Algerian border dispute of 1963. President Fidel Castro is also supposed to have made contact with Agostinho Neto's MPLA as early as 1964. Support for the MPLA grew to the point of 14,000 Cuban troops being sent to Angola to assist in the fight against remnants of Portuguese colonialism and, later, South African forces and to establish the Neto regime in Angola. Cuban forces, totaling approximately 17,000, have also been instrumental in defending Ethiopia against Somalian incursions in the Ogaden.

In sub-Saharan Africa, Nigeria and South Africa are the principal military powers. South African forces have operated in Angola, Namibia, Mozambique, and Zimbabwe. They are the most powerful military force in southern Africa. Nigeria's oil resources, large population, strategic geographic position, and aspiring regional-leadership role in the Organization of African Unity (OAU) afford it an important voice in African politics and make it an attractive alliance partner. The United States, for example, is currently in debt to Nigeria to the tune of $14 billion, primarily because of the importation of oil. Fifteen percent of U.S. oil imports come from Nigeria. Lagos officials insist that the continuation of good relations with Washington will depend on U.S. policy toward South Africa. Like the Arab oil producers, the Nigerians are threatening to use oil for political purposes, although their objectives differ considerably from those of the Middle East states.

Influence over the Outcomes of Intrastate Conflict. The capacity to influence the kinds of regimes that will govern abroad and, as in Angola or Indochina, to install a government or leadership group in power are additional marks of the growing importance of developing states in international security. If a regional tour of the world is again made, one is impressed by the level of activity of developing states in penetrating politically and intervening militarily in the affairs of other states and the array of security assets at their disposal to shape political events and security policies abroad.

In Asia, North Vietnam has been notably successful in imposing its will on South Vietnam after a struggle covering thirty years. It has also installed puppet regimes in Cambodia and Laos over the resistance of a militarily superior China and the United States. Its large cache of U.S.-made weapons, captured after the fall of Saigon, provides it means to influence events in the Persian Gulf and in Central America where U.S. arms are in demand. Its dependence on Soviet assistance potentially places constraints on its maneuverability, but its reserve in extending permanent base rights to the Soviets suggests that Hanoi still maintains a considerable degree of autonomy and initiative. Similarly, and as already noted, India has much to say about what government will control Bangladesh and its foreign and security policies have a critical impact on the Pakistani government. The Pakistani defeat in 1971 led to the fall of the Khan regime. The regime of President Zia depends implicitly on the good will of New Delhi.

The Middle East has also been rife with intrigue. North and South Yemen are pulled in opposite directions. Saudi money and U.S.-bought arms keep the North Yemen government tenuously afloat while Soviet arms and Libyan assistance support the Marxist regime in South Yemen. (On the other hand, North Yemen is apparently using some of its newly acquired wealth to play a double game by buying some Soviet arms.) Previously, a more politically radical Egypt under Nasser sent troops to support the Yemenese insurgents. For a time, the shah's Iran underwrote the Sultan of Oman. Syria maintains an iron grip over parts of Lebanon and has not recoiled from using its superior military strength, based on Soviet arms, to impress its will on a recalcitrant PLO. For its part, Israel extends a protective cover over Lebanese Christians, who provide a barrier against PLO and Arab infiltrators.

From North Africa, Libya extends a mischievous hand throughout the region and well beyond. It has been implicated in assassination plots in Egypt. It also assisted in returning President Jaafar M. al Nemery of Sudan to power after an aborted Communist coup d'etat, although relations between Khartoum and Tripoli have subsequently cooled. For a while, Libyan troops kept Idi Amin in power in Uganda—until his overthrow by domestic opponents supported by an expeditionary force from Tanzania.

The most dramatic success to date of the Quaddafi government has been in Chad. Six thousand Libyan troops, supported by tanks and armor, seized N'jamena in 1980 and tipped the scales of the Chadian civil war in favor of President Goukouni Oueddei over the forces of Prime Minister Hissire Habre. On the other hand, Libyan action has been checked partially by the opposition engendered among its neighbors, including Nigeria, which are concerned about Libyan expansionism.

On the other hand, France, in league with Moroccan troops ferried by American air transports and partially underwritten by Saudi financial resources, intervened in Zaire to save the Mobutu regime.[31] Meanwhile, the outcome of the conflict between Morocco and the Polisario depends largely on Algeria and to a lesser extent Libya.

The victory of Robert Mugabe in Zimbabwe can be attributed in great part to the support that the black-independence movement received from developing states. Arms filtered to the rebels from the Soviet Union through Mozambique, Zambia, and Angola to Joshua Nkomo's forces, while Mugabe's ZANU (Zimbabwe African National Union) movement enjoyed Chinese patronage. The willingness of the two revolutionary leaders to accept a negotiated solution derived in considerable measure from the pressures exerted by the front-line states on Mugabe and Nkomo to seek a peaceful settlement of the conflict. Mozambique was particularly strained by the war and drained by having to provide sanctuary and scarce resources for the battle.[32]

When attention is turned toward Latin America, Cuban foreign policy obviously provides the most striking evidence of the importance of developing states in regime change. The Marxist governments in Angola and Ethiopia can be said to be products of Cuban military intervention and its continued presence in these countries. Cubans also advise Marxist or Marxist-leaning regimes in Congo-Brazzaville, Libya, Mozambique, and Benin.[33] Cuban attempts to export revolution have been less successful despite closer geographic and ethnic affinities. Che Guevara was eventually killed in his attempt to foment revolution in Bolivia. Nicaragua and El Salvador have furnished more favorable terrain for Cuban intervention. If State Department charges are correct, Havana has used its connections in Honduras and Nicaragua to ship arms to the Salvadoran rebels, and it has been instrumental in organizing rebel forces into effective fighting units.[34]

Influence over the International Agenda of Security Issues. Developing states increasingly control the issues that will be on the international-security agenda. As the superpowers and the European states have settled their differences in Europe, the developing world has become the focus of big-power and middle-power competition. But unlike previous periods, the developing states are exercising more influence over the scope, timing, articulation, management, and resolution of regional international-security issues. Their greater influence and initiative derive from the increasingly impressive security assets at their disposal to use directly, to invest in other developing states or revolutionary movements, or to "lend" to developed powers.

Vietnam and Cuba may be aligned with the Soviet Union, but they have often taken initiatives that apparently are riskier than those that Moscow would have approved. Israel has also been able to maintain a sizable margin of maneuverability relative to Washington despite its dependency for arms and economic assistance on the United States. However much the Soviet Union might have wished to discourage the Iraqi attack on Iran, it has been powerless to control fully the course of events in the Persian Gulf. After more than a year in Afghanistan, it has still not been able to quell the rebellion. South Africa exercises a hold on the security interests of the Western democracies. Sizeable economic investments are at stake. As the superpower contest threatens to become more tense, the strategic geographic position and resources of the South African regime also become more attractive.

Developing States and
International Security

The growing military weight, economic power, and political influence of developing states require a reexamination of prevailing assumptions about their role and impact on regional and global security. Conflicts and disruptive influences around the globe are not easily reduced to the superpower struggle. Notions, such as those of the Third World, also impede our understanding of the implications of new forces in international politics and how they create and impact on security issues. The developed world, including the superpowers, is as much a prisoner of events and of initiatives taken by developing states as it is a determiner of regional and international security arrangements.

Of particular interest has been the rise of regional powers that can exercise considerable local and even trans-regional influence on security issues. The developed states can ignore the claims of these states only at the peril of their security needs. These include India in South Asia, Vietnam in Southeast Asia, Brazil in Latin America, and Israel and Egypt in the Middle East. Lesser, but still crucial, players like Cuba, Argentina, and Venezuela in Latin America, Pakistan in South Asia, Indonesia in East Asia, Iraq, Iran, Syria, and Saudi Arabia in the Middle East, Libya and Algeria in North Africa, and South Africa and Nigeria in sub-Saharan Africa have a demonstrated capacity to shape their own environments and the security prospects of other states, including the superpowers.

The increased military resources in the hands of developing states and their willingness to use their resources implies that regional and international security systems are becoming progressively more decentralized and yet inter-dependent. Such a system, characterized by a heightened accent on military force, threatens to grow progressively out of control. Initiative lies increasingly in the hands of a larger number of players possessing augmented military capabilities and acting under variable conditions of freedom and restraint. Never before have so many states been so inter-dependent for their security and yet so bereft of means and mechanisms to harmonize their actions—if for no other reason than to minimize the mutual harm and damage that they can inflict on each other. Conflicts are thus widened horizontally among developing states and extended vertically to include developed states and the superpowers. One is thus confronted with a larger number of competing states with more military force at their respective disposal than ever before to influence this competition. The unintended result of this circumstance is that no one state or group of states can provide stability at a regional or global level. Security issues gain ascendancy over questions of economic and political development as states must be preoccupied with their security needs in a world of shifting alliances and alignments. The increasing number of influential players in the security game are then more parts of the problem of creating regional and global stability than they are solutions to it.

This volume offers little support for the optimism of Nye and Keohane that complex interdependence leads to the decreased play of force in international relations.[35] Security relations still frame and inform international transactions, although they must be understood in wider and subtler terms than the crude employment of violence. Building stable regional and international regimes requires the integration of security, economic, and political factors, not an approach that presumes the independence of these factors in shaping the exterior behavior of other states. Even less persuasive is the view that economic forces are gaining ascendancy. Evidence and logic suggest that the distinction between low and high politics should be reexamined. We should merely view them as different dimensions of the security dilemma facing nation-states today. The international system thus remains divided against itself. As Kenneth Waltz reminds us, it is still a self-help system.[36]

The very dimensions of the global-security system, and the dynamics of contemporary and intrastate security relations pose new problems for students and practitioners alike. We still know little about the specific factors that influence and shape the security policies of the states comprising the international system or about the effect of these policies on the behavior of the actors. We know even less how to control or manage armed conflict, to lower threat levels, and to resolve differences short of hostilities. We need to revise our strategic maps by integrating the strategic policies and behavior of developing and developed states within a common framework of analysis. As the preceding discussion suggests, work on this task is long overdue, and the present effort may be said to have merely scratched the surface.

Notes

1. For a general discussion of comparative foreign-policy analysis, see Wolfram Hanrieder, *Comparative Foreign Policy* (New York: McKay, 1971).

2. Probably the best general work cataloguing and discussing all the various elements of grand strategy is John Collins, *Grand Strategy: Principles and Practices* (Annapolis, Md.: Naval Institute Press, 1973).

3. One recent, interesting discussion of the demarcation between high and low politics is in Daniel Patrick Moynihan, *A Dangerous Place* (Boston: Little, Brown, 1978), esp. pp. 10-12.

4. See Hans Morgenthau, *Power Among Nations,* 5th ed. (New York: Knopf, 1968), chaps. 8-10; and A.F.K. Organski, *World Politics*, 2nd ed. (New York: Knopf, 1968), chaps. 6-9.

5. See, for instance, Robert O. Keohane and Joseph S. Nye, *Power and Interdependence* (Boston: Little, Brown, 1977); and Edward L. Morse, *Modernization and the Transformation of International Relations* (New York: Free Press, 1976).

6. This point is made in Geoffrey Kemp, "The New Strategic Map," *Survival* 19 (March/April 1977):50-59.

7. Probably the best recent summary of the corpus of traditional geopolitical theory is Colin Gray, *The Geopolitics of the Nuclear Era* (New York: Crane, Russak, 1977). Also valuable is Robert E. Walters, *The Nuclear Trap* (Baltimore, Md.: Penguin, 1974); and for a more complex development, see Saul Cohen, *Geography and Politics in a World Divided* (New York: Oxford University Press, 1973), chaps. 1, 2.

8. This terminology is utilized in Hans Weigert, *Principles of Political Geography* (New York: Appleton-Century-Crofts, 1957).

9. The growing importance of such small islands to contemporary strategy is highlighted in Kemp, "The New Strategic Map"; and in P.M. Dadant, "Shrinking International Airspace as a Problem for Future Air Movements—A Briefing," Report R-2178-AF (Santa Monica, Calif.: Rand Corporation, 1978).

10. For recent analyses of what may now finally be an unraveling of the nuclear nonproliferation, see the various articles in the symposium edition of *International Organization* 35, no. 1 (Winter 1981); and also John

Kerry King, ed., *International Political Effects of the Spread of Nuclear Weapons* (Washington, D.C.: U.S. Government Printing Office, 1979), a collection of essays sponsored by the CIA and the Department of Defense.

11. See Robert E. Harkavy, "Pariah States and Nuclear Proliferation," *International Organization,* 35, no. 1 (Winter 1981):135-163.

12. This is discussed in the context of the historical evolution of international law (read "custom") in William Coplin, "International Law and Assumptions about the State System," *World Politics* 17 (July 1965):615-634. The U.N.'s role as an instrument of legitimization (or delegitimization) is analyzed in Inis Claude, "Collective Legitimization as a Political Function of the United Nations," *International Organization* 20, no. 3 (Summer 1966):367-379.

13. For an elaboration of the view that power has become a very elusive and unmeasurable concept, see Stanley Hoffmann, "Notes on the Elusiveness of Power," *International Journal,* 30 (Spring 1975):183-206.

14. Regarding the power bases of earlier maritime empires, see, *inter alia,* George Modelski, "The Theory of Long Cycles and U.S. Strategic Policy," *American Security Policy and Policy-Making* in eds. R. Harkavy and E. Kolodziej (Lexington, Mass.: Lexington Books, D.C. Heath and Company, 1980), pp. 3-19. The various works of the historian C.R. Boxer and the sociologist Immanuel Wallerstein are also useful in this area.

15. See Richard Burt, "Pakistan Said to Offer to Base Troops on Saudi Soil" *The New York Times,* 20 Aug. 1980, p. A5.

16. Probably the most useful, comprehensive, and general treatment of the subject of national-power measurements is Klaus Knorr, *The Power of Nations* (New York: Basic Books, 1975).

17. On the relationships between indigenous arms production capability, GNP., and per capital GNP., see R.E. Harkavy, *The Arms Trade and International Systems* (Cambridge, Mass.: Ballinger, 1975), chap. 6.

18. For a more general analysis of this phenomenon, see Geoffrey Kemp, "Arms Transfers and the 'Back-End' Problem in Developing Countries," in *Arms Transfers in the Modern World,* eds. S. Neuman and R. Harkavy (New York: Praeger, 1979), pp. 264-275.

19. The general extent and importance of such relationships, that is, that of linkage politics, have been much argued over regarding the "levels of analysis" problem and what some allege to be a consistent determinism deriving from the external environment. Morgenthau and those of his school, for instance, tend to denigrate the importance of internal politics in determining security policies. On levels of analysis, see J. David Singer, "The Level of Analysis Problem in International Relations," in *The International System: Theoretical Essays,* eds. Klaus Knorr and Sidney Verba (Princeton: Princeton University Press, 1961), pp. 77-78. Useful for com-

parative analysis are Morris Janowitz, *Military Institutions and Coercion in the Developing Nations* (Chicago: University of Chicago Press, 1977); and Samuel E. Finer, *The Man on Horseback* (London: Pall Mall, 1962).

20. For one good history and analysis, see John Toland, *The Rising Sun: The Decline and Fall of the Japanese Empire, 1936-1945* (New York: Random House, 1970).

21. Scott A. Boorman, *The Protracted Game: A Wei-Ch'i Interpretation of Maoist Revolutionary Strategy* (New York: Oxford University Press, 1969).

22. For an exception, see Ken Booth's seminal analysis of ethnocentric strategic policymaking, *Strategy and Ethnocentrism* (London: Holmes and Meier, 1979).

23. On the possible importance of purely and specifically cultural factors in determining Arab perceptions of the threat from Israel, see Y. Harkabi, *Arab Attitudes to Israel* (New York: Hart, 1972); and Gil Carl Alroy, *Behind the Middle East Conflict: The Real Impasse Between Arab and Jew* (New York: Putnam, 1975).

24. Two works that might be profitably read in this regard are: Alexander George and Richard Smoke, *Deterrence in American Foreign Policy: Theory and Practice* (New York: Columbia University Press, 1974); Richard Ned Lebow, *Between Peace and War* (Baltimore: Johns Hopkins, 1981).

25. For historical perspective on this point, see Jacob Viner, "Power Versus Plenty as Objectives of Foreign Policy in the Seventeenth and Eighteenth Centuries," *World Politics* 1 (October 1948):1-29; and Viner, *International Economics* (Glencoe, Ill.: Free Press, 1951), chap. 3.

26. In a more elaborate discussion of these processes than can be presented here, see E. Kolodziej and R.E. Harkavy, "Developing States and the International Security System," *Journal of International Affairs* 34 (Spring/Summer 1980):59-87.

27. "Airlift to Ethiopia," *Newsweek*, 23 January 1978, pp. 35-36.

28. *The New York Times*, 6 February 1981, p. 4.

29. Ibid., 24 February 1981, p. 6.

30. Ibid., 6 February 1981, p. 4.

31. The circumstances of the Shaba interventions are described in Peter Mangold, "Shaba I and Shaba II," *Survival* (May/June 1979):107-115. Also useful is Julian Crandall Hollick, "French Intervention in Africa in 1978," *The World Today* 35 (February 1979): 71-80. Also consult, James O. Goldsborough, "Dateline Paris: Africa's Policeman," *Foreign Policy* 33 (Winter, 1978-1979):174-190.

32. This analysis is not meant to slight the British contribution to the settlement, but to emphasize the indispensable role of Chinese guns, the threat of Soviet and Cuban intervention, and the offices of the front-line

states in producing a solution for independence and black rule through the ballot box and not by bullets. For a useful review, see Xan Smiley, "Zimbabwe, Southern Africa and the Rise of Robert Mugabe," *Foreign Affairs* 58 (Summer 1980):1060-1083.

33. Pierre Lellouche and Dominque Moisi, "French Policy in Africa: A Lonely Battle against Destabilization," *International Security* 3 (Spring 1979):108-133.

34. *The New York Times,* 24 February 1981, p. 6.

35. Keohane and Nye, *Power and Interdependence.*

36. Kenneth N. Waltz, *Theory of International Politics* (New York: Addison-Wesley, 1979). See also his stimulating essay, "The Myth of National Interdependence," *The International Corporation,* ed. Charles P. Kindleberger (Cambridge: MIT Press, 1970), pp. 205-223.

Appendix

Argentina

Population: 27,000,000.
Military Service: Army and Air Force 1 year, Navy 14 months.
Total armed forces: 139,500 (92,000 conscripts).
Estimated GNP 1978: $45 bn.[a]
Defense expenditure 1979: 3,713 bn pesos ($2.8 bn).[a]
$1 = 1,317 pesos (1979), 795.8 pesos (1978).[b]

Army: 85,000 (65,000 conscripts).
4 army corps.
2 armd bdes (6 armd car regts).
6 inf bdes (1 mech, 4 mot, 1 jungle).
3 mountain bdes.
1 airmobile bde.
1 indep armd car regt.
6 AD bns.
1 aviation bn.
100 M-4 *Sherman*, 100 *TAM* med, 120 AMX-13 lt tks; 250 M-113, 60 Mowag, 300 AMX-VCTP, 75 M-3 APC; 200 105mm and 155mm towed, 20 M-7 105mm SP guns; 105mm pack, 90 M-114 155mm towed, 24 Mk F3, 6 M-109 155mm SP how; 81mm, 120mm mor; 50 *Kuerassier* 105mm SP ATK guns; 75mm, 90mm, 105mm RCL; SS-11/12, *Bantam, Cobra, Mamba* ATGW; 30mm, 35mm, 40mm, 90mm AA guns; *Tigercat* SAM; 5 *Turbo-Commander* 690A, 3 *Turbo-Porter*, 2 DHC-6, 3 G-222, 4 *Merlin* IIIA, 4 *Queen Air*, 1 *Sabreliner*, 5 Cessna 207, 15 Cessna 182, 1 *Citation*, 20 U-17A/B ac; 9 A-109, 7 Bell 206, 4 FH-1100, 18 UH-1H, 4 Bell 47G, 2 Bell 212, 6 SA-315 *Lama* hel.
(On order: 120 *TAM* med tks; 120 *Kuerassier* SP ATK guns; 12 SA-330 *Puma* 12 *Lama* hel.)

Reserves: 250,000: 200,000 National Guard, 50,000 Territorial Guard.

Navy: 35,000 (17,000 conscripts), incl Naval Air Force and Marines.
4 submarines: 2 Type 209, 2 ex-US *Guppy*.
1 ex-Br *Colossus* aircraft carrier (capacity 14 A-4, 6 S-2 ac, 4 S-61 hel).
1 ex-US *Brooklyn* cruiser with *Seacat* SAM, 2 hel.
8 destroyers: 1 Type 42 with *Sea Dart* SAM, 1 *Lynx* hel; 7 ex-US (3 *Summer*, 1 *Gearing*; 3 *Fletcher* with *Exocet* SSM).
2 ex-Fr A-69 corvettes with *Exocet* SSM.
7 patrol ships: 2 ex-US *Cherokee*, 2 *King*) 1 trg), 3 ex-US *Sotoyomo*.
2 large patrol craft.
4 *Dabur* FAC(P).
2 TNC-45 FAC(G).
2 ex-US *Higgins* FAC(T)<.
6 ex-Br *Ton* coastal minesweeper/hunters.
1 LSD, 2 LST, 27 ex-US landing craft<.
(On order: 6 submarines, 1 Type 42 destroyer, 4 *Meko* 360 frigates, 1 A-69, 2 *Meko* 140 corvettes.)

Bases: Puerto Belgrano, Mar del Plata, Buenos Aires, Ushuaia.

Naval Air Force: 3,000; 23 combat aircraft.
1 FB sqn with 11 A-4Q.
1 MR sqn with 9 S-2A/E, 3 SP-2H.
Tpts incl 3 *Electra*, 1 HS-125, 3 I-28.
Other ac incl 8 *King Air*, 4 *Queen Air*, 3 *Turbo-Porter*.
Hel incl 5 S-61D/NR, 9 *Alouette* A-103(III), 2 WG-13 (*Lynx*), 3 *Puma*.
Trainers incl 7 EMB-326GB, 15 T-34C, 12 T-6/-28, 2 C-45.
(On order: 14 *Super Etendard* fighters, 8 WG-13 (*Lynx*) hel.)

Marines: 10,000.
5 inf bns.
1 cdo bn.
1 amph bn.
1 fd arty bn.
1 AD bn.
2 security bns.

By permission of the International Institute for Strategic Studies, *The Military Balance*, 1980-1981 (London, 1981).

[a]Rapid inflation makes defense expenditure and GNP figures in local currency and dollar terms unreliable.

[b]Year average exchange rates.

1 sigs bn.
6 indep inf coys.
22 LVTP-7, 15 LARC-5, 6 Mowag APC; 105mm, 155mm how; 81mm, 106mm mor; 75mm, 105mm RCL; *Bantam* ATGW; 30mm AA guns; 10 *Tigercat* SAM.

Air Force: 19,500 (10,000 conscripts); 236 combat aircraft.
1 bbr sqn with 9 *Canberra* B-62, 2 T-64.
4 FB sqns with 60 A-4P *Skyhawk*.
1 FB sqn with 18 F-86F.
6 FGA sqns: 2 with 21 *Nesher*, 1 with 17 *Mirage* 5, 3 with 48 MS-760A *Paris* II.
1 interceptor sqn with 22 *Mirage* IIIEA, 2 IIIDA.
2 COIN sqns with 37 IA-58 *Pucará*.
1 assault hel sqn with 14 Hughes 500 M, 8 UH-1H.
1 SAR sqn with 12 *Lama*, 2 S-58T, 2 S-61NR hel.
5 tpt sqns with 1 Boeing 707-320B, 7 C-130E/H, 2 KC-130, 1 *Sabreliner*, 2 *Learjet* 35A, 3 G-222, 13 C-47, 10 F-27, 6 F-28, 5 DHC-6, 22 IA-50 *Guaraní* II, 2 *Merlin* IVA.
1 Antarctic sqn with 2 DHC-2, 3 DHC-3, 1 LC-47 ac, 1 S-61R hel.
1 comms sqn with 4 *Commander*, 14 *Shrike Commander, Paris,* T-34, IA-35 *Huanquero.*
Hel incl 4 UH-1D, 3 UH-19, 3 Bell 47G.
Trainers incl 35 T-34C, 12 *Paris*, 37 Cessna 182.
AAM: R-530. ASM: AS-11/-12.
(On order: 8 *Mirage* 5 fighters; 20 IA-58 *Pucará* COIN; 16 *Turbo-Commander* tpts; 2 KC-130 tankers; 3 CH-47C, 8 Bell 212, 9 *Puma* hel.)

Para-Military Forces: 42,000. Gendarmerie: 11,000; Shorland armd cars, M-113 APC, 20 lt ac, 10 hel under Army command, mainly for frontier duties. Argentine Naval Prefecture (coastguard): 9,000; 2 patrol ships, 25 large patrol craft, 30 patrol vessels, 5 aircraft, 6 hel. Federal Police: 22,000; APC, 4 hel.

Brazil

Population: 126,000,000.
Military service: 1 year.
Total armed forces: 272,550 (113,000 conscripts).
Estimated GDP 1978: $201 bn.

Defense expenditure 1979: 47.3 bn cruzeiros ($2.09 bn).
$1 = 22.65 cruzeiros (1979), 16.9 cruzeiros (1978).

Army: 182,750 (110,000 conscripts).
4 army, 2 indep comd HQ.
8 divs: each up to 6 armd, 4 mech or mot inf bdes.
2 indep inf bdes.
1 indep para bde.
5 lt 'jungle' inf bns.
60 M-4, some M-47 med, 250 M-3A1, 250 M-41 lt tks; 120 EE-9 *Cascavel*, M-8 armd cars; EE-11 *Urutu*, M-59, 600 M-113 APC; 500 M-116 75mm pack, 375 105mm, 90 M-114 155mm towed, 50 M-7, 100 M-108 105mm SP how; 81mm mor; 3.5-in RL, 108mm MRL; 106mm RCL; *Cobra* ATGW; 30 35mm, 30 40mm, 40 90mm AA guns; 4 *Roland* SAM; 40 L-42 *Regente*, O-1E lt ac; 10 AB-206A hel.
(On order: 80 X-1A2 med tks.)

Reserves: 60,000 first line; 500,000 second line.

Navy: 47,000, incl 13,500 Naval Air Force, Marines and Auxiliary Corps, 3,000 conscripts.
8 submarines: 3 *Oberon*, 5 ex-US *Guppy* II/III.
1 ex-Br *Colossus* aircraft carrier (capacity 20 ac, incl 7 S-2A ASW ac, 4 *Sea King* hel).
12 destroyers: 5 ex-US *Fletcher* (1 with *Seacat* SAM), 5 ex-US *Sumner* (1 with *Seacat*), 2 ex-US *Gearing* with *ASROC*.
6 *Niteroi* frigates: 2 with *Seacat* SAM, *Ikara*, 1 *Lynx* hel; 4 with *Exocet* SSM.
10 *Imperial Marinheiro* patrol vessels.
6 river patrol ships: 2 *Pedro Teixeira*, 3 *Roraima*, 1 monitor.
6 *Piratini* large patrol craft.
6 *Schütze* coastal minesweepers.
10 river patrol craft< (6 *Anchova*).
2 ex-US LST.
4 LCU.

Bases: Rio de Janeiro, Aratu, Belem, Natal, Ladario.

Naval Air Force: no combat aircraft.
1 ASW sqn with 5 SH-3D *Sea King* hel.
1 utility sqn with 5 *Whirlwind*, 7 *Wasp*, 6 AS-350M *Ecureuil*, 18 AB-206B, 9 *Lynx* hel.
1 trg sqn with 10 Hughes 269/300 hel.

Marines: 12,000.
1 div (bde) with 3 inf, 1 amph assault, 1 arty, 1 engr bns. LVTP-7 APC.

Air Force: 42,800; 173 combat aircraft.
1 interceptor sqn with 14 *Mirage* IIIEBR, 3
DBR.
2 FGA sqns with 33 F-5E, 5 F-5B.
8 COIN/recce sqns with 70 AT-26 *Xavante*,
19 T-25 ac, 11 UH-1D, 4 Bell 206, 4 OH-
6A hel.
1 ASW sqn with 8 S-2E, 9 S-2A (7 in carrier).
1 MR sqn with 12 EMB-111 M.
4 SAR sqns with 7 HU-16B *Albatross*, 3 RC-
130E, 7 PBY-5A ac, 5 SH-1D, 2 Bell 47G
hel.
12 tpt sqns with 2 Boeing 737, 9 C-130E/H, 2
KC-130H, 13 HS-125, 1 *Viscount*, 12
HS-748, 20 DHC-5, 96 EMB-110
Bandeirante (78 C-95, 6 R-95, 4 EC-95, 8
C-95A), 5 EMB-121 *Xingu*, 10 C-47 ac, 6
AB-206, 6 SA-330 *Puma* hel.
3 liaison sqns with L-42, T-25, O-1E, 10 EMB-
810C (*Seneca* II) ac, 30 UH-1D/H hel.
Trainers incl 62 T-23 *Uirapuru*, 130 T-25
Universal, 10 T-33, 82 AT-26.
AAM: R-530.
(On order: 20 EMB-110 (C-95A) tpts, 20
AT-26 trg ac.)

Para-Military Forces: Some 185,000 Public
Security Forces; state militias in addition.

Cuba

Population: 9,900,000.
Military service: 3 years.
Total armed forces: 206,000.
Estimated GNP 1978: $12.5 bn.
Estimated defense expenditure 1980: 811 m
pesos ($1.1 bn).
$1 = 0.72 pesos (1980), 0.76 pesos (1978).

Army: 180,000.
3 armd bdes.
15 inf divs (bdes), (some mech).
Some indep bns.
Over 600 tks, incl 60 IS-2 hy, T-34/-54/-55,
50 T-62 med, PT-76 lt; BRDM-1 armd
cars; BMP MICV, 400 BTR-40/-60/-152
APC; M-116 75mm pack, 122mm,
130mm, 152mm guns/how; 100 SU-100
SP guns; 45 *FROG*-4 SSM; 57mm, 76mm,
85mm ATK guns; 57mm RCL; *Snapper,
Sagger* ATGW; ZU-23, 37mm, 57mm,
85mm, 100mm towed, ZSU-23-4 SP AA
guns; SA-7 SAM.

Deployment: *Angola:* 19,000; *Ethiopia:*
16,500.

Reserves: 90,000.

Navy: 10,000
3 ex-Sov submarines: 2 F-, W-class.
14 ex-Sov large patrol craft: 10 SO-1, 4
Kronshtadt.
27 ex-Sov FAC(M) with *Styx* SSM: 6 *OSA*-I
5 *OSA*-II, 16 *Komar<*.
26 ex-Sov FAC(T): 2 *Turya*, 12 P-6<, 12
P-4<.
12 ex-Sov *Zhuk* FAC(P)<.
12 coastal patrol craft.
3 minesweepers: 2 ex-Sov *Yevgenya,* ex-
Pol K-8.
7 T-4 LCM.
Some 50 *Samlet* coast-defense SSM.

Bases: Cienfuegos, Havana, Mariel, Punta
Ballenatos, Canasi.

Air Force: 16,000, incl Air Defense Forces;
168 combat aircraft.
3 FB sqns: 2 with 30 MiG-17, with 10 MiG-23.
8 interceptor sqns: 3 with 48 MiG-21F, 2 with
30 MiG-21 MF, 2 with 40 MiG-19, 1 with
10 MiG-23.
1 trg sqn with 15 MiG-15UTI.
Tpts incl 10 Il-14, 12 An-2, 4 An-24, 20
An-26.
Hel incl 5 Mi-1, 24 Mi-4, 20 Mi-8, Mi-24.
Trainers incl 2 MiG-23U, 10 Zlin 326.
AAM: AA-2 *Atoll.*
24 SAM bns with 144 SA-2/3, SA-6.

Para-Military Forces: 15,000 State Security
troops; 3,000 border guards; 100,000 People's Militia.

Pakistan

Population: 82,700,000.
Military service: voluntary.
Total armed forces: 438,600.
Estimated GNP 1978: $18.5 bn.
Defense expenditure 1979: 11.68 bn rupees
($1.18bn).
$1 = 9.9 rupees (1978, 1979).

Army: 408,000 (incl 29,000 *Azad Kashmir*
troops).
6 Corps HQ.
2 armd divs.
16 inf divs.
4 indep armd bdes.
4 indep inf bdes.
6 arty bdes.
2 AA arty bdes.
6 armd recce regts.
6 SAM sqns with *Crotale.*

1 Special Services Group.
5 army aviation sqns.
M-4, 250 M-47/-48, 50 T-54/-55, 700 T-59
   med, 15 PT-76, Type 60, 50 M-24 lt tks;
   550 M-113, K-63 APC; about 1,000 75mm
   pack, 25-pdr, 100mm, 105mm, 130mm
   and 155mm towed, 12 M-7 105mm SP
   guns/how; 270 107mm, 120mm mor;
   57mm, 100mm towed, 8 M-36 90mm SP
   ATK guns; 75mm, 106mm RCL; *Cobra*
   ATGW; ZU-2-/4 23 mm, 30mm, 37mm,
   60 40mm, 57mm, 15 90mm, 3.7-in AA
   guns; 6 *Crotale* SAM; 40 O-1E, 30 Saab
   Supporter lt ac; 12 Mi-8, 35 *Puma*, 20
   Alouette III, 12 UH-1, 15 Bell 47G hel.
(On order: *TAM* med tks; M-113 APC; *TOW*
   ATGW.)

Reserves: 500,000.

Navy: 13,000.
6 submarines: 2 *Agosta*, 4 *Daphne*.
5 SX-404 midget submarines.
1 ex-Br *Dido* cruiser (cadet trg ship).
6 destroyers: 2 ex-US *Gearing*, 4 ex-Br (1
   Battle, 1 CH, 2 CR).
1 ex-Br Type 16 frigate.
3 large patrol craft: 1 *Town*, 2 ex-Ch *Hai Nan*.
12 ex-Ch *Shanghai*-II FAC(G).
4 ex-Ch *Hu Chwan* hydrofoil (FAC(T) < .
7 ex-US *Adjutant* and 268-class coastal minesweepers.
1 ASW/MR sqn with 3 *Atlantic*, 2 HU-16B.
3 *Alouette* III, 6 *Sea King* ASW/SAR hel.
ASM: AM-39.
(On order: 40 *ASROC* ASW msls.)

Base: Karachi.

Reserve: 5,000.

Air Force: 17,600; 256 combat aircraft.
1 lt bbr sqn with 11 B-57B (*Canberra*).
12 FGA sqns: 4 with 17 *Mirage* IIIEP, 38
   Mirage 5PA/DP; 5 with 140 MiG-19/F-6;
   3 with 40 F-86F/*Sabre* 6.
1 recce sqn with 10 *Mirage* IIIRP.
2 tpt sqns with 14 C-130B/E, 1 L-100, 1 *Falcon* 20, 1 F-27, 1 *Super King Air*, 1
   Bonanza.
Hel: 10 HH-34B, 4 *Super Frelon*, 14 *Alouette*
   III, 1 *Puma*, 12 Bell 47G.
Trainers incl 5 MiG-15UTI, 24 MiG-17/F-4,
   5 *Mirage* IIIDP, 23 Saab *Supporter*, 20
   T-33A, 50 T-37-C.
AAM: *Sidewinder*, R-530, R-550 *Magic*.
(On order: 32 *Mirage*, 5, 18 *Mirage* III FGA;
   25 *Supporter* trg ac.)

Reserves: 8,000.

Para-Military Forces: 109,000: 22,000 National Guard, 65,000 Frontier Corps,
   15,000 Pakistan Rangers, 2,000 Coastguard, 5,100 Frontier Constabulary.

India

Population: 672,000,000.
Military service: voluntary.
Total armed forces: 1,104,000.
Estimated GNP 1979: $96 bn.
Defense expenditure 1980-81: 36 bn rupees.
   ($4.4 bn).
   $1 = 8.17 rupees (1980), 8.19 rupees
   (1979).

Army: 944,000.
2 armd divs.
17 inf divs.
10 mountain divs.
5 indep armd bdes.
1 indep inf bde.
2 para bdes, 1 cdo bde.
14 indep arty bdes, incl about 20 AA, 4 arty
   observation sqns and indep flts.
950 T-54/-55, 70 T-72, 1,100 *Vijayanta* med,
   50 PT-76, AMX-13 lt tks; 700
   BTR-50/-152, OT-62A/-64A APC; about
   2,000 75mm, 25-pdr (mostly towed),
   about 300 100mm, 105mm (incl pack, *Ab-
   bot* SP how), 550 130mm, 5.5-in, 155mm,
   203mm guns/how; 500 120mm, 160mm
   mor; 106mm RCL; SS-11, *ENTAC*
   ATGW; 57mm, 100mm ATK guns;
   30mm, 40mm towed, ZSU-23-4 SP AA
   guns; 40 *Tigercat* SAM; 40 *Krishak*, 20
   Auster AOP-9 lt ac; some *Alouette* III, 38
   Cheetah (Lama) hel.
(On order: 700 T-72 med tks, 75 *Cheetah* hel.)

Reserves: 200,000. Territorial Army 40,000.

Navy: 47,000, incl Naval Air Force.
8 ex-Sov F-class submarines.
1 ex-Br *Majestic*-class aircraft carrier (capacity 18 *Sea Hawk*, 4 *Alizé*).
1 ex-Br *Fiji*-class cruiser (trg).
29 frigates: 6 *Leander* with *Seacat* SAM, 1
   hel; 2 ex-Br *Whitby* with *Styx* SSM; 12 ex-
   Sov *Petya* II; 7 trg (3 ex-Br *Leopard*, 1
   Hunt, 2 *Black Swan*, 1 *River*); 2 ex-Br
   Blackwood (coastguard).
4 ex-Sov *Nanuchka* corvettes with SSM,
   SAM.
16 ex-Sov *Osa*-I/II FAC(M) with *Styx* SSM.
1 *Abhay* large patrol craft.
5 *Poluchat* large patrol craft (coastguard).

4 ex-Sov *Natya* ocean, 4 ex-Br *Ton* coastal, 3 *Ham* inshore minesweepers.
1 ex-Br LST.
6 ex-Sov *Polnocny* LCT.
(On order: 3 *Kashin* destroyers, 2 modified *Leander* frigates, 2 *Nanuchka* corvettes, FAC(M), 2 *Natya* minesweepers, 6 *Polnocny* LCT.)

Bases: Bombay, Vishakapatnam, Cochin, Calcutta, Goa, Port Blair.

Naval Air Force: 2,000; 50 combat aircraft.
1 attack sqn with 25 *Sea Hawk* (10 in carrier).
1 ASW sqn with 17 *Alizé* (4 in carrier).
2 MR sqns with 5 *Super Constellation*, 3 Il-38.
4 ASW hel sqns with 15 *Sea King*, 5 Ka-25.
1 SAR/liaison hel sqn with 10 *Alouette* III.
3 trg/comms sqns with 7 HJT-16 *Kiran*, 4 *Vampire* T-55, 5 *Defender*, 2 *Devon* ac, 4 Hughes 300 hel.
(On order: 8 *Sea Harrier* FGA, 1 Il-38 MR, 8 *Kiran* COIN/trg ac.)

Air Force: 113,000; some 630 combat aircraft.
3 lt bbr sqns with 60 *Canberra* B(I)58/B(I)12/B-66.
17 FGA sqns: 4 with 64 Su-7BM/U, 4 with 64 *Hunter* F-56/-56A, 3 with 50 HF-24 *Marut* 1/1T, 5 with 80 *Gnat* Mk 1, 1 with 16 Jaguar GR-1, 2 T2.
14 interceptor/FGA sqns with 252 MiG-21PF/FL/PFMA/MF/M/bis/U.
1 recce sqn with 18 *Canberra* PR-57 (to be replaced by MiG-25).
OCU with 24 *Hunter* F-56/T-66/T-66D.
Trg and conversion sqn with *Canberra* T-4/T-13/T-67, *Hunter* F-56/T-66, MiG-21, Su-7, *Gnat*.
11 tpt sqns: 1 with 16 HS-748, 2 with 32 C-119G, 2 with 28 An-12, 2 with 24 DHC-3, 3 with 40 C-47, 1 with 14 DHC-4.
1 comms sqn with 2 Tu-124, 6 HS-748, C-47, *Devon*.
12 hel units: 6 with 40 Mi-4, 3 with 40 Mi-8 3 with 60 *Chetak* (*Alouette* III).
Trainers incl 70 HT-2, 110 *Kiran* 1/1A, 15 *Marut*, 45 *Iskra*, 20 HS-748 ac, *Chetak* hel.
AAM: AA-2 *Atoll*.
ASM: AS-30.
20 SAM sqns with 120 SA-2/-3.
(On order: 150 *Jaguar* 110 to be locally built), MiG-21/bis, 100 *Ajeet* (*Gnat* Mk 2)

fighters; 5 MiG-25 recce; An-32, 10 HS-748 tpts; 40 *Iskra* trainers; 45 *Chetak* hel.)

Para-Military Forces: About 200,000 Border Security Force, 100,000 in other organizations.

Vietnam

Population: 60,000,000.
Military service: 2 years minimum.
Total armed forces: 1,029,000.
Estimated GNP 1979: $8.5 bn.

Army: 1,000,000.
1 armd div.
38 inf divs.[c]
2 fd, 1 AA arty divs.
5 engr, 3 construction divs.
1 transport div.
5 indep fd, 4 indep AA arty bdes.
4 indep engr bdes.
5 indep armd regts.
25 SAM regts (10 with 180 SA-2, 10 with 180 SA-3, 5 with 45 SA-6).
1,500 T-34/85, T-54, T-55, T-62 and Type 59, 400 M-47 and M-48 med, 450 PT-76 and Type 60, Types 62/63, 150 M-41 lt tks; BRDM, M-8, M-20 armd cars; 1,500 BTR-40/-50/-60/-152, Type 56, K-63, 800 M-113, V-100 *Commando* APC; 300 76mm, 85mm, 100mm and 105mm, 800 122mm, 200 130mm, 100 152mm (all ex-Sov), 800 ex-US M-101/-102 105mm and M-114 155mm guns/how; 90 SU-76, SU-100, ISU-122, 200 M-108 105mm, M-109 155mm, M-107 175mm and M-110 203mm SP guns/how; 82mm, 100mm, 107mm, 120mm, 160mm mor; 107mm, 122mm, 140mm RL; *Sagger* ATGW; 4,000 23mm, 37mm, 57mm, 85mm, 100mm and 130mm towed, ZSU-23-4, ZSU-57-2 SP AA guns; SA-2/-3/-6/-7/-9 SAM.

Deployment: 40,000 (3 inf divs and spt tps) in Laos (numbers fluctuate), 180-200,000 in Kampuchea.

Navy: 4,000.
3 frigates: 2 ex-Sov *Petya*, 1 ex-US *Barnegat*.
2 ex-US *Admirable* corvettes.
10 FAC(M) with *Styx* SSM: 8 ex-Sov *Osa*, 2 *Komar* <.

---

[c]Inf divs, normally totalling 8-10,000 men, include 1 tk bn, 3 inf, 1 arty regts and spt elements.

21 large patrol craft: 3 ex-Sov SO-1, 18 ex-US PGM-59/-71.
12 FAC(T)<:6 ex-Sov P-4, 6 ex-Ch P-6.
22 ex-Ch FAC(G): 8 *Shanghai*, 14 *Swatow* <.
About 80 coastal patrol craft <.
28 MCM craft.
3 501-1152 LST, 11 LSM, 18 LCU (all ex-US).
Some 360 river patrol, gun, troop carrier and spt craft.
10 Mi-4 SAR hel.

Air Force: 25,000; 485 combat aircraft.
1 lt bbr sqn with 10 Il-28.
20 FGA sqns with 90 Mig-17/F-4, 60 MiG-19/ F-6, 60 Su-7/-20, 25 F-5A, 60 A-37B.
12 interceptor sqns with 160 MiG-21bis, 120 MiG-21F/PF.
Tpts incl 35 An-2 and Li-2, An-12, 9 An-24, 12 Il-14, 4 Il-18, C-130.
Hel incl 20 Mi-4, 10 Mi-6, 60 Mi-8, 20 CH-47, 100 UH-1.
About 60 trainers incl Yak-11/-18, MiG-15/UTI/-21U.
AAM: AA-2 *Atoll*.

Para-Military Forces: 70,000 Frontier, Coast Security and People's Armed Security Forces; Armed Militia of about 1,500,000.

Indonesia

Population: 149,600,000.
Military service: selective.
Total armed forces: 241,800.
Estimated GDP 1979: $43.1 bn.
Defense budget 1980: 1,300 bn rupiahs ($2.07 bn).
$1 = 627.8 rupiahs (1980), 625 rupiahs (1979).

Army: 181,000.[d]
1 armd cav bde (1 tk bn, spt units).[e]
13 inf bdes (90 inf, 14 arty, 13 AA, 10 engr bns, 1 bn in KOSTRAD).
2 AB inf bdes (6 bns).[e]
4 fd arty regts. 4 AA arty regts.
1 engr regt.

Army Aviation: 1 composite sqn; 1 hel sqn.
100 M-3A1, 350 AMX-13, 75 PT-76 lt tks; 75 *Saladin* armd, 55 *Ferret* scout cars; 1,000

AMX-VCI MICV, *Saracen*, 60 V-150 *Commando*, 130 BTR-40/-152 APC; 50 76mm, 40 105mm (incl 105mm lt), 122mm guns/how; 81mm, 200 120mm mor; 106mm RCL; *ENTAC* ATGW; 20mm, 40mm, 200 57mm AA guns; 2 C-47, 2 Aero *Commander* 680, 1 Beech 18, Cessna 185, 18 *Gelatik* ac; 16 Bell 205, 7 *Alouette* III, 6 BO-105 hel.[f]

Navy: 35,800, incl Naval Air Force and 12,000 Marines.[f]
4 submarines: 2 ex-Sov W-class, 2 Type 209.
7 frigates: 4 ex-US *Jones*, 3 ex-Sov *Riga* (2 *Pattimura* in reserve).
3 *Fata Hilla* corvettes with *Exocet* SSM.
22 large patrol craft: 6 ex-Sov *Kronshtadt* (1 in reserve), 3 ex-US PC-461 (2 in reserve), 5 ex-Yug *Kraljevica*, 3 *Kelabang*, 2 *Attack*, 3 ex-US PGM-39.
4 PSSM Mk 5 FAC(M) with *Exocet* SSM.
4 Lürssen TNC-45 FAC(T).
8 coastal patrol craft<: 2 *Spear*, 6 Australian De Havilland.
5 ex-Sov T-43 ocean minesweepers (2 R-class coastal in reserve).
3 comd/spt ships.
9 LST, 3 LCU, 38 LCM.
1 marine bde (2 regts).

Bases: Gorontalo, Jakarta, Surabaya.

Naval Air Force: 1,000; 12 combat aircraft.
2 MR sqns with 12 *Nomad*.
5 HU-16, 6 C-47, 3 Aero *Commander* ac; 4 Bell 47G, 6 *Alouette* II/III, 4 BO-105 hel.
(On order: 1 trg frigate, 6 *Nomad* MR ac.)

Air Force: 25,000; 48 combat aircraft.
3 FGA sqns with 12 F-5E, 4 F-5F, 16 CA-27 *Avon-Sabre*.
1 COIN sqn with 16 OV-10F.
Tpts incl 10 C-130B, 1 L-100-30, 1 C-140 *Jetstar*, 21 C-47, 1 *Skyvan*, 8 F-27, 7 DHC-3, 6 CASA C-212, 2 Aero *Commander*, 12 Cessna 207/401/402, 18 *Gelatik*.
2 hel sqns with 4 UH-34D, 2 Bell 204B, 17 *Puma*, 28 Bell 47.
Trainers incl 4 T-6, 10 T-33A, 16 T-34C1, *Airtourer*, 30 LT-200.
(On order: 14 A-4, 2 TA-4 FGA; 25 CASA C-212, 3 Transall C-160 tpts; 8 *Hawk* T-53, 20 AS-202 *Bravo* trg ac; 21 *Musketeer*, 2 *King Air* lt ac; 16 BO-105, 6 *Puma* hel.)

[d]About one-third of the army is engaged in civil and administrative duties.

[e]In KOSTRAD (Strategic Reserve Command).

[f]Some equipment and ships nonoperational for lack of spares.

(In storage: 22 Tu-16, 10 Il-28, 40 MiG-15/
-17, 35 MiG-19, 15 MiG-21 ac, 20 Mi-4, 9
Mi-6 hel.)

Para-Military Forces: 12,000 Police Mobile
bde; about 100,000 Militia.

Egypt

Population: 40,460,000.
Military service: 1 year
Total armed forces: 367,000.
Estimated GDP 1979: $16.5 bn.
Defense expenditure 1979-80: £E 1.5 bn.
($2.17 bn).
$1 = £E 0.692 (1979).

Army: 320,000, incl Air Defense Command.
2 armd divs (each with 1 armd, 2 mech
bdes).
3 mech inf divs.
5 inf divs (each with 2 inf bdes).
1 Republican Guard Brigade (div).
3 indep armd bdes.
7 indep inf bdes.
2 airmobile bdes.
1 para bde.
4 arty bdes.
2 hy mor bdes.
1 ATGW bde.
6 cdo gps.
2 SSM regts (up to 24 *Scud*).
850 T-54/-55, 750 T-62 med, 80 PT-76
lt tks; 300 BRDM-1/-2 scout cars; 200
BMP-1 MICV, 2,500 OT-62/-64, BTR-40/
-50/-60/-152, *Walid*, 50 M-113A2 APC;
1,300 76mm, 100mm, 122mm, 130mm,
152mm and 180mm guns/how; about 200
SU-100 and ISU-152 SP guns; 300
120mm, 160mm and 240mm mor; 300
122mm, 132mm, 140mm and 240mm RL;
30 *FROG*-4/-7, 24 *Scud* B, *Samlet* SSM;
900 57mm, 85mm and 100mm ATK guns;
900 82mm and 107mm RCL; 1,000 *Sagger, Snaper, Swatter, Milan, Beeswing,
Swingfire* and *TOW* ATGW; 350 ZSU-
23-4 and ZSU-57-2 SP AA guns; 20
SA-7/-9, *Crotale* SAM.[g]
(On order: 244 M-60 med tks; 550 M-113A2
APC; 100 M-106A2 and M-125A2 mor
carriers; *Swingfire* ATGW; 12 btys *Improved HAWK* SAM.)

Air Defense Command (75,000): 360 SA-2,
200 SA-3, 75 SA-6 SAM; 2,500 20mm,
23mm, 37mm, 40mm, 57mm, 85mm and
100mm AA guns; missile, gun and EW
radars.[g]

Reserves: about 500,000.

Navy: 20,000.[g]
10 ex-Sov submarines: 6 W- (1 in reserve), 4
R-class.
5 destroyers: 4 ex-Sov *Skory* with *Styx*
SSM, 1 ex-Br Z-class.
3 ex-Br frigates: 1 *Black Swan*, 1 *Hunt*,
1 *River* (sub spt ship).
18 FAC(M): 8 ex-Sov (4 *Osa*-1 with SA-7,
4 *Komar* < with *Styx* SSM), 9 *October*
6 <,1 *Ramadan* < with *Otomat* SSM.
12 ex-Sov SO-1 large patrol craft.
26 ex-Sov FAC(T): 2 *Shershen*, 20 P-6<,
4 P-4<.
4 ex-Sov *Shershen* FAC(G).
14 ex-Sov minesweepers: 10 ocean (6 T-43, 4
Yurka), 4 inshore (2 T-301, 2 K-8).
3 SRN-6 hovercraft.
3 ex-Sov *Polnocny* LCT.
14 ex-Sov LCU: 10 *Vydra*, 4 SMB1.
6 *Sea King* ASW hel.
(On order: 5 Vosper *Ramadan* FAC(M), 15
SRN-6 hovercraft, *Otomat* SSM.)

Bases: Alexandria, Por Said, Mersa Matruh,
Port Suez, Hurghada, Safaqa.

Reserves: about 15,000.

Air Force: 27,000; about 363 combat aircraft.[g]
1 bbr regt with 23 Tu-16 (some with AS-5
ASM).
4 FB regts: 2 with 35 F-4E, 50 MiG-21/
PFM/F, 40 Ch F-6; 1 with 30 MiG-17F; 1
with 46 *Mirage* IIIEE/DE.
4 FGA/strike sqns: 3 with 60 Su-7BM; 1
with 18 Su-20, 14 *Mirage* 5.
3 interceptor sqns with 45 MiG-21MF/U.
(Further ac in reserve incl up to 100 MiG-21,
20 MiG-23S/U, 100 MiG-17, 60 Su-7, 25
Su-20.)
ELINT ac: 2 EC-130H.
Tpts incl 20 C-130H, 26 Il-14, 16 An-12,
1 *Falcon*, 1 Boeing 707, 1 Boeing 737.
Hel incl 20 Mi-4, 12 Mi-6, 55 Mi-8, 27 *Commando*, 54 *Gazelle*.
Trainers incl 50 MiG-15UTI, 100 L-29, 40
Gomhouria, 36 Yak-11.
AAM: AA-2 *Atoll*, R-530, *Sparrow*, *Sidewinder*.

[g]Spares for Soviet equipment are scarce: active holdings being reduced to 1/3 of listed total;
replacement by Western material planned.

ASM: AS-1 *Kennel,* AS-5 *Kelt, Maverick.*
(On order: 40 F-16, 20 F-6, 30 F-7 fighters;
20 *Gazelle* hel; *Sparrow, Sidewinder*
AAM; *Maverick* ASM; Ch CSA-1 SAM.)

Reserves: About 20,000.

Para-Military Forces: 49,000: National
Guard 6,000, Frontier Crops 6,000,
Defense and Security 30,000, Coast
Guard 7,000.

Israel

Population: 3,900,000.
Military service: men 36 months, women 24
months (Jews and Druses only; Muslims and Christians may volunteer). Annual training for reservists thereafter up
to age 54 for men, up to 25 for women.
Total armed forces: 169,600 (125,300 conscripts); mobilization to 400,000 in about
24 hours.
Estimated GDP 1979: $16.4 bn.
Defense expenditure 1980-81: £I 21bn. (5.2
bn).
$1 = S 40.31 (1980), £I 25.44 (1979).[h]

Army: 135,000 (120,000 conscripts, male
and female), 375,000 on mobilization.
24 armd bdes.[i]
9 mech bdes.[i]
9 inf bdes.[i]
9 arty bdes.[i]
5 para bdes.[i]
3,050 med tks, incl 1,000 *Centurion,* 650
M-48, 810 M-60, 400 T-54/-55, 150 T-62,
Merkava I/II; 65 PT-76 lt tks; about
4,000 AFV, incl AML-60, 15 AML-90
armd cars; RBY *Ramta,* BRDM recce
vehs; M-2/-3/-113, BTR-40/-50P(OT-
62)/-60P/-152, *Walid* APC; 500 105mm,
450 122mm, 130mm and 155mm towed,
120 M-109 155mm, L-33 155mm, 60 M-
107 175mm, 48 M-110 203mm SP guns/
how; 900 81mm, 120mm and 160mm mor
(some SP); 122mm, 135mm, 240mm RL;
Lance, Ze'ev (*Wolf*) SSM; 106mm RCL;
TOW, Cobra, Dragon, SS-11, *Sagger,
Picket* ATGW; about 900 *Vulcan/
Chaparral* 20mm msl/gun systems, 30mm
and 40mm AA guns; *Redeye* SAM.
(On order: 325 M-60 med tks; 800 M-113
APC; 175mm towed, 200 M-109A1B

155mm, M-107 175mm SP guns; *Lance*
SSM; *TOW, Dragon* ATGW.)

Navy: 6,600 (3,300 conscripts), 10,000
on mobilization.
3 Type 206 submarines.
22 FAC(M): 10 *Reshef* with *Gabriel* and
Harpoon SSM, 12 *Saar* with *Gabriel.*
38 coastal patrol craft<:35 *Dabur,* 3 ex-
US PBR.
3 ex-US LSM, 6 LCT.
3 *Westwind* 1124N MR ac.
Naval cdo: 300.
(On order: 3 *Reshef* FAC(M), 2 Qu-9-35
corvettes, 2 *Flagstaff* II hydrofoils with
Harpoon SSM, 3 *Westwind* MR ac.)

Coastguard: 4 patrol craft<.

Bases: Haifa, Ashdod, Sharm-el-Sheikh,
Eilat.

Air Force: 28,000 (2,000 conscripts, AD
only), 37,000 on mobilization; 535 combat aircraft.
12 FGA/interceptor sqns: 1 with 25 F/TF-
15, 5 with 130 F-4E, 3 with 30 *Mirage*
IIICJ/BJ, 3 with 80 *Kfir*-C2.
6 FGA sqns with 200 A-4E/H/M/N *Skyhawk.*
1 recce sqn with 12 RF-4E, 2 OV-1E; 4E-
2C AEW ac.
Tpts incl 10 Boeing 707, 24 C-130E/H,
20 C-47, 2 KC-130H (tankers), 14 *Arava,*
2 *Islander.*
Liaison: 23 Do-27, 15 Do-28D, 5 Cessna
U-206, 3 *Westwind.*
Trainers incl 24 TA-4H, 50 *Kfir,* 70 *Ma-
gister,* 16 *Queen Air,* 30 *Super Cub.*
Hel incl 11 *Super Frelon,* 35 CH-53G, 6
AH-1G/S, 23 Bell 205A, 20 Bell 206, 12
Bell 212, 25 UH-1D, 19 *Alouette* II/III.
15 SAM bns with *Improved Hawk.*
AAM: *Sidewinder,* AIM-7E/F *Sparrow,
Shafrir.*
ASM: *Luz, Maverick, Shrike, Walleye,
Bullpup.*
(On order: 15 F-15, 67 F-16A, 8 F-16B
fighters; 30 Hughes 500 hel gunships; 600
Maverick ASM; 600 *Sidewinder* AAM.)

Reserves (all services: 460,000.

Para-Military Forces: 4,500 Border Guards
and 5,000 *Nahal* Militia.

[h]The Israeli £ was replaced by the Shekel, at the rate of 10 to 1, in early 1980.
[i]11 bdes (5 armd, 4 inf, 2 para) normally kept near full strength; 6 (1 armd, 4 mech, 1 para) between 50% and full strength; the rest at cadre strength.

Iraq

Population: 13,110,000.
Military service: 21-24 months.
Total armed forces: 242,250 (177,200 conscripts).
Estimated GNP 1979: $21.4 bn.
Defense expenditure 1979: 789.3 m dinars ($2.67 bn).
$1 = 0.295 dinars (1979).

Army: 200,000 (150,000 conscripts).
3 corps HQ.
4 armd divs (each with 2 armd, 1 mech bdes).
4 mech divs.
4 mountain inf divs.
1 Republican Guard armd bde.
2 special forces bdes.
100 T-34, 2,500 T-54/-55/-62, 50 T-72, 100 AMX-30 med, 100 PT-76 lt tks; about 2,500 AFV, incl 200 BMP MICV, BTR-50/-60/-152, OT-62, VCR APC; 800 75mm, 85mm, 122mm, 130mm and 152mm guns/how; 120 SU-100, 120 ISU-122 SP guns; 120mm, 160mm mor; BM-21 122mm MRL; 26 *FROG*-7, 12 *Scud* B SSM; *Sagger*, SS-11, *Milan* ATGW; 1,200 23mm, 37mm, 57mm, 85mm, 100mm towed, ZSU-23-4 and ZSU-57-2 SP AA guns; SA-7 SAM.
(On order: T-62, AMX-30 med tks; *Sucuri* SP ATK guns; EE-9 *Cascavel, Jararaca* armd cars; Panhard, EE-11 *Urutu* APC; SP-74, SP-73 SP how; *Scud* B SSM; SS-11, 360 *HOT* ATGW.)

Reserves: 250,000.

Navy: 4,250 (3,200 conscripts).
12 ex-Sov FAC(M) with *Styx* SSM: 4 *OSA*-I, 8 *Osa*-II.
5 ex-Sov large patrol craft: 3 SO-1, 2 Poluchat<.
12 ex-Sov P-6 FAC(T)<.
10 ex-Sov coastal patrol craft: 4 *Nyryat* II, 6 (2 PO-2, 4 *Zhuk*).
5 ex-Sov minesweepers: 2 T-43 ocean, 3 *Yevgenya* inshore.
4 ex-Sov *Polnocny* LCT.
(On order: 1 Yug, 4 *Lupo* frigates, 6 corvettes, 1 spt ship.)
Bases: Basra, Umm Qasr.

Air Force: 38,000 (10,000 AD personnel); 332 combat aircraft.

1 bbr sqn with 12 Tu-22.
1 lt bbr sqn with 10 Il-28.
12 FGA sqns: 4 with 80 MiG-23B, 3 with 40 Su-7B, 4 with 60 Su-20, 1 with 15 *Hunter* FB-59/FR-10.
5 interceptor sqns with 115 MiG-21.
2 tpt sqns with 9 An-2, 8 An-12, 8 An-24, 2 An-26, 12 Il-76 (6 civilian), 2 Tu-124, 13 Il-14, 2 *Heron*.
11 hel sqns with 35 Mi-4, 15 Mi-6, 78 Mi-8, 41 Mi-24, 47 *Alouette* III, 10 *Super Frelon*, 40 *Gazelle*, 3 *Puma*, 7 *Wessex* Mk 52.
Trainers incl MiG-15/-21/-23U, Su-7U, *Hunter* T-69, 10 Yak-11, 40 L-29, 50 L-39, 48 AS-202/18A, 16 *Flamingo*.
AAM: AA-2 *Atoll*. ASM: AS-11/-12, AM-39.
SAM: SA-2, SA-3, 25 SA-6.
(On order: 150, MiG-23/-25/-27, 60 *Mirage* F-1C/-1B fighters; C-160 tpts; 40 PC-7 *Turbo-Trainer*; *Super Frelon, Gazelle, Lynx,* 36 *Puma*, 3 Mi-8, Mi-24, 6 AS-61TS, 8 AB-212 ASW hel; *Super* 530 AAM.)

Para-Military Forces: 4,800 security troops, 75,000 People's Army.

Iran

Population: 38,250,000.
Military service: 18 months.
Total armed forces: 240,000.[j]
Estimated GNP 1978: $76.1 bn.
Defense expenditure 1980: 300 bn rials ($4.2 bn).
$1 = 71.5 rials (1980). 70.45 rials (1978).

Army: 150,000.[j]
3 armd divs.
3 inf divs.
4 indep bdes (1 armd, 1 inf, 1 AB, 1 special force).
4 SAM bns with *HAWK*.
Army Aviation Command.
875 *Chieftain*, 400 M-47/-48, 460 M-60A1 med, 250 *Scorpion* lt tks; BMP MICV, about 325 M-113, 500 BTR-40/-50/-60/152 APC; 1,000 + guns/how, incl 75mm pack, 330 M-101 105mm, 130mm, 112 M-114 155mm, 14 M-115 203mm towed, 440 M-109 155mm, 38 M-107 175mm, 14 M-110 203mm SP; 72 BM-21 122mm MRL; 106mm RCL; *ENTAC*, SS-11, SS-12, *Dragon*, *TOW* ATGW; 1,800

---

[j]Pre-1979 manpower and holdings shown. Present totals are believed to be considerably less, and serviceability, particularly of ships and aircraft is low.

23mm, 35mm, 40mm, 57mm and 85mm towed, 100 ZSU-23-4 and ZSU-57-2 SP AA guns; *HAWK* SAM.

AC incl 40 Cessna 185, 6 Cessna 310, 10 O-2A, 2 F-27, 5 *Shrike Commander*, 2 *Falcon*.

205 AH-1J, 295 Bell 214A, 50 AB-205A, 20 AB-206, 90 CH-47C hel.

Reserves: 400,000.

Navy: 20,000, incl Naval Air.[j]
3 destroyers with *Standard* SSM: 1 ex-Br *Battle* with *Seacat* SAM, 2 ex-US *Sumner* with 1 hel.
4 *Saam* frigates with *Seakiller* SSM and *Seacat* SAM.
4 ex-US PF-103 corvettes.
9 *Kaman* FAC(M) with *Harpoon* SSM.
7 large patrol craft: 3 *Improved* PGM-71, 4 *Cape*.
3 ex-US coastal, 2 inshore minesweepers.
14 hovercraft: 8 SRN-6, 6 BH-7.
2 landing ships, 1 ex-US LCU.
1 replenishment, 2 fleet supply ships.
3 Marine bns.

Bases: Bandar Abbas, Booshehr, Kharg Island, Korramshar, Bandar-e-Enzli.

Naval Air:[j]
1 MR sqn with 6 P-3F *Orion*.
1 assault hel sqn with 6 S-65A.
1 ASW hel sqn with 20 SH-3D.
1 MCM hel sqn with 6 RH-53D.
1 tpt sqn with 6 *Shrike Commander*, 4 F-27, 1 *Mystère* 20.
Hel incl 4 AB-205A, 14 AB-206, 6 AB-212.

Air Force: 70,000; 445 combat ac.[j]
10 FGA sqns with 188 F-4D/E.
8 FGA sqns with 166 F-5E/F.
4 interceptor/FGA sqns with 77 F-14A.
1 recce sqn with 14 RF-4E.
2 tanker/tpt sqns with 13 Boeing 707, 9 Boeing 747.
5 tpt sqns: 4 with 54 C-130E/H; 1 with 18 F-27, 3 Aero *Commander* 690, 4 *Falcon* 20.
Hel: 10 HH-34F, 10 AB-206A, 5 AB-212, 39 Bell 214C, 2 CH-47C, 16 *Super Frelon*, 2 S-61A4.
Trainers incl 45 F33A/C *Bonanza*, 9 T-33.
AAM: *Phoenix, Sidewinder, Sparrow*.
ASM: AS-12, *Maverick, Condor*.
5 SAM sqns with *Rapier*, 25 *Tigercat*.

Para-Military Forces: 75,000. Gendarmerie and Revolutionary Guards with Cessna

185/310 lt ac, 32 AB-205/-206 hel, 32 patrol boats.

Syria

Population: 8,800,000.
Military service: 30 months.
Total armed forces: 247,500.
Estimated GDP 1979: $9.2 bn.
Defense expenditure 1980: £Syr 15.87 bn ($4.04 bn).
$1 = £Syr 3.93 (1979, 1980).

Army: 200,000, incl 140,000 conscripts.
3 armd divs (each 2 armd, 1 mech bde).
2 mech divs (each 1 armd, 2 mech bdes).
2 indep armd bdes.
4 indep mech bdes.
2 arty bdes.
5 cdo regts.
1 para regt.
2 SSM regts: 1 with *Scud*, 1 with *FROG*.
32 SAM btys with SA-2/-3/-6/-9.
2,200 T-54/-55, 600 T-62, 120 T-72 med tks; BRDM recce vehs; BMP MICV, 1,600 BTR-40/-50/-60/-152, OT-64 APC; 800 122mm, 130mm, 152mm and 180mm guns/how; ISU-122/-152 SP guns; 122mm, 140mm, 240mm MRL; 15 *FROG*, 36 *Scud* SSM; 82mm, 120mm, 160mm mor; 57mm, 85mm, 100mm ATK guns; *Snapper, Sagger, Swatter, Milan* ATGW; 23mm, 37mm, 57mm, 85mm, 100mm towed, ZSU-23-4, ZSU-57-2 SP AA guns; SA-7/-9 SAM; 25 *Gazelle* hel.
(On order: 130 T-72 med tks, SP arty, *FROG* SSM, *HOT* ATGW, SA-6/-8/-9 SAM, *Gazelle* hel.)

Deployment: *Lebanon:* (Arab Deterrent Force): 35,000.

Reserves: 100,000.

Navy: 2,500.
2 ex-Sov *Petya* I frigates.
18 FAC(M) with *Styx* SSM: 6 ex-Sov *Osa*-I, 6 *Osa*-II, 6 *Komar* <.
8 ex-Sov P-4 FAC(T) <.
1 ex-Fr CH large patrol craft.
3 ex-Sov minesweepers: 1 T-43 ocean, 2 *Vanya* coastal.
(On order: FAC(M).)

Bases: Latakia, Tartus.

Reserves: 2,500.

Air Force: 45,000 (incl AD command); about 395 combat ac.[k]

---

[k]Some aircraft believed to be in storage.

7 FGA sqns: 4 with 60 MiG-17, 1 with 20 Su-7, 2 with 30 Su-20.

4 FGA/interceptor sqns with 60 MiG-23.

12 interceptor sqns: 1 with 25 MiG-25, 11 with 200 MiG-21PF/MF.

2 tpt wings with 2 An-12, 3 An-24, 4 An-26, 2 *Mystere* 20F.

Trainers incl 60 L-29, MiG-15UTI, 32 MBB-223 *Flamingo*.

Hel incl 4 Mi-2, 8 Mi-4, 70 Mi-8, 4 Ka-25 ASW, 35 *Gazelle*.

AAM: AA-2 *Atoll*.

(On order: MiG-23/-27 fighters, 18 AB-212, 21 *Super Frelon* hel, AAM.)

Air Defense Command:[1] 15,000.

50 SAM btys with SA-2/-3, 25 with SA-6, AA arty, and radar.

Para-Military Forces: 9,500: 8,000 Gendarmerie, 1,500 Desert Guard (Frontier Force). Palestine Liberation Army Brigade of 6,000 with Syrian officers (nominally under PLO). 500,000 workers militia.

Nigeria

Population: 76,420,000.
Military service: voluntary.
Total armed forces: 146,000.
Estimated GDP 1978: $35 bn.
Defense expenditure 1980: 987 m naira ($1.7 bn).
$1 = 0.58 naira (1980), 0.64 naira (1979).

Army: 130,000[m]
4 inf divs.
1 Guards bde.
4 arty bdes.
4 engr bdes.
4 recce regts.
64 T-55 med, 50 *Scorpion* lt tks; 20 *Saladin*, 15 AML-60/-90 armd, 75 *Fox* scout cars; 8 *Saracen* APC; 32 105mm, 122mm, 130mm guns/how; 81mm mor; 76mm ATK guns; 20mm, 40mm towed, ZSU-23-4 SP AA guns.

Deployment: *Lebanon:* (UNIFIL): 1 bn (700).

Navy: 8,000.
1 *Nigeria*-class ASW frigate.

4 *Hippo*-class corvettes (2 Vosper Thorneycroft Mk 9 with *Seacat*, 2 Mk 3).

8 large patrol craft (4 Brooke Marine, 4 Abeking & Rasmussen).

2 RoRo 1300 LST.

6 coastpatrol boats.

(On order: 1 *Meko* 360 frigate; 6 FAC(M) (3 Lurssen S-143 with *Otomat*, 3 *La Combattante* with *Exocet* SSM); *Seacat* SAM.)

Bases: Apapa (Lagos), Calabar.

Reserves: 2,000.

Air Force: 8,000; 21 combat aircraft.

3 FGA/interceptor sqns: 1 with 3 MiG-17, 2 with 18 MiG-21MF.

2 tpt sqns with 6 C-130H, 1 F-27, 3 F-28, 1 *Gulfstream* II.

Hel incl: 20 BO-105C/D, 13 *Puma*, 10 *Alouette* III, 3 *Whirlwind*.

3 trg/service sqns with 2 MiG-15UTI, 2 MiG-21U, 25 *Bulldog*, 15 Do-27/-28, 3 *Navajo*, 20 L-29.

AAM: AA-2 *Atoll*.

(On order: 12 *AlphaJet* FGA, 6 CH-47C hel.)

South Africa

Population: 28,800,000.
Military service: 24 months.
Total armed forces: 86,050 (66,250 conscripts; total mobilizable strength 404,500).
Estimated GNP 1979: $54.3 bn.
Defense expenditure 1980: 2.07 bn rand ($2.56 bn).
$1 = 0.81 rand (1980), 1.85 rand (1979).

Army: 71,000 (6,000 White, 3,000 Black and Colored regulars, 2,000 women, 60,000 conscripts).
1 corps, 2 div HQ (1 armd, 1 inf).
1 armd bde.[n]
2 mech bdes.[n]
4 mot bdes.[n]
1 para bde.
9 fd, 4 med, 7 lt AA arty regts.[n]
1 missile regt.
15 fd engr sqns.[n]
3 sigs regts, 3 sigs sqns.
Some 250 *Centurion*, 40 *Sherman*, 20 *Comet* med tks; 1,600 AML *Eland* Mk IV armd cars; 230 scout cars incl *Ferret*; 1,000

---

[1]Under Army Command, with Army and Air Force manpower.

[m]Planned to reduce to 120,000 in 1980.

[n]Cadre units, forming 2 divs when brought to full strength on mobilization of Citizen Force.

Ratel, 280 *Saracen* APC, 500 lt APC incl *Hippo*, *Rhino*; 125 25-pdr, 15 5.5in, G-5 150mm towed, 50 *Sexton* 25-pdr, 15 M-7 105mm SP guns; 40 155mm towed, 50 M-109A1 155mm SP how; 127 mm MRL; 81mm, 200 120mm mor; 900 6-pdr (57mm) and 17-pdr (76mm) ATK guns; M-67 90mm, 106mm RCL; SS-11, *EN-TAC* ATGW; 20mm, 55 K-63 twin 35mm, 25 L/70 40mm, 15 3.7-in AA guns; 18 *Cactus* (*Crotale*), 54 *Tigercat* SAM.

Reserves: 120,000 Active Reserve (Citizen Force). Reservists serve 30 days per year for 8 years.

Navy: 4,750 (1,250 conscripts).
3 *Daphne* submarines.
3 *President* ASW frigates (each with 1 *Wasp* hel).
6 *Minister* (*Reshef*) FAC(M) with *Gabriel* SSM.
6 *DVORA* FAC(M) with single *Gabriel* SSM.
5 ex-Br *Ford* large patrol craft (1 survey vessel).
10 ex-Br *Ton* minesweepers (some as patrol craft).
(On order: 6 *Minister* FAC(M).)

Bases: Simonstown, Durban.

Reserves: 10,000 Citizen Force.

Air Force: 10,300 (4,000 conscripts); 204 combat aircraft (incl 96 with Citizen Force).
Strike Command:
   2 lt bbr sqns: 1 with 6 *Canberra* B(I)12, 3 T-4; 1 with 6 *Buccaneer* S-50.
   1 fighter sqn with 32 *Mirage* F-1AZ.

2 AWX/FGA recce sqns: 1 with 22 *Mirage* IIICZ/BZ/RZ/RD2Z, 1 with 14 *Mirage* F-1CZ.
Maritime Command:
   2 MR sqns: 1 with 7 *Shackleton* MR-3, 1 with 18 Piaggio P-166S.
   1 tpt spt sqn with 11 C-47B.
   1 ASW flt with 11 *Wasp* HAS-1, *Alouette* II (trg).
Transport Command:
   3 tpt sqns: 1 with 7 C-130B, 9 Transall C-160Z; 1 with 5 DC-4, 15 C-47; 1 with 4 HS-125 *Mercurius*, 3 C-47, 1 *Viscount* 781, 5 Swearingen *Merlin* IVA.
   5 hel sqns: 2 with 40 *Alouette* III, 2 with 40 *Puma*, 1 with 15 *Super Frelon*.
   Other hel incl 17 *Alouette* III, 40 SA-330, 25 AB-205A.
Light Aircraft Command (army assigned):
   4 liaison sqns: 20 Cessna 185A/D/E, 20 AM-3C *Bosbok*, 30 C-4M *Kudu*.
Training Command:
   Training schools with 60 T-6G *Harvard*, 100 MB-326M/K *Impala* I/II, 29 *Mirage* III (16 EZ, 10 D2Z, 3 DZ), 5 C-47 ac, 10 *Alouette* III hel.
AAM: R-530, R-550 *Magic*. ASM: AS-20/-30.

Reserves: 25,000 Active Citizen Force; 6 COIN/trg sqns with 96 *Impala* I, T-6G.

Para-Military Forces: 110,000 Commandos; inf bn-type protective units in formations of 5+; 12 months initial, 19 days annual trg. 13 Air Cdo sqns with private ac. 35,500 South African Police (19,500 White, 16,000 Non-white), 20,000 Police Reserves.

Index of Names

Index of Subjects

About the Contributors

Gabriel Ben-Dor is associate professor of political science and former chairman of the Department of Political Science at the Institute of Middle Eastern Studies at the University of Haifa. Presently he is visiting professor of political science and international affairs at Carleton University in Ottawa, Canada. He is author of the *Druses in Israel: A Political Study*, editor of *The Palestinians and the Middle East Conflict*, and coeditor of *Political Participation in Turkey*. He has also published numerous articles in scientific journals on Middle East politics, political development, and the Arab-Israeli conflict.

Gary J. Buckley is associate professor of political science and acting dean, College of Public and Environmental Service, at Northern Arizona University, Flagstaff, Arizona. He received the doctorate in international relations from the Graduate School of International Studies at the University of Denver. His specialties include U.S. foreign policy, particularly defense issues.

Stephen Philip Cohen is professor of political science and Asian studies at the University of Illinois, Urbana. He is the author of *The Indian Army*, a forthcoming book on the Pakistan army, coauthor of *India: Emergent Power?* and *The Andhra Cyclone of 1977*, and author of numerous articles on South Asian security problems and U.S. policy in the region. Professor Cohen is codirector of the University's Office of Arms Control, Disarmament, and International Security.

John F. Devlin, of Middle East Research Associates, Washington, D.C., is the author of *The Ba'th Party: A History from Its Origins to 1966*. His special interest is the modern history of the Fertile Crescent area.

Lee Dowdy is a research associate with Dalhousie University's Centre for Foreign Policy Studies. An international relations specialist concentrating on security issues in the Indian Ocean area, he has received degrees from Duke and Tulane Universities. He has published several articles on third-world defense policies and is coauthoring a book entitled *Regional Navies of the Indian Ocean*, forthcoming in 1982.

Peter Lyon is a professor of political science at the University of London and a member of the Institute of Commonwealth Studies. He has published several books and numerous articles about international security and political and security problems in Africa and Asia.

Edward S. Milenky is a foreign affairs officer with the Office of International Affairs, U.S. Department of Energy. He is the author of *Argentina's Foreign Policies* (1978), *The Politics of Regional Organization in Latin America* (1972), and numerous articles. He has been a visiting researcher at the Inter-American Development Bank, Buenos Aires, and a consultant to the Department of State.

David J. Myers received the Ph.D. from the University of California at Los Angeles. He is associate professor of political science and director of the Telecommunications Program for the Americas at The Pennsylvania State University. He contributed two chapters to the American Enterprise Institute's volume, *Venezuela at the Polls* (Washington, D.C., 1980). He has published in the areas of electoral politics in Latin America, and his countries of major interest are Brazil and Venezuela. His other specialties include policymaking in national security and urban development.

John M. Ostheimer, associate professor of political science at Northern Arizona University, received the doctorate from Yale University. Having traveled extensively throughout Africa, he is the author of *Nigerian Politics* and *The Politics of the Western Indian Ocean Islands* as well as articles on several topics related to the region.

Itamar Rabinovich is head of the Shiloah Center for Middle Eastern and African Studies and associate professor of Middle Eastern history at Tel Aviv University. He is author of *Syria under the Ba'th, 1963-1966*, coeditor of *From June to October*, and coauthor of *The Middle East and the United States*.

Bernard Reich is professor of political science and international affairs and chairman of the Department of Political Science at George Washington University. He is the author of *Quest for Peace: United States-Israel Relations and the Arab-Israeli Conflict* (1977) and coeditor of *The Government and Politics of the Middle East and North Africa* (1980) in addition to numerous articles and chapters on various aspects of Middle East politics.

Carla Anne Robbins is a specialist in international relations with particular interest in Latin America. She has lectured at American University and has recently published in *Foreign Affairs*. She is currently completing a book on Cuban foreign policy.

Ann T. Schulz is research associate professor of political science at Clark University. She is the author of *Local Politics and Nation-States: Case Studies in Politics and Policy, International and Regional Politics in the*

Middle East and North Africa: A Guide to Information Sources, and co-editor of *Nuclear Proliferation and the Near Nuclear Countries*.

Timothy Shaw is associate professor of political science at Dalhousie University and has lectured and written extensively on African politics and foreign policy. He is the author of *Dependence and Underdevelopment: The Development and Foreign Policies of Zambia* and editor of *The Politics of Africa*.

Sheldon Simon is professor of political science and director of the Center for Asian Studies at Arizona State University. Under a grant from the Hoover Institution he has recently completed his fifth book on Asian security issues, entitled *The ASEAN States and Regional Security*.

Raju G.C. Thomas is associate professor of political science at Marquette University and the author of *The Defence of India: A Budgetary Perspective of Strategy and Politics*. He is a frequent contributor to journals on South Asian security issues.

About the Editors

Edward A. Kolodziej is a former head of the Department of Government and Foreign Affairs at University of Virginia, former head of the Department of Political Science at University of Illinois, and codirector of the Office of Arms Control, Disarmament and International Security. He is the author of *French International Policy under De Gaulle and Pompidou: The Politics of Grandeur* and *The Uncommon Defense and Congress: 1945-1963*. He is also coeditor (with Robert Harkavy) of *American Security Policy and Policy-Making: The Dilemmas of Using and Controlling Military Force*. He is completing a book on French arms transfers and international relations and is a frequent contributor to professional journals, especially in the areas of U.S. and European security and foreign policy and policymaking.

Robert E. Harkavy is associate professor of political science at The Pennsylvania State University. He earlier served with the U.S. Atomic Energy Commission (1966-1968) and the U.S. Arms Control and Disarmament Agency (1975-1977), taught at Kalamazoo College, and was a senior research associate at the Cornell University Center for International Studies. He is the author of *The Arms Trade and International Systems*, *Spectre of a Middle Eastern Holocaust: The Strategic and Diplomatic Implications of the Israeli Nuclear Weapons Program*, and a forthcoming book entitled *Great Power Competition for Overseas Bases*. He is coeditor (with Edward Kolodziej) of *American Security Policy and Policy-Making: The Dilemmas of Using and Controlling Military Force* and (with Stephanie Neuman) of *Arms Transfers in the Modern World*, as well as author of additional writings on defense and arms-control issues.